Living Language

FRENCH

ALL THE WAY™

THE LIVING LANGUAGE™ SERIES

Living Language™ Basic Courses, Revised & Updated
Spanish*   *Japanese**
French*   *Russian*
German*   *Portuguese (Brazilian)*
Italian*   *Portuguese (Continental)*
Inglés/English for Spanish Speakers

Living Language™ Intermediate Courses
Spanish 2/In-Tense™ (1996)
French 2/In-Tense™ (1996)
German 2/In-Tense™ (1996)
Italian 2/In-Tense™ (1996)

Living Language™ Advanced Courses
Spanish   *French*

Living Language™ All the Way™
Spanish*   *Spanish 2**   *Japanese (1996)**
French*   *French 2**
German*   *German 2**
Italian*   *Inglés/English for Spanish Speakers (1996)**

Living Language™ Children's Courses
Spanish   *French*

Living Language™ Conversational English
for Chinese Speakers   *for Korean Speakers*
for Japanese Speakers   *for Spanish Speakers*
for Russian Speakers

Living Language™ Fast & Easy
Spanish   *Inglés/English for Spanish Speakers*
French   *Portuguese*
Italian   *Korean*
German   *Mandarin Chinese*
Japanese   *Hungarian*
Hebrew   *Arabic*
Russian   *Czech*
Polish

Living Language™ Speak Up!® Accent Elimination Courses
American Regional
Spanish
Asian, Indian and Middle Eastern

Living Language Traveltalk™
Spanish   *Japanese*
French   *Russian*
German   *Portuguese*
Italian

LIVING LANGUAGE MULTIMEDIA™ TriplePlay*Plus!*
Spanish   *English*
French   *Hebrew*
German

LIVING LANGUAGE MULTIMEDIA™ Your Way
Spanish   *French*   *Inglés*

LIVING LANGUAGE MULTIMEDIA™ Let's Talk
Spanish, French, German, Italian
English

*Available on Cassette and Compact Disc

Living Language™

FRENCH
ALL THE WAY™

CONVERSATION / GRAMMAR / CULTURE /

READING / WRITING

Annie Heminway
Alliance Française, New York

CROWN PUBLISHERS, INC., NEW YORK

Published by Crown Publishers, Inc., 201 East 50th Street,
New York, New York 10022.
Member of the Crown Publishing Group.
Random House, Inc. New York, Toronto, London, Sydney, Auckland
http://www.fodors.com/
Living Language, All the Way, and colophon are trademarks of
Crown Publishers, Inc.

Manufactured in the United States of America

Library of Congress Cataloging-in-Publication Data
Heminway, Annie.
       Living language French all the way: Annie Heminway.
       1. French language—Textbooks for foreign speakers—English.
    I. Title.
    PC2129.E5H45   1994
    448.2'421—dc20   93-9000
                                                                          CIP

ISBN 0-517-59566-4

10   9   8   7   6   5   4

First Edition

ACKNOWLEDGMENTS

Thanks to Crown Publishers' Living Language™ staff: Kathryn Mintz, Helga Schier, Victoria Su, Eveyln Ch'ien, Ana Suffredini, Peter Davis, Jennifer Harper, and Susan Cane. Special thanks to Liliane Lazar, Alexandra Leaf, Suzanne Nairne and Jeffrey Shenk.

CONTENTS

Living Language™

FRENCH
ALL THE WAY™

INTRODUCTION

Living Language™ *French All the Way*™ is a practical and enjoyable way to learn French. The complete course consists of this text and eight hours of recordings. You can, however, use the text on its own if you already know how to pronounce French.

With *French All the Way*™, you'll speak French from the very beginning. Each lesson starts with a dialogue about common situations that you are likely to experience at home or abroad. You'll learn the most common and useful expressions for everyday conversation.

Key grammatical structures introduced in the dialogue are clearly explained in a separate section. The lessons build on one another. The material you've already studied is "recycled," or used again, in later lessons as you learn new words, phrases, and grammatical forms. This method helps you gradually increase your language skills while reinforcing and perfecting material learned previously.

In addition, brief notes on cultural topics will add to your understanding of French and French-speaking people.

COURSE MATERIALS

THE MANUAL

Living Language French™ *All the Way*™ consists of forty lessons, eight review sections, and four reading sections. The review sections appear after every five lessons, and the reading sections after every ten lessons. Read and study each lesson before listening to it on the recordings.

DIALOGUE (Dialogue): Each lesson begins with a dialogue presenting a realistic situation in a French locale. The dialogue is followed by a translation in colloquial English. Note that while there are many regional dialects and accents, we will be using standard French grammar and vocabulary throughout the course.

PRONONCIATION (Pronunciation): In lessons 1 through 10, you will learn the correct pronunciation of vowels and diphthongs, as well as consonants and consonant combinations.

GRAMMAIRE ET USAGE (Grammar and Usage): This section explains the major grammatical points covered in the lesson. The heading of each topic corresponds to its listing in the table of contents.

VOCABULAIRE (Vocabulary): In this section you can review the words and expressions from the dialogue and learn additional vocabulary.

EXERCICES (Exercises): These exercises test your mastery of the lesson's essential vocabulary and structures. You can check your answers in the *LA CLÉ DES EXERCICES* (Answer Key) section.

NOTE CULTURELLE (Cultural Note): These brief notes about French customs put the language in its cultural context. Cultural awareness will enrich your understanding of French and your ability to communicate effectively.

REVISION (Review): Review sections appear after every five lessons. These sections are similar to the exercises in format but integrate material of all the lessons you have studied to that point.

LECTURE (Reading Passage): The four reading passages are not translated. However, the material covered in the preceding lessons, along with the vocabulary notes that accompany the reading, will enable you to infer the meaning, just as you would when reading a newspaper abroad.

APPENDIXES: There are four appendixes—a glossary of Countries, Nationalities, and Continents; a Grammar Summary; Verb Charts; and a section on Letter Writing.

GLOSSARY: Be sure to make use of the two-way glossary in the back of the manual to check the meanings and connotations of new words.

INDEX: The manual ends with an index of all the grammar points covered in the lessons.

The appendixes, glossary, and index make this manual an excellent source for future reference and study.

RECORDINGS (SETS A & B)

This course provides you with eight hours of audio practice. There are two sets of complementary recordings: the first is designed for use with the manual, while the second may be used without it. By listening to and imitating the native speakers, you'll be able to improve your pronunciation and comprehension while learning to use new phrases and structures.

RECORDINGS FOR USE WITH THE MANUAL (SET A)

This set of recordings gives you four hours of audio practice in French only, with translations in the manual. The dialogue of each lesson, the pronunciation sections of lessons 1 through 10, the vocabulary section, and parts of the grammar section are featured on these recordings. All the words and expressions that are recorded appear in **boldfaced type** in your manual.

First, you will hear native French speakers read the complete dialogue at a normal conversational pace without interruption; then you'll have a chance to listen to the dialogue a second time and repeat each phrase in the pauses provided.

Next, listen carefully to learn the sounds from the pronunciation sections. By repeating after the native speakers, you will gradually master the sounds.

You will then have the opportunity to practice some of the most important grammatical forms from the *Grammaire et Usage* section.

Finally, the most important and commonly used vocabulary will also be modeled by the native speakers for you to repeat in the pauses provided.

After studying each lesson and practicing with Set A, you can go on to the second set of recordings (Set B), which you can use on the go—while driving, jogging, or doing housework.

RECORDINGS FOR USE ON THE GO (SET B)

The "On the Go" recordings give you four hours of audio practice in French and English. Because they are bilingual, Set B recordings may be used without the manual, anywhere it's convenient to learn.

The 40 lessons on Set B correspond to those in the text. A bilingual narrator leads you through the four sections of each lesson:

The first section presents the most important phrases from the original dialogue. You will first hear the abridged dialogue at normal conversational speed. You'll then hear it again, phrase by phrase, with English translations and pauses for you to repeat after the native French speakers.

The second section reviews and expands upon the vocabulary in the dialogue. Additional expressions show how the words may be used in other contexts. Again, you are given time to repeat the French phrases.

In the third section, you'll explore the lesson's most important grammatical structures. After a quick review of the rules, you can practice with illustrative phrases and sentences.

The exercises in the last section integrate what you've learned and help you generate sentences in French on your own. You'll take part in brief conversations, respond to questions, transform sentences, and occasionally translate from English into French. After you respond, you'll hear the correct answer from a native speaker.

The interactive approach on this set of recordings will teach you to speak, understand and *think* in French.

Now it's time to begin . . .

PRONUNCIATION CHART

While the rules of French pronunciation will be explained in the first ten chapters of the manual, this chart will serve as a quick reference guide.

CONSONANTS

French Spelling	Approximate Sound	Example
b, d, k, l, m, n, p, s, t, v, z	same as in English	
c (before e, i, y)	s	<u>c</u>inéma
c (before a, o, u)	k	<u>c</u>ave
ç (appears only before a, o, u)	s	fran<u>ç</u>ais
ch	sh	<u>ch</u>aud
g (before e, i, y)	s (as in measure)	â<u>g</u>e
g (before a, o, u)	g in game	<u>g</u>âteau
gn	ny in onion	a<u>gn</u>eau
h	always silent	<u>h</u>omme
j	s in measure	<u>J</u>acques
qu, final q	k	<u>q</u>ui
r	pronounced in back of mouth, rolled like light gargling sound	Pa<u>r</u>is
ss	s	ta<u>ss</u>e
s (beginning of word or before consonant)	s	<u>s</u>alle di<u>s</u>que
s (between vowels)	z in Zelda	mai<u>s</u>on
th	t	<u>th</u>é
x	x in exact	e<u>x</u>act
x	x in excellent	e<u>x</u>cellent
ll	y in yes	volai<u>ll</u>e
ll	as in ill	e<u>ll</u>e

VOWELS

French Spelling	Approximate Sound	Example
a, à, â	a in father	*la*
é, er, ez (end of word)	ay in lay	*thé*
		parler
		allez
e plus final pronounced consonant	e in met	*belle* (l is the final pronounced consonant)
è, ai, aî	e in met	*père*
		chaîne
e, eu	u in put	*le*
i	ee in beet	*ici*
i plus vowel	y in yesterday	*lion*
o, au, eau, ô	o in both	*mot*
		chaud
		beau
		hôte
ou	oo in toot	*vous*
oi, oy	wa in watt	*moi*
u	no equivalent in English —say ee, then round your lips	*tu* *fumeurs*
ui	wee as in week	*lui*
euille	no equivalent in English —say uh and follow it with y	*feuille*
eille	ay as in hay	*merveilleux*

NASAL VOWELS

Nasal vowels are sounds produced when air is expelled from both the mouth and the nose. In French, a consonant that follows a nasal vowel is not fully pronounced. For example, the French word *on:* We pronounce the nasal vowel *o* through the mouth and nose, but we do not sound the following consonant *n* or *m.* That is, we do not touch the roof of our mouth with the tip of the tongue.

French Spelling	Approximate Sound	Example
an, en	vowel in balm	*France*
em	vowel in balm	*emmener*
in, ain, ein	vowel in man	*fin*
im, aim	vowel in man	*faim*
ien	y̱ + vowel in men	*bien*
ion	y̱ + vowel in song	*station*
oin	w̱ + vowel in man	*loin*
on	vowel in song	*bon*
om	vowel in song	*tomber*
un	vowel in lung	*un*

LEÇON 1

LES PRÉSENTATIONS. Introductions.

A. DIALOGUE

Dans l'autobus.

FLORENCE: **Bonjour, Christophe.**

CHRISTOPHE: **Florence! Quelle bonne surprise! Comment vas-tu?**

FLORENCE: **Ça va, et toi?**

CHRISTOPHE: **Très bien, merci. Florence, je te présente Stéphanie.**

FLORENCE: **Enchantée de faire votre connaissance.**

STÉPHANIE: **Enchantée.**

CHRISTOPHE: **Stéphanie est italienne. Elle étudie la musique baroque au Conservatoire.**

FLORENCE: **Ah . . . C'est très intéressant. . . . Christophe, tu parles italien?**

CHRISTOPHE: **Euh . . . non, mais Stéphanie parle très bien le français.**

FLORENCE: **Stéphanie, vous avez le temps de profiter de Paris?**

STÉPHANIE: **Oui, bien sûr, mais j'ai beaucoup de cours.**

CHRISTOPHE: **Oh . . . nous sommes place de la Concorde. . . . Au revoir, Florence.**

FLORENCE: **Au revoir et à bientôt.**

On the Bus.

FLORENCE: Hi, Christophe.

CHRISTOPHE: Florence! What a nice surprise! How are you?

FLORENCE: I am fine. What about you?

CHRISTOPHE: Very well, thank you. Florence, this is Stéphanie.

FLORENCE: Pleased to meet you.

STÉPHANIE: Nice to meet you.

CHRISTOPHE: Stéphanie is Italian. She studies baroque music at the Conservatory.

FLORENCE: Oh . . . That's very interesting. . . . Christophe, do you speak Italian?

CHRISTOPHE: Uh . . . no, but Stéphanie speaks French very well.

FLORENCE: Stéphanie, do you have time to enjoy Paris?

STÉPHANIE: Yes, of course, but I have a lot of classes.

CHRISTOPHE: Oh . . . we are at Place de la Concorde. . . . Good-bye, Florence.

FLORENCE: Good-bye. See you soon.

B. PRONONCIATION
(Pronunciation)

1. GENERAL PRINCIPLES

In French, each sound is pronounced clearly. Each syllable is stressed equally, with slightly greater stress falling on the last syllable of a word:

bonjour, connaissance, ami, présente

English and French share many sounds, but French pronunciation is quite different from the English. French has many spellings for one sound. Use the pronunciation section in the manual and listen carefully to the tape for practice.

2. VOWELS

a. French vowels often take accents:
the acute accent *(l'accent aigu):* é
the grave accent *(l'accent grave):* à, è, ù
the circumflex *(l'accent circonflexe):* â, ê, î, ô, û
These accents do not indicate stress of voice, but they may affect pronunciation. There are no accents on capital letters.

b. Here are some French vowels with typical spellings, their English equivalent, and some words in which they occur.

a, à, â	like a (ah) in f<u>a</u>ther	**ami, baroque, à, âge**
e	like <u>u</u> in b<u>u</u>rn	**le, de**

10

é	like <u>ay</u> in day, but not drawn out	**étudier, présenter, Stéphanie**
e (followed by r or z)	same as <u>é</u>	**profiter, voulez**
è, ai, aî	like <u>e</u> (eh) in g<u>e</u>t	**très, connaissance, plaît**

An unaccented e at the end of a word is usually mute *(e muet):*

elle, être, Christophe, parle, surprise, Concorde

This is also true of an unaccented e followed by one or more silent consonants at the end of a word:

êtes, sommes, parlent

3. CONSONANTS

Most French consonants are pronounced like their English equivalents; you will study the exceptions in this and later lessons.

Final consonants are usually not pronounced in French, except for *c, r, f, l* (the consonants in CaReFuL).

Silent final consonants are:

vas, nous, français, beaucoup, intéressant, bientôt, avez.

Pronounced final consonants are:

avec, parc, bonjour, revoir, neuf, chef, il, seul.

In verb forms, the final *-ent* of the third-person plural is silent:

parlent, profitent

In the verb form *est* (is), only the e is voiced:

est (like *è*).

The final s of a word is pronounced like a z, if followed by a word beginning with a vowel. This is called *liaison* (linking):

vousVêtes, nousVétudions, vousVavez, trèsVintéressant

11

The letter *c* has several different pronunciations:

c + *e* or *i*	pronounced like s̲ in s̲ing	**ce, place, merci**
c + *a, o, u*	like the English k̲	**café, comment, cours**
ç (*c* cedilla)	like s̲ in s̲ing	**ça, français, François**
c + consonant	like the English k̲	**Christophe, classe, article**

The letter j is pronounced *zh:*

j	like s̲ in plea̲s̲ure	**je, Japon, bonjour**

C. GRAMMAIRE ET USAGE
(Grammar and Usage)

1. SUBJECT PRONOUNS

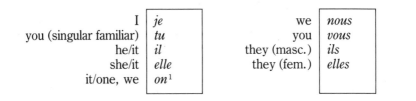

I	*je*	we	*nous*
you (singular familiar)	*tu*	you	*vous*
he/it	*il*	they (masc.)	*ils*
she/it	*elle*	they (fem.)	*elles*
it/one, we	*on*[1]		

Note that the pronoun *ils* is also used as the subject pronoun when the subject is both masculine and feminine.

Florence et Christophe sont à Paris. = *Ils sont à Paris.*

2. *TU* AND *VOUS*

There are two forms for the pronoun "you" in French, *tu* and *vous*.
Tu is the singular, familiar form. It is used with family members, close friends, long-time acquaintants, children, and when addressing animals. *Vous,* on the other hand, is used when addressing more than one person. It is also used to address someone you don't know well or to maintain a degree of respect toward an older person or colleague.

3. THE AUXILIARIES *ÊTRE* AND *AVOIR*

Être (to be) and *avoir* (to have) are extremely important verbs in French. You will need to memorize their conjugations and be ready to use them in almost every conversation.

[1] The idiomatic use of *on* will be discussed in *Leçon 8*.

12

	ÊTRE TO BE		*AVOIR* TO HAVE
I am	*je suis*	I have	*j'ai*
you are	*tu es*	you have	*tu as*
he/she/one is	*il/elle/on est*	he/she/one has	*il/elle/on a*
we are	*nous sommes*	we have	*nous avons*
you are	*vous êtes*	you have	*vous avez*
they are	*ils/elles sont*	they have	*ils/elles ont*

Elle est italienne.
She is Italian.

Je suis américain.
I am American.

Ils sont architectes.
They are architects.

Vous êtes française.
You are French.

Nous avons le livre italien.
We have the Italian book.

Vous avez le plan?
Do you have the map?

Il a la réponse.
He has the answer.

4. THE PRESENT TENSE OF REGULAR *-ER* VERBS

French verbs are divided into three groups. The first group of verbs ends in *-er*. Some are regular, some irregular. Regular *-er* verbs are all conjugated according to the following pattern. You just need to memorize the ending for each person and attach it to the root of the verb. The root is obtained by dropping *-er* from the infinitive (*parler* → *parl*).

PARLER TO SPEAK

I speak	*je parle*	we speak	*nous parlons*
you speak	*tu parles*	you speak	*vous parlez*
he/she/one speaks	*il/elle/on parle*	they speak	*ils/elles parlent*

VISITER TO VISIT

I visit	*je visite*		we visit	*nous visitons*
you visit	*tu visites*		you visit	*vous visitez*
he/she/one visits	*il/elle/on visite*		they visit	*ils/elles visitent*

ÉTUDIER TO STUDY

I study	*j'étudie*		we study	*nous étudions*
you study	*tu étudies*		you study	*vous étudiez*
he/she/one studies	*il/elle/on étudie*		they study	*ils/elles étudient*

Elle parle français.
 She speaks French.

Vous parlez très bien l'espagnol.
 You speak Spanish very well.

Tu visites les Cloîtres.
 You visit the Cloisters.

J'étudie au Conservatoire.
 I study at the Conservatory.

Vous étudiez l'histoire médiévale?
 Do you study medieval history?

Note that the French present tense can be translated in two ways:

Je parle.
 I speak; I am speaking.

VOCABULAIRE (Vocabulary)

Bonjour.	Hello. Good morning. Good afternoon.
Bonsoir.	Good evening.
Bonne nuit.	Good night.
Au revoir.	See you later. Good-bye.
Salut!	Hi! Hello! (informal greeting among friends)
À bientôt.	See you soon.
À demain.	See you tomorrow.
enchanté(*e*)	delighted

Enchanté de faire votre connaissance.	Pleased to meet you.
Je me présente . . .	Let me introduce myself . . .
Comment allez-vous?	How are you?
Très bien, merci.	Very well, thanks.
Ça va.	I am fine.
Pas mal, merci.	Not too bad, thanks.
Merci.	Thank you.
bien sûr.	of course.
la musique	music
baroque	baroque
le conservatoire	conservatory
le temps	time
la surprise	surprise
beaucoup de cours	a lot of classes
intéressant	interesting
italien*(ne)*	Italian
le plan	map
profiter de	to enjoy, to take advantage of

EXERCICES (Exercises)

A. *Compléter avec le pronom qui convient.* (Fill in the appropriate pronoun.)

MODÈLE: _____ *suis japonais.*
          Je suis japonais.

1. _____ *parlons espagnol.*
2. _____ *visites le Conservatoire.*
3. _____ *étudiez l'architecture.*
4. _____ *parlent très bien.*
5. _____ *visite la Tour Eiffel.*

B. *Compléter avec le verbe "être."* (Fill in the verb *être*.)

MODÈLE: Pierre _____ *architecte.*
          Pierre est architecte.

1. *Vous* _____ *japonaise.*
2. *Tu* _____ *italien.*
3. *Elle* _____ *musicienne.*
4. *Nous* _____ *français.*
5. *Je* _____ *enchanté.*

C. *Compléter avec le verbe "avoir."* (Fill in the verb to have.)

MODÈLE: Ils _____ le temps.
Ils ont le temps.

1. *Nous _____ l'article.*
2. *Elle _____ le livre espagnol.*
3. *J' _____ le plan de Paris.*
4. *Vous _____ la réponse.*
5. *Il _____ beaucoup de cours.*

NOTE CULTURELLE (Cultural Note)

In France, the moment you enter a store or a restaurant, step into an elevator, or approach a clerk for information, you are likely to be greeted by people saying *"Bonjour Monsieur"* or *"Bonjour Madame."*

When they address each other, the French distinguish between the pronouns *vous* and *tu*. *Vous* is the formal form of address. When you greet someone for the first time, have a business meeting, purchase something in a store, or ask the concierge for directions, you should be using *vous*.

Tu is reserved for friends, children, and intimacy. Once a relationship is established, you are expected to use *tu*. In general, it is good for foreigners to wait until the person they know begins to address them with *tu*. They should then reply in the same way.

No rule applies in every situation. If you travel in certain circles, you may meet married couples who address each other with *vous*. Simone de Beauvoir and Jean-Paul Sartre "voued" each other all their life! On the other hand, young people who are introduced to each other for the first time might use the *tu* form right away.

The French shake hands when greeting and when leaving someone. Among friends and family, men and women kiss each other on each cheek.

LA CLÉ DES EXERCICES (Answer Key)

A. 1. *Nous* 2. *Tu* 3. *Vous* 4. *Ils, elles* 5. *Je* or *il/elle*
B. 1. *êtes* 2. *es* 3. *est* 4. *sommes* 5. *suis*
C. 1. *avons* 2. *a* 3. *ai* 4. *avez* 5. *a*

LEÇON 2

DÉCRIRE LES GENS ET LES CHOSES.   Describing People and Things.

A. DIALOGUE

Dans le hall d'un hôtel.

MME RENAUD: **Excusez-moi, Monsieur. Je cherche une amie.**

CONCIERGE: **Une amie?**

MME RENAUD: **Oui . . . Elle est anglaise, elle arrive de Rome.**

CONCIERGE: **Une dame brune? Elle porte un grand chapeau?**

MME RENAUD: **Non, elle est blonde.**

CONCIERGE: **Comment s'appelle-t-elle?**

MME RENAUD: **Julie Austen.**

CONCIERGE: **Ah, c'est la jeune femme avec deux petits chiens adorables?**

MME RENAUD: **Oui, c'est ça. Où est-elle?**

CONCIERGE: **Elle est dans le Jardin du Luxembourg avec les deux chiens.**

MME RENAUD: **Quel[1] est le numéro de sa[2] chambre, s'il vous plaît?**

CONCIERGE: **Chambre 10.**

MME RENAUD: **Merci.**

CONCIERGE: **Je vous en prie.**

In a Hotel Lobby.

MRS. RENAUD: Excuse me, sir. I am looking for a friend.

CONCIERGE: A friend?

MRS. RENAUD: Yes. She is English. She is arriving from Rome.

CONCIERGE: A dark-haired woman? She is wearing a large hat?

MRS. RENAUD: No, she is blond.

CONCIERGE: What's her name?

MRS. RENAUD: Julie Austen.

[1] Interrogative pronouns will be discussed in detail in *Leçon* 7.

[2] See possessive adjectives in *Leçon* 5.

CONCIERGE: Ah. . . . It's the young woman with the two adorable little dogs?

MRS. RENAUD: Yes, that's right. Where is she?

CONCIERGE: She is in the Luxembourg Gardens with the two dogs.

MRS. RENAUD: What's her room number, please?

CONCIERGE: Room 10.

MRS. RENAUD: Thank you.

CONCIERGE: You're welcome.

B. PRONONCIATION
(Pronunciation)

1. VOWELS

i	like <u>ee</u> in b<u>ee</u>t but cut off	**petit, arrive, Christophe**
i (with a vowel)	like <u>y</u> in <u>y</u>es	**lion, amie, prie**
o, au, eau, ô (last sound)	like <u>o</u> in g<u>o</u> but cut off	**trop, au, chapeau, bientôt**
o (with a consonant)	like <u>o</u> in f<u>o</u>r but shorter	**baroque, Rome, adorable**
ou	like <u>oo</u> in f<u>oo</u>d	**vous, nous, bonjour, cours**
u	no true English equivalent; say <u>ee</u> with rounded lips	**numéro, tu, excuser**

2. ELISION

An elision is the omission of the last vowel of a word when the next word begins with a vowel or an *h*. This is most commonly used with the definite articles *le* and *la*.

le Anglais	**l'Anglais**
la Américaine	**l'Américaine**
le hôtel	**l'hôtel**
si il	**s'il**

18

3. LIAISON

In lesson 1 you learned that the final *s* of a word is pronounced like a *z*, if followed by a word beginning with a vowel or the silent *h*. This is called *liaison* or linking. *Liaison* also occurs with a few other consonant-vowel combinations:

Elle est italienne.
She is Italian.

Comment allez-vous?
How are you?

un ami
a friend

The sound of certain consonants changes with liaison.

s → *z*	**ils étudient**	*f* → *v*	**neuf étudiants**
x → *z*	**six étudiants**	*d* → *t*	**grand ami**

In some cases liaison is optional. A speaker may say:

il est étudiant or *il est* → *étudiant.*

The t of *et,* however, is never linked:

et / il arrive
et / un petit chien

C. GRAMMAIRE ET USAGE
(Grammar and Usage)

1. THE GENDER OF NOUNS AND THE DEFINITE ARTICLE

a. All French nouns have a gender. They are either masculine or feminine, whether they refer to a person, a thing, an animal, or an abstract notion. Thus, while English has only one definite article, "the," French uses *le* for masculine singular nouns, and *la* for feminine singular nouns.

	MASCULINE		FEMININE
the garden	*le jardin*	the woman	*la femme*
the dog	*le chien*	the bedroom	*la chambre*

b. *Le* and *la* become *l'* in front of nouns starting with a vowel or a mute *h*.

	MASCULINE			FEMININE
the hotel	*l'hôtel*		the friend	*l'amie*
the Englishman	*l'Anglais*		the Englishwoman	*l'Anglaise*

c. How can you tell whether a noun is masculine or feminine? The ending of a noun provides a general rule of thumb.

Nouns ending in *-age* and *-ment* tend to be masculine.

le langage	language	*le gouvernement*	government
le courage	courage	*le document*	document

Nouns ending in *-ure, -sion, -tion, -ence, -ance, -té, -ette* tend to be feminine.

la nature	nature	*la balance*	scale
la télévision	television	*la beauté*	beauty
la nation	nation	*la clarinette*	clarinette
la transparence	transparency		

Nouns ending with a consonant are generally masculine.

le restaurant	restaurant
le chocolat	chocolate

d. Some nouns have both a masculine and a feminine form. To obtain the feminine form, add an *e* to the masculine form.

	MASCULINE			FEMININE
friend	*l'ami*		friend	*l'amie*
Frenchman	*le Français*		Frenchwoman	*la Française*

e. Some nouns have irregular endings for masculine and feminine forms.

MASCULINE	FEMININE	
le danseur	*la danseuse*	dancer
le chanteur	*la chanteuse*	singer
l'acteur	*l'actrice*	actor/actress
le directeur	*la directrice*	director

le passager	la passagère	passenger
l'étranger	l'étrangère	foreigner
le Parisien	la Parisienne	Parisian
l'Italien	l'Italienne	Italian

f. Some nouns bear one meaning when masculine and another when feminine.

le livre	book	la livre	pound
le poêle	stove	la poêle	frying pan
le moule	mold/form	la moule	mussel
le rose	rose (the color)	la rose	rose (the flower)
le page	pageboy	la page	page

2. THE PLURAL OF NOUNS

a. To form the plural, add an *s* to singular nouns, just as with most English words. The articles *le, la* and *l'* become *les* in the plural.

	SINGULAR		PLURAL
garden	*le jardin*	gardens	*les jardins*
room	*la chambre*	rooms	*les chambres*
hotel	*l'hôtel*	hotels	*les hôtels*
friend	*l'amie*	friends	*les amies*

b. If a noun in the plural begins with a vowel or an *h,* liaison occurs.

| *les hôtels* | hotels | *les histoires* | histories |
| *les architectes* | architects | *les Anglais* | English people |

3. ADJECTIVE AGREEMENT

a. Adjectives agree in gender and number with the noun they modify. The feminine form of most adjectives ends in -*e.*

| *Christophe est français.* | Christophe is French. |
| *Caroline est française.* | Caroline is French. |

| *Jérôme est blond.* | Jérôme is blond. |
| *Véronique est blonde.* | Véronique is blond. |

| *le grand chapeau* | the big hat |
| *la grande chambre* | the big room |

21

le petit chien	the small dog (masculine)
la petite chienne	the small dog (feminine)

b. If a masculine adjective ends in -*e,* the feminine form is the same.

le jeune Français	the young Frenchman
la jeune amie	the young friend (feminine)

le document énorme	the enormous document
la différence énorme	the enormous difference

c. If an adjective ends in -*é* or any other vowel in the masculine, add an *e* to form the feminine. This does not change the pronunciation of the word.

Il est désolé.	He is sorry.
Elle est désolée.	She is sorry.

C'est joli.	It is pretty.
Elle est jolie.	She is pretty.

d. Some adjectives have an irregular feminine form.

le beau livre	the beautiful book
la belle dame	the beautiful woman

le nouveau restaurant	the new restaurant
la nouvelle amie	the new friend

le vieux château	the old castle
la vieille clarinette	the old clarinette

le chapeau blanc	the white hat
la Maison Blanche	the White House

le bon chocolat	the good chocolate
la bonne soupe	the good soup

le château ancien	the ancient castle
l'histoire ancienne	ancient history

e. For the plural of adjectives, add an *s* to the singular form. The *s* remains silent.

le bon chocolat	the good chocolate
les bons chocolats	the good chocolates

le petit chien	the small dog
les petits chiens	the small dogs
l'énorme document	the enormous document
les énormes documents	the enormous documents
la bonne amie	the good friend
les bonnes amies	the good friends

    f. A singular adjective ending in *s* remains the same in the plural.

l'ami français	the French friend
les amis français	the French friends
le voyageur irlandais	the Irish traveler
les voyageurs irlandais	the Irish travelers

4. THE NUMBERS 0–10

0	**zéro**	4	**quatre**	8	**huit**
1	**un**	5	**cinq**	9	**neuf**
2	**deux**	6	**six**	10	**dix**
3	**trois**	7	**sept**		

When the following numbers precede a vowel, *liaison* is used:

trois Italiens	s → z
deux étudiants, six étudiants,	x → z
dix étudiants	
neuf amis	f → v

When the numbers 5, 6, 8, and 10 are followed by a consonant, their final consonant is not sounded:

cinq journalistes	*huit professeurs*
six cours	*dix collègues*

5. C'EST

C'est is used to describe someone or something and means "it is" or "this is."

C'est bon.	It's good.
C'est petit.	It's small.

It is also used for emphasis. Instead of saying, *"le chocolat est bon,"* you can stress the statement by saying, *"le chocolat, c'est bon."*

La musique baroque, c'est magnifique!
Baroque music, it's magnificent!

La grammaire, c'est difficile!
Grammar, it's difficult!

VOCABULAIRE (Vocabulary)

l'ami(e)	friend
la femme	woman
la chambre	room
la clé	key
le chapeau	hat
le chien	dog
le jardin	garden
le langage	language
le courage	courage
le gouvernement	government
le livre	book
jeune	young
petit	small
grand	tall, big
blond	blond
brun	dark-haired
anglais	English
chercher	to look for
porter	to wear
appeler	to call
arriver	to arrive
Comment vous appelez-vous?	What is your name?
Je m'appelle . . .	I am . . . My name is . . .
Je vous en prie.	You're welcome.
Où est-elle?	Where is she?

EXERCICES (Exercises)

A. *Employer l'article défini qui convient devant le nom.* (Use the appropriate definite article before the noun.)

MODÈLE: Elle est dans _____ hall de l'hôtel.
Elle est dans le hall de l'hôtel.

1. *Il parle très bien _____ japonais.*
2. *Tu étudies _____ architecture à l'université.*
3. *Vous cherchez _____ hôtel.*
4. *Nous visitons _____ Jardin des Plantes.*
5. *Vous rencontrez _____ amie de Christophe.*

B. *Relier chaque nom à l'adjectif qui correspond.* (Link each noun with a corresponding adjective.)

MODÈLE: Le chapeau est _____.
Le chapeau est vieux.

1. *Carole est _____.*   a. *blonds*
2. *Les amis de Julien sont _____.*   b. *américain*
3. *Le chien est _____.*   c. *grandes*
4. *L'architecte de François est _____.*   d. *brune*
5. *Véronique et Florence sont _____.*   e. *petit*

C. *Compléter les phrases avec le verbe "chercher."* (Fill in the sentences with the verb *chercher*.)

MODÈLE: Elle _____ les petits chiens.
Elle cherche les petits chiens.

1. *Nous _____ un livre d'Albert Camus.*
2. *Je _____ mon amie Christine.*
3. *Ils _____ un bon restaurant.*
4. *Tu _____ le courage.*
5. *Vous _____ un hôtel à Paris.*

NOTE CULTURELLE (Cultural Note)

Whether you live in an apartment or stay in a hotel, the one person indispensable to making your visit pleasant is the concierge. When you need advice about the best restaurants, ask the concierge of your hotel. Need theater tickets? Ask the concierge! How about those last-minute reservations? Well, concierges have been known to work miracles. Can't figure out how to make your way through the metro system? Expecting an important package, need help with a phone call, or somebody to carry out a service? Again, try the concierge. If s/he can't arrange what you need, then the President of the Republic probably can't help you either.

LA CLÉ DES EXERCICES (Answer Key)

A. 1. *le*   2. *l'*   3. *l'*   4. *le*   5. *l'*
B. 1. *brune*   2. *blonds*   3. *petit*   4. *américain*   5. *grandes*
C. 1. *cherchons*   2. *cherche*   3. *cherchent*   4. *cherches*   5. *cherchez*

LEÇON 3

REMPLIR UN FORMULAIRE.   Filling out Forms.

A. DIALOGUE

Les inscriptions.

M. CLÉMENT: **Comment vous appelez-vous?**

STEWART: **Stewart Stevenson.**

M. CLÉMENT: **Comment épelez-vous votre nom?**

STEWART: **S-T-E-W-A-R-T S-T-E-V-E-N-S-O-N.**

M. CLÉMENT: **Date et lieu de naissance?**

STEWART: **18 septembre 1960 à Paris.**

M. CLÉMENT: **Vous êtes né à Paris?**

STEWART: **Oui. Je suis né à Paris, Texas, aux États-Unis.**

M. CLÉMENT: **Ah, j'ai une cousine en Californie.**

STEWART: **Ah bon? Elle habite dans quelle ville?**

M. CLÉMENT: **Elle habite dans une petite ville près de San Diego. Je rêve d'aller en Californie! Bon. Quelle est votre adresse à Paris?**

STEWART: **44, boulevard Voltaire dans le 11ème arrondissement.**

M. CLÉMENT: **Quelle est la durée de votre séjour en France?**

STEWART: **Je passe trois semaines à Paris. Ensuite, je vais en Alsace pour un stage de quatre semaines dans une entreprise.**

M. CLÉMENT: **Et les vacances?**

STEWART: **Une semaine au Sénégal à la fin du stage.**

M. CLÉMENT: **Ah, formidable! Bon séjour et bonnes vacances!**

Registration.

MR. CLÉMENT: What is your name?

STEWART: Stewart Stevenson.

MR. CLÉMENT: How do you spell your name?

STEWART: S-T-E-W-A-R-T S-T-E-V-E-N-S-O-N.

MR. CLÉMENT: Date and place of birth?

STEWART: September 18, 1960, in Paris.

MR. CLÉMENT: You were born in Paris?

STEWART: Yes. In Paris, Texas, in the United States.

MR. CLÉMENT: Oh! I have a cousin in California.

STEWART: Is that right? In what city does she live?

MR. CLÉMENT: She lives in a small town near San Diego. I dream of going to California! Good. What is your address in Paris?

STEWART: 44 Boulevard Voltaire in the 11th arrondissement.

MR. CLÉMENT: How long will you stay in France?

STEWART: I'll spend three weeks in Paris. Then, I'll go to Alsace for a four-week internship in a firm.

MR. CLÉMENT: What about a vacation?

STEWART: A week in Senegal at the end of the training.

MR. CLÉMENT: Great! Enjoy your stay and have a nice vacation!

B. PRONONCIATION
(Pronunciation)

1. SYLLABIFICATION

In French, syllables within a word generally end in a vowel sound. Compare:

ENGLISH	FRENCH
gov-ern-ment	**gou-ver-ne-ment**
A-mer-i-can	**a-mé-ri-cain**
a-dor-able	**a-do-ra-ble**

When several consonants come together in a French word, the syllables are usually divided between the consonants: *par-ler, nais-sance.*

2. VOWELS AND DIPHTHONGS

a. Diphthongs are a combination of two adjacent vowels, or a vowel and a consonant, which change the pronunciation of a syllable. Some syllables formed with a vowel and *n* or *m* create a nasal vowel sound. The *n* or *m* that follows these nasal vowels is not fully pronounced. An *(n)* will be used to indicate the diphthong.

an, am, en, em	ah(n)	*en France*	in France
ain, aim,	a(n)	*américain*	American
in, im, ym		*inscription*	registration
ien	ya(n)	*chien*	dog
on, om	oh(n)	*bon*	good
un, um	uh(n)	*un*	one

If *i* or *y* precedes a nasal vowel, it sounds like *y* in *yes* and is pronounced with the vowel in one syllable: *étudiant, bien, profession, Lyon.*

The combination *oin* sounds like the English *w* followed by the vowel *a* as in m*a*n: *loin, moins, point.*

A vowel + *n* or *m* + another vowel is not nasal:

a	année	*i*	Christine
e	semaine	*u*	une, numéro
e	aime, américaine	*o*	sommes, comment

The word *pays* (country) is pronounced *pay* + *ee*.

3. CONSONANTS

a. The letter *q* (usually *qu*) is like the English *k:*

quelle, quatre, quinze.

b. The letter *s* can be pronounced in different ways.

ss	like s in sing	**adresse, professeur**
s (at the beginning of a word)	like s in so	**suis, sont, séjour**
s (between vowels)	like *z*	**présente, française, plaisir**

c. The letter *z* is like the English *z:*

zéro, onze, quinze.

d. The letter *h* is never pronounced in French; it is always mute:

habiter, hôtel, hôtesse.

When *h* begins a word, elision and liaison occur with the preceding consonant and the following vowel:

j'habite, nous habitons, l'hôtel, les hôtels.

C. GRAMMAIRE ET USAGE
(Grammar and Usage)

1. THE INDEFINITE ARTICLE

In addition to the definite articles you studied in the previous lesson, French has two indefinite articles: *un* for the masculine nouns, and *une* for the feminine nouns. The indefinite article translates as "a" or "an," or the number "one."

	MASCULINE			FEMININE
a/one cousin	*un cousin*		a/one week	*une semaine*
an/one desk	*un bureau*		a/one company	*une entreprise*

The plural of *un* and *une* is *des:*

	MASCULINE			FEMININE
cousins	*des cousins*		weeks	*des semaines*
desks	*des bureaux*		companies	*des entreprises*

2. THE VERB *ALLER*

Aller (to go) is an irregular *-er* verb.

	ALLER TO GO			
I go	*je vais*		we go	*nous allons*
you go	*tu vas*		you go	*vous allez*
he/she/one goes	*il/elle/on va*		they go	*ils/elles vont*

Je vais en Grèce.
I am going to Greece.

Vous allez au conservatoire.
You are going to the conservatory.

Tu vas à l'opéra.
You are going to the opera.

Aller is used in many idiomatic expressions, some of which you may already know.

Comment vas-tu?
How are you?

Ça va?
How is it going? How are things?

Comment allez-vous?
How are you?

Ce chapeau vous va bien.
This hat looks good on you.

Je vais au bureau à pied.
I walk to the office.

3. THE PREPOSITION *À* + DEFINITE ARTICLE

The preposition *à* combined with the definite article is used in the same way as the English "at," "in" or "to"; it is also used for an implied "to":

Je vais à la maison.   I go (to) home.

It takes the following forms:

à + le = au

Je vais à + le cinéma. = Je vais au cinéma.
I am going to the movies.

à + la = à la

Elle va à + la maison. = Elle va à la maison.
She is going home.

à + l' = à l'

Ils sont à + l'opéra. = Ils sont à l'opéra.
They are at the opera.

à + les = aux

Ils vont à + les Antilles. = Ils vont aux Antilles.
They are going to the Antilles.

4. THE PREPOSITION *DE*

De with the definite article is used to express the English "from" or "about."

31

de + le = du

Elle est de + le Canada. = Elle est du Canada.
    She is from Canada.

de + la = de la

Je parle de + la maison. = Je parle de la maison.
    I am talking about the house.

de + l' = de l'

Je parle de + l'hôtel. = Je parle de l'hôtel.
    I am talking about the hotel.

de + les = des

Ils viennent de + les USA. = Ils viennent des USA.
    They come from the United States.

5. THE GENDER OF COUNTRIES

In French, countries, continents, states, provinces, etc., have, like everything else, a gender. France is feminine, Japan is masculine. How can one determine the gender? Most of the time, by its ending. Countries and regions ending in *e* tend to be feminine: *la France, la Chine, la Norvège, la Provence, la Californie, l'Asie.* But Mexico, *le Mexique,* is masculine. Countries and regions ending in a consonant or another vowel tend to be masculine: *le Japon, le Canada, le Maroc, le Languedoc, le Texas, le Montana.*

6. OTHER PREPOSITIONS

a. Prepositions preceding countries and regions.

En is used in front of a feminine country or region.

Je vais en Allemagne.
    I am going to Germany.

Ils habitent en Italie.
    They live in Italy.

Elles arrivent en Indonésie.
    They arrive in Indonesia.

Il est en Floride.
    He is in Florida.

Au is used in front of a masculine country or region.

Elles sont au Venezuela.
　　They are in Venezuela.

Tu vas au Luxembourg.
　　You are going to Luxembourg.

Il habite au Québec.
　　He lives in Quebec.

Aux is used in front of plural countries or regions.

Amélie habite aux États-Unis.
　　Amélie lives in the United States.

Nous allons aux Antilles.
　　We are going to the Antilles.

　　b.　Prepositions preceding cities.

The preposition *à,* meaning "in," "at" or "to," is used with cities.

Il va à Paris.
　　He is going to Paris.

Elle est à Moscou.
　　She is in Moscow.

Nous sommes à Tokyo.
　　We are in Tokyo.

A few cities have an article: *La Nouvelle-Orléans, Le Havre.*

Il habite à La Nouvelle-Orléans.
　　He lives in New Orleans.

Elle va au Havre.
　　She is going to Le Havre.

　　c.　The preposition *de* used with cities and countries means "from." If the country is masculine or plural, *de* is contracted with the article (*du,* masculine; *des,* plural). For the feminine, only *de* or *d'* is used.

Before a feminine country:

J'arrive de France.
　　I arrive from France.

Elle arrive d'Italie.
　　She arrives from Italy.

Before a masculine country:

Je suis du Brésil.
   I am from Brazil.

Il est du Guatemala.
   He is from Guatemala.

Before a plural country:

Ils arrivent des États-Unis.
   They arrive from the United States.

Before a city:

Elle est de Bordeaux.
   She is from Bordeaux.

   d. The preposition *dans* means "in." Its usage is varied.

Marc est dans la chambre.
   Marc is in the room.

Elle est dans la boutique.
   She is in the shop.

7. THE NUMBERS 11–19

11	**onze**		16	**seize**
12	**douze**		17	**dix-sept**
13	**treize**		18	**dix-huit**
14	**quatorze**		19	**dix-neuf**
15	**quinze**			

VOCABULAIRE (Vocabulary)

le nom	name
le prénom	first name
l'adresse	address
le pays	country
le lieu de naissance	place of birth
la date de naissance	date of birth
Quelle est votre date de naissance?	When is your date of birth?
Quelle âge avez-vous?	How old are you?
J'ai dix-neuf ans.	I am nineteen years old.

le jour	day
la semaine	week
le mois	month
l'année *(f.)*	year
les vacances	vacation
aller en vacances	to go on vacation
prendre des vacances	to take a vacation
le chapeau	hat
le bureau	office
la rue	street
l'avenue *(f.)*	avenue
le boulevard	boulevard
le code postal	zip code
la ville	city, town
J'habite dans un village.	I live in a village.
J'habite dans une ville.	I live in a city/town.
la province	province
L'état	state
la région	region
aller	to go
appeler	to call
épeler	to spell
Comment épelez-vous votre nom?	How do you spell your name?
être né	to be born
Où êtes-vous né(e)?	Where were you born?
Je suis né(e) à Paris.	I was born in Paris.
rêver	to dream
habiter	to live

EXERCICES (Exercises)

A. *Conjuguer le verbe "aller."* (Conjugate the verb *aller.*)

MODÈLE: *Il _____ en Pennsylvanie.*
        Il va en Pennsylvanie.

1. *Nous _____ en Amérique latine.*
2. *Tu _____ au théâtre.*
3. *Elles _____ au Club Med.*
4. *Je _____ à la bibliothèque.*
5. *Vous _____ en Inde.*

B. *Compléter en utilisant la préposition qui convient.* (Fill in using the appropriate preposition.)

MODÈLE: Nous allons _____ Égypte.
Nous allons en Égypte.

1. *Il va _____ Chine.*
2. *Elle habite _____ Canada.*
3. *Ils sont _____ États-Unis.*
4. *Je suis _____ Maroc.*
5. *Elles vont _____ Asie.*

C. *Compléter en utilisant l'article défini.* (Fill in using the definite article.)

MODÈLE: _____ Grèce est très jolie.
La Grèce est très jolie.

1. *_____ Californie est un grand État.*
2. *_____ France est en Europe.*
3. *_____ Québec est en Amérique du nord.*
4. *_____ Provence est une province magnifique.*
5. *_____ Japon est un petit pays.*

D. *Compléter avec la préposition à et l'article défini.* (Fill in with the preposition *à* and the definite article.)

MODÈLE: Ils vont _____ conservatoire.
Ils vont au conservatoire.

1. *Marie va _____ cinéma.*
2. *Il est _____ opéra.*
3. *Nous sommes _____ maison.*
4. *Ils sont _____ hôtel.*
5. *Vous allez _____ Halles de Paris.*

E. *Compter en français.* (Add in French.)

MODÈLE: Douze et trois font _____.
Douze et trois font quinze.

1. *Huit et cinq font _____.*
2. *Dix et huit font _____.*
3. *Onze et cinq font _____.*
4. *Dix-huit et un font _____.*
5. *Deux et treize font _____.*

NOTE CULTURELLE (Cultural Note)

The saying goes that if you die and want to know whether you are in heaven or in hell, find out who runs the bureaucracy. If it is the French, then you are in trouble. Filling out forms is a French sport. A socialized state provides many essential services, but makes you fill out endless forms. Although the French no longer need their passports to go from one country to another in the European Community, they need to carry an identification card, *carte d'identité,* at all times. A visitor also should always carry some form of identification.

LA CLÉ DES EXERCICES (Answer Key)

A. 1. *allons* 2. *vas* 3. *vont* 4. *vais* 5. *allez*
B. 1. *en* 2. *au* 3. *aux* 4. *au* 5. *en*
C. 1. *La* 2. *La* 3. *Le* 4. *La* 5. *Le*
D. 1. *au* 2. *à l'* 3. *à la* 4. *à l'* 5. *aux*
E. 1. *treize* 2. *dix-huit* 3. *seize* 4. *dix-neuf* 5. *quinze*

LEÇON 4

FIXER UN RENDEZ-VOUS. Making a Date.

A. DIALOGUE

Une surprise-party.

MÉLANIE: **Est-ce que vous êtes libres vendredi prochain?**

PATRICK: **Oui, pourquoi?**

MÉLANIE: **C'est l'anniversaire de Nathalie.**

JÉRÔME: **Vendredi, le 25? C'est impossible.**

MÉLANIE: **Tu n'es pas libre vendredi? Pourquoi?**

JÉRÔME: **Euh . . . Je vais à un match de basket-ball.**

PATRICK: **Toi et le basket!!! Bon, alors, samedi?**

MÉLANIE: **Non, ce n'est pas possible. Je sors samedi soir.**

PATRICK: **Tu sors avec qui?**

MÉLANIE: **Je suis invitée à une soirée chez Christian.**

PATRICK: **Ah bon?**

MÉLANIE: **Jérôme, à quelle heure finit le match vendredi?**

JÉRÔME: **Le match ne finit pas avant 21 heures 30.**

MÉLANIE: **Bon, rendez-vous chez moi à 10 heures. Jérôme, tu achètes un gâteau?**

JÉRÔME: **D'accord, j'achète un gâteau au chocolat!**

PATRICK: **Est-ce que j'apporte une bouteille de champagne?**

MÉLANIE: **Excellente idée!**

A Surprise Party.

MÉLANIE: Are you free next Friday?

PATRICK: Yes, why?

MÉLANIE: It's Nathalie's birthday.

JÉRÔME: Friday, the 25th? It's impossible.

MÉLANIE: You are not free on Friday? Why?

JÉRÔME: Uh . . . I am going to a basketball game.

PATRICK: You and basketball!!! So, what about Saturday?

MÉLANIE: No, it's not possible. I'm going out Saturday night.

PATRICK: With whom are you going out?

MÉLANIE: I'm invited to a party at Christian's.

PATRICK: Is that right?

MÉLANIE: Jérôme, at what time does the game end on Friday?

JÉRÔME: The game does not end until 9:30 P.M.

MÉLANIE: All right, let's meet at my place at ten o'clock. Jérôme, are you buying a cake?

JÉRÔME: Okay, I'll buy a chocolate cake!

PATRICK: Shall I bring a bottle of champagne?

MÉLANIE: Excellent idea!

B. PRONONCIATION
(Pronunciation)

1. INTONATION

In French sentences, the last syllable receives a slight downward inflection.

Je suis libre le dix-sept.
I'm free on the 17th.

Je sors samedi soir.
I am going out Saturday night.

The last syllable before a comma receives a slight upward inflection.

Alors, tu apportes du champagne.
So, you're bringing champagne.

D'accord, j'apporte une bouteille.
Okay, I'll bring a bottle.

The last syllable in a question receives a slight upward inflection.

Le 15, ça vous va?
Is the 15th all right?

Est-ce que vous êtes libre mardi?
Are you free on Tuesday?

2. VOWELS

eu	closed like <u>u</u> in p<u>u</u>t	**peu, deux, jeudi**
eu	open like <u>u</u> in f<u>u</u>n	**neuf, seul**
oi	like <u>wa</u> in <u>wa</u>tch	**moi, pourquoi, trois**
oy	like <u>wa</u> in watch + ee	**voyage, voyelle**
ui	like wee	**suis, huit, suisse**
oui	like oo + ee	**oui, Louis**

3. CONSONANTS

The French *r* is very different from the English *r*. It is pronounced at the back of the mouth and it is slightly rolled:

très, libre, français, Florence, sortir, partir.

C. GRAMMAIRE ET USAGE
(Grammar and Usage)

1. THE PRESENT TENSE OF *-IR* VERBS

The second group of verbs ends in *-ir*. These verbs have two different conjugation patterns: The first type of *-ir* verbs removes the *-ir* ending of the verb, keeps the root, and adds the endings shown below. Note the insertion of an *-iss-* in the plural forms of the present tense.

FINIR   TO FINISH

I finish	*je finis*		we finish	*nous finissons*
you finish	*tu finis*		you finish	*vous finissez*
he/she/one finishes	*il/elle/on finit*		they finish	*ils/elles finissent*

À quelle heure finit le match?
At what time does the game end?

Other verbs following this pattern are: *choisir* (to choose), and *réussir* (to succeed).

Ils choisissent un gâteau au chocolat.
They choose a chocolate cake.

Nous finissons le vingt et un.
We finish on the twenty-first.

Ils finissent avant 18 heures.
They'll be finished before 6 P.M.

Je choisis le numéro trente.
I choose number thirty.

Tu choisis une bouteille de champagne.
You choose a bottle of champagne.

Elles réussissent les gâteaux.
They make great cakes.

Il réussit tout.
He succeeds in everything.

The second type of *-ir* verbs drops the *-ir* ending and the last consonant of the root and adds the endings shown below.

PARTIR TO LEAVE

I leave	*je pars*		we leave	*nous partons*
you leave	*tu pars*		you leave	*vous partez*
he/she/one leaves	*il/elle/on part*		they leave	*ils/elles partent*

Other verbs following this pattern are *sortir* (to go out, to come out), and *dormir* (to sleep).

Je sors samedi soir.
I am going out Saturday night.

Elle sort du palais des sports.
She is leaving the sports stadium.

Nous partons le dix-neuf.
We leave on the 19th.

Tu pars pour la France?
Are you leaving for France?

Il dort pendant le match.
He sleeps during the game.

Ils dorment après la soirée.
They sleep after the party.

2. THE INTERROGATIVE FORM

There are several ways of asking a question in French.

a. *Est-ce que* + subject + verb (familiar form)

Est-ce que vous êtes libre?
Are you free?

Est-ce que vous aimez l'opéra?
Do you like opera?

b. Inversion: verb + subject

Etes-vous libre?
Are you free?

Aimez-vous l'opéra?
Do you like opera?

In the inversion of the third person singular a -*t*- is inserted to make the pronunciation clearer.

Achète-t-elle un cadeau?
Is she buying a present?

Va-t-il au festival?
Is he going to the festival?

Organise-t-il une soirée?
Is he organizing a party?

c. Upward intonation without any change in sentence structure

Vous êtes libre?
Are you free?

Vous aimez l'opéra?
Do you like opera?

Ça va?
How are you?

3. NEGATION

To make a sentence negative, *ne . . . pas* is placed around the verb.

Je suis libre.
I am free.

Je ne suis pas libre.
I am not free.

Il parle portugais.
He speaks Portuguese.

Il ne parle pas portugais.
He does not speak Portuguese.

Nous finissons le dessert.
We are finishing the dessert.

Nous ne finissons pas le dessert.
We are not finishing the dessert.

Vous cherchez la rue Colbert.
You are looking for Rue Colbert.

Vous ne cherchez pas la rue Colbert.
You are not looking for Rue Colbert.

If *ne* precedes a verb starting with a vowel or a mute *h,* the *e* of *ne* is dropped.

Il habite à Berlin.
He lives in Berlin.

Il n'habite pas à Berlin.
He doesn't live in Berlin.

Vous étudiez la musique.
You study music.

Vous n'étudiez pas la musique.
You don't study music.

Elle est suisse.
She is Swiss.

Elle n'est pas suisse.
She is not Swiss.

Nous avons le temps.
We have time.

Nous n'avons pas le temps.
We don't have time.

4. THE NUMBERS 20–69

20	**vingt**	23	**vingt-trois**
21	**vingt et un**	24	*vingt-quatre*
22	**vingt-deux**	25	*vingt-cinq*

26	*vingt-six*	42	**quarante-deux**
27	*vingt-sept*	43	*quarante-trois*
28	*vingt-huit*	44	*quarante-quatre*
29	*vingt-neuf*	50	*cinquante*
30	*trente*	51	*cinquante et un*
31	*trente et un*	52	*cinquante-deux*
32	*trente-deux*	53	*cinquante-trois*
33	*trente-trois*	57	**cinquante-sept**
34	**trente-quatre**	58	**cinquante-huit**
40	**quarante**	59	**cinquante-neuf**
41	**quarante et un**	60	**soixante**

5. THE DAYS OF THE WEEK

The days of the week are masculine. They are not capitalized. In France, as in most other European countries, the week starts with Monday.

lundi	Monday	**vendredi**	Friday
mardi	Tuesday	**samedi**	Saturday
mercredi	Wednesday	**dimanche**	Sunday
jeudi	Thursday		

The use of the definite article with weekdays varies according to the meaning. The definite article is not used when a sentence implies that an action will happen only once on a certain day.

Je vais à Strasbourg lundi.
I am going to Strasbourg on Monday.

Il arrive samedi.
He is arriving on Saturday.

The definite article is used when it is implied that the action takes place repeatedly on a particular day of the week.

Je vais à l'école de danse le mardi et le jeudi.
I go to dance school on Tuesdays and Thursdays.

Ils dînent au restaurant le vendredi.
They have dinner in a restaurant on Fridays.

Note that in French, only the first of the month takes the ordinal number, unlike English, which uses ordinal numbers on all days.

Nous allons à Paris le premier septembre.
We are going to Paris on the first of September.

L'anniversaire de Jacques est le premier décembre.
Jacques' birthday is the first of December.

Vous allez à Bruxelles le trois octobre.
You are going to Brussels on the third of October.

Rendez-vous à Nice le quinze novembre.
Let's meet in Nice on the fifteenth of November.

VOCABULAIRE (Vocabulary)

la surprise-party	surprise party
la soirée	party
la fête	festival, holiday
l'invité*(e)*	guest
l'hôte*(sse)*	host, hostess
le rendez-vous	appointment
l'anniversaire	birthday
Quelle est la date de votre anniversaire?	When is your birthday?
le gâteau	cake
le café	coffee
le cadeau	gift
la bouteille	bottle
aimer	to like, to love
apporter	to bring
acheter	to buy
décider	to decide
organiser	to organize
libre	free
l'idée	idea
Pourquoi?	Why?
Alors?	Then? Well then?
D'accord.	All right. Okay.
Ah bon?	Is that right?
avant	before
le match	game
le palais des sports	sports stadium
finir	to finish
sortir	to go out
partir	to leave
choisir	to choose
réussir	to succeed

EXERCICES (Exercises)

A. *Mettre les phrases à la forme interrogative en utilisant l'inversion et la forme* est-ce que. (Put the sentences in the interrogative form using inversion and *est-ce que.*)

MODÈLE: Vous êtes français.
Etes-vous français? / Est-ce que vous êtes français?

1. *Vous habitez dans un appartement.*
2. *Tu es américaine.*
3. *Il est content de sa chambre d'hôtel.*
4. *Nous parlons de la politique internationale.*
5. *Elle est dans le jardin.*

B. *Mettre les phrases à la forme négative.* (Put the sentences in the negative form.)

MODÈLE: Nous finissons le gâteau.
Nous ne finissons pas le gâteau.

1. *Il arrive le premier septembre.*
2. *Elle est anglaise.*
3. *Nous parlons très bien le français.*
4. *Elle porte le chapeau de sa cousine.*
5. *Vous allez à une soirée jeudi.*

C. *Répondre à la forme négative.* (Answer in the negative.)

MODÈLE: Vous êtes fatigué?
Non, je ne suis pas fatigué.

1. *Elles étudient l'architecture?*
2. *Est-ce que vous êtes américain?*
3. *Nous sommes libres le cinq?*
4. *Allez-vous à la classe de danse mercredi?*
5. *Parle-t-il espagnol?*

D. *Additions et soustractions.* (Addition and subtraction.)

MODÈLE: Trente-deux moins trois font _____.
Trente-deux moins trois font vingt-neuf.

1. *Cinquante-neuf moins quatre font _____.*
2. *Trente-huit plus trois font _____.*
3. *Quarante-quatre plus cinq font _____.*
4. *Soixante et un moins trente-deux font _____.*
5. *Quarante-trois moins quinze font _____.*

E. *Compléter avec la forme correcte du verbe.* (Fill in with the correct verb form.)

MODÈLE: Elles _____ mardi pour la France. (partir)
Elles partent mardi pour la France.

1. *Vous étudiez et vous _____. (réussir)*
2. *Je travaille le matin et je _____ à midi. (finir)*
3. *Nous _____ la date de la soirée. (choisir)*
4. *Le cours _____ le vingt-huit. (finir)*
5. *Ils _____ à midi et demi. (finir)*

NOTE CULTURELLE (Cultural Note)

For Americans, the term *rendez-vous* has a romantic connotation: a candlelight dinner for two, a walk along the Seine. But in France, the term *rendez-vous* has many practical meanings as well: a dental appointment, a business meeting, a visit to the hairdresser's, or lunch with a friend.

If you are about to rendezvous with friends or acquaintances and want to bring a gift, a bottle of wine or champagne, candy or chocolate, as well as flowers are always welcome. Don't be surprised if your hosts open the gift you gave them right away. In France, gifts are opened in front of you. Do not buy gifts for expectant mothers or brides-to-be, however, as the French believe that this will inevitably bring bad luck. Chrysanthemums mean bad luck as well, so choose a different flower instead.

LA CLÉ DES EXERCICES (Answer Key)

A. 1. *Habitez-vous dans un appartement? / Est-ce que vous habitez dans un appartement? 2. Es-tu américaine? / Est-ce que tu es américaine? 3. Est-il content de sa chambre d'hôtel? / Est-ce qu'il est content de sa chambre d'hôtel? 4. Parlons-nous de la politique internationale? / Est-ce que nous parlons de la politique internationale? 5. Est-elle dans le jardin? / Est-ce qu'elle est dans le jardin?*
B. 1. *Il n'arrive pas le premier septembre. 2. Elle n'est pas anglaise. 3. Nous ne parlons pas très bien le français. 4. Elle ne porte pas le chapeau de sa cousine. 5. Vous n'allez pas à une soirée jeudi.*
C. 1. *Non, elles n'étudient pas l'architecture. 2. Non, je ne suis pas américain. 3. Non, nous ne sommes pas libres le cinq. 4. Non, je ne vais pas à la classe de danse mercredi. 5. Non, il ne parle pas espagnol.*
D. 1. *cinquante-cinq* 2. *quarante et un* 3. *quarante-neuf* 4. *vingt-neuf* 5. *vingt-huit*
E. 1. *réussissez* 2. *finis* 3. *choisissons* 4. *finit* 5. *finissent*

LEÇON 5
LES OBJETS DE LA MAISON. Household Objects.

A. DIALOGUE

Chez un antiquaire.

LA VENDEUSE: **Vous cherchez quelque chose?**

MME LEROI: **Nous cherchons des meubles pour notre maison de campagne.**

LA VENDEUSE: **Qu'est-ce que vous cherchez exactement? Un lit, une armoire, une commode?**

M. LEROI: **Un fauteuil pour mon secrétaire dans le salon.**

MME LEROI: **Et des chaises de salle à manger.**

LA VENDEUSE: **Voici un fauteuil très confortable pour votre salon.**

M. LEROI: **C'est vraiment un fauteuil magnifique.**

MME LEROI: **Oui, mais il est beaucoup trop grand pour ton secrétaire. Vous savez, notre maison n'est pas très grande.**

M. LEROI: **Et ce petit fauteuil vert?**

MME LEROI: **Cette couleur ne va pas du tout avec le décor. Avez-vous des chaises de salle à manger rustiques?**

LA VENDEUSE: **Nous n'avons pas de chaises rustiques en ce moment.**

M. LEROI: **Chérie, regarde ce récamier!**

MME LEROI: **Ah, mon Dieu! Il est superbe! Tu sais, il est parfait pour notre chambre, juste en face du lit, près de la fenêtre.**

In an Antique Shop.

SALESPERSON: May I help you?

MRS. LEROI: We're looking for furniture for our country house.

SALESPERSON: What are you looking for exactly? A bed, an armoire, a dresser?

MR. LEROI: An armchair for my desk in the living room.

MRS. LEROI: And some dining room chairs.

SALESPERSON: Here is a very comfortable armchair for your living room.

MR. LEROI: It's really a wonderful armchair.

MRS. LEROI: Yes, but it's far too big for your desk. You know, our house is not very large.

MR. LEROI: What about this small green armchair?

MRS. LEROI: This green does not go at all with the decor. Do you have country-style dining-room chairs?

SALESPERSON: We don't have any country-style chairs at this moment.

MR. LEROI: Darling, look at this récamier!

MRS. LEROI: Ah! My goodness, it's superb! You know, it is perfect for our bedroom, just across the bed, next to the window.

B. PRONONCIATION
(Pronunciation)

1. LIAISON

In lesson 2, you learned that many final consonants are linked to a vowel that follows: **vous → avez; les → appartements; sont → amis; dix → architectes.**

Liaison with the vowel that follows occurs after *h,* because *h* is silent: **les → hôtels; ils → habitent.**

The indefinite article *un* (a, an) is linked to a vowel or *h* that follows it; *un* is still nasal, but the *n* is then pronounced: **un → appartement; un → hôtel.**

Adjectives that precede a noun are linked to a vowel that follows: **un grand → appartement** (d = t); **un bon → ami; un mauvais → hotel** (s = z).

A final *t* is commonly linked to a vowel that follows: **c'est → un vieux fauteuil; ils sont → intéressants.**

2. CONSONANTS

a. The letter *l* is usually pronounced like the English equivalent, though with more vigor and distinctness. However, *ill* and a final *il* are often pronounced like the *y* in *yes.*

travail	like <u>a</u> in f<u>a</u>ther + *y*
soleil, fauteuil	*è* + *y*

49

vieil	$y + è + y$
bouteille	$ee + y$

Before a vowel, *il* is linked like the *y* in *yes*:

un vieil ami, un vieil homme *(vyèy)*

b. The letters *ch* are usually pronounced like the English *sh:*

chambre; chien; chapeau; architecte.

Occcasionally *ch* is sounded like the English *k:*

Christine   orchestre   archéologue

3. OMISSIONS

You learned in lesson 1 that an unaccented *e* at the end of a word is usually not pronounced, with the exception of short words like *je*.

Silent: **regrette, possible, trente, une**

Pronounced: **je, ne, le, ce**

In addition, an unaccented *e* within certain words is not pronounced:

avenue; mademoiselle; acheter; samedi.

Also, in certain combinations of words, the short words like *je* may create a silent *e*.

ce n'est pas
beaucoup de meubles
qu'est-ce qu'il y a
pas de fenêtre

In casual daily speech omissions such as these also occur:

un petit secrétaire
au revoir

C. GRAMMAIRE ET USAGE
(Grammar and Usage)

1. POSSESSIVE ADJECTIVES

Like all adjectives, the possessive adjectives agree in gender and number with the noun they modify. They agree with the thing possessed, not the possessor.

	MASCULINE SINGULAR	FEMININE SINGULAR	MASCULINE AND FEMININE PLURAL
my	mon salon	ma maison	mes livres
your	ton salon	ta maison	tes livres
his/her/its	son salon	sa maison	ses livres
our	notre salon	notre maison	nos livres
your	votre salon	votre maison	vos livres
their	leur salon	leur maison	leurs livres

C'est ma chambre.
　　It is my room.

Leurs livres sont intéressants.
　　Their books are interesting.

Son chien est dans le jardin.
　　His/her dog is in the garden.

The forms *mon, ton,* and *son* are used with *all* nouns that begin with a vowel or *h,* masculine and feminine alike.

	MASCULINE		FEMININE
my hotel	mon hôtel	your wardrobe	ton armoire
his/her friend	son ami	his/her idea	son idée

Note that *son, sa, ses* can mean either "his" or "her."

son fauteuil	his/her armchair
sa chambre	his/her room
ses chapeaux	his/her hats

Unlike in English, where the possessive adjective may refer to two or more connected nouns, French uses a possessive adjective with each individual noun.

C'est mon piano et ma clarinette.
　　It's my piano and my clarinet.

2. DEMONSTRATIVE ADJECTIVES

Demonstrative adjectives (this, that, these, those) are used to point out a thing or a person. Like all adjectives they agree in gender and number with the noun they modify.

	SINGULAR		PLURAL	
MASCULINE	*ce chapeau*	this hat	*ces chapeaux*	these hats
MASCULINE	*cet architecte*	this architect	*ces architectes*	these architects
FEMININE	*cette femme*	this woman	*ces femmes*	these women

The masculine singular *ce* adds a *t* when a vowel or *h* sound follows.

Ce danseur s'appelle Jérôme Leduc.
This dancer is called Jérôme Leduc.

Cette femme parle cinq langues.
This woman speaks five languages.

Ces gâteaux sont excellents.
These cakes are excellent.

Demonstrative adjectives can be used to make a distinction or clarify a choice between things by adding the suffix *-ci* to the first noun and *-là* to the second.

Préférez-vous cette chaise-ci ou cette chaise-là?
Do you prefer this or that chair?

Aimez-vous cette commode-ci ou cette commode-là?
Do you like this dresser or that one?

3. THE POSITION OF ADJECTIVES

In English, the adjective precedes the noun, whereas in French most descriptive adjectives follow the noun.

une armoire magnifique	a beautiful armoire
une salle à manger rustique	a country-style dining room
un architecte espagnol	a Spanish architect

Il achète des livres français.
He buys French books.

Nous aimons les meubles anglais.
We like English furniture.

Ils choisissent le fauteuil vert.
They choose the green armchair.

Ce secrétaire italien est superbe.
This Italian bureau is superb.

Certain common short adjectives are placed before the noun they modify.

un petit hôtel	a small hotel
un grand chapeau	a big hat
une jeune femme	a young woman
un vieux fauteuil	an old armchair
un bon ami	a good friend
une mauvaise réponse	a bad answer

Voilà un beau jardin!
Here's a beautiful garden!

Ils cherchent une jolie maison.
They are looking for a nice house.

Elle choisit un nouveau restaurant.
She chooses a new restaurant.

4. THE VERB *SAVOIR*

The English verb "to know" has two different translations in French: *savoir* and *connaître*. *Savoir* is used to indicate to know how to do something or to have a skill acquired through the repetition of an act. *Connaître,* on the other hand, implies familiarity with a person or place. In this chapter we will concentrate on *savoir*. *Connaître* will be dealt with in a later lesson.[1]

SAVOIR   TO KNOW

I know	*je sais*	we know	*nous savons*
you know	*tu sais*	you know	*vous savez*
he/she/one knows	*il/elle/on sait*	they know	*ils/elles savent*

Savez-vous la réponse?
Do you know the answer?

Il sait danser.
He knows how to dance.

Sais-tu comment elle s'appelle?
Do you know her name?

[1] Please refer to *Leçon* 37.

VOCABULAIRE (Vocabulary)

les objets ménagers *(m. pl.)*	household objects
la maison	house
la maison de campagne	country house
la campagne	countryside
la porte	door
la fenêtre	window
le salon	living room
la salle à manger	dining room
la cuisine	kitchen
la chambre	room, bedroom
les meubles	furniture
le décor	decor
l'armoire	wardrobe, armoire
la table	table
la chaise	chair
le fauteuil	armchair
la lampe	lamp
le secrétaire	secretary, writing desk
le sofa	sofa
le lit	bed
la commode	dresser
l'antiquaire	antique shop
le vendeur	salesperson
le couple	couple
savoir	to know, to know how
chercher	to look for
danser	to dance
vert	green
grand	large, big, tall
petit	small
bon	good
mauvais	bad
jeune	young
vieux	old
rustique	country-style
joli	pretty
confortable	comfortable
voici	here is, here are
voilà	there is, there are
cette chaise-ci	this chair
cette chaise-là	that chair

beaucoup de
en face

much, a lot (of), many
in front of, opposite

EXERCICES (Exercises)

A. *Compléter les phrases suivantes par l'adjectif possessif.* (Fill in the appropriate possessive adjective.)

MODÈLE: Elle invite _____ amis à la campagne.
Elle invite ses amis à la campagne.

1. *Nous aimons _____ salon.*
2. *Il cherche _____ clés.*
3. *Elle porte _____ chapeau vert.*
4. *Vous regardez _____ fauteuil favori.*
5. *Je vais dans _____ chambre.*

B. *Compléter avec le verbe "savoir."* (Fill in the verb *savoir*.)

MODÈLE: Elle _____ le numéro de la chambre.
Elle sait le numéro de la chambre.

1. *Tu _____ parler français.*
2. *_____-vous comment s'appelle ce danseur?*
3. *Nous _____ la réponse.*
4. *Est-ce que vous _____ la couleur du fauteuil?*
5. *Ils _____ acheter des antiquités.*

C. *Compléter avec l'adjectif démonstratif qui convient.* (Fill in the appropriate demonstrative adjective.)

MODÈLE: Nous regardons _____ secrétaire.
Nous regardons ce secrétaire.

1. *Tu achètes _____ armoire?*
2. *Nous aimons _____ chaises rustiques.*
3. *_____ lit est très confortable.*
4. *Ils préfèrent _____ hôtel.*
5. *_____ salon est magnifique.*

D. *Insérer les adjectifs à la place qui convient.* (Insert the adjectives at the appropriate place.)

MODÈLE: La cuisine est très jolie. (rustique)
La cuisine rustique est très jolie.

1. *Cette maison est à la campagne.*   *(petite)*
2. *Ce danseur habite à Paris.*   *(italien)*

3. *Ces meubles sont français.*   *(vieux)*
4. *Ce couple cherche des meubles.*   *(français)*
5. *Le salon a une fenêtre.*   *(grande)*

NOTE CULTURELLE (Cultural Note)

The love of furniture is immediately noticeable when you enter a French home or hotel. The focal point of a room may be a piece that has been passed down from generation to generation. If you are fortunate enough to be invited to someone's country home, you may end up in a restored barn or a 14th-century manor house.

A trip to Paris should include a visit to the antique stores on the left bank at the Carré Rive Gauche and near the Palais Royal. If you decide to purchase an antique, it should be carefully crated before it is shipped home.

LA CLÉ DES EXERCICES (Answer Key)

A. 1. *notre*   2. *ses*   3. *son*   4. *votre*   5. *ma*
B. 1. *sais*   2. *Savez*   3. *savons*   4. *savez*   5. *savent*
C. 1. *cette*   2. *ces*   3. *Ce*   4. *cet*   5.   *Ce*
D. 1. *Cette petite maison est à la campagne.* 2. *Ce danseur italien habite à Paris.* 3. *Ces vieux meubles sont français.* 4. *Ce couple français cherche des meubles.* 5. *Le salon a une grande fenêtre.*

PREMIÈRE RÉVISION (First Review)

A. *Compléter les phrases avec le verbe "être."* (Complete the sentences with the verb *être*.)

1. *Nous _____ étudiants.*
2. *Michèle _____ professeur.*
3. *Est-ce que vous _____ libre aujourd'hui?*

B. *Compléter avec le verbe "travailler."* (Fill in the verb *travailler*.)

1. *Je _____ à Paris.*
2. *Est-ce que vous _____ aux États-Unis?*
3. *Nous _____ samedi prochain.*

C. *Compléter avec la préposition "à" et l'article défini.* (Fill in the preposition *à* and the definite article.)

MODÈLE: Elle va _____ cinéma.
        Elle va au cinéma.

1. *Il est _____ match de basket-ball.*
2. *Vous habitez _____ États-Unis.*
3. *Je reste _____ maison.*

D. *Ecrire les chiffres en toutes lettres.* (Write out the numbers in French.)

1. 21
2. 49
3. 35

E. *Mettre les phrases à la forme negative.* (Put the sentences in the negative.)

1. *Il va à Paris.*
2. *Nous avons des cassettes.*
3. *Je suis français.*

F. *Compléter avec le verbe "avoir."* (Fill in the verb *avoir.*)

1. *Ils _____ des amis français.*
2. *Je _____ un travail intéressant.*
3. *Est-ce que vous _____ des amis en France?*

G. *Mettre les adjectifs à la place qui convient.* (Put the adjectives in the correct place.)

1. *Corrine a une maison. (petite)*
2. *Luc est un ami. (difficile)*
3. *Il a un fauteuil. (vieux)*
4. *Nous avons des amis. (sympathiques)*

H. *Compléter avec le verbe "finir."* (Fill in the verb *finir.*)

1. *Je _____ le travail.*
2. *Nous _____ la leçon.*
3. *Vous _____ votre stage.*

I. *Compléter avec le verbe "aller."* (Fill in the verb *aller.*)

1. *Ils _____ au Jardin du Luxembourg.*
2. *Est-ce que tu _____ à Lyon?*
3. *Vous _____ en Italie.*

J. *Relier le français et l'anglais.* (Match the French and the English.)

1. *Comment allez-vous?*
2. *Je vous en prie.*
3. *Je m'appelle Marie.*
4. *Je vous présente Laurence.*
5. *A bientôt.*

a. My name is Marie.
b. See you soon.
c. You are welcome.
d. How are you?
e. Let me introduce Laurence.

LA CLÉ DES EXERCICES (Answer Key)

A. 1. *sommes*   2. *est*   3. *êtes*
B. 1. *travaille*   2. *travaillez*   3. *travaillons*
C. 1. *au*   2. *aux*   3. *à la*
D. 1. *vingt et un*   2. *quarante-neuf*   3. *trente-cinq*
E. 1. *Il ne va pas à Paris.* 2. *Nous n'avons pas de cassettes.* 3. *Je ne suis pas français.*
F. 1. *ont*   2. *J'ai*   3. *avez*
G. 1. *Corrine a une petite maison.* 2. *Luc est un ami difficile.* 3. *Il a un vieux fauteuil.* 4. *Nous avons des amis sympathiques.*
H. 1. *finis*   2. *finissons*   3. *finissez*
I. 1. *vont*   2. *vas*   3. *allez*
J. 1.—d   2.—c   3.—a   4.—e   5.—b

LEÇON 6

CE QUE J'AIME, CE QUE JE N'AIME PAS.   Expressing Likes and Dislikes.

A. DIALOGUE

Le temps.

JULIE: **Vous partez en vacances?**

ANDRÉ: **Non, je vais chez mon cousin pour le week-end.**

JULIE: **Vous avez de la chance! Il fait si chaud à Paris cet été. Où habite votre cousin?**

ANDRÉ: **Il habite dans une vieille maison normande. Et vous, vous allez partir cet été?**

JULIE: **Non, je vais prendre mes vacances dans les Hautes-Alpes en octobre.**

ANDRÉ: **Il fait froid dans les Alpes à cette saison!**

JULIE: **Parfois il pleut! Mais j'adore la montagne à toutes les saisons. Et vous, quand partez-vous?**

ANDRÉ: **Nous allons voyager en Tunisie en novembre et à Tahiti en mars.**

JULIE: **Vous n'avez pas peur de la chaleur?**

ANDRÉ: **Personnellement, je préfère la neige, les sports d'hiver . . . Mais ma femme déteste le froid et adore le soleil.**

JULIE: **Bon, j'espère que vous allez passer un bon week-end!**

ANDRÉ: **Merci. À la semaine prochaine.**

The Weather.

JULIE: Are you going on vacation?

ANDRÉ: No, I am going to my cousin's for the weekend.

JULIE: How lucky you are! It's so hot in Paris this summer. Where does your cousin live?

ANDRÉ: He lives in an old Norman-style house. And you, are you going away this summer?

JULIE: No, I'll take my vacation in the Hautes-Alpes in October.

ANDRÉ: It's cold in the Alps during that season!

JULIE: Sometimes it rains! But I love the mountains during any season. And you? When are you going away?

ANDRÉ: We are going to travel to Tunisia in November and to Tahiti in March.

JULIE: You're not afraid of the heat?

ANDRÉ: Personally, I prefer snow, winter sports. . . . But my wife hates the cold and loves the sun.

JULIE: Well, I hope you have a great weekend.

ANDRÉ: Thank you. See you next week.

B. PRONONCIATION

1. MASCULINE AND FEMININE FORMS OF NOUNS AND ADJECTIVES

When a masculine noun or adjective ending in a silent consonant adds an *e* in the feminine, the preceding consonant is pronounced.

français, française
étudiant, étudiante

Masculine words ending in a nasal vowel lose the nasal vowel when the feminine ending *-e* is added and sound the preceding consonant.

américain, américaine
un, une

Some of these words double the final *n* in the feminine.

parisien, parisienne
bon, bonne

Masculine adjectives ending in *-eux* change to *-euse* in the feminine.

heureux, heureuse
merveilleux, merveilleuse

Masculine forms ending in *-er* (sounded *é)* change to *-ère* (sounded *è* + *r*) in the feminine.

premier, première
étranger, étrangère

2. CONSONANTS

The letter *t* + *ion* is sounded like *ss:*

nation, nationalité, *sensationnel.*

The letters *gn* are pronounced like the *n* in "onion":

campagne, dignité, *signal, cognac.*

3. THE VERBS *PRÉFÉRER AND ESPÉRER*

There is a difference in sound between the singular and plural forms of *préférer* (to prefer).

SINGULAR

je préfère
tu préfères
il/elle/on préfère

PLURAL

nous préférons
vous préférez
ils/elles préfèrent

Because the *s* of *ils* is silent, the third-person forms sound alike.

il parle/ils parlent
elle préfère/elles préfèrent

Notice, however, the difference in the sound if the verb begins with an *e* or *h:*

il espère/ils → espèrent
elle habite/elles → habitent

C. GRAMMAIRE ET USAGE

1. THE VERB *FAIRE*

The verb *faire* (to do) is one of the most important verbs, and it is used in many idiomatic expressions.

I make	*je fais*	we make	*nous faisons*
you make	*tu fais*	you make	*vous faites*
he/she/one makes	*il/elle/on fait*	they make	*ils/elles font*

Je fais un gâteau.
  I'm making a cake.

Qu'est-ce que vous faites?
  What are you doing?

Nous faisons un voyage.
  We're taking a trip.

Faire is also used in most expressions describing the weather.

Il fait beau.
  The weather is nice.

Il fait du soleil.
  It is sunny.

Il fait du vent.
  It is windy.

Il fait frais.
  It is cool.

Il fait froid.
  It is cold.

Il fait chaud.
  It is hot.

Il fait doux.
  It is mild.

2. THE VERBS *ESPÉRER* AND *ACHETER*

Espérer (to hope) and *acheter* (to buy) are two *-er* verbs with changes in the accented *e* in all but the first and second persons plural.

ESPÉRER   TO HOPE

I hope	*j'espère*	we hope	*nous espérons*
you hope	*tu espères*	you hope	*vous espérez*
he/she/one hopes	*il/elle/on espère*	they hope	*ils/elles espèrent*

Nous espérons que vous allez bien.
We hope you're feeling well.

J'espère qu'il fait beau à Paris.
I hope the weather is nice in Paris.

While the accented *é aigu* in the root of the verb *espérer* changes to an accented *è grave*, *acheter* adds an *accent grave* in all but the first and second persons plural.

ACHETER   TO BUY

I buy	*j'achète*	we buy	*nous achetons*
you buy	*tu achètes*	you buy	*vous achetez*
he/she/one buys	*il/elle/on achète*	they buy	*ils/elles achètent*

Il achète un livre français.
He buys a French book.

Vous achetez ce chapeau?
Are you buying this hat?

3. THE IMMEDIATE FUTURE/*ALLER* + INFINITIVE

The immediate future is formed using the verb *aller* followed by an infinitive. It is used to express future plans and intentions. It often replaces the real future in familiar conversation and would most commonly be translated into English as "going to."

Je vais voyager à Tahiti.
I am going to travel to Tahiti.

Nous allons acheter une maison.
We're going to buy a house.

Tu vas avoir froid.
You're going to be cold.

The immediate future can be used with impersonal expressions.

Il va faire chaud cet été.
It's going to be hot this summer.

Est-ce qu'il va pleuvoir?
Is it going to rain?

4. THE SEASONS AND MONTHS OF THE YEAR

Like the French words for the days of the week, the seasons and the months are not capitalized. They are all masculine and are used with the definite article.

LES SAISONS
le printemps
l'été
l'automne
l'hiver

THE SEASONS
spring
summer
fall
winter

L'automne est splendide.
The fall is wonderful.

Je préfère le printemps.
I prefer spring.

LES MOIS	THE MONTHS	*LES MOIS*	THE MONTHS
janvier	January	*juillet*	July
février	February	*août*	August
mars	March	*septembre*	September
avril	April	*octobre*	October
mai	May	*novembre*	November
juin	June	*décembre*	December

With seasons and months, use *en* for "in the," with exception of "in spring," which is *au printemps.*

Julie aime Paris en automne.
Julie likes Paris in the fall.

Les cours finissent en juin.
The classes end in June.

André va voyager au printemps.
André will travel in the spring.

5. IRREGULAR FEMININE ADJECTIVES

Most feminine forms of adjectives end in *e.* Some adjectives, however, are irregular in the feminine form. These irregular adjectives change their endings in a number of ways. Once you familiarize yourself with the variations, you will be quick to know the right ending.

a. *-if/-ive*

MASCULINE	FEMININE	
actif	*active*	active
neuf	*neuve*	new
créatif	*créative*	creative
	une femme active	an active woman

b. *-eux/-euse*

MASCULINE	FEMININE	
heureux	*heureuse*	happy
nombreux	*nombreuse*	numerous
merveilleux	*merveilleuse*	wonderful
	une musique merveilleuse	a wonderful piece of music

c. *-el/-elle*

MASCULINE	FEMININE	
naturel	*naturelle*	natural
tel	*telle*	such
exceptionnel	*exceptionnelle*	exceptional
	une saison exceptionnelle	an exceptional season

d. Some common adjectives have an irregular feminine form that must be memorized.

MASCULINE	FEMININE	
bon	*bonne*	good
blanc	*blanche*	white
doux	*douce*	soft
épais	*épaisse*	thick
gentil	*gentille*	nice
frais	*fraîche*	fresh
long	*longue*	long
sec	*sèche*	dry
	de longues vacances	long vacation
	une chaleur sèche	a dry heat
	une bonne idée	a good idea

e. Some irregular adjectives have two irregular forms, one for the feminine and one for the masculine singular, if the word it directly precedes begins with a vowel or a mute *h*.

le vieux document	the old document
le vieil architecte	the old architect

les vieux livres	the old books
les vieilles rues	the old streets
le beau jardin	the beautiful garden
le bel hôtel	the beautiful hotel
les beaux livres	the beautiful books
les belles maisons	the beautiful houses
le nouveau livre	the new book
le nouvel ami	the new friend
les nouveaux amis	the new friends

6. IRREGULAR MASCULINE PLURAL ADJECTIVES

a. Masculine singular adjectives ending in *-al* have a plural in *-aux*.

un programme international	an international program
des programmes internationaux	international programs
un journal régional	a regional paper
des journaux régionaux	regional papers

b. Masculine singular adjectives ending in *s* or *x* do not change in the plural.

un ami français	a French friend
des amis français	French friends
un hiver doux	a mild winter
des hivers doux	mild winters
un voyageur heureux	a happy traveler
des voyageurs heureux	happy travelers

VOCABULAIRE

l'année *(f.)*	the year
la saison	season
le printemps	spring
l'été *(m.)*	summer
l'automne *(m.)*	autumn, fall
l'hiver *(m.)*	winter
le mois	month
la semaine	week
le week-end	weekend
la mer	sea
la montagne	mountain, the mountains

le soleil	sun
la chaleur	heat
le froid	cold
le vent	wind
la neige	snow
le temps	weather
faire	to do, to make
l'air *(m.)*	air
la voiture	car
devant	in front of
prochain	next
espérer	to hope
préférer	to prefer
adorer	to love, to adore
charger	to load
passer	to spend (time)
prendre	to take
je vais prendre	I am going to take
avoir peur *(de)*	to be afraid (of)
beau, bel, belle	beautiful, lovely, fine
bon, bonne	good
doux, douce	soft, mellow, mild
frais, fraîche	fresh
heureux, heureuse	happy
merveilleux, merveilleuse	marvelous, wonderful
nouveau, nouvel, nouvelle	new
sensationnel, sensationnelle	sensational, fantastic
sportif, sportive	athletic
vieux, vieil, vieille	old

EXERCICES

A. *Faire correspondre les colonnes A et B.*

COLONNE A

COLONNE B

Maryse et moi
tu
M. et Mme Leblanc
je
nous

achètent
achète
achetons
achètes
achetons

COLONNE A	COLONNE B
Je	*espère*
Vous	*espèrent*
Marc et sa soeur	*espérez*
Nous	*espère*
Elle	*espérons*

B. *Compléter en utilisant le verbe "faire."*

MODÈLE: Il _____ chaud en été.
        Il fait chaud en été.

1. *Nous _____ un voyage en septembre.*
2. *Il _____ froid au mois de décembre.*
3. *Vous _____ un gâteau au chocolat.*
4. *Qu'est-ce que tu _____ ce soir?*
5. *Il _____ beau au Maroc toute l'année.*

C. *Mettre les adjectifs au féminin.*

MODÈLE: Il est français.
        Elle est française.

1. *Jacques est sportif.*
   Sandra est _____.
2. *Jacques n'est pas heureux.*
   Christine n'est pas _____.
3. *Le temps est exceptionnel.*
   La cuisine est _____.
4. *L'air est doux.*
   La saison est _____.
5. *André est gentil.*
   Julie est_____.

D. *Mettre les phrases suivantes au futur immédiat.*

MODÈLE: Il étudie l'architecture.
        Il va étudier l'architecture.

1. *Nous voyageons au Mexique.*
2. *Elles partent à midi.*
3. *J'achète un livre d'histoire.*
4. *Vous regardez les documents.*
5. *Il fait chaud à Tahiti.*

E. *Répondre aux questions suivantes.*

1. *Quelle saison commence le 21 mars?*
2. *Quelle est la date de votre anniversaire?*
3. *Quelle est la date de la fête nationale?*
4. *Quelle est la date du Nouvel An?*

NOTE CULTURELLE

La Provence is one of the most charming regions of France. It is a dry, hilly region in the Southeast just north of the French Riviera, the *Côte d'Azur*. It is dotted with tiny villages and covered with vineyards. It is known for the friendliness of its inhabitants, the warmth of its climate, and its seclusion. It is a favorite spot for vacationers who do not enjoy the crowds and bustle of the *Côte d'Azur*.

The French have about five weeks of paid vacation. They usually take three to four weeks during the summer and the rest at some other time of the year. In the winter, the French either go skiing or look for warm weather in the south of France, Northern Africa or faraway destinations.

LA CLÉ DES EXERCICES

A. *Maryse et moi achetons* *J'espère*
   Tu achètes *Vous espérez*
   M. et Mme Leblanc achètent *Marc et sa soeur espèrent*
   J'achète *Nous espérons*
   Nous achetons *Elle espère*

B. 1. *faisons* 2. *fait* 3. *faites* 4. *fais* 5. *fait*

C. 1. *sportive* 2. *heureuse* 3. *exceptionnelle* 4. *douce* 5. *gentille*

D. 1. *Nous allons voyager au Mexique.* 2. *Elles vont partir à midi.* 3. *Je vais acheter un livre d'histoire.* 4. *Vous allez regarder les documents.* 5. *Il va faire chaud à Tahiti.*

E. 1. *Le printemps commence le 21 mars.* 2. *La date de mon anniversaire est . . . . .* 3. *La fête de la Bastille est le 14 juillet.* 4. *Le Nouvel An est le 1er janvier.*

LEÇON 7

À LA GARE.   At the Train Station.

A. DIALOGUE

À la Gare de l'Est.

CAROLINE: **Je voudrais faire une réservation, s'il vous plaît.**

EMPLOYÉ: **Quelle est votre destination?**

CAROLINE: **Je voudrais aller à Strasbourg demain matin.**

EMPLOYÉ: **Il y a un rapide à 8 h 55 et un TGV[1] à 10 h 40.**

CAROLINE: **À quelle heure est-ce que le TGV arrive à Strasbourg? J'ai un rendez-vous d'affaires à 14 heures.**

EMPLOYÉ: **Il arrive à Strasbourg à 12 h 40.**

CAROLINE: **Très bien. Je voudrais réserver une place.**

EMPLOYÉ: **Aller simple ou aller-retour?**

CAROLINE: **Un aller-retour, s'il vous plaît.**

EMPLOYÉ: **En première ou en seconde?**

CAROLINE: **En seconde, s'il vous plaît.**

EMPLOYÉ: **Fumeur ou non-fumeur?**

CAROLINE: **Non-fumeur.**

EMPLOYÉ: **Quelle est la date de votre retour?**

CAROLINE: **Je voudrais être de retour vendredi vers midi.**

EMPLOYÉ: **Il y a un TGV vendredi à 8 h du matin. Il arrive à 11 h 22.**

CAROLINE: **C'est parfait!**

EMPLOYÉ: **Bon, départ mardi à 10 h 40, retour vendredi à 11 h 22. Votre place est réservée. Voilà votre billet. Bon voyage!**

———————————

At the *Gare de l'Est.*

CAROLINE: I would like to make a reservation, please.

EMPLOYEE: What is your destination?

[1] *Le TGV, le Train à Grande Vitesse* (Super Express Train), is a high-speed train connecting the major cities in France and Europe.

CAROLINE: I would like to go to Strasbourg tomorrow morning.

EMPLOYEE: There is an express train at 8:55 A.M. and a TGV at 10:40 A.M.

CAROLINE: At what time does the TGV arrive in Strasbourg? I have a business meeting at 2 P.M.

EMPLOYEE: It arrives at 12:40 A.M.

CAROLINE: Great! I'd like to reserve a seat.

EMPLOYEE: One way or round trip?

CAROLINE: Round trip, please.

EMPLOYEE: First or second class?

CAROLINE: Second class, please.

EMPLOYEE: Smoking or non-smoking?

CAROLINE: Non-smoking.

EMPLOYEE: When are you coming back?

CAROLINE: I'd like to be back Friday around noon.

EMPLOYEE: There is a TGV Friday at 8 in the morning. It arrives at 11:22.

CAROLINE: Perfect!

EMPLOYEE: So, you're leaving Tuesday at 10:40 A.M. and coming back Friday at 11:22 A.M. Your seat is reserved. Here is your ticket. Have a nice trip!

B. PRONONCIATION

1. THE FRENCH ALPHABET

To spell words and abbreviations (like *le TGV*) in French you need to know the alphabet.

letter	sound	letter	sound	letter	sound
a	*a*	j	*jee*	s	*éss*
b	*bé*	k	*ka*	t	*té*
c	*sé*	l	*èl*	u	*u*
d	*dé*	m	*èm*	v	*vé*
e	*e*	n	*èn*	w	*double vè*
f	*èf*	o	*o*	x	*eeks*
g	*jé*	p	*pé*	y	*i grec*
h	*ash*	q	*ku*	z	*zèd*
i	*ee*	r	*èr*		

2. CONSONANTS

g + a, o, u	like g in go	**gare, golf**
g + consonant	like g in go	**grand, agréable**
g + e, i	like s in pleasure	**manger, concierge**

3. VOWELS

The final *e* is not pronounced in these sentences.

Il est une heure et demie.
Il est une heure moins le quart.
Il est quatre heures.
Je voudrais un billet aller-retour.
Je voudrais revenir.

C. GRAMMAIRE ET USAGE

1. *IL Y A*

Il y a is a very common idiomatic expression which means both "there is" and "there are."

Il y a un train à 10 heures.
    There is a train at 10 P.M.

Il y a quatre fauteuils.
    There are four armchairs.

Est-ce qu'il y a du champagne?
    Is there any champagne?

Combien de mois y a-t-il dans l'année?
    How many months are there in a year?

2. THE POLITE FORM *JE VOUDRAIS*

Je voudrais is used to ask for something politely. It is a form of the verb *vouloir* (to want) and equivalent to the English, "I would like." (Vouloir will be conjugated and discussed in lesson 9.) Like its English equivalent, *je voudrais* can be used with both a noun and an infinitive.

Je voudrais un billet.
    I would like a ticket.

Je voudrais un café.
    I would like some coffee.

Je voudrais aller à Lyon.
    I would like to go to Lyon.

Je voudrais partir lundi.
    I would like to leave Monday.

3. THE INTERROGATIVE ADJECTIVE *QUEL*

	SINGULAR		PLURAL
MASCULINE	*quel*	what, which	*quels*
FEMININE	*quelle*	what, which	*quelles*

Quel is used in interrogative sentences. Like other adjectives, *quel* agrees in gender and number with the noun it modifies.

Quel jour sommes-nous?
    What day is it? / What's today?

À quelle heure partez-vous?
    At what time are you leaving?

Quels sont vos sports favoris?
    What are your favorite sports?

It is also used in exclamatory sentences.

Quelle soirée magnifique!
    What a wonderful evening!

Quelle chaleur!
    How hot it is!

4. *QU'EST-CE QUE C'EST*

When you need the definition of a word you ask:

Qu'est-ce que c'est?
    What is it?

Qu'est-ce que c'est que le TGV?
    What is the TGV?

5. TELLING TIME

To ask or tell the time, use the expressions:

Quelle heure est-il?	What time is it?
Il est . . .	It is . . .
Il est une heure.	It is one o'clock.
Il est deux heures.	It is two o'clock.
Il est sept heures.	It is seven o'clock.
Il est deux heures cinq.	It is five past two.
Il est deux heures dix.	It is ten past two.
Il est deux heures et quart.	It is a quarter past two.
Il est deux heures et demie.	It is half past two.
Il est trois heures moins vingt-cinq.	It is twenty-five to three.
Il est trois heures moins vingt.	It is twenty to three.
Il est trois heures moins le quart.	It is a quarter to three.
Il est trois heures moins dix.	It is ten to three.
Il est midi.	It's noon.
Il est midi et demi.	It is twelve thirty.
Il est minuit.	It's midnight.

To ask when something will happen, use *à*.

À quelle heure part le train?
At what time does the train leave?

À quelle heure finissent-ils?
At what time will they be finished?

There is no A.M./P.M. system in French. In conversation, use:

Il est sept heures du matin.
It is 7 A.M.

Il est quatre heures de l'après-midi.
It is 4 P.M.

Il est huit heures du soir.
It is 8 P.M.

Official time, the 24-hour clock, is used for train, plane, and bus schedules, as well as on the radio and on television.

Le programme commence à 20 h.
The show starts at 8 P.M.

Le train part à dix-sept heures vingt.
The train leaves at 5:20 P.M.

74

6. EXPRESSIONS OF TIME

aujourd'hui	today
hier	yesterday
demain	tomorrow
avant-hier	the day before yesterday
après-demain	the day after tomorrow
la semaine prochaine	next week
la semaine dernière	last week
le mois prochain	next month
le mois dernier	last month
l'année prochaine	next year
l'année dernière	last year
dans une quinzaine	in two weeks (in 15 days)
dans un mois	in a month
dans deux ans	in two years

VOCABULAIRE

la gare	train station
les renseignements *(m. pl.)*	information
le guichet	(ticket) booth
le quai	platform
le billet	ticket
le voyage	trip
la destination	destination
un aller simple	a one-way ticket
un aller-retour	a round-trip ticket
le départ	departure
l'arrivée *(f.)*	arrival
le retour	return
la correspondance	transfer
le TGV *(le Train à Grande Vitesse)*	The Super Express Train
le chemin de fer	railroad
Est-ce qu'il y a une correspondance à Lyon?	Is there a transfer at Lyon?
le train du matin	morning train
le train du soir	evening train
une réservation	a reservation
réserver	to reserve
Je voudrais réserver une place.	I'd like to reserve a seat.
première classe	first class
seconde classe	second class
fumeur	smoking section

non-fumeur	non-smoking section
le compartiment	compartment
la consigne	baggage room
la place	seat
Cette place est libre *(occupée).*	This seat is free (taken).
arriver	to arrive
désirer	to wish, to want
je voudrais . . .	I would like . . .
le matin	morning
l'après-midi *(m.)*	afternoon
le soir	evening
la nuit	night
l'heure *(f.)*	hour
hier	yesterday
demain	tomorrow
aujourd'hui	today
il y a . . .	there is . . . , there are . . .
Quelle heure est-il?	What time is it?
quel, quelle *(m., f.)*	what, which
quand	when

EXERCICES

A. *Répéter la phrase avec "je voudrais."*

MODÈLE: *Une place non-fumeur.*
Je voudrais une place non-fumeur.

1. *Un aller-retour pour Lyon.*
2. *Aller à Strasbourg.*
3. *Etre de retour dimanche.*
4. *Revenir vendredi.*
5. *Réserver une place.*

B. *Compléter les phrases suivantes.*

1. *Jacques voudrait un _____ pour Lyon.*
2. *Départ lundi et _____ vendredi.*
3. *Le train de Lyon _____ à dix-neuf heures.*
4. *Voilà le _____ des réservations.*
5. *Votre _____ est réservée.*

a. *part*
b. *guichet*
c. *aller-retour*
d. *place*
e. *retour*

C. *Écrire l'heure en français.* (Write the time in French.)

MODÈLE: 8:40 P.M.
        Neuf heures moins vingt.

1. 12:30 P.M.
2. 9:45 A.M.
3. 7:50 P.M.
4. 11:15 A.M.
5. 6:40 A.M.

6. 8:20 A.M.
7. 3:55 P.M.
8. 9:12 P.M.
9. 12:30 A.M.
10. 5:35 P.M.

D. *Écrire l'heure officielle en français.* (Write the official time in French.)

MODÈLE: 8:20 P.M.
        Vingt heures vingt.

1. 1:15 P.M.
2. 4:20 P.M.
3. 8:50 A.M.
4. 3:47 P.M.
5. 5:38 P.M.

6. 11:14 A.M.
7. 10:26 P.M.
8. 5:35 A.M.
9. 12:10 A.M.
10. 6:30 P.M.

E. *Traduire.* (Translate)

1. There are three tickets.
2. Is there a train at 8:30 A.M.?
3. There are three apartments on this floor.
4. Is there a party tomorrow?
5. There is a good program the day after tomorrow.

F. *Compléter en utilisant l'adjectif interrogatif "quel."*

1. _____ *sont vos livres favoris?*
2. _____ *programme regardes-tu à la télévision aujourd'hui?*
3. _____ *maison voudrais-tu acheter?*
4. _____ *chapeau allez-vous acheter?*
5. *À* _____ *heure part le train?*

NOTE CULTURELLE

Trains are a favorite mode of transportation in France. The railway system is extensive and serves both large and small cities throughout the country. The TGV (*le Train à Grande Vitesse,* or high-speed train) also contributes greatly to the popularity of trains. It goes from Paris to Lyon (250 miles) in a mere two hours and now links most important cities in France and in Europe. If you want to go on the TGV, you need a reservation. On the TGV, you pay a supplement but, as on all French trains, you can choose between first and second class (coach). American travelers can buy discount passes in the United States.

LA CLÉ DES EXERCICES

A. 1. *Je voudrais un aller-retour pour Lyon.* 2. *Je voudrais aller à Strasbourg.* 3. *Je voudrais être de retour dimanche.* 4. *Je voudrais revenir vendredi.* 5. *Je voudrais réserver une place.*
B. 1. *aller-retour* 2. *retour* 3. *part* 4. *guichet* 5. *place*
C. 1. *Midi et demi.* 2. *Dix heures moins le quart.* 3. *Huit heures moins dix.* 4. *Onze heures et quart.* 5. *Sept heures moins vingt.* 6. *Huit heures vingt.* 7. *Quatre heures moins cinq.* 8. *Neuf heures douze.* 9. *Minuit et demi.* 10. *Six heures moins vingt-cinq.*
D. 1. *Treize heures quinze.* 2. *Seize heures vingt.* 3. *Huit heures cinquante.* 4. *Quinze heures quarante-sept.* 5. *Dix-sept heures trente-huit.* 6. *Onze heures quatorze.* 7. *Vingt-deux heures vingt-six.* 8. *Cinq heures trente-cinq.* 9. *Zéro heure dix.* 10. *Dix-huit heures trente.*
E. 1. *Il y a trois billets.* 2. *Y a-t-il un train à huit heures trente?* 3. *Il y a trois appartements à cet étage.* 4. *Y a-t-il une soirée demain?* 5. *Il y a un bon programme après-demain.*
F. 1. *Quels* 2. *Quel* 3. *Quelle* 4. *Quel* 5. *Quelle*

LEÇON 8

AU RESTAURANT. At a Restaurant.

A. DIALOGUE

Dîner avec des amis.

LAURE: Bertrand, qu'est-ce que tu prends?

BERTRAND: Euh . . . j'hésite entre le carré d'agneau et le homard. Qu'est-ce que tu recommandes?

CAROLINE: La spécialité de la maison, c'est les crustacés. Ce homard a vraiment l'air délicieux. . . .

LAURE: J'ai envie d'une côte de bœuf avec des frites.

CAROLINE: Laure, tu manges trop de viande rouge!

BERTRAND: Laure a besoin de protéines. Son travail est très stressant. . . .

LAURE: Bertrand a raison. Et toi, tu manges trop de desserts!

CAROLINE: Je suis au régime. Pas de graisse, pas de sucre.

BERTRAND: Tu bois du vin, j'espère?

CAROLINE: Le vin rouge, c'est bon pour la santé et ça ne fait pas grossir. . . .

BERTRAND: Mesdames, par quoi voulez-vous commencer?

LAURE: On partage des hors-d'œuvre? Les escargots ont l'air succulent.

CAROLINE: Bon, deux douzaines d'escargots et des artichauts.

BERTRAND: Et qu'est-ce qu'on boit avec ça?

LAURE: Monsieur, apportez-nous[1] une bonne bouteille de Bourgogne.

BERTRAND: Bon appétit!

Dinner with Friends.

LAURE: Bertrand, what are you having?

BERNARD: I can't decide (literally: hesitate) between the rack of lamb and the lobster. What do you suggest?

CAROLINE: Shellfish is the house speciality. This lobster looks really delicious.

---

[1] The imperative forms will be discussed in *Leçon* 12.

LAURE: I feel like having ribs with french fries.

CAROLINE: Laure, you eat too much red meat!

BERTRAND: Laure needs protein. Her job is very stressful. . . .

LAURE: Bertrand is right . . . And you, you eat too many desserts!

CAROLINE: I am on a diet. No fat, no sugar.

BERTRAND: You'll drink some wine, I hope?

CAROLINE: Red wine is good for your health and does not make you gain weight.

BERTRAND: Ladies, what are we starting with?

LAURE: What about sharing some appetizers? The snails look delicious.

CAROLINE: O.K., two dozen snails and some artichokes.

BERTRAND: What are we drinking with this?

LAURE: Waiter, bring us a good bottle of Bourgogne.

BERTRAND: Enjoy your meal!

B. PRONONCIATION

1. THE VERB *PRENDRE*

Note the varied sounds of *e* in the irregular verb *prendre* (to take).

je prends	**nous prenons**
tu prends	**vous prenez**
il/elle/on prend	**ils/elles prennent**

Notice the sound of the third-person forms in the inversion.

Prend-il?   **Prennent-ils?**

2. CONSONANTS

You learned in lesson 3 that the letter *h* is never pronounced in French, and that elision and liaison occur with the vowel that follows it. This is called the "muted h." Some examples are: *l'hiver; aujourd'hui; l'hôtel; j'habite; trois → heures.*

However, there are a number of exceptions when you do not use an elision or liaison. It's just a matter of memorizing the list. Some examples are: *les hors-d'oeuvre; le hot-dog; le homard; les haricots; les Halles.*

Je ne prends pas de hors-d'oeuvre.
Il achète deux kilos de/haricots aux/Halles.

In the glossary, these exceptions will be preceded by an asterisk:
· *les *hors-d'oeuvre*

3. VOWELS: A REVIEW

a. *e/é/è*

E	É	È
je	*régime*	*très*
ce	*spécialité*	*ces*
le	*appétit*	*près*

b. open and closed *o*

OPEN	CLOSED
chapeau	*escargot*
soleil	*artichaut*
adore	*bonne*
joli	*bientôt*

c. closed and open *eu*

OPEN	CLOSED
veux	*veulent*
ceux	*heure*
deux	*peur*
meubles	*beurre*

d. *ou* and *u*

OU	U
douzaine	*du*
bouteille	*juste*
jour	*tu*
vous	*rustique*

e. nasal vowels

a	*moins*
an	*année, an*
moi	*en, train, on, un*

C. GRAMMAIRE ET USAGE

1. THE VERB *PRENDRE*

Prendre is an irregular verb which means "to take," "to have something to eat," or "to have something to drink."

PRENDRE TO TAKE

I take	*je prends*	we take	*nous prenons*
you take	*tu prends*	you take	*vous prenez*
he/she/one takes	*il/elle/on prend*	they take	*ils/elles prennent*

A few key verbs, *comprendre* (to understand) and *apprendre* (to learn), follow the same pattern.

J'apprends le français.
  I learn French.

Elle apprend à manger les escargots.
  She learns to eat snails.

Tu comprends son accent?
  Do you understand his accent?

Il comprend très bien l'anglais.
  He understands English very well.

Comprenez-vous?
  Do you understand?

Je prends des vacances.
  I am taking a vacation.

Je prends un café.
  I'll have coffee.

2. THE *-ER* VERBS *MANGER* AND *COMMENCER*

Although *manger* (to eat) and *commencer* (to begin) conjugate regularly, spelling changes occur in the *nous* form.

Manger adds an *e* to the stem *mang-* in order to keep the soft pronunciation of the *g*.

MANGER TO EAT

I eat	*je mange*	we eat	*nous mangeons*
you eat	*tu manges*	you eat	*vous mangez*
he/she/one eats	*il/elle/on mange*	they eat	*ils/elles mangent*

On mange bien ici.
One eats well here.

Nous mangeons beaucoup.
We eat a lot.

Commencer takes a cedilla on the *c* to keep the soft pronunciation of the *c*.

COMMENCER TO BEGIN

I begin	*je commence*	we begin	*nous commençons*
you begin	*tu commences*	you begin	*vous commencez*
he/she/one begins	*il/elle/on commence*	they begin	*ils/elles commencent*

Il commence un livre intéressant.
He is starting an interesting book.

Nous commençons un long voyage.
We're starting a long journey.

3. THE VERB *BOIRE*

Boire (to drink) has the following irregular forms.

BOIRE TO DRINK

I drink	*je bois*	we drink	*nous buvons*
you drink	*tu bois*	you drink	*vous buvez*
he/she/one drinks	*il/elle/on boit*	they drink	*ils/elles boivent*

Vous buvez du vin rouge?
Are you drinking red wine?

Ils boivent du café.
They drink coffee.

83

4. THE PARTITIVE ARTICLE

The partitive article designates a part of a whole. Its equivalent in English is "some" or "any." In French, it is: *du* (masculine singular); *de l'* (masculine and feminine singular); *de la* (feminine singular); *des* (masculine and feminine singular).

The partitive indicates an unspecified quantity of a given noun. Although the partitive article is often omitted in English, it is always used in French.

Je bois de l'eau.
I drink water.

Elle prend des escargots.
She's having some snails.

Je voudrais des frites.
I'd like some French fries.

Apportez-moi une bouteille d'eau.
Bring me a bottle of water.

J'ai de la chance.
I am lucky.

Do not use the partitive article after verbs of liking and disliking; use the definite article instead.

J'aime le poisson.
I like fish.

Elle adore la salade.
She loves salad.

Il déteste les légumes.
He hates vegetables.

The negative of the partitive article is *pas de* + noun.

Je ne mange pas de pain.
I don't eat bread.

Elle ne mange pas de salade.
She does not eat salad.

Ils ne boivent pas d'eau.
They don't drink water.

5. IDIOMATIC EXPRESSIONS WITH *AVOIR*

Avoir (to have), is used in many idiomatic expressions, such as:

avoir besoin de	to need
avoir faim	to be hungry
avoir soif	to be thirsty
avoir chaud	to be hot
avoir froid	to be cold
avoir 15 ans	to be 15 years old
avoir du mal à	to have trouble (doing)
avoir de la chance	to be lucky
avoir peur	to be afraid
avoir mal à	to have a pain
avoir raison	to be right
avoir le temps	to have time
avoir l'air	to seem/to look
avoir honte	to be ashamed

Elle a de la chance au casino.
> She has luck at the casino.

Il a du mal à comprendre.
> He has trouble understanding.

Ils ont l'air fatigué.
> They look tired.

Quel âge a-t-elle?
> How old is she?

Tu n'as pas honte?
> Aren't you ashamed?

In the verbal expression *avoir envie de, de* remains invariable if it refers to a general notion.

J'ai envie de fraises.
> I feel like strawberries.

J'ai envie de salade.
> I feel like salad.

J'ai envie de pommes.
> I feel like having apples.

J'ai envie d'eau.
> I feel like drinking water.

This expression can be used with the indefinite article: *de* is then elided to *d'*.

Nous avons envie de steak.
    We feel like having steak.

Laure a envie d'une tarte.
    Laure feels like having a pie.

    Avoir envie de can also be used with an infinitive.

Nous avons envie de voyager.
    We feel like traveling.

J'ai envie de dormir.
    I feel sleepy.

6. THE PRONOUN *ON*

    On (one, they) is used to indicate a general fact or rule.

Dans une pharmacie, on vend des médicaments.
    In a pharmacy, one sells medicine.

On parle français à Québec.
    They speak/one speaks French in Quebec.

En Angleterre, on boit du thé.
    In England, they drink tea.

    On is also used to mean "we," although it is grammatically singular and is always followed by the third person singular form of the verb.

On commande des escargots?
    Shall we order snails?

On dîne au restaurant ce soir.
    We're eating out tonight.

    Remember, as *on* is an understood "we," any adjective must agree in gender and number with the implied subject, *nous*.

On est ravis de sa visite.
    We're delighted to see him.

On est italiens.
    We are Italians.

le repas	meal
le petit déjeuner	breakfast
le déjeuner	lunch
le dîner	dinner
le régime	diet
la santé	health
à votre santé	to your health, cheers
bon appétit	enjoy your meal
la graisse	fat
le sucre	sugar
le pain	bread
le beurre	butter
le sel	salt
le poivre	pepper
le restaurant	restaurant
le menu	menu
les *hors-d'œuvre *(m. pl.)*	hors d'oeuvres, appetizers
le plat principal	main course
la viande	meat
l'agneau *(m.)*	lamb
le steak	steak
le bœuf	beef
le poulet	chicken
le veau	veal
le porc	pork
le foie	liver
le poisson	fish
le homard	lobster
les crustacés	shellfish
les escargots	snails
la salade	salad
le pain	bread
les légumes *(m.)*	vegetables
l'artichaut *(m.)*	artichoke
les frites *(f.)*	French fries
la pomme de terre	potato
le chou-fleur	cauliflower
les *haricots *(m.)*	beans
le dessert	dessert
le fromage	cheese
les fruits	fruit
un fruit	a piece of fruit

le gâteau	cake
une tarte aux pommes	an apple pie
la boisson	beverage
le vin rouge	red wine
le vin blanc	white wine
l'eau *(f.)*	water
une carafe	a pitcher
le café/un café	coffee, a cup of coffee, a café
le serveur/la serveuse	waiter, waitress
l'addition *(f.)*	the bill
avoir faim	to be hungry
avoir soif	to be thirsty
avoir envie de	to feel like (having or doing something)
avoir raison	to be right
avoir tort	to be wrong
avoir besoin de	to need
inviter	to invite
commander	to order
recommander	to recommend, to suggest
commencer par	to begin with
prendre	to take, to have something to eat or drink
manger	to eat
boire	to drink
si	yes (contradicting a negative)
ici	here
comprendre	to understand
apprendre	to learn

EXERCICES

A. *Compléter en utilisant l'article partitif correct.* (Answer with the proper partitive article.)

MODÈLE: Comme boisson, vous prenez _____? (le vin)
Comme boisson, vous prenez du vin?

1. *Comme hors-d'oeuvre, vous prenez _____? (la salade)*
2. *Comme plat principal, vous prenez _____? (le poisson)*
3. *Comme boisson, vous prenez _____? (l'eau)*
4. *Comme dessert, vous prenez _____? (la tarte)*
5. *Comme entrée, vous prenez _____? (les escargots)*

B. *Conjuguer le verbe "prendre."* (Conjugate the verb *prendre.*)

MODÈLE: Il _____ une côte de bœuf.
Il prend une côte de bœuf.

1. *Nous _____ un carré d'agneau.*
2. *J'ai envie de _____ un gâteau au chocolat.*
3. *Je _____ de la salade.*
4. *Tu _____ des frites?*
5. *Qu'est ce que vous _____ pour le petit déjeuner?*

C. *Utiliser le verbe "boire."* (Use the verb *boire.*)

MODÈLE: Il _____ de la bière.
Il boit de la bière.

1. *Je _____ du vin ce soir.*
2. *Nous _____ un thé.*
3. *Ils _____ du café le matin.*
4. *Vous _____ du vin blanc?*
5. *Elle ne _____ pas de soda.*
6. *Tu veux _____ de l'eau?*

D. *Relier les phrases correspondantes.* (Connect the following sentences.)

1. *Je voudrais un steak et des frites.*   a. *Elle a envie de dormir.*
2. *Je prends une salade verte.*   b. *Il a très soif.*
3. *Jean adore les voyages.*   c. *Je n'ai pas faim.*
4. *Catherine est très fatiguée.*   d. *Il a envie de voyager.*
5. *Il demande de l'eau.*   e. *J'ai très faim.*

E. *Conjuguer les verbes entre parenthèses.*

1. *Nous _____ par des hors-d'œuvre. (commencer)*
2. *Ils _____ du poisson? (manger)*
3. *Elle _____ le repas. (commencer)*
4. *Nous _____ beaucoup de fruits. (manger)*
5. *La célébration _____ à vingt heures. (commencer)*

NOTE CULTURELLE

Not without reason are the French well-known for their food. French breakfasts are light and often just consist of a delicious, fresh croissant from the baker around the corner. Lunches are losing ground as fast-food restaurants are mushrooming all over. However, sandwiches (baguette and cold cuts) and light meals (soup and salad) are available in *brasseries.* Dinner remains the most important meal in France, and most families eat at around seven or eight in the evening.

French cooking varies greatly from region to region, and it is always a good idea to ask for *la spécialité de la maison,* if you are eating at one of the many restaurants France has to offer. To find out which is the best restaurant of the region, refer to the *Michelin Guide* or the *Gault Millaut.*

When you do go to a restaurant, don't be surprised if you see an elderly, or not so elderly, lady with her dog seated at the table, waiting to be served. A waiter who values his tips will serve the dog first—and hope the animal does not send the dish back to the kitchen. No one indulges their beloved canines more than the French. You will see dogs in department stores, grocery stores, at the butcher's, the baker's, and in cafés and restaurants. When the former mayor of Paris, Jacques Chirac, tried a curb-your-dog campaign, everybody, whether master or dog, ignored it.

LA CLÉ DES EXERCICES

A. 1. *de la salade*   2. *du poisson*   3. *de l'eau*   4. *de la tarte*   5. *des escargots*
B. 1. *prenons*   2. *prendre*   3. *prends*   4. *prends*   5. *prenez*
C. 1. *bois*   2. *buvons*   3. *boivent*   4. *buvez*   5. *boit*   6. *boire*
D. 1.—*e*   2.—*c*   3.—*d*   4.—*a*   5.—*b*
E. 1. *commençons*   2. *mangent*   3. *commence*   4. *mangeons*   5. *commence*

LEÇON 9
À LA PHARMACIE.   At the Pharmacy.

A. DIALOGUE

Lutter contre les allergies.

ANNE: **À vos souhaits!**

MARK: **Merci.**

ANNE: **À vos souhaits! Vous avez l'air d'avoir un bon rhume! Qu'est-ce que je peux faire pour vous?**

MARK: **Je voudrais des médicaments contre les allergies. J'ai mal à la tête et je ne peux pas respirer.**

ANNE: **À quoi êtes-vous allergique, Monsieur?**

MARK: **Je ne sais pas. . . . Je suis un peu allergique aux chats, c'est tout. Qu'est-ce que vous me conseillez de prendre?**

ANNE: **Veuillez attendre un instant, je vais vous montrer les différents remèdes. Voilà.**

MARK: **Ah, ce sont des antihistamines?**

ANNE: **C'est exact. Vous pourriez aussi prendre du sirop ou ces médicaments.**

MARK: **Je vais prendre des antihistamines pour commencer. Et est-ce que vous vendez du dentifrice et de la mousse à raser?**

ANNE: **Bien sûr. C'est à votre gauche, sur la deuxième étagère.**

MARK: **Ah, merci. Ça fait combien?**

ANNE: **Quatre-vingt-quinze francs. Au revoir Monsieur et meilleure santé!**

Fighting allergies.

ANNE: Bless you!

MARK: Thanks.

ANNE: Bless you! You seem to have a serious cold. What can I do for you?

MARK: I would like some medicine for allergies. I have a headache, and I cannot breathe.

ANNE: What are you allergic to, sir?

MARK: I don't know. . . . I am a bit allergic to cats, that's all. What do you advise me to take?

ANNE: Wait just a moment, I'll show you different remedies. Here we are.

MARK: Are these antihistamines?

ANNE: That's right. You can also take some syrup or this medicine.

MARK: I'll take some antihistamines to start. Do you sell toothpaste and shaving cream?

ANNE: Of course. It's on your left, on the second shelf.

MARK: Thanks. How much does this come to?

ANNE: Ninety-five francs. Good-bye and feel better!

B. PRONONCIATION

1. SYLLABLE STRESS

In English, one syllable of each word is more heavily stressed than the others: na-tion, me-di-cine. Words of several syllables may even have a primary and a secondary stress. In the word re-ser-va-tion, the first syllable receives the secondary stress, and the third syllable the primary stress. In French, on the other hand, words normally receive a mild stress only on the last pronounced syllable: ré-ser-va-tion. Compare the stress of these pairs of similar words:

ENGLISH	FRENCH
reservation	**réservation**
nationality	**nationalité**
pronunciation	**prononciation**
detergent	**détergent**
aspirin	**aspirine**
deodorant	**déodorant**
sensational	**sensationnel**

2. THE VERB *VENDRE*

Compare the sound of the singular and plural forms of *vendre,* "to sell."

VENDRE   TO SELL

I sell	**je vends**	we sell	**nous vendons**
you sell	**tu vends**	you sell	**vous vendez**
he/she/one sells	**il/elle/on vend**	they sell	**ils/elles vendent**

Note that the third-person singular and plural forms can be distinguished by sound.

In inversion the third-person singular and plural forms can also be distinguished by sound.

Vend-il?   **Vendent-ils?**

In the singular the *d* is linked like a *t.* In the plural both a *d* and a *t* are pronounced.

3. THE VERBS *VOULOIR* AND *POUVOIR*

The singular forms of these verbs end with the closed *eu.*

VOULOIR (TO WANT TO)	*POUVOIR* (TO BE ABLE TO)
je veux	**je peux**
tu veux	**tu peux**
on veut	**on peut**

But the third-person plural forms have an open *eu* sound + consonant.

elles veulent   **elles peuvent**

C. GRAMMAIRE ET USAGE

1. THE PRESENT TENSE OF *-RE* VERBS

Several verbs which end in *-re, vendre* (to sell), *entendre* (to hear), *répondre* (to answer), *perdre* (to lose), *attendre* (to wait), and *rendre* (to return something), are conjugated according to the following pattern:

VENDRE   TO SELL

I sell	*je vends*	we sell	*nous vendons*
you sell	*tu vends*	you sell	*vous vendez*
he/she/one sells	*il/elle/on vend*	they sell	*ils/elles vendent*

ATTENDRE   TO WAIT

I wait	*j'attends*	we wait	*nous attendons*
you wait	*tu attends*	you wait	*vous attendez*
he/she/one waits	*il/elle/on attend*	they wait	*ils/elles attendent*

Nous vendons du dentifrice.
We sell toothpaste.

Elle attend un instant.
She is waiting for a minute.

Attendez-vous l'autobus?
Are you waiting for the bus?

Vous ne répondez pas au téléphone?
Aren't you answering the phone?

Tu rends le livre à la bibliothèque.
You return the book to the library.

Ils perdent le match.
They are losing the game.

Il n'entend pas très bien.
He doesn't hear very well.

2. THE VERBS *VOULOIR* AND *POUVOIR*

The verb *vouloir* means "to want," "to desire." The verb *pouvoir* means "can," "may," "to be able to." It expresses ability and capability. *Pouvoir* is generally followed by another verb in the infinitive form. Both verbs are frequently used in the conditional tense to politely make a request or express a desire. They are conjugated in the same pattern.

VOULOIR   TO WANT

I want	*je veux*	we want	*nous voulons*
you want	*tu veux*	you want	*vous voulez*
he/she/one wants	*il/elle/on veut*	they want	*ils/elles veulent*

POUVOIR   CAN

I can	*je peux*	we can	*nous pouvons*
you can	*tu peux*	you can	*vous pouvez*
he/she/one can	*il/elle/on peut*	they can	*ils/elles peuvent*

Tu peux faire cet exercice?
Can you do this exercise?

Je ne peux pas respirer.
I can't breathe.

Je veux une aspirine.
I want an aspirin.

Vous voulez acheter du dentifrice?
Do you want to buy toothpaste?

Nous pouvons partir demain.
We can leave tomorrow.

Elles ne veulent pas de chats.
They don't want cats.

Pouvoir is also used to ask permission. In this case, the first person can take a different form. Note the difference:

Puis-je vous poser une question?
May I ask you a question?

Puis-je vous aider?
May I help you?

Est-ce que je peux vous poser une question?
May I ask you a question?

Est-ce que je peux vous aider?
May I help you?

Another way to ask permission or to suggest that someone do something is to use *pourriez-vous* ("could you?"). This is a conditional tense and will be discussed in lesson 32.

Pourriez-vous me conseiller?
Could you give me some advice?

Pourriez-vous me montrer les médicaments contre les allergies?
Could you show me the anti-allergy medicine?

Vouloir is used to express what you want; in the polite forms the conditional tense is most commonly used. It conveys a sense of diplomacy. Compare:

Je veux des médicaments contre les allergies.
I want anti-allergy medicine.

Je voudrais des médicaments contre les allergies.
I would like anti-allergy medicine.

3. THE NUMBERS 70–100

The numbers 60–79 are based on 60. You just need to do a bit of calculation: 78 = 60 + 18!

70	**soixante-dix**	72	**soixante-douze**
71	**soixante et onze**	73	**soixante-treize**

74	**soixante-quatorze**	77	**soixante-dix-sept**
75	**soixante-quinze**	78	**soixante-dix-huit**
76	**soixante-seize**	79	**soixante-dix-neuf**

The number 80 is really 4 times 20, and thus the numbers from 81 to 99 are based on *quatre-vingts*.

80	*quatre-vingts*	91	*quatre-vingt-onze*
81	*quatre-vingt-un*	92	*quatre-vingt-douze*
82	*quatre-vingt-deux*	93	*quatre-vingt-treize*
83	**quatre-vingt-trois**	94	*quatre-vingt-quatorze*
84	**quatre-vingt-quatre**	95	*quatre-vingt-quinze*
85	**quatre-vingt-cinq**	96	**quatre-vingt-seize**
86	*quatre-vingt-six*	97	**quatre-vingt-dix-sept**
87	*quatre-vingt-sept*	98	**quatre-vingt-dix-huit**
88	*quatre-vingt-huit*	99	**quatre-vingt-dix-neuf**
89	*quatre-vingt-neuf*	100	**cent**
90	*quatre-vingt-dix*		

4. *OUI* VERSUS *SI*

Oui and *si* are both translated as "yes." *Si,* however, is used to contradict a negative statement or question.

Vous prenez du vin? Oui.
Are you having wine? Yes.

Vous ne buvez pas de vin? Si.
You don't drink wine? Yes, I do.

Il n'a pas besoin de maigrir? Mais si!
He does not need to lose weight? Oh yes, he does!

VOCABULAIRE

le magasin	store
la pharmacie	pharmacy
le*(la)* **pharmacien***(ne)*	pharmacist
l'ordonnance *(f.)*	prescription
le médicament	medicine
le remède	remedy
avoir un rhume	to have a cold
la grippe	flu
avoir mal à la tête	to have a headache
l'expiration *(f.)*	expiration

À vos souhaits!	Bless you!
respirer	to breathe
allergique	allergic
l'aspirine *(f.)*	aspirin
le sirop	syrup
le savon	soap
le dentifrice	toothpaste
la mousse à raser	shaving cream
le shampooing	shampoo
les cheveux *(m.)*	hair
le déodorant	deodorant
la parfumerie	perfumerie
les produits de beauté	beauty products, cosmetics
le parfum	perfume
le maquillage	makeup
une marque	a brand
le produit	product
le chat	cat
où	where
à gauche	on the left
à droite	on the right
l'étagère *(f.)*	shelf
montrer	to show
tousser	to cough
commencer	to begin
conseiller	to advise
vendre	to sell
pouvoir	to be able to
vouloir	to want to, to desire
attendre	to wait (for)
répondre	to answer
perdre	to lose
rendre	to return something

EXERCICES

A. *Compléter les phrases avec la forme correcte du verbe entre parenthèses.*

MODÈLE: *Nous _____ le cadeau. (rendre)*
       Nous rendons le cadeau.

   1. *Vous _____ le pharmacien. (attendre)*
   2. *On _____ du parfum ici. (vendre)*

3. *Anne* _____ *à la question. (répondre)*
4. *Nous* _____ *une minute. (attendre)*
5. *Il* _____ *son temps. (perdre)*

B. *Compléter les phrases avec la forme correcte du verbe "pouvoir."*

MODÈLE: *Je veux acheter ce parfum mais je ne* _____ *pas le trouver.*
       Je veux acheter ce parfum mais je ne peux pas le trouver.

1. *Ils veulent aller en France, mais ils ne* _____ *pas.*
2. *Nous voulons sortir ce soir mais nous ne* _____ *pas.*
3. *Elle veut partir mais elle ne* _____ *pas.*
4. *Je veux rester à la campagne, mais je ne* _____ *pas.*
5. *Vous voulez voyager au Japon mais vous ne* _____ *pas.*

C. *Compléter les phrases avec la forme correcte du verbe "vouloir."*

MODÈLE: *Je* _____ *de l'aspirine.*
      Je veux de l'aspirine.

1. *Elle doit aller au bureau, mais elle* _____ *dormir.*
2. *Nous* _____ *acheter du parfum.*
3. *Je* _____ *aussi du dentifrice.*
4. *Tu* _____ *dîner au restaurant ce soir?*
5. *Il* _____ *de la mousse à raser.*

D. *Additionner ou soustraire.* (Add or substract.)

1. *Quatre-vingts plus dix font* _____.
2. *Cent moins quinze font* _____.
3. *Cinquante plus trente-trois font* _____.
4. *Quatre-vingt-dix-huit moins vingt-six font* _____.
5. *Soixante dix-neuf plus vingt font* _____.

NOTE CULTURELLE

Pharmacies are very important in France. Pharmacists receive training similar to that of doctors, and they are licensed not only to sell medicines but also to give medical advice about minor health problems and to help in an emergency. Many people go to the pharmacist with a minor ailment rather than to a doctor. S/he will even examine the wild mushrooms you've picked in the woods and tell you whether they are safe to eat! The pharmacist doesn't prepare prescriptions; in France medicine is pre-packaged. Cosmetics sold in a pharmacy are usually hypoallergenic and "natural."

How do you find a pharmacy? Look for the green cross emblem. During the weekend it will be lit if it's open; it not, a sign will be posted indicating the nearest pharmacist on duty.

LA CLÉ DES EXERCICES

A. 1. *attendez* 2. *vend* 3. *répond* 4. *attendons* 5. *perd*
B. 1. *peuvent* 2. *pouvons* 3. *peut* 4. *peux* 5. *pouvez*
C. 1. *veut* 2. *voulons* 3. *veux* 4. *veux* 5. *veut*
D. 1. *Quatre-vingt-dix* 2. *Quatre-vingt-cinq* 3. *Quatre-vingt-trois*
   4. *Soixante-douze* 5. *Quatre-vingt-dix-neuf*

LEÇON 10

LE WEEK-END.   The Weekend.

A. DIALOGUE

Les activités du week-end.

VIRGINIE: **Allô, Patrick?**

PATRICK: **Ah! Bonjour Virginie! Ça va?**

VIRGINIE: **Très bien. Il fait un temps magnifique ce matin. Tu veux aller faire du jogging avec nous?**

PATRICK: **Ce matin? C'est impossible. Je vais faire de la planche à voile sur le lac.**

VIRGINIE: **Tu n'es jamais libre!**

PATRICK: **Si, j'ai beaucoup de loisirs car je ne travaille plus le vendredi. Je joue du piano, je fais de l'équitation, de la voile.**

VIRGINIE: **Alors, tu veux participer à un mini-marathon avec nous demain?**

PATRICK: **Un marathon? Vous êtes beaucoup trop rapides pour moi!**

VIRGINIE: **Mais tu es un très bon coureur.**

PATRICK: **Tu plaisantes. Je cours moins vite que vous. D'ailleurs, vous êtes plus entraînés que moi.**

VIRGINIE: **Cela ne fait rien. C'est simplement un marathon pour amateurs.**

PATRICK: **Bon, d'accord. À quelle heure on se retrouve?**

VIRGINIE: **Rendez-vous à dix heures au club.**

PATRICK: **Et après le marathon, on prend un verre chez moi.**

VIRGINIE: **Pour fêter notre victoire!**

Weekend activities.

VIRGINIE: Hello! Patrick?

PATRICK: Hi! Virginie! How are you?

VIRGINIE: Very well. The weather is gorgeous this morning. Do you want to go jogging with us?

PATRICK: This morning? It's not possible. I am going windsurfing on the lake.

VIRGINIE: You're never free!

CLAUDE: Yes, I am! I have a lot of free time because I don't work on Fridays anymore. I play the piano, go horseback riding, sailing.

VIRGINIE: Well, do you want to take part in a mini-marathon with us tomorrow?

PATRICK: A marathon? You're too fast for me.

VIRGINIE: But you are a very good runner.

PATRICK: You're kidding. I don't run as fast as you do. Besides, you're in better shape than I am.

VIRGINIE: It does not matter. It's only a marathon for amateurs.

PATRICK: O.K., I'll go. At what time shall we meet?

VIRGINIE: Let's meet at the club at ten o'clock.

PATRICK: And after the marathon, we'll have a drink at my place.

VIRGINIE: To toast our victory!

B. PRONONCIATION

1. THE VERB *FAIRE*

Note the varied sounds of *ai* in the irregular verb *faire* (to do, to make).

je fais	
tu fais	*è* sound
on fait	
nous faisons	like *e* in *le*
vous faites	*è*
ils font	nasal *on*

2. CONSONANTS

The combination of *t* and *h* is pronounced like the *t* in "tea":

marathon, théâtre, Nathalie, Thibault.

At the end of a word the letter *x* is silent unless followed by a word beginning with a vowel, then it is pronounced as a z:

veux, deux, cheveux.

Deux → (z) **étagères de médicaments.**

Je veux → (z) **acheter du dentifrice.**

Within a word, *x* has two sounds:

x + vowel = gz	**exercice, exemple, exactement**
x + consonant = ks	**excellent, excuser, expiration**

3. OMISSIONS

a. When *de* is used with an adverb of quantity, the *e* is silent:

beaucoup de choses, trop de loisirs.

Note also the silent *e* in these words and sentences:

promenade, franchement, régulièrement.

Je ne fais jamais de sport.

Ce n'est pas bien.

b. Adverbs of adjectives ending in *-ent* and *-ant*.

Adjectives ending in *-ent* and *-ant* have the nasal *en* ending:

patient, récent, constant, élégant.

When they form their adverbs, the vowel before the double consonant becomes like the <u>a</u> in f<u>a</u>ther; it is not pronounced with a nasal sound.

patiemment	pa-sya-men
récemment	ré-sa-men
constamment	con-sta-men
élégamment	é-lé-ga-men
intelligemment	un-té-li-gea-men

4. HOMONYMS

Homonyms are words that are pronounced the same but differ in spelling and meaning. In English, the words "to", "two" and "too" are homonyms.

French has many homonyms. You already know some of the words in the following list; others you will learn. As you pronounce them, observe the different spellings of the same vowel sounds, and how many final consonants are silent. (Verb forms in English are given with the personal pronoun.)

eau (water)	**haut** (high)	**au** (at)	**aux** (at)
cent (100)	**sans** (without)	**sent** (he smells)	
en (in)	**an** (year)		
moi (me)	**mois** (month)		
on (one, we)	**ont** (they have)		
son (his/her)	**sont** (they are)		
vin (wine)	**vingt** (20)	**vain** (vain)	
pain (bread)	**pin** (pine)		
sept (seven)	**cette** (this)		
ça (this)	**sa** (his/her)		
es (you are)	**est** (he is)		
temps (time)	**tant** (so much)		
mais (but)	**mai** (May)	**mets** (dish)	
la (the)	**là** (there)		
ou (or)	**où** (where)	**août** (August)	
ces (these)	**ses** (his/her)		
peu (a little)	**peux** (I/you can)	**peut** (he/she can)	
car (bus)	**quart** (quarter)		
leur (their)	**l'heure** (hour)		

C. GRAMMAIRE ET USAGE

1. COMPARATIVES

In comparing two things of the same nature, you will need to use comparatives of superiority (more than) or inferiority (less than).[1]

The book is more interesting than the movie.

Claude runs less quickly than Patrick.

The comparative of superiority is formed by placing *plus* (more) before the adjective or adverb which is modified and *que* after it. For the comparative of inferiority, you use *moins* (less) before and *que* after.

Il est rapide.
He is fast.

[1] Other comparatives will be discussed in *Leçon* 19.

Il est plus rapide que Patrick.
    He is faster than Patrick.

Elle court vite.
    She runs fast.

Elle court plus vite que Virginie.
    She runs faster than Virginie.

Jacques est grand.
    Jacques is tall.

Jacques est plus grand que Pierre.
    Jacques is taller than Pierre.

Je suis entraîné.
    I am trained.

Je suis moins entraîné que vous.
    I am less trained than you.

Il joue bien.
    He plays well.

Il joue moins bien que Pierre.
    He does not play as well as Pierre.

La cuisine est grande.
    The kitchen is big.

La cuisine est plus grande que le salon.
    The kitchen is bigger than the living room.

The adjectives *bon* (good) and *mauvais* (bad) have an irregular form for the comparative of superiority.

Ce gâteau est bon.
    This cake is good.

Ce gâteau est meilleur que l'autre.
    This cake is better than the other.

Ce vin est mauvais.
    This wine is bad.

Ce vin-ci est plus mauvais que ce vin-là.
    This wine is worse than that wine.

When talking about concrete things, one tends to use *plus mauvais*.

Le temps est plus mauvais à Paris qu'à Nice.
    The weather is worse in Paris than in Nice.

Ce gâteau-ci est plus mauvais que ce gâteau-là.
    This cake is worse than that cake.

When talking about abstractions, the comparative of superiority of *mauvais* is a different word altogether: *pire*.

La situation est mauvaise.
The situation is bad.

La situation est pire à Bordeaux qu'à Lyon.
The situation is worse in Bordeaux than in Lyon.

Le remède est pire que le mal.
The cure is worse than the disease.

2. NEGATIONS

You have already encountered the negation *ne . . . pas* in lesson 4. Here are a few other negations: *Ne . . . jamais* (never), *ne . . . rien* (nothing), and *ne . . . plus* (no more, no longer). In all negative sentences, *ne* is placed right before the conjugated verb and *pas* right after.

a. *Ne . . . jamais.*

Elle participe au marathon.
She runs in the marathon.

Elle ne participe jamais au marathon.
She never runs in the marathon.

Il travaille le vendredi.
He works on Fridays.

Il ne travaille jamais le vendredi.
He never works on Fridays.

b. *Ne . . . plus*

Il court dans le parc.
He runs in the park.

Il ne court plus dans le parc.
He no longer runs in the park.

Il est libre le dimanche.
He is free on Sundays.

Il n'est plus libre le dimanche.
He is no longer free on Sundays.

c. *Ne . . . rien*

Je mange quelque chose le matin.
I eat something in the morning.

Je ne mange rien le matin.
  I eat nothing in the morning.

Il prend un verre.
  He is having a drink.

Il ne prend rien.
  He is not having anything.

3. *JOUER DE / JOUER À*

Jouer (to play) is followed either by the preposition *de* or *à*. *Jouer de* is used with musical instruments, *jouer à* with sports and any other expression.

Il joue du piano.
  He plays the piano.

Elle joue du violon.
  She plays the violin.

Vous jouez du saxophone?
  You play the saxophone?

Ils jouent des cymbales.
  They play cymbals.

Je joue de la guitare.
  I play the guitar.

Ils jouent au tennis.
  They play tennis.

Tu joues au base-ball?
  You play baseball?

Nous jouons au golf.
  We play golf.

Elle joue aux échecs.
  She plays chess.

Ils jouent au chat et à la souris.
  They're playing cat and mouse.

4. THE VERB *FAIRE*

You have been introduced to the verb *faire* (to do, to make) with expressions of weather in lesson 6. You have just learned a few other expressions in the preceding dialogue *(faire du jogging)*. *Faire* is a multifaceted verb in French, comparable to the verb "to get" in English. Here are a few more uses to add to your list:

faire la cuisine	to cook
faire le ménage	to do the housework
faire la vaisselle	to do the dishes
faire la lessive	to do the laundry
faire les courses	to do the shopping, to run errands
faire une promenade	to take a walk
faire sa toilette	to wash (oneself)
faire du sport	to exercise, to practice a sport
faire du tennis	to play tennis
faire de l'exercice	to exercise
faire attention	to pay attention
faire la queue	to stand in line
faire le plein	to fill up the tank

Je fais le ménage le samedi.
 I do the housework on Saturday.

Tu sais faire la cuisine?
 Do you know how to cook?

Nous faisons une promenade.
 We are taking a walk.

Elle aime faire les courses.
 She loves to shop.

Il fait la lessive le dimanche.
 He does the laundry on Sundays.

5. QUANTITY EXPRESSIONS

To indicate quantity, you can use one of the following expressions:

beaucoup de	a lot, much	*encore*	more
peu de	little	*trop de*	too much, too many
un peu de	a little	*tellement de*	so much, so many
assez de	enough	*bien des*	many
plus de	more	*la plupart des*	most

Il ne fait pas beaucoup de sport.
 He doesn't play a lot of sports.

La plupart des coureurs sont bien entraînés.
 Most of the runners are well trained.

Avez vous un peu de temps libre ce soir?
Do you have a little free time this evening?

Ils ont tellement de loisirs!
They have so much leisure time!

VOCABULAIRE

le sport	sport
le marathon	marathon
la victoire	victory
faire	to make, to do
faire la cuisine	to cook, to do the cooking
faire le ménage	to do the house-cleaning
faire les courses	to do the shopping, to run errands
faire du sport	to do/practice a sport
faire du tennis	to play tennis
faire du jogging	to go jogging, to jog
faire de la planche à voile	to windsurf
faire de la voile	to sail
faire du ski	to ski
faire du ski nautique	to water ski
faire de la plongée	to go diving
faire de l'équitation	to go horseback riding
faire une promenade	to take a walk
les loisirs *(m. pl.)*	leisure time
le coureur	runner
courir	to run
jouer	to play
entraîner	to train
travailler	to work
participer	to take part
plaisanter	to joke
se retrouver	to meet (planned ahead of time)
prendre un verre	to have a drink
fêter	to celebrate
un peu de	a little of
assez de	enough of
trop de	too much of
beaucoup de	a lot of
ne . . . jamais	never
ne . . . rien	nothing
d'ailleurs	besides

EXERCICES

A. *Utiliser la négation.*

MODÈLE: *Il mange après neuf heures. (rien).*
Il ne mange rien après neuf heures.

1. *Il comprend. (rien)*
2. *Vous travaillez le samedi. (jamais)*
3. *Ils font de la planche à voile (plus).*
4. *Nous jouons au tennis le jeudi matin. (jamais)*
5. *Je fais de la planche à voile. (plus)*

B. *Comparer les deux éléments suivants en utilisant "plus" ou "moins."*

MODÈLE: *L'autobus / Le train (rapide)*
L'autobus est moins rapide que le train.

1. *La ville de Paris / La ville de Bordeaux (grand)*
2. *L'été / L'hiver (chaud)*
3. *La chaise / Le fauteuil (confortable)*
4. *Un coureur amateur / Un coureur professionnel (rapide)*
5. *Le gâteau au chocolat / La soupe (meilleur)*

C. *Relier les deux colonnes.*

1. *Elle prépare le dîner.*
2. *Elle est dans un magasin.*
3. *Elle fait du tennis.*
4. *Elle attend.*
5. *Elle marche dans le parc.*

a. *Elle aime le sport.*
b. *Elle fait une promenade.*
c. *Elle fait la cuisine.*
d. *Elle fait les courses.*
e. *Elle fait la queue.*

D. *Compléter avec la préposition qui convient.*

MODÈLE: *Elle joue _____ trompette.*
Elle joue de la trompette.

1. *Je joue _____ football.*
2. *Nous jouons _____ guitare.*
3. *Vous jouez _____ tennis.*
4. *Il joue _____ clarinette.*
5. *Ils jouent _____ hockey.*

NOTE CULTURELLE

You can practice a wide variety of sports in France. As the country is surrounded by water (the Atlantic Ocean, the Mediterranean Sea, the English Channel), water sports such as sailing, windsurfing, and diving are rather popular among the French. One of the most famous sailing regattas starts from *Les Sables d'Olonne* in *Vendée*. Other well-known sporting events are the *Tour de France,* the biking race, and *Le Mans,* the car race held every June.

As France is an alpine country, winter sports, such as cross-country and downhill skiing, enjoy popularity as well. The 1992 Winter Olympics were held in Albertville, France.

LA CLÉ DES EXERCICES

A. 1. *Il ne comprend rien.* 2. *Vous ne travaillez jamais le samedi.* 3. *Ils ne font plus de planche à voile.* 4. *Nous ne jouons jamais au tennis le jeudi matin.* 5. *Je ne fais plus de planche à voile.*
B. 1. *La ville de Paris est plus grande que la ville de Bordeaux.* 2. *L'été est plus chaud que l'hiver.* 3. *La chaise est moins confortable que le fauteuil.* 4. *Un coureur amateur est moins rapide qu'un coureur professionnel.* 5. *Le gâteau au chocolat est meilleur que la soupe.*
C. 1. —c   2. —d   3. —a   4. —e   5. —b
D. 1. *au*   2. *de la*   3. *au*   4. *de la*   5. *au*

DEUXIÈME RÉVISION

A. *Quelle heure est-il?* (What time is it?)

1. 6:30
2. 8:15
3. 5:20
4. 2:45
5. 11:50

B. *Compléter les phrases en mettant l'adjectif à la forme qui convient.*

1. *Christine n'est pas _____ (sportif).*
2. *Sandra est _____ à Paris. (heureux)*
3. *Elle habite dans une _____ maison. (vieux)*
4. *Suzanne est _____ (canadien).*
5. *Il trouve un _____ appartement. (nouveau)*

C. *Mettre les verbes au présent.*

1. *Jean-Luc _____ aller à Lyon. (préférer)*
2. *Nous _____ à sept heures. (manger)*
3. *Qu'est-ce que vous _____ boire? (vouloir)*
4. *Il _____ aller à Paris cet été. (espérer)*
5. *Je ne _____ pas vous conseiller. (pouvoir)*
6. *Nous _____ la troisième leçon. (commencer)*
7. *Ils _____ dîner à 19 heures. (vouloir)*
8. *_____-vous nous indiquer la route? (pouvoir)*

D. *Compléter les phrases avec l'article défini, indéfini ou partitif.*

MODÈLE: *Ils mangent . . . fromage.*
Ils mangent du fromage.

1. *Sophie aime beaucoup _____ sport.*
2. *Il prend _____ viande comme plat principal.*
3. *J'ai _____ amis français.*
4. *Pierre a _____ appartement à Cannes.*
5. *Nous buvons _____ eau.*

E. *Poser la question avec "quel."*

MODÈLE: *J'aime la cuisine chinoise.*
Quelle cuisine aimez-vous?

1. *Il est trois heures et demie.*
2. *Je prends le train de sept heures.*
3. *Je préfère le mois de mai.*
4. *Je suis libre mardi et jeudi.*
5. *Je voudrais ces chaises.*

F. *Compléter les phrases avec le verbe "faire."*

1. *Bruno _____ des courses le week-end.*
2. *Maryse et Denis _____ de la planche à voile le dimanche.*
3. *Nous ne _____ pas assez de sport.*
4. *Est-ce que tu _____ de l'équitation?*
5. *Qu'est que vous _____ demain?*

G. *Compléter les phrases avec une préposition.*

1. *J'aime Paris _____ octobre.*
2. *Il va _____ Paris le mois prochain.*
3. *Les étrangers adorent Paris _____ mai.*
4. *Nous allons voyager _____ printemps.*
5. *Est-ce qu'il fait très chaud sur la Côte d'Azur _____ été?*

H. *Compléter les phrases avec la forme correcte du verbe.*

1. On _____ du shampooing dans une pharmacie. (vendre)
2. Ils _____ le train. (attendre)
3. Est-ce que vous _____ des journaux étrangers? (vendre)
4. Le pharmacien _____ à la question du client. (répondre)
5. Nous _____ votre visite avec impatience. (attendre)

LA CLÉ DES EXERCICES

A. 1. *Il est six heures et demie.* 2. *Il est huit heures et quart.* 3. *Il est cinq heures vingt.* 4. *Il est trois heures moins le quart.* 5. *Il est midi moins dix.*
B. 1. *sportive* 2. *heureuse* 3. *vieille* 4. *canadienne* 5. *nouvel*
C. 1. *préfère* 2. *mangeons* 3. *voulez* 4. *espère* 5. *peux*
   6. *commençons* 7. *veulent* 8. *Pouvez*
D. 1. *le* 2. *de la* 3. *des* 4. *un* 5. *de l'*
E. 1. *Quelle heure est-il?* 2. *Quel train prenez-vous?* 3. *Quel mois préférez-vous?* 4. *Quels jours êtes-vous libre?* 5. *Quelles chaises voulez-vous?*
F. 1. *fait* 2. *font* 3. *faisons* 4. *fais* 5. *faites*
G. 1. *en* 2. *à* 3. *en* 4. *au* 5. *en*
H. 1. *vend* 2. *attendent* 3. *vendez* 4. *répond* 5. *attendons*

LECTURE

Now you're ready to practice your reading skills! While indeed you've been reading the dialogs, the four *Lecture* sections offer you the chance to practice reading as you would read a newspaper article or essay. First, read through each passage without referring to the accompanying vocabulary notes. Try to understand the main idea of the text, inferring the meanings of new words from context. Don't worry if a passage seems long or if you don't know each word; you can go back and reread it, checking the vocabulary notes to learn the exact meaning of new words and phrases. Now, let's begin!

À LA POSTE

Isabelle arrive à la poste.[1] *Elle achète des timbres*[2] *pour des lettres*[3] *et une douzaine*[4] *de cartes postales.*[5] *Elle veut envoyer*[6] *deux lettres aux États-Unis par avion,*[7] *une douzaine de cartes postales, et une lettre à Rome par exprès.*[8] *Elle désire aussi envoyer un petit paquet*[9] *à son amie Carole.*

Ensuite, elle va chercher son courrier[10] *à la poste restante.*[11] *Elle reçoit toujours beaucoup de courrier: plusieurs cartes postales, un mandat-poste,*[12] *une lettre recommandée*[13] *et quelques imprimés.*[14] *Avant de partir, elle achète une télécarte pour téléphoner*[15] *des cabines téléphoniques.*[16]

VOCABULAIRE

1. *la poste* — the post office
2. *le timbre* — stamp
3. *la lettre* — letter
4. *la douzaine* — dozen
5. *la carte postale* — postcard
6. *envoyer* — to send
7. *par avion* — air mail
8. *par exprès* — by special delivery
9. *le paquet* — package
10. *le courrier* — mail
11. *la poste restante* — the general delivery
12. *le mandat-poste* — postal money order
13. *une lettre recommandée* — registered letter
14. *les imprimés* — printed matter
15. *téléphoner* — to telephone
16. *la cabine téléphonique* — phone booth

LEÇON 11

LA FAMILLE.   The Family.

A. DIALOGUE

Les photos de famille.

MÉLANIE: C'est à toi, ce vieil album de photos, Catherine?

JEANNE: Non, Mélanie, c'est à moi.

MÉLANIE: Qui sont tous ces gens, tante Jeanne?

JEANNE: Ces gens? C'est ta famille! Au milieu, c'est ton grand-père Julien.

MÉLANIE: Et à côté de lui?

JEANNE: Ta grand-mère Amélie et ton oncle Georges.

MÉLANIE: Et cette dame au chapeau fleuri?

JEANNE: C'est une cousine éloignée ou la belle-mère d'un parent, je ne sais plus vraiment.

MÉLANIE: Et toi, tu n'es pas sur la photo?

JEANNE: Si, je suis là, entre mon frère Jacques et ma soeur Marceline.

MÉLANIE: Ce n'est pas mon père à côté de toi!

JEANNE: Mais si, c'est lui.

MÉLANIE: Quel âge a-t-il sur cette photo?

JEANNE: Environ huit ans et demi.

MÉLANIE: Il est plus beau aujourd'hui!

JEANNE: Moi aussi?

MÉLANIE: Oui, toi aussi, tante Jeanne.

Family Pictures.

MÉLANIE: This old photo album, is it yours, Catherine?

JEANNE: No, Mélanie, it's mine.

MÉLANIE: Who are these people, Aunt Jeanne?

JEANNE: These people? They're your family! In the middle is your grandfather Julien.

MÉLANIE: And next to him?

JEANNE: Your grandmother Amélie and your uncle Georges.

MÉLANIE: And the lady with the flowered hat?

JEANNE: It's a distant cousin or the mother-in-law of a relative. I don't really know anymore.

MÉLANIE: And you, aren't you in the picture?

JEANNE: Yes, I'm there, between my brother Jacques and my sister Marceline.

MÉLANIE: That's not my father next to you!

JEANNE: Yes, it's him!

MÉLANIE: How old was he when this photo was taken?

JEANNE: About eight and a half.

MÉLANIE: He is more handsome today.

JEANNE: What about me?

MÉLANIE: Yes, you too, Aunt Jeanne.

B. GRAMMAIRE ET USAGE

1. STRESSED PRONOUNS

Stressed pronouns *(pronoms toniques)* are used when you want to call attention to yourself or to what you are doing or saying.

me	*moi*		us	*nous*
you	*toi*		you	*vous*
him	*lui*		them (masculine)	*eux*
her	*elle*		them (feminine)	*elles*

The stressed pronouns are emphatic pronouns. There are many ways to use them.

a. To emphasize a subject pronoun.

Et toi, tu n'es pas sur la photo?
And you, aren't you in the picture?

Mon frère a huit ans. Moi, j'ai dix ans!
My brother is eight. I am ten!

115

b. After prepositions.

Mon père est à côté de toi.
My father is next to you.

Nous voyageons avec eux.
We travel with them.

Il est assis entre lui et elle.
He is sitting between him and her.

c. In comparisons.

Tu es plus beau que lui.
You look better than he.

Elle est plus grande que toi.
She is taller than you.

d. After *c'est* or *ce sont*.

C'est toi sur la photo?
It's you in the picture?

Ce sont eux là-bas!
It's them over there!

e. When used alone in response to questions.

Qui est là?—Moi.
Who's there?—Me.

Qui veut du café?—Nous!
Who wants coffee?—We do!

f. In the following expressions.

René aime le café.—Moi aussi.
René likes coffee.—So do I.

René n'aime pas le café.—Moi non plus.
René does not like coffee.—Neither do I.

Sa cousine prend des photos en vacances.—Lui aussi.
His cousin takes pictures on vacation.—So does he.

Sa cousine ne prend jamais de photos en vacances.—Lui non plus.
His cousin never takes pictures on vacation.—Neither does he.

2. TELLING YOUR AGE

To talk about age, the French use the verb *avoir:* you "have" years, while in English you "are" so many years old.

Quel âge avez-vous?
How old are you?

J'ai vingt-deux ans.
I'm twenty-two.

Quel âge a-t-elle?
How old is she?

Elle a douze ans.
She's twelve.

3. WITH

The preposition "with" presents a number of problems for an English-speaking student. Although the general translation of "with" is *avec,* most of the time "with" cannot be translated this simply. An analysis of its real meaning is needed in each sentence.

a. When "with" implies doing something or going along with someone, it can be translated by *avec.*

Je regarde l'album de photos avec ma grand-mère.
I am looking at the photo album with my grandmother.

Je vais au Canada avec ma belle-sœur.
I am going to Canada with my sister-in-law.

b. In many idiomatic expressions "with" is *de.* These need to be memorized.

Je suis content de mon appartement.
I am pleased with my apartment.

La voiture est couverte de neige.
The car is covered with snow.

c. In phrases of manner, *"with"* is also translated as *de.*

Il regarde sa montre d'un air inquiet.
He is looking at his watch with a worried look.

Il me remercie d'un sourire.
He thanks me with a smile.

d. When it refers to someone's attribute, "with" is either *au, à la,* or *aux.*

La dame au chapeau fleuri, c'est une cousine éloignée.
The lady with the flowered hat, she's a distant cousin.

La femme aux cheveux roux est scandinave.
The lady with red hair is Scandinavian.

e. To describe the way one carries oneself, no extra word is used in French.

Il marche, les mains dans les poches.
He is walking with his hands in his pockets.

Elle dort, la bouche ouverte.
She sleeps with her mouth open.

f. When "with" means "as far as such and such is concerned," it is translated by *chez.*

Chez Baudelaire, tous les sens se répondent.
With Baudelaire, all the senses respond to each other.

Chez cet enfant, tout est pathologique.
With this child, everything is pathological.

4. CHEZ

Now, let's compare *chez* as mentioned above with *chez* meaning "at someone's home, or place of work."

Je vais chez ma tante ce week-end.
I am going to my aunt's this weekend.

Le restaurant Chez Henri est le meilleur du quartier.
The restaurant Henri's is the best in the neighborhood.

Va chercher du pain chez le boulanger.
Go get some bread at the baker's.

VOCABULAIRE

la famille	the family
le parent	relative
les parents	parents, mother and father
les gens	people
le père	father
la mère	mother

le mari	husband
la femme	wife, woman
l'homme	man
la sœur	sister
le frère	brother
l'enfant *(m. f.)*	child
le fils	son
la fille	daughter, girl
le garçon	boy
les grands-parents *(m. pl.)*	grandparents
le grand-père	grandfather
la grand-mère	grandmother
l'oncle *(m.)*	uncle
la tante	aunt
le neveu	nephew
la nièce	niece
le cousin/la cousine	cousin
l'âge *(m.)*	age
Quel âge avez-vous?	How old are you?
J'ai trente ans.	I'm thirty.
la photo	photograph
l'album *(m.)*	album
à côté	next to
entre	between
éloigné	far, remote
vraiment	really, truly
environ	about

EXERCICES

A. *Traduire.*

    1. *Il n'aime pas le chocolat blanc.* Neither does she.
    2. *Je préfère le vin rouge.* So do I.
    3. *Tu n'as pas d'album.* Neither do I.
    4. *Nous prenons des photos en vacances.* So do we.
    5. *Elle a un frère et deux soeurs.* So does he.

B. *Compléter avec le pronom tonique.*

MODÈLE: C'est _____ *sur la photo?* (you, polite)
       C'est vous sur la photo?

1. *Je suis assis à côté de _____.* (them)
2. *Il voyage avec _____ en été.* (us)
3. *Elle est plus active que _____.* (you, familiar)
4. *C'est _____ sur la photo?* (her)
5. *Il a plus de chance que _____.* (me)

C. *Répondre en employant un pronom.*

MODÈLE: *Vous dînez avec moi? (oui)*
        Oui, je dîne avec vous.

1. *Vous sortez avec sa soeur? (oui)*
2. *Vous travaillez avec votre mari? (oui)*
3. *C'est toi sur la photo? (non)*
4. *Vous allez chez vos grands-parents? (oui)*
5. *Elle parle de vos soeurs? (non)*

D. *Compléter en utilisant la préposition qui convient.*

1. *La dame _____ cheveux bruns est italienne.*
2. *_____ Mozart, tout est harmonie.*
3. *Elle voyage au Brésil _____ sa cousine.*
4. *Nous achetons notre vin _____ un marchand de vins du quartier.*
5. *Vous regardez le programme _____ un air content.*

NOTE CULTURELLE

Although French families are no longer very large (1.7 children per family according to statistics), they are still very close. Because of decentralization, family members are often scattered throughout France but get together on holidays. Children sometimes spend Christmas, Easter, and part of the summer vacation at their grandparents' house outside the cities.

The French government continues to support childbearing by allocating government subsidies *(allocations familiales)* for families with children and by providing free day care for working parents.

Taking pictures is a custom during holidays. If you happen to be visiting French friends, there is a good chance you'll end up in the family album.

LA CLÉ DES EXERCICES

A. 1. *Elle non plus.* 2. *Moi aussi.* 3. *Moi non plus.* 4. *Nous aussi.* 5. *Lui aussi.*
B. 1. *d'eux* 2. *nous* 3. *toi* 4. *elle* 5. *moi*
C. 1. *Oui, je sors avec elle.* 2. *Oui, je travaille avec lui.* 3. *Non, ce n'est pas moi.* 4. *Oui, je vais chez eux.* 5. *Non, elle ne parle pas d'elles.*
D. 1. *aux* 2. *Chez* 3. *avec* 4. *chez* 5. *d'*

LEÇON 12

DEMANDER SA ROUTE. Asking for Directions.

A. DIALOGUE

Quelle route faut-il prendre?

JACQUES: La route pour aller au château de Chenonceau, s'il vous plaît?

POMPISTE: Ah, mais Monsieur, vous n'êtes pas sur la bonne route . . .

JACQUES: Quelle route faut-il prendre?

POMPISTE: Prenez la première route à droite et allez tout droit jusqu'aux feux. Ensuite, vous allez voir un pont sur votre gauche.

JACQUES: Il faut traverser le pont?

POMPISTE: Non, non, il vaut mieux continuer tout droit et traverser le pont dans la ville suivante. Il y a moins de circulation.

JACQUES: C'est loin d'ici?

POMPISTE: Non, c'est à une dizaine de kilomètres d'ici.

JACQUES: Donc je traverse le pont et . . .

POMPISTE: Oui. Et après le pont, tournez à droite et le château est à cinq cents mètres.

JACQUES: Ah, merci Monsieur.

POMPISTE: D'où venez-vous?

JACQUES: Je viens de Chicago.

POMPISTE: Combien de temps restez-vous dans la région?

JACQUES: Environ quatre jours.

POMPISTE: Ne manquez pas le spectacle de Son et Lumière au château!

Which Road Do I Take?

JACQUES: Which way to the Chenonceau castle, please?

GAS STATION ATTENDANT: Oh, sir, you are on the wrong road.

JACQUES: What road should I take?

GAS STATION ATTENDANT: Take the first road to the right, then go straight up to the light. Then, you'll see a bridge on your left.

JACQUES: Should I cross the bridge?

GAS STATION ATTENDANT: No, no, it's better to continue straight ahead and cross the bridge in the next town. There's less traffic.

JACQUES: Is it far from here?

GAS STATION ATTENDANT: No, it's about ten kilometers from here.

JACQUES: So, I cross the bridge and . . .

GAS STATION ATTENDANT: Yes, and after the bridge, turn right and the chateau is about five hundred meters away.

JACQUES: Thank you, sir.

GAS STATION ATTENDANT: Where do you come from?

JACQUES: I come from Chicago.

GAS STATION ATTENDANT: How long will you stay in the region?

JACQUES: About four days.

GAS STATION ATTENDANT: Do not miss the Sound and Light show at the castle!

B. GRAMMAIRE ET USAGE

1. THE VERB *VENIR*

Venir (to come) is an irregular verb which is used in many different ways.[1] First, let's look at the present tense.

VENIR   TO COME

I come	*je viens*		we come	*nous venons*
you come	*tu viens*		you come	*vous venez*
he/she/one comes	*il/elle/on vient*		they come	*ils/elles viennent*

D'où venez-vous?
    Where are you from?

Je viens de Chicago.
    I come from Chicago.

Revenir (to come back) and *devenir* (to become) follow the same pattern.

---

[1] See also *Leçon* 14.

I come back	*je reviens*		we come back	*nous revenons*
you come back	*tu reviens*		you come back	*vous revenez*
he/she/one comes back	*il/elle/on revient*		they come back	*ils/elles reviennent*

Ils reviennent de vacances lundi.
They're coming back from vacation on Monday.

Ce pianiste va devenir célèbre.
This pianist will become famous.

Qu'est-ce que tu deviens?
What are you up to?

2. THE IMPERATIVE FORM

Verbs in the imperative form are used to give orders and make requests. They are formed like the *tu, nous, vous* forms of the present tense of verbs, except that the *s* ending of the *tu* form is dropped in all *-er* verbs. Following are the forms for the familiar singular "you," the plural "we," and the polite or plural of "you."

a. Regular *-er* verbs.

Traverse le pont. (familiar)
Cross the bridge.

Traversons le pont. (we)
Let's cross the bridge.

Traversez le pont. (polite or plural of "you")
Cross the bridge.

b. *Aller.*

Va chez Henri.
Go to Henri's.

Allons chez Henri.
Let's go to Henri's.

Allez chez Henri.
Go to Henri's.

c. *-re* verbs like *attendre.*

Attends une minute.
Wait a minute.

Attendons une minute.
Let's wait a minute.

Attendez une minute.
Wait a minute.

d. *-ir* verbs like *partir*.

Pars tout de suite.
Leave right away.

Partons tout de suite.
Let's leave right away.

Partez tout de suite.
Leave right away.

e. *-ir* verbs like *choisir*.

Choisis un chapeau.
Choose a hat.

Choisissons un chapeau.
Let's choose a hat.

Choisissez un chapeau.
Choose a hat.

f. *Être.*

Sois à l'heure.
Be on time.

Soyons à l'heure.
Let's be on time.

Soyez à l'heure.
Be on time.

g. *Avoir.*

Aie plus de patience.
Be more patient.

Ayons plus de patience.
Let's be more patient.

Ayez plus de patience.
Be more patient.

h. To form the negative, you simply put the negation around the verb.

Traversez le pont.
Cross the bridge.

Ne traversez pas le pont.
Don't cross the bridge.

Va voir le spectacle.
Go see the show.

Ne va pas voir le spectacle.
Don't go see the show.

3. THE NUMBERS 100–1,000,000

We have learned the numbers up to 100. Now, let's keep going. It's just a matter of adding on.

100	**cent**
101	**cent un**
102	**cent deux**
103	**cent trois**
104	**cent quatre**

Add an *s* to *cent* when counting above one hundred.

200	**deux cents**
300	**trois cents**
900	**neuf cents**

But do not add an *s* when *cent* is followed by another number.

213	**deux cent treize**
434	**quatre cent trente-quatre**

Mille is pronounced like *ville:* the *l* is sounded. It takes no *s*.

1 000	**mille**
2 000	**deux mille**
2 001	**deux mille un**
1 000 000	**un million**

Note that in counting, French uses spaces where English uses commas.

4. EXPRESSING DISTANCES

In France and in most European countries, distance is expressed in meters and kilometers. A meter is a little over a yard; a kilometer is a thousand meters or approximately three-fifths of a mile. In a city there are no "blocks"; distance is measured in meters or minutes. The prepositions *à* and *de* are used.

C'est à cinq cents mètres d'ici.
   It's five hundred meters from here.

C'est à deux kilomètres.
   It's two kilometers away.

5. IMPERSONAL VERBS

   a. *Il faut* + infinitive.

Il faut (it is necessary, one must) is used with an infinitive. *Il faut* is not conjugated.

Il faut traverser le pont.
   You must cross the bridge.

Il faut tourner à droite.
   You have to turn right.

   b. *Il vaut mieux* + infinitive.

Il vaut mieux (it is better) is also followed by an infinitive.

Il vaut mieux continuer tout droit.
   It's better to continue straight ahead.

Il vaut mieux prendre le train.
   You'd do better to take the train.

VOCABULAIRE

la ville	city, town
la rue	street
la route	road, way
l'avenue *(f.)*	avenue
le boulevard	boulevard
la place	square
le pont	bridge
le musée	museum

le château	castle
la circulation	traffic
les feux de circulation	traffic lights
demander sa route	asking for directions
tout droit	straight ahead
à droite	on the right; right
à gauche	on the left; left
Tournez à droite	Turn right.
Tournez à gauche.	Turn left.
Allez jusqu'à . . .	go (all the way) to . . .
	go as far as . . .
venir	to come
revenir (like *venir*)	to come back
chercher	to search for, to look for
traverser	to cross
ralentir	to slow down
doubler	to pass (car)
rester	to stay
manquer	to miss
il faut	one/you must
Il vaut mieux	it is better
Quel est le chemin le plus court?	What is the shortest way?
Il y a des déviations?	Are there detours?
Avez-vous une carte routière?	Do you have a road map?
À quelle distance . . . ?	How far . . . ?
jusqu'à	as far as, all the way to, until
ensuite	afterward
combien de temps	how long
suivant	following, next

EXERCICES

A. *Répondre à la question avec "il faut."*

MODÈLE: *Je tourne à gauche?*
Oui, il faut tourner à gauche.

1. *Je traverse le pont?*
2. *Je prends la première à droite?*
3. *Je tourne à gauche?*
4. *Je prends l'autoroute?*
5. *Je vais tout droit jusqu'aux feux?*

B. *Dire à un ami de . . .* (Tell a friend to . . .)

MODÈLE: aller au spectacle.
      Va au spectacle.

1. *prendre la première à gauche.*
2. *choisir un bouquet de fleurs.*
3. *tourner à droite.*
4. *être à l'heure.*
5. *regarder le château.*

C. *Dire à un étranger de . . .*

MODÈLE: traverser la rue.
      Traversez la rue.

1. *être prudent.*
2. *aller tout droit jusqu'aux feux.*
3. *avoir de la patience.*
4. *prendre la deuxième à gauche.*
5. *(ne . . . pas) traverser le pont.*

D. *Compléter les phrases avec le verbe "venir."*

1. *Julien* _____ *de Chicago.*
2. *Vous* _____ *chez mes amis.*
3. *Ils* _____ *de New York.*
4. *D'où* _____ *vous?*
5. *Elle va* _____ *nous voir en septembre.*

E. *Donner des conseils en utilisant "il vaut mieux."*

MODÈLE: Nous sommes fatigués. (dormir une heure ou deux)
      Il vaut mieux dormir une heure ou deux.

1. *Le château est loin. (prendre un taxi)*
2. *Je n'aime pas ce restaurant. (aller dans un autre restaurant)*
3. *Il est tard. (partir)*
4. *Nous ne sommes pas sur la bonne route. (demander notre route)*
5. *Il y a beaucoup de circulation. (prendre une autre route)*

F. *Écrire les nombres en lettres.*

1. 203
2. 786
3. 1,580
4. 2,642
5. 5,567

NOTE CULTURELLE

France has quite an elaborate road system comparable to the American system of expressways *(autoroutes),* state highways *(routes nationales),* and country roads *(chemins de campagne).* Although there is a speed limit in France, it is much higher than in the United States. Europeans in general drive faster than Americans. France still has a lot of roads with three lanes only, which can be quite dangerous when passing.

The French are rather passionate behind the wheel and often seem to forget their good manners. Don't be surprised if you hear drivers yelling and swearing at each other.

LA CLÉ DES EXERCICES

A. 1. *Oui, il faut traverser le pont.* 2. *Oui, il faut prendre la première à droite.* 3. *Oui, il faut tourner à gauche.* 4. *Oui, il faut prendre l'autoroute.* 5. *Oui, il faut aller tout droit jusqu'aux feux.*

B. 1. *Prends la première à gauche.* 2. *Choisis un bouquet de fleurs.* 3. *Tourne à droite.* 4. *Sois à l'heure.* 5. *Regarde le château.*

C. 1. *Soyez prudent.* 2. *Allez tout droit jusqu'aux feux.* 3. *Ayez de la patience.* 4. *Prenez la deuxième à gauche.* 5. *Ne traversez pas le pont.*

D. 1. *vient* 2. *venez* 3. *viennent* 4. *venez* 5. *venir*

E. 1. *Il vaut mieux prendre un taxi.* 2. *Il vaut mieux aller dans un autre restaurant.* 3. *Il vaut mieux partir.* 4. *Il vaut mieux demander notre route.* 5. *Il vaut mieux prendre une autre route.*

F. 1. *deux cent trois* 2. *sept cent quatre-vingt-six* 3. *mille cinq cent quatre-vingts* 4. *deux mille six cent quarante-deux* 5. *cinq mille cinq cent soixante-sept*

LEÇON 13
LA VIE QUOTIDIENNE.   Everyday Life.

A. DIALOGUE

Les habitudes.

JEAN-CLAUDE: **Bonsoir Bernard!**

BERNARD: **Jean-Claude! Asseyez-vous donc avec moi un moment.**

JEAN-CLAUDE: **Quel plaisir de vous revoir! Qu'est-ce que vous devenez?**

BERNARD: **Toujours la même routine, métro-boulot-dodo![1] Je n'ai pas le temps de m'ennuyer! Je suis très occupé et je n'ai pas l'occasion de sortir beaucoup.**

JEAN-CLAUDE: **Oui, mais il faut se distraire!**

GÉRALDINE: **Alors, les hommes, vous vous amusez bien?**

JEAN-CLAUDE: **Quelle soirée Géraldine! Vos hors-d'oeuvre sont exquis.**

GÉRALDINE: **Ah, mon nouveau chef est sensationnel. Il peut préparer un dîner pour dix personnes en cinq minutes.**

JEAN-CLAUDE: **Je pourrais manger toute la soirée.**

BERNARD: **Moi aussi. Malheureusement, je travaille demain et je ne peux pas me coucher trop tard.**

JEAN-CLAUDE: **Je vais aussi être obligé de partir bientôt. Je me lève tôt le samedi matin car je joue au golf. Je vous[2] dépose, Bernard?**

GÉRALDINE: **Vous allez bien prendre une tasse de café?**

BERNARD: **Bon, d'accord, une tasse de café et on part dans un quart d'heure.**

Habits.

JEAN-CLAUDE: Good evening, Bernard.

BERNARD: Jean-Claude! Come sit with me for a moment.

[1] This is a rather common colloquial expression.

[2] Direct objects will be discussed in *Leçon* 15.

JEAN-CLAUDE: What a pleasure to see you again! What are you up to?

BERNARD: Always the same routine, subway-work-sleep. I don't have time to get bored! I'm very busy, and I don't have a chance to go out much.

JEAN-CLAUDE: But one must have some fun!

GÉRALDINE: Are you men enjoying yourselves?

JEAN-CLAUDE: What an evening, Géraldine! Your hors-d'oeuvres are delicious.

GÉRALDINE: Ah, my new chef is sensational. He can prepare a dinner for ten people in five minutes.

JEAN-CLAUDE: I could eat all evening.

BERNARD: So could I. Unfortunately, I work tomorrow, and I can't go to sleep too late.

JEAN-CLAUDE: I also have to leave soon. I get up early on Saturday morning to play golf. Can I drop you off, Bernard?

GÉRALDINE: Aren't you going to have a cup of coffee?

BERNARD: O.K., a cup of coffee and we'll leave in 15 minutes.

B. GRAMMAIRE ET USAGE

1. THE PRESENT TENSE OF REFLEXIVE VERBS

a. Reflexive verbs are verbs whose object pronouns refer or reflect back to the same person. You use them to talk about things you do to or for yourself. In French, this type of verb is conjugated with a reflexive pronoun *(me, te, se, nous, vous, se)* placed between the subject and the verb. Not all verbs that are reflexive in French are reflexive in English. While the English equivalent to *se laver,* to "wash oneself," does take the reflexive pronoun "oneself," the English equivalent to *se lever,* "to get up," does not. The reflexive verb *se lever* has the same spelling changes as the verb *acheter.*

SE LEVER TO GET UP

I get up	*je me lève*
you get up	*tu te lèves*
he/she/one gets up	*il/elle/on se lève*
we get up	*nous nous levons*
you get up	*vous vous levez*
they get up	*ils/elles se lèvent*

Note that the reflexive pronoun *se* remains the same for masculine and feminine singular and plural.

Je me lève tard le dimanche.
I get up late on Sundays.

Nous nous couchons tôt.
We go to sleep early.

À quelle heure vous levez-vous?
At what time do you get up?

b. The pronouns *me, te, se* drop the *e* before *h* or a vowel.

S'AMUSER TO ENJOY ONESELF

I enjoy myself	*je m'amuse*
you enjoy yourself	*tu t'amuses*
he/she/one enjoys him/her/oneself	*il/elle/on s'amuse*
we enjoy ourselves	*nous nous amusons*
you enjoy yourselves	*vous vous amusez*
they enjoy themselves	*ils/elles s'amusent*

Je m'amuse avec mes amis.
I enjoy myself with my friends.

Tu t'amuses bien?
Are you having a good time?

c. In the negative form, *ne* is placed after the subject pronoun and *pas* right after the verb.

Il ne se lève pas tôt le week-end.
He does not get up early on weekends.

Nous ne nous couchons pas avant minuit.
We don't go to sleep before midnight.

d. In the interrogative form, the reflexive pronoun remains before the verb. Only the subject goes after.

Comment vous appelez-vous?
What is your name?

Pourquoi te couches-tu si tard?
Why do you go to sleep so late?

e. In the imperative, the reflexive pronoun is placed after the verb; in the *tu* form it changes from *te* to *toi* in the affirmative only.

Lève-toi.	Get up.	*Ne te lève pas.*	Don't get up.
Levons-nous.	Let's get up.	*Ne nous levons pas.*	Let's not get up.
Levez-vous.	Get up.	*Ne vous levez pas.*	Don't get up.

f. In the infinitive, the reflexive verb keeps its reflexive pronoun in the same person as the subject of the verb.

Je me lève tôt.
  I get up early.

J'aime me lever tard.
  I like to get up late.

Nous nous couchons.
  We go to sleep.

Nous voulons nous coucher.
  We want to go to sleep.

Il se distrait.
  He is enjoying himself.

Il sait se distraire.
  He knows how to enjoy himself.

Vous vous amusez.
  You are having fun.

Vous allez vous amuser.
  You are going to have fun.

g. In impersonal constructions such as *il faut* and *il est impossible de* or when stating a general rule, the reflexive pronoun is *se*.

Il ne faut pas s'asseoir ici.
  One must not sit down here.

Ils sont amusants; il est impossible de s'ennuyer avec eux.
  They are funny; it is impossible to be bored with them.

2. THE VERB *S'ASSEOIR*

S'asseoir (to sit down) has two forms, A and B, in the present tense. Both forms are used. Yet, for the *nous* and *vous* forms, form A is more common in modern usage.

A	B

	A	B
I sit down	*je m'assieds*	*je m'assois*
you sit down	*tu t'assieds*	*tu t'assois*
he/she/one sits down	*il/elle/on s'assied*	*il/elle/on s'assoit*
we sit down	*nous nous asseyons*	*nous nous assoyons*
you sit down	*vous vous asseyez*	*vous vous assoyez*
they sit down	*ils/elles s'asseyent*	*ils/elles s'assoient*

Elle s'assoit à côté de Marc.
She sits down next to Marc.

Asseyez-vous, s'il vous plaît.
Sit down, please.

Ne t'assieds pas dans ce vieux fauteuil.
Don't sit in this old armchair.

3. EXCLAMATIONS WITH *QUEL*

The interrogative adjective *quel* (what, which) is also used in exclamations.

Quel plaisir! *(m.)*
What a pleasure!

Quelle soirée! *(f.)*
What an evening!

Quels beaux enfants! *(m. pl.)*
What beautiful children!

Quelles habitudes étranges! *(f. pl.)*
What strange habits!

4. EXPRESSIONS OF TIME WITH *EN* AND *DANS*

Both *en* and *dans* mean "in," but they are used differently.
a. The preposition *en* expresses the length of time an action takes.

Mon chef peut préparer un dîner en cinq minutes.
My chef can prepare a dinner in five minutes.

Je peux lire un livre en une heure.
I can read a book in an hour.

b. The preposition *dans* indicates the time when an action will begin.

Nous partons dans une demi-heure.
We'll leave in a half hour.

134

Je reviens dans cinq minutes.
I'll be back in five minutes.

VOCABULAIRE

l'habitude *(f.)*	habit
la vie	life
la connaissance	acquaintance, knowledge
la routine	routine
le boulot *(fam.)*	job
se réveiller	to wake up
se lever	to get up, to stand up
préparer	to prepare
se préparer	to get ready
s'habiller	to get dressed
se coucher	to go to bed
s'endormir	to fall asleep
se reposer	to rest, to relax
se dépêcher	to hurry
se promener	to take a walk
s'amuser	to enjoy oneself
amusant	funny
se distraire	to have fun
travailler	to work
avoir le temps de (+ infinitive)	to have time to (do something)
avoir l'occasion	to have the opportunity
s'asseoir	to sit down
rencontrer	to meet
s'ennuyer	to get bored
être obligé	to have to
être occupé	to be busy
déposer	to drop off (someone)
revoir	to see again
tôt	early
tard	late
de bonne heure	early
toujours	always
bientôt	soon
malheureusement	unfortunately
la soirée	evening, party
le plaisir	pleasure
une tasse de café	a cup of coffee
sensationnel*(le)*	sensational

EXERCICES

A. *Compléter avec le pronom réfléchi.*

MODÈLE: *Elle* _____ *amuse à la soirée.*
　　　　Elle s'amuse à la soirée.

1. *Nous* _____ *amusons chez Bernard.*
2. *Il faut* _____ *distraire dans la vie.*
3. _____ *levez-vous tôt le matin?*
4. *Ils* _____ *préparent à partir en vacances.*
5. *Est-ce que tu* _____ *couches tard le samedi soir?*

B. *Que fait Jean-Claude? Utiliser les suggestions entre parenthèses.*

MODÈLE: *Le matin, Jean-Claude* _____. *(se lever à 7 heures)*
　　　　Le matin, Jean-Claude se lève à 7 heures.

1. *Le week-end, Jean-Claude* _____. *(se coucher tard)*
2. *Le soir, Jean-Claude* _____. *(s'asseoir devant la télé)*
3. *Après le dîner, Jean-Claude* _____. *(se préparer pour sortir)*
4. *Le week-end, Jean-Claude* _____. *(s'amuser avec ses amis)*
5. *Le dimanche, Jean-Claude* _____. *(se promener à la campagne)*

C. *Mettre les phrases à la forme négative.*

MODÈLE: *Il se repose aujourd'hui.*
　　　　Il ne se repose pas aujourd'hui.

1. *Je me lève tard tous les jours.*
2. *Vous vous reposez bien.*
3. *Nous nous asseyons dans le train.*
4. *Il s'ennuie en vacances.*
5. *Les enfants se couchent de bonne heure.*

D. *Dire à un ami de . . .*

MODÈLE: *s'amuser avec le chien.*
　　　　Amuse-toi avec le chien!

1. *se lever à huit heures.*
2. *se coucher plus tôt.*
3. *se dépêcher.*
4. *s'asseoir dans le fauteuil.*
5. *se promener dans le Jardin du Luxembourg.*

E. *Mettre à la forme négative.*

MODÈLE: *Levez-vous.*
　　　　Ne vous levez pas.

1. *Dépêchez-vous.*
2. *Asseyons-nous dans le salon.*
3. *Couche-toi avant minuit.*
4. *Préparez-vous.*
5. *Réveille-toi de bonne heure.*

F. *Réécrire la phrase avec une exclamation.*

MODÈLE: *C'est une belle maison.*
       Quelle belle maison!

1. *C'est un beau château.*
2. *C'est une soirée magnifique.*
3. *Ce sont des habitudes bizarres.*
4. *C'est une belle journée.*
5. *C'est un plaisir de vous revoir.*

NOTE CULTURELLE

A regular workday in France lasts from nine to five as it does in the United States. More and more employees, however, only take a short break for lunch and continue to work in their lunch hour *(la journée continue)*. This allows them either to go to work later or to leave earlier.

The French end the day rather late: dinner is usually served at eight o'clock in the evening. The news programs on television start at eight, and the evening's entertainment starts at eight-thirty or nine.

LA CLÉ DES EXERCICES

A. 1. *nous* 2. *se* 3. *Vous* 4. *se* 5. *te*
B. 1. *Le week-end, Jean-Claude se couche tard.* 2. *Le soir, Jean-Claude s'assied/s'assoit devant la télé.* 3. *Après le dîner, Jean-Claude se prépare pour sortir.* 4. *Le week-end, Jean-Claude s'amuse avec ses amis.* 5. *Le dimanche, Jean-Claude se promène à la campagne.*
C. 1. *Je ne me lève pas tard tous les jours.* 2. *Vous ne vous reposez pas bien.* 3. *Nous ne nous asseyons pas dans le train.* 4. *Il ne s'ennuie pas en vacances.* 5. *Les enfants ne se couchent pas de bonne heure.*
D. 1. *Lève-toi à huit heures!* 2. *Couche-toi plus tôt!* 3. *Dépêche-toi!* 4. *Assieds-toi dans le fauteuil.* 5. *Promène-toi dans le Jardin du Luxembourg.*
E. 1. *Ne vous dépêchez pas.* 2. *Ne nous asseyons pas dans le salon.* 3. *Ne te couche pas avant minuit.* 4. *Ne vous préparez pas.* 5. *Ne te réveille pas de bonne heure.*
F. 1. *Quel beau château!* 2. *Quelle soirée magnifique!* 3. *Quelles habitudes bizarres!* 4. *Quelle belle journée!* 5. *Quel plaisir de vous revoir!*

LEÇON 14

AU TRAVAIL. At Work.

A. DIALOGUE

Dans un salon de la gastronomie.

ÉMILIE: Alors, vous travaillez pour *Choco Suisse* maintenant?

WOLFGANG: Oui, c'est une société très dynamique.

ÉMILIE: Depuis combien de temps habitez-vous à Lausanne?

WOLFGANG: J'y habite depuis trois mois. Et vous, vous travaillez toujours pour *Les Vins de France?*

ÉMILIE: Non, je viens de commencer à travailler pour *La Comtesse du Périgord.*

WOLFGANG: Vous vendez du foie gras! C'est fantastique! De plus, c'est une société en pleine expansion.

ÉMILIE: Oui, nous venons d'ouvrir des boutiques dans plusieurs grands magasins.

WOLFGANG: Alors, vous n'habitez plus à Paris?

ÉMILIE: Non, il y a six mois que j'habite dans le Sud-Ouest! La région est très agréable et il y a beaucoup plus de soleil!

WOLFGANG: Vous venez souvent à Paris?

ÉMILIE: Non, j'y viens rarement.

WOLFGANG: Vous savez, le prochain Salon International a lieu en Suisse.

ÉMILIE: Oui, j'ai l'intention d'y aller.

WOLFGANG: C'est formidable! Voilà ma nouvelle carte de visite. Passez-moi un coup de fil à votre arrivée!

At a Food Show.

ÉMILIE: So, you are working for *Choco Suisse* now?

WOLFGANG: Yes, it's a very dynamic company.

ÉMILIE: How long have you been living in Lausanne?

WOLFGANG: I have been living there for three months. And you, are you still working for *Les Vins de France?*

ÉMILIE: No, I just started working for *La Comtesse du Périgord*.

WOLFGANG: You sell goose liver pâté! That's fantastic! And besides, it's a growing company.

ÉMILIE: Yes, we just opened boutiques in several large department stores.

WOLFGANG: Then you no longer live in Paris.

ÉMILIE: No, I've been living in the Southwest for six months. The region is very pleasant and there is much more sunshine.

WOLFGANG: Do you come to Paris often?

ÉMILIE: No, I seldom come here.

WOLFGANG: You know, the next international show will take place in Switzerland.

ÉMILIE: Yes, I plan to go there.

WOLFGANG: Wonderful! Here's my new business card. Give me a call when you get there!

B. GRAMMAIRE ET USAGE

1. *DEPUIS* AND *IL Y A . . . QUE* WITH THE PRESENT TENSE

a. To express an action or a situation that began in the past and is still going on in the present, French uses the present tense + *depuis* or *il y a . . . que* with the date or length of time. Note that French uses the present tense where English uses the present perfect.

Je travaille pour cette société depuis trois mois.
I have been working for this company for three months.

Il y a trois mois que je travaille pour cette société.
I have been working for this company for three months.

Il habite à Lausanne depuis un an.
He has been living in Lausanne for a year.

Il y a un an qu'il habite à Lausanne.
He has been living in Lausanne for a year.

b. The questions that evoke an answer with *depuis* or *il y a . . . que* are:

Depuis combien de temps . . . ? (How long . . . ?)

Depuis quand . . . ? (Since when . . . ?)[1]

---

[1] When answering a question with *depuis quand,* use *depuis* and not *il y a . . . que,* which only refers to a length of time and not a date.

Depuis combien de temps travaillez-vous à Marseille?
How long have you been working in Marseille?

Depuis quand êtes-vous à Paris?
Since when have you been in Paris?

> When using *depuis combien de temps,* the answer will be given in minutes, hours, months, years, etc., as it refers to a length of time.

Depuis combien de temps m'attendez-vous?
How long have you been waiting for me?

Je vous attends depuis dix minutes.
I have been waiting for you for ten minutes.

> When using *depuis quand,* the answer will be a specific point in time: a day, a date, a month.

Depuis quand ouvrez-vous votre magasin le dimanche?
Since when have you been opening your store on Sundays?

Depuis septembre.
Since September.

Depuis quand es-tu malade?
Since when have you been sick?

Je suis malade depuis hier.
I have been sick since yesterday.

2. THE IMMEDIATE PAST

You remember the immediate future: *aller* + infinitive. The immediate past is built in a similar manner. You use *venir* (to come) in the present tense + *de* + infinitive. Although it is in the present, it conveys an idea in the past in English. First, let's review the verb *venir:*

VENIR TO COME

I come	*je viens*	we come	*nous venons*
you come	*tu viens*	you come	*vous venez*
he/she/one comes	*il/elle/on vient*	they come	*ils/elles viennent*

Je viens de commencer à travailler pour La Comtesse du Périgord.
I've just started working for *La Comtesse du Périgord.*

Nous venons d'ouvrir trois magasins.
We've just opened three stores.

Elle vient de vendre sa voiture.
She has just sold her car.

Vous venez d'acheter une nouvelle maison!
You've just bought a new house!

3. ADVERBS OF TIME

toujours	always, still
encore	still, more
ne pas . . . encore	not yet
jamais	ever
ne . . . jamais	never
ne . . . plus	no longer, no more
souvent	often
rarement	rarely, seldom
maintenant	now
longtemps	long, for a long time
lors	then, during
tôt	early
tard	late
bientôt	soon
aujourd'hui	today
hier	yesterday
demain	tomorrow
avant-hier	the day before yesterday
après-demain	the day after tomorrow
autrefois	formerly

Vous n'habitez plus à Paris?
You no longer live in Paris?

Vous travaillez toujours pour Les Vins de France?
You're still working for *Les Vins de France?*

Vous venez souvent à Lausanne?
Do you often come to Lausanne?

Ils voyagent rarement.
They seldom travel.

Je ne sais pas encore.
I don't know yet.

4. THE LOCATION PRONOUN Y

Y is a pronoun which replaces a location. It is used to express "there" when a place has already been mentioned. Otherwise, the pronoun *là* is used.

Depuis quand habitez-vous à Lausanne?
How long have you been living in Lausanne?

J'y habite depuis mars dernier.
I have been living there since last March.

Avez-vous l'intention d'aller au Salon?
Do you intend to go to the trade show?

Oui, j'ai l'intention d'y aller.
Yes, I intend to go there.

Allez-vous chez Hubert ce soir?
Are you going to Hubert's tonight?

Non, je n'y vais pas.
No, I am not going.

VOCABULAIRE

la société	company
le grand magasin	department store
la carte de visite	business card
un salon	trade show; living room
un salon gastronomique	food show
le foie gras	goose liver pâté
la Suisse	Switzerland
suisse	Swiss
le soleil	sun
dynamique	dynamic
agréable	pleasant
en pleine expansion	growing
vendre	to sell
travailler	to work
habiter	to live
avoir lieu	to take place
passer un coup de fil	to give a call *(fam.)*
avoir l'intention	to intend
ouvrir	to open
depuis	since, for
souvent	often
rarement	seldom, rarely
toujours	always, still
ne . . . plus	no more, no longer
de plus	moreover, in addition
y	there
fantastique	fantastic

| nouveau *(nouvelle)* | new |
| prochain*(e)* | next |

EXERCICES

A. *Répondre aux questions en utilisant "depuis" et ensuite "il y a . . . que."*
(Answer the questions using *depuis,* then *il y a . . . que.*)

MODÈLE: *Depuis combien de temps habitez-vous à Paris? (trois mois)*
       J'habite à Paris depuis trois mois.
       Il y a trois mois que j'habite à Paris.

   1. *Depuis combien de temps travaillez-vous pour M. Mazure? (six mois)*
   2. *Depuis combien de temps prenez-vous vos vacances en Suisse? (deux ans)*
   3. *Depuis combien de temps habitez-vous dans cette maison? (dix ans)*
   4. *Depuis combien de temps jouez-vous au golf? (trois semaines)*
   5. *Depuis combien de temps avez-vous cette voiture? (un an et demi)*

B. *Répondre aux questions en utilisant "depuis."*

MODÈLE: *Depuis quand est-il en vacances? (la semaine dernière)*
       Il est en vacances depuis la semaine dernière.

   1. *Depuis quand est-il malade? (mercredi)*
   2. *Depuis quand vendez-vous du vin aux Japonais? (le printemps dernier)*
   3. *Depuis quand sait-elle la nouvelle? (hier)*
   4. *Depuis quand ont-ils cette armoire? (l'automne)*
   5. *Depuis quand l'attendez-vous? (midi)*

C. *Transformer les phrases en utilisant le passé immédiat.*

MODÈLE: *Il achète du foie gras.*
       Il vient d'acheter du foie gras.

   1. *Nous vendons notre maison.*
   2. *Ils ouvrent un nouveau magasin.*
   3. *Elle prend une photo.*
   4. *Il tourne à gauche.*
   5. *Vous commencez à travailler dans une autre société?*

D. *Utiliser le pronom "y."*

MODÈLE: *Elle habite à Paris.*
       Elle y habite.

   1. *Il va au Salon de la Gastronomie.*
   2. *Nous allons à la campagne.*
   3. *Vous avez l'intention d'aller en Italie?*
   4. *Elle habite dans le Sud-Ouest.*
   5. *Vous allez au Conservatoire?*

NOTE CULTURELLE

In February and September, fashion and boutique shows take place in Paris. Fashion designers, clothing buyers, and the press gather at the top hotels or in the immense Exposition Hall at the Porte de Versailles. While Milan, Tokyo, London, and New York vie with Paris for fashion dominance, nothing stirs up the fashion world like the "bad boys of fashion," Christian Lacroix and Jean-Paul Gaultier, whose exuberant styles manage to shock the fashion world year in and year out.

Throughout the year, a wide range of trade shows takes place in Paris. In addition to these, the wine shows in Lyon and in Bordeaux *(Vin Expo)* attract a large number of people.

LA CLÉ DES EXERCICES

A. 1. *Je travaille pour M. Mazure depuis six mois. / Il y a six mois que je travaille pour M. Mazure. 2. Je prends mes vacances en Suisse depuis deux ans. / Il y a deux ans que je prends mes vacances en Suisse. 3. J'habite dans cette maison depuis dix ans. / Il y a dix ans que j'habite dans cette maison. 4. Je joue au golf depuis trois semaines. / Il y a trois semaines que je joue au golf. 5. J'ai cette voiture depuis un an et demi. / Il y a un an et demi que j'ai cette voiture.*

B. 1. *Il est malade depuis mercredi. 2. Je vends du vin aux Japonais depuis le printemps dernier. 3. Elle sait la nouvelle depuis hier. 4. Ils ont cette armoire depuis l'automne. 5. Je l'attends depuis midi.*

C. 1. *Nous venons de vendre notre maison. 2. Ils viennent d'ouvrir un nouveau magasin. 3. Elle vient de prendre une photo. 4. Il vient de tourner à gauche. 5. Vous venez de commencer à travailler dans une autre société?*

D. 1. *Il y va. 2. Nous y allons. 3. J'ai l'intention d'y aller. 4. Elle y habite. 5. J'y vais.*

LEÇON 15

DANS UN GRAND MAGASIN. In a Department Store.

A. DIALOGUE

Faire les courses.

SOPHIE: **Regarde ce chemisier!**

ÉRIC: **Celui-ci?**

SOPHIE: **Non, le chemisier rose pâle juste à côté.**

ÉRIC: **C'est trop clair pour ton teint. Ce chemisier aubergine est ravissant.**

SOPHIE: **C'est trop triste! J'ai horreur des couleurs foncées!**

ÉRIC: **Et ce chemisier jaune à fleurs, comment le trouves-tu?**

SOPHIE: **Je le trouve assez joli.**

ÉRIC: **Bon, essaie-les tous les deux! Quelle taille fais-tu?**

SOPHIE: **Quarante ou quarante-deux . . . j'espère qu'ils ont ma taille . . . Voilà, je vais les essayer.**

ÉRIC: **Madame, s'il vous plaît, où sont les cabines d'essayage?**

VENDEUSE: **Au fond du magasin. Si vous voulez bien me suivre . . .**

ÉRIC: **Alors Sophie, quel chemisier est-ce que tu préfères?**

SOPHIE: **Tu sais, j'adore le rose. Je vais le prendre.**

VENDEUSE: **Il est en solde cette semaine. C'est une très bonne affaire!**

SOPHIE: **C'est parfait!**

Shopping for Clothes.

SOPHIE: Look at that blouse!

ÉRIC: This one?

SOPHIE: No, the light rose blouse just next to it.

ÉRIC: It's too light for your complexion. This aubergine blouse is beautiful.

SOPHIE: It's too somber! I hate dark colors.

ÉRIC: What about this yellow blouse with flowers, how do you like it?

SOPHIE: I find it rather nice.

145

ÉRIC: Try them both. What's your size?

SOPHIE: Eight or ten . . . I hope they have my size. Here we are, I am going to try them on.

ÉRIC: Madame, where are the dressing rooms?

SALESWOMAN: In the back of the store. Please follow me.

ÉRIC: Well, Sophie, which blouse do you prefer?

SOPHIE: You know, I love the rose-colored one. I'll take it.

SALESWOMAN: It is on sale this week. It's a very good buy.

SOPHIE: It's perfect!

B. GRAMMAIRE ET USAGE

1. DEMONSTRATIVE PRONOUNS

a. We have studied the demonstrative adjectives "this" and "these" *(ce, cet, cette, ces)* in lesson 5. A demonstrative pronoun replaces a demonstrative adjective and its noun:

Je vais essayer ce chemisier.
I'm going to try on this blouse.

Je vais essayer celui-ci.
I'm going to try on this one.

Like other pronouns, demonstrative pronouns agree in gender and number with the nouns they replace.

	MASCULINE	FEMININE
singular	*celui*	*celle*
plural	*ceux*	*celles*

b. Demonstrative pronouns are used to compare things of the same nature. When you need to make a distinction between two things, just add *-ci* and *-là* to the pronoun.

Regardez ces chemisiers! Préférez-vous celui-ci ou celui-là?
Look at these blouses! Do you prefer this one or that one?

Quelle cabine d'essayage est libre? Celle-ci ou celle-là?
Which dressing room is free? This one or that one?

Quelles belles chaussures! Tu veux acheter celles-ci ou celles-là?
What beautiful shoes! Do you want to buy these or those?

146

Tu prends ceux-ci ou ceux-là?
  Are you taking these or those?

c. The demonstrative pronouns used without *-ci* or *-là* are used in dependent clauses introduced by *qui* or *que* (that, which) which will be discussed in depth in lesson 27.

Celui que je voudrais acheter coûte trop cher.
  The one that I would like to buy costs too much.

Ceux qui sont sur cette étagère sont en solde.
  Those which are on this shelf are on sale.

Je préfère ce chapeau à celui que tu viens d'acheter.
  I prefer this hat to the one you've just bought.

d. The indefinite demonstrative pronouns *ceci* (this), *cela* (that), and *ça* (this/that, familiar) refer to indefinite things or ideas.

Prenez ceci. Ne prenez pas cela.
  Take this. Don't take that.

Je préfère ceci.
  I prefer this.

Je préfère ça.
  I prefer this/that.

Nous n'aimons pas ça.
  We don't like that.

2. DIRECT OBJECT PRONOUNS

a. The direct object pronouns are:

me	*me*	us	*nous*
you	*te*	you	*vous*
him	*le*	them	*les*
her	*la*		
him/her/it	*l'*		

b. Just as in English, direct object pronouns replace direct object nouns. An object is called direct if it goes directly from the verb to the noun without a preposition.

Je prends → le chemisier jaune.
  I take → the yellow blouse.

When a direct object noun is replaced by the direct object pronoun, the direct object pronoun precedes the verb. If *me, te, le, la* are followed by a verb starting with a vowel or a silent *h*, they become *m', t', l'*.

Je prends le chemisier jaune.
  I take the yellow blouse.

Je le prends.
  I take it.

Tu achètes la robe bleue.
  You buy the blue dress.

Tu l'achètes.
  You buy it.

Ils ont ma taille.
  They have my size.

Ils l'ont.
  They have it.

Nous aimons ces couleurs.
  We like these colors.

Nous les aimons.
  We like them.

Note that some verbs that take direct objects in French may take indirect objects (preceded by a preposition) in English.

Nous regardons → les boutiques.
  We are looking → at → the shops.

Nous les regardons.
  We are looking at them.

Je cherche mon amie.
  I am looking for my friend.

Je la cherche.
  I am looking for her.

Elle demande l'adresse.
  She is asking for the address.

Elle la demande.
  She is asking for it.

c. In a question, the direct object pronoun still comes immediately before the verb.

Quelles belles chaussures!
  What beautiful shoes!

Est-ce que vous les prenez?
Will you take them?

d. In a negative sentence, the direct object pronoun also comes immediately before the verb.

Ils n'ont pas sa taille.
They don't have her size.

Ils ne l'ont pas.
They don't have it.

Je n'aime pas le jaune.
I don't like the color yellow.

Je ne l'aime pas.
I don't like it.

e. In sentences with a verb + infinitive, the object pronoun is placed immediately before the infinitive.

Je vais acheter cette robe.
I am going to buy this dress.

Je vais l'acheter.
I am going to buy it.

Tu veux acheter cette cravate?
You want to buy this tie?

Tu veux l'acheter?
You want to buy it?

Elle espère trouver sa taille.
She hopes to find her size.

Elle espère la trouver.
She hopes to find it.

f. In the positive imperative, the direct object pronoun follows the verb.

Prenez ce chemisier.
Take this blouse.

Prenez-le.
Take it.

Achète ces chaussures.
Buy these shoes.

Achète-les.
Buy them.

In the negative imperative, the direct object pronoun remains before the verb.

Ne prenez pas ce pantalon.
Don't take these pants.

Ne le prenez pas.
Don't take them.

N'attendez pas Sophie.
Don't wait for Sophie.

Ne l'attendez pas.
Don't wait for her.

3. THE -*ER* VERB *ESSAYER*

Verbs like *essayer* (vowel + *y* + -*er*) have spelling changes in the present tense.

ESSAYER TO TRY, TO TRY ON

I try	*j'essaie*	we try	*nous essayons*
you try	*tu essaies*	you try	*vous essayez*
he/she/one tries	*il/elle/on essaie*	they try	*ils essaient*

Tu essaies cette robe.
You're trying on this dress.

Essayez ces chaussures.
Try on these shoes.

Payer (to pay, to pay for) is conjugated like *essayer*.

Je paie le billet.
I'm paying for the ticket.

Nous payons 500 francs par jour.
We pay 500 francs a day.

4. COLORS

The names of colors (see the vocabulary) are placed after the noun they modify. Being adjectives, they agree in gender and number with the noun modified.

un pantalon blanc	a pair of white pants
une robe bleue	a blue dress
des chaussures noires	black shoes

Marron (brown) and *orange* (orange) do not agree.

des robes orange	orange dresses
une chemise marron	a brown shirt

When modified by *foncé* (dark) or *clair* (light), all colors become invariable.

une cravate vert clair	a light green tie
un pantalon bleu foncé	a dark blue pair of pants

When used as a noun, the name of a color is preceded by *le*.

J'aime le bleu.
I like blue.

Préférez-vous le rouge?
Do you prefer red?

VOCABULAIRE

le grand magasin	department store
les vêtements *(m.)*	clothes
un pantalon	pair of pants
un costume	man's suit
une chemise	man's shirt
une cravate	a tie
une robe	a dress
une jupe	skirt
un chemisier	blouse
la soie	silk
la dentelle	lace
la laine	wool
un tailleur	woman's suit
un manteau	coat
un imperméable	raincoat
une veste	jacket
un pull	sweater
une ceinture	belt
un collant	pantyhose
une paire de chaussettes	a pair of socks
un maillot de bain	bathing suit
des chaussures *(f. pl.)*	shoes
la couleur	color
blanc, blanche	white
bleu, bleue	blue

rouge	red
vert, verte	green
jaune	yellow
orange	orange
marron	brown
gris, grise	grey
noir, noire	black
clair	clear, light (colored)
foncé	dark (color)
triste	somber
le vendeur *(m.)*, la vendeuse *(f.)*	salesperson
la taille	size (for clothes), waist
la pointure	shoe, glove size
le teint	complexion
essayer	to try, to try on
suivre	to follow
adorer	to love
avoir horreur de	to hate
faire les courses	to shop
le salon d'essayage	dressing room
en solde	on sale
une bonne affaire	bargain
celui-ci	this one
celui-là	that one
assez	enough, fairly
au fond du magasin	in the back of the store
parfait	perfect
ravissant	beautiful

EXERCICES

A. *Réécrire les phrases proposées avec un pronom démonstratif.*

MODÈLE: J'aime cette robe.
J'aime celle-ci.

1. *Je voudrais ce pantalon.*
2. *Catherine préfère cette chemise.*
3. *Je déteste ces chapeaux.*
4. *Je n'aime pas cette couleur.*
5. *Ces voitures-ci sont américaines.*

B. *Répondre aux questions avec un pronom objet direct.*

MODÈLE: *Est-ce que Paul aime les chaussures marron? (oui)*
    Oui, il les aime.

1. *Est-ce que Sophie aime le tailleur bleu? (oui)*
2. *Est-ce qu'Ariane aime la cravate à fleurs? (non)*
3. *Est-ce que Murielle essaie les tailleurs de printemps? (non)*
4. *Est-ce que la vendeuse a la taille de Monique? (oui)*
5. *Est-ce que Jérôme aime les couleurs foncées? (oui)*

C. *Compléter les phrases avec la forme correcte du verbe.*

1. *Nous _____ des chaussures. (essayer)*
2. *Il _____ un pantalon. (essayer)*
3. *Je _____ les vêtements. (payer)*
4. *Vous _____ le chemisier? (essayer)*
5. *Tu _____ le chapeau? (payer)*

D. *Accorder les noms et les couleurs.* (Match the nouns and the colors.)

1. *Des robes / noir*
2. *Une chemise / blanc*
3. *Des chaussures / marron*
4. *Des chemisiers / jaune*
5. *Des chapeaux / orange*

NOTE CULTURELLE

There are many large department stores *(les grands magasins)* in France. The most well known are *les Galeries Lafayette, le Printemps, le Bon Marché,* and *La Samaritaine.* They are generally open all day, from 9:30 A.M. to 7 P.M. Smaller stores and shops often close at lunch time.

New shopping centers are opening up in towers and complexes such as *La Grande Arche, le Palais des Congrès, le Centre Beaubourg* and in the *Tour Montparnasse.* The discount stores in the southwest of Paris, near the subway stop Alesia, are great for bargain hunters.

When you are shopping for clothes, you need to know that French sizes *(la taille)* are different from American sizes. Here are a few comparative charts:

Ladies' dresses and tops:

France	36	38	40	42	44	46	48	
USA	4	6	8	10	12	14	16	

Men's suits:

France	36	38	40	42	44	46	48	50
USA	35	36	37	38	39	40	41	42

Men's shirts:

France	37	38	39	40	41	42
USA	14	15	15	16	16	17

A. 1. *Je voudrais celui-ci.* 2. *Catherine préfère celle-ci.* 3. *Je déteste ceux-ci.*
    4. *Je n'aime pas celle-ci.* 5. *Celles-ci sont américaines.*
B. 1. *Oui, elle l'aime.* 2. *Non, elle ne l'aime pas.* 3. *Non, elle ne les essaie pas.*
    4. *Oui, elle l'a.* 5. *Oui, il les aime.*
C. 1. *essayons* 2. *essaie* 3. *paie* 4. *essayez* 5. *paies*
D. 1. *noires* 2. *blanche* 3. *marron* 4. *jaunes* 5. *orange*

TROISIÈME RÉVISION

A. *Compléter les phrases avec la forme correcte du verbe suggéré.*

    1. *Est-ce qu'ils* _____ *avec nous? (venir)*
    2. *Il va* _____ *ministre des finances. (devenir)*
    3. *Vous* _____ *mercredi? (revenir)*
    4. *Elle* _____ *d'une très vieille famille. (venir)*
    5. *Attendez, je* _____ *tout de suite. (revenir)*

B. *Répondre en utilisant les pronoms toniques.*

MODÈLE: *Tu viens avec nous? (non)*
          Non, je ne viens pas avec vous.

    1. *Mélanie va chez sa tante. (non)*
    2. *Sophie achète des cadeaux pour ses neveux. (oui)*
    3. *Émilie travaille avec Wolfgang. (non)*
    4. *Est-ce que ces photos sont à Ariane? (oui)*
    5. *Vous rentrez chez vous? (oui)*

C. *Faire des phrases complètes.*

MODÈLE: *Ils / s'asseoir / dans un café.*
          Ils s'asseoient dans un café.

    1. *Géraldine / se lever / de bonne heure.*
    2. *Je / se coucher / très tard le samedi soir.*
    3. *Vous / se reposer / le week-end.*
    4. *Tu / s'amuser / toujours avec tes amis.*
    5. *Il / s'ennuyer / à la campagne.*

D. *Utiliser l'impératif pour donner un conseil.*

MODÈLE: *J'adore cette couleur. (Essayer ce modèle)*
          Essayez ce modèle!

    1. *La cathédrale est loin! (prendre un taxi)*
    2. *Je suis fatigué! (s'asseoir)*

3. *Il faut partir! (être patient)*
4. *J'ai soif! (boire du vin)*
5. *Où se trouve le château? (tourner à droite)*

E. *Relier le français et l'anglais.* (Match the French and the English.)

1. *Il fait chaud.*
2. *Tournez à droite.*
3. *C'est tout droit.*
4. *Il pleut.*
5. *C'est tout près.*
6. *Il fait mauvais.*
7. *Il neige.*

a. It's straight ahead.
b. It's raining.
c. It's snowing.
d. It's quite near.
e. The weather is bad.
f. Turn right.
g. It's hot.

F. *Répondre aux phrases en utilisant un pronom démonstratif.* (Answer the sentences using a demonstrative pronoun.)

MODÈLE: Quelle robe voulez-vous acheter?
Je veux acheter celle-ci.

1. *Quels vins recommandez-vous?*
2. *Quel cours suivez-vous?*
3. *Quelle commode aimez-vous?*
4. *Quel chemisier préférez-vous?*
5. *Quelles régions allez-vous visiter?*

G. *Mettre les verbes au passé-immédiat.*

MODÈLE: J'achète un chemisier à fleurs.
Je viens d'acheter un chemisier à fleurs.

1. *Nous dînons dans un excellent restaurant.*
2. *Vous visitez le Salon de la Gastronomie.*
3. *Tu fais un voyage en Asie.*
4. *Elle prépare un grand dîner pour ses invités.*
5. *J'essaie une taille plus petite.*

H. *Répondre aux questions.*

MODÈLE: Depuis combien de temps suivez-vous ce cours de danse? (trois mois)
Je suis ce cours de danse depuis trois mois.

1. *Depuis quand travaillez-vous dans cette société? (six mois)*
2. *Depuis combien de temps étudiez-vous le français? (un mois)*
3. *Depuis combien de temps attendez-vous le train? (dix minutes)*
4. *Depuis quand jouez-vous au tennis? (1990)*
5. *Depuis quand habitez-vous dans le Sud-Ouest? (mars)*

I. *Remplacer les mots soulignés par un pronom objet direct.* (Replace the underlined words with a direct object pronoun.)

MODÈLE: *Vous traversez le pont de Nantes.*
   Vous le traversez.

1. *J'aime beaucoup le café au lait.*
2. *Mélanie trouve les couleurs foncées tristes.*
3. *Il donne sa carte de visite à Ariane.*
4. *Nous regardons les photos de famille.*
5. *Vous prenez le chapeau fleuri.*

LA CLÉ DES EXERCICES

A. 1. *viennent* 2. *devenir* 3. *revenez* 4. *vient* 5. *reviens*

B. 1. *Non, Mélanie ne va pas chez elle.* 2. *Oui, Sophie achète des cadeaux pour eux.* 3. *Non, Émilie ne travaille pas avec lui.* 4. *Oui, ces photos sont à elles.* 5. *Oui, je rentre chez moi.*

C. 1. *Géraldine se lève de bonne heure.* 2. *Je me couche très tard le samedi soir.* 3. *Vous vous reposez le week-end.* 4. *Tu t'amuses toujours avec tes amis.* 5. *Il s'ennuie à la campagne.*

D. 1. *Prenez un taxi!* 2. *Asseyez-vous!* 3. *Soyez patient!* 4. *Buvez du vin!* 5. *Tournez à droite!*

E. 1.—g 2.—f 3.—a 4.—b 5.—d 6.—e 7.—c

F. 1. *Je recommande ceux-ci.* 2. *Je suis celui-ci.* 3. *J'aime celle-ci.* 4. *Je préfère celui-ci.* 5. *Je vais visiter celles-ci.*

G. 1. *Nous venons de dîner dans un excellent restaurant.* 2. *Vous venez de visiter le Salon de la Gastronomie.* 3. *Tu viens de faire un voyage en Asie.* 4. *Elle vient de préparer un grand dîner pour ses invités.* 5. *Je viens d'essayer une taille plus petite.*

H. 1. *Je travaille dans cette société depuis six mois.* 2. *J'étudie le français depuis un mois.* 3. *J'attends le train depuis dix minutes.* 4. *Je joue au tennis depuis 1990.* 5. *J'habite dans le Sud-Ouest depuis mars.*

I. 1. *Je l'aime beaucoup.* 2. *Mélanie les trouve tristes.* 3. *Il la donne à Ariane.* 4. *Nous les regardons.* 5. *Vous le prenez.*

LEÇON 16

LE TÉLÉPHONE. The Telephone.

A. DIALOGUE

Au téléphone.

LA RÉCEPTIONNISTE: **GlobeInfo, bonjour.**

M. BENOÎT: **Je voudrais parler à monsieur Chabrol.**

LA RÉCEPTIONNISTE: **C'est de la part de qui, s'il vous plaît?**

M. BENOÎT: **C'est Pierre Benoît à l'appareil.**

LA RÉCEPTIONNISTE: **Ne quittez pas. Je regrette, la ligne est occupée. Voulez-vous lui laisser un message?**

M. BENOÎT: **Pourriez-vous lui dire de m'appeler cet après-midi?**

LA RÉCEPTIONNISTE: **Bien sûr, quel est votre numéro de téléphone?**

M. BENOÎT: **Il peut me joindre au 44 76 99 67 jusqu'à 15 heures, ensuite au bureau—41 58 14 81.**

Plus tard.

M. CHABROL: **Allô, est-ce que je pourrais parler à Monsieur Benoît.**

LA SECRÉTAIRE: **Ne quittez pas, je vous le passe.**

M. BENOÎT: **Allô, Christian, vous m'entendez?**

M. CHABROL: **Non, je ne vous entends pas très bien. On se rappelle ce soir?**

M. BENOÎT: **Non, non, raccrochez. Je vous rappelle tout de suite. Je veux vous parler d'un nouveau projet.**

On the Telephone.

RECEPTIONIST: GlobeInfo, good morning.

MR. BENOÎT: I would like to speak to Mr. Chabrol.

RECEPTIONIST: Who should I say is calling?

MR. BENOÎT: It's Pierre Benoit speaking.

RECEPTIONIST: Hold on. I'm sorry, his line is busy. Do you want to leave a message?

MR. BENOÎT: Could you tell him to call me this afternoon?

RECEPTIONIST: Certainly. What is your telephone number?

MR. BENOÎT: He can reach me at 44 76 99 67 until 3 P.M. After that, at the office, 41 58 14 81.

Later.

MR. CHABROL: Hello, may I speak to Mr. Benoît?

SECRETARY: Hold on, I'll connect you.

MR. BENOÎT: Hello, Christian, can you hear me?

MR. CHABROL: No, I can't hear you very well. Shall we call each other this evening?

MR. BENOÎT: No, no, hang up. I'll call you right back. I want to speak to you about a new project.

B. GRAMMAIRE ET USAGE

1. THE -ER VERB APPELER

You were first introduced to *appeler* (to call) in lesson 3 with the expression *"Comment vous appelez-vous?"* ("What's your name?"). It has an irregular conjugation.

The verb *appeler* doubles its *l* in all but the *nous* and *vous* forms of the present tense.

APPELER   TO CALL

I call	*j'appelle*		we call	*nous appelons*
you call	*tu appelles*		you call	*vous appelez*
he/she/one calls	*il/elle/on appelle*		they call	*ils appellent*

M. Benoît appelle M. Chabrol.
Mr. Benoît calls Mr. Chabrol.

Elle appelle le médecin.
She calls the doctor.

Je vais l'appeler ce soir.
I am going to call him/her tonight.

158

Rappeler (to call back) and *s'appeller* (to call oneself, to be named) are conjugated the same way.

Je vous rappelle dans un instant.
I'll call you right back.

Comment s'appelle-t-elle?
What is her name?

2. THE VERB *DIRE*

The verb *dire* (to say), like *faire,* is irregular only in the *vous* form *(vous faites).*

DIRE   TO SAY

I say	*je dis*		we say	*nous disons*
you say	*tu dis*		you say	*vous dites*
he/she/one says	*il/elle/on dit*		they say	*ils/elles disent*

Il dit bonjour.
He says good morning.

Elles ne disent rien.
They say nothing.

Ne dites pas cela.
Don't say that.

Qu'est-ce que vous dites?
What are you saying?

3. INDIRECT OBJECT PRONOUNS

After the direct object pronouns studied in the previous chapter, let's take a look at the indirect object pronouns.

a. The indirect object pronouns are:

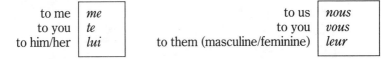

to me	*me*		to us	*nous*
to you	*te*		to you	*vous*
to him/her	*lui*	to them (masculine/feminine)	*leur*

b. An indirect object pronoun replaces an indirect object noun.
An object is called indirect if a preposition is needed to connect the verb and the object.

Je parle → à → M. Benoît.
I talk to Mr. Benoît.

Je lui parle.
I talk to him.

c. Indirect object pronouns, like direct object pronouns, are placed immediately before their verb.

Elle laisse un message à Paul.
She leaves a message for Paul.

Elle lui laisse un message.
She leaves a message for him.

Il répond à Julien.
He replies to Julien.

Il lui répond.
He replies to him.

d. In sentences with verb + an infinitive, the indirect object pronoun is placed immediately before the infinitive.

Je veux lui laisser un message.
I want to leave a message for him.

Nous allons leur téléphoner.
We're going to call them.

Il peut me joindre à mon bureau.
He can reach me at my office.

e. In the imperative form, the indirect object pronoun follows the same rule as the direct object pronoun. It is placed after the verb in a positive command and precedes the verb in a negative command.

Laisse-moi un message avant 19 heures.
Leave me a message before 7 P.M.

Dis-lui d'arriver à l'heure.
Tell him to be on time.

Ne me demande pas l'impossible.
Don't ask me for the impossible.

Ne leur téléphonez pas avant 10 heures.
Don't call them before 10 o'clock.

4. RECIPROCAL VERBS

The subjects of reflexive verbs act on themselves, whereas the subjects of reciprocal verbs act on one another.

Reflexive: We look at ourselves in the mirror.

Reciprocal: We look at each other.

In French, some reflexive verbs express a reciprocal action.

On se rappelle à midi.
We'll call each other at noon.

Ils se regardent.
They are looking at each other.

Bruno et Luc se parlent.
Bruno and Luc talk to each other.

Ils se voient le dimanche.
They see each other on Sundays.

5. *PARLER À / PARLER DE*

Parler à means to talk to someone, whereas *parler de* means to talk about someone or something.

Je parle au directeur.
I am talking to the director.

Nous parlons à Christian.
We are talking to Christian.

Vous voulez leur parler?
Do you want to talk to them?

De quoi parlez-vous?
What are you talking about?

Elle parle de son voyage.
She is talking about her trip.

Il parle de son projet.
He is talking about his project.

le téléphone	telephone
faire un appel à l'étranger	to make an international call
le numéro de téléphone	telephone number
consulter l'annuaire *(m.)*	to consult the telephone book
composer un numéro	to dial a number
Quel est votre numéro?	What's your telephone number?
le poste 203	extension 203
Vous n'avez pas le bon numéro.	You've got the wrong number.
La ligne est occupée.	The line is busy.
Qui est à l'appareil?	Who's calling?
C'est de la part de qui?	Who should I say is calling?
C'est Monsieur Benoît à l'appareil.	It's Mr. Benoît speaking.
Ne quittez pas, s'il vous plaît.	Please hold.
Je voudrais parler à . . .	I would like to speak to . . .
Je voudrais laisser un message.	I'd like to leave a message.
donner un coup de fil	to make a phone call
téléphoner *(à)*	to call someone on the phone
appeler	to call, to call on the telephone
raccrocher	to hang up
rappeler	to call back
répondre au téléphone	to answer the telephone
quitter	to leave
joindre	to reach someone, to meet
regretter	to be sorry
parler à	to talk to
parler de	to talk about
dire	to say, to tell
laisser	to leave
partir	to leave, to go away
entendre	to hear
la réceptionniste	receptionist
le/la secrétaire	secretary
PDG	CEO
Président-directeur général	Chief Executive Officer
tout de suite	right away, immediately
le bureau	office; desk
le/la collègue	colleague
l'employé*(e)*	employee
la lettre	letter
le document	document

EXERCICES

A. *Répondre aux questions avec un pronom objet indirect.*

MODÈLE: *Est-ce que Julie parle à Christine? (oui)*
Oui, elle lui parle.

1. *Est-ce que la secrétaire donne le message à Julien? (oui)*
2. *Est-ce que Cloé parle à M. Benoît? (oui)*
3. *Est-ce que M. Boissard et M. Bresson laissent un message à Jacques? (non)*
4. *Est-ce qu'elle répond au directeur? (non)*
5. *Est-ce que vous demandez l'impossible à vos employés? (non)*

B. *Compléter avec le pronom indirect.*

MODÈLE: *Il va laisser un message à Julien.*
Il va lui laisser un message.

1. *Elle veut envoyer une lettre à sa belle-mère.*
2. *Tu veux demander ce service à Gérard?*
3. *Nous pouvons téléphoner à Julie et Bertrand après six heures.*
4. *Il vient d'envoyer des fleurs à sa mère.*
5. *Vous allez répondre à M. Chabrol.*

C. *Compléter avec l'objet indirect.*

MODÈLE: *Téléphone à Pierre.*
Téléphone-lui.

1. *Répondez à la secrétaire.*
2. *Ne parlez pas au directeur.*
3. *Demandez aux clients.*
4. *Téléphonez à vos collègues.*
5. *Ne répondez pas à Christian.*

D. *Compléter avec l'objet direct ou indirect.*

MODÈLE: *Je donne des fleurs (à ma secrétaire).*
Je lui donne des fleurs.

1. *Tu demandes le document (au secrétaire).*
2. *Il prend (les messages).*
3. *Elle donne un coup de fil (à sa mère).*
4. *Nous demandons (le document).*
5. *Il répond (à ses collègues.)*

E. *Faire une phrase en utilisant un verbe réciproque.*

MODÈLE: *Bruno / Yves / se regarder.*
Bruno et Yves se regardent.

1. *M. Benoît / M. Chabrol / se parler chaque jour.*
2. *Marie / moi / se voir le jeudi soir.*
3. *Le directeur / l'assistant / se rencontrer dans le café.*
4. *Le secrétaire / la réceptionniste / se voir* (negative) *le week-end.*
5. *Mme Dubois / M. Leblanc / se rappeler avant cinq heures.*

F. *Compléter avec le verbe "dire" ou "appeler."*

1. *Est-ce qu'il te _____ tout? (dire)*
2. *Est-ce que vous _____ (appeler) le médécin?*
3. *_____ lui de ne pas téléphoner. (dire)* (fam.)
4. *Nous ne _____ rien. (dire)*
5. *Elle _____ sa secrétaire. (appeler)*

G. *Compléter avec "parler à" ou "parler de" suivant le sens.*

MODÈLE: *Elle parle _____ Paul.*
          Elle parle à Paul.

1. *Ils parlent _____ leurs vacances.*
2. *Il parle _____ Joséphine de son projet.*
3. *Nous parlons _____ son nouveau livre.*
4. *N'en parlez pas _____ Bruno dimanche prochain.*
5. *Tu parles _____ la conférence aux employés.*

NOTE CULTURELLE

Unlike in the United States, telecommunications in France are run by a single, state-owned company, France Télécom. Pay phones can be found easily in the *P&Ts* ("Post and Telecommunication" offices), which provide both postal and telecommunication services. While France still uses some coin operated phones, most of them are being replaced by phones using magnetic cards *(la télécarte)*. These cards can be purchased at the post office or in tobacco shops. All French phone numbers have eight digits. For international calls from France, dial 19, then the country code, the area code, and the number. The country code for the United States is 1.

LA CLÉ DES EXERCICES

A. 1. *Oui, elle lui donne le message.* 2. *Oui, elle lui parle.* 3. *Non, ils ne lui laissent pas un message.* 4. *Non, elle ne lui répond pas.* 5. *Non, je ne leur demande pas l'impossible.*
B. 1. *Elle veut lui envoyer une lettre.* 2. *Tu veux lui demander ce service?* 3. *Nous pouvons leur téléphoner après six heures.* 4. *Il vient de lui envoyer des fleurs.* 5. *Vous allez lui répondre.*
C. 1. *Répondez-lui.* 2. *Ne lui parlez pas.* 3. *Demandez-leur.* 4. *Téléphonez-leur.* 5. *Ne lui répondez pas.*

D. 1. *Tu lui demandes le document.* 2. *Il les prend.* 3. *Elle lui donne un coup de fil.* 4. *Nous le demandons.* 5. *Il leur répond.*

E. 1. *M. Benoît et M. Chabrol se parlent chaque jour.* 2. *Marie et moi, nous nous voyons le jeudi soir.* 3. *Le directeur et l'assistant se rencontrent dans le café.* 4. *Le secrétaire et la réceptionniste ne se voient pas le week-end.* 5. *Mme Dubois et M. Leblanc se rappellent avant cinq heures.*

F. 1. *Est-ce qu'il te dit tout?* 2. *Est-ce que vous appelez le médécin?* 3. *Dis-lui de ne pas téléphoner.* 4. *Nous ne disons rien.* 5. *Elle appelle sa secrétaire.*

G. 1. *Ils parlent de leurs vacances.* 2. *Il parle à Joséphine de son projet.* 3. *Nous parlons de son nouveau livre.* 4. *N'en parlez pas à Bruno dimanche prochain.* 5. *Tu parles de la conférence aux employés.*

LEÇON 17

À LA BANQUE.   At the Bank.

A. DIALOGUE

Changer de l'argent.

LE GARDIEN: **Monsieur?**

ÉRIC: **Où se trouve le guichet pour changer des devises étrangères?**

LE GARDIEN: **Guichet trois, juste en face de la caisse.**

ÉRIC: **Je voudrais changer des chèques de voyage. Quel est le taux de change aujourd'hui?**

LE GUICHETIER: **Le dollar est à 5 francs 50. Combien voulez-vous changer?**

ÉRIC: **200 dollars.**

LE GUICHETIER: **Veuillez me montrer votre passeport et signer en bas à droite. Je vous donne des petites coupures?**

ÉRIC: **Donnez-moi trois billets de 200 francs, quatre billets de 100 francs, et de la petite monnaie. Au fait, à quelle heure ouvrez-vous demain?**

LE GUICHETIER: **Monsieur, demain, c'est un jour férié! C'est le premier mai. La banque ferme pendant trois jours mais le bureau de change de la Gare Saint-Lazare est ouvert vingt-quatre heures sur vingt-quatre.**

Exchanging Currency.

THE GUARD: Sir?

ÉRIC: Where is the exchange window for foreign currency?

THE GUARD: Window three, across from the cashier.

ÉRIC: I would like to change some traveler's checks. What is the rate of exchange today?

THE TELLER: The dollar is at 5 francs, 50 centimes. How much would you like to change?

ÉRIC: 200 dollars.

THE TELLER: Please show me your passport and sign on the lower right-hand corner. Shall I give you small bills?

ÉRIC: Please give me three 200-franc bills, four 100-franc bills and some change. By the way, at what time do you open tomorrow?

THE TELLER: Sir, tomorrow is a holiday! It's May Day. The bank will be closed for three days, but the exchange bureau at the Saint Lazare train station is open around the clock.

B. GRAMMAIRE ET USAGE

1. THE VERB *OUVRIR*

One of the irregular -*ir* verbs, *ouvrir* (to open) is conjugated according to the following pattern. *Offrir* (to offer) and *souffrir* (to suffer) have the same conjugation.

OUVRIR TO OPEN

I open	*j'ouvre*	we open	*nous ouvrons*
you open	*tu ouvres*	you open	*vous ouvrez*
he/she/one opens	*il/elle/on ouvre*	they open	*ils/elles ouvrent*

Éric ouvre un compte.
Eric opens an account.

À quelle heure ouvrez-vous?
At what time do you open?

La banque ouvre à 9 heures.
The bank opens at 9 A.M.

2. THE VERB *CHANGER*

Changer (to change), like *manger* (lesson 8), adds an *e* in the *nous* form of the present tense.

CHANGER TO CHANGE

I change	*je change*	we change	*nous changeons*
you change	*tu changes*	you change	*vous changez*
he/she/one changes	*il/elle/on change*	they change	*ils/elles changent*

The verb *changer* has different constructions depending on its meaning.

a. When it is a matter of changing money, the verb *changer* is used with the preposition *de*.

Elle change de l'argent.
She's changing money.

Nous changeons des dollars.
We're changing dollars.

b. When *changer* means to transform something, it is used without the preposition *de*.

Il change ses projets.
He is changing his plans.

Cela ne change rien.
It does not change anything.

c. When *changer* means to swap one thing for another of the same nature, one uses *changer* + *de* + a singular noun.

Elle va changer de banque.
She is going to change banks.

Je veux changer de robe.
I want to change my dress.

Il change souvent d'avis.
He often changes his mind.

3. ASKING QUESTIONS

Here are the most common French question words.

comment	how
combien	how much
quand	when
pourquoi	why
que	what
où	where

Comment allez-vous?
How are you doing?

Combien voulez-vous changer?
How much do you want to change?

Quand partons-nous?
When do we leave?

Pourquoi sort-il?
Why is he going out?

Que désirez-vous?
What would you like?

Où se trouve la caisse?
Where is the cashier's window?

In sentences with question words, it is often possible to use the familiar question form by intonation, placing the question word at the end of the sentence. Though common in everyday speech, this is not acceptable in written French.

Nous partons quand?
When do we leave?

Vous allez où?
Where are you going?

Tu as combien de temps?
How much time do you have?

Inversion is not normally used with *je,* except with certain verbs such as *devoir* and *pouvoir.* When using the inverted approach, the *je* form of *pouvoir* becomes *puis.*

Que dois-je faire?
What must I do?

Puis-je vous aider?
May I help you?

4. PREPOSITIONS

a. Like the preposition "with" (lesson 11), *sur* presents a few difficulties. *Sur* is not always translated by "on" in English and vice versa. Let's look at the following examples.

Le bureau de change est ouvert vingt-quatre heures sur vingt-quatre.
The exchange bureau is open twenty-four hours a day.

Elle est assise sur la chaise.
She is sitting on the chair.

Il travaille cinq jours sur sept.
He works five days out of seven.

En mai, un week-end sur deux est férié.
In May, one weekend out of two is a holiday.

Elle fait du jogging un jour sur deux.
She jogs every second day.

Il travaille le samedi.
He works on Saturdays.

Elle habite au deuxième étage.
She lives on the second floor.

    b. Here are some other common prepositions.

sous	under
entre	between
vers	toward, about
envers	toward
à côté de	next to
près de	near
loin de	far from
en face de	across
au-dessus de[1]	above
au-dessous de[1]	under
devant	in front of
derrière	behind
en bas	at the bottom
en haut	at the top

Le guichet trois est en face de la caisse.
The window number three is across from the cashier's.

Signez en bas à gauche.
Sign on the lower left hand corner.

La banque est à côté de la poste.
The bank is next to the post office.

5. FRENCH MONEY

There are eight French coins *(les pièces):* 5-, 10-, 20-, and 50-centime coins, and 1-, 2-, 5-, and 10-franc coins. One hundred centimes equal one franc.

J'ai une pièce de cinq francs.
I have a five-franc coin.

Avez-vous des pièces d'un franc?
Do you have any one-franc coins?

---

[1] Please note that pronunciation is extremely important to distinguish these phrases.

To ask for change *(la monnaie)*, use the following expression:

Avez-vous la monnaie de cent francs?
Have you got change for one hundred francs?

There are bills *(les billets)* for 20, 50, 100, 200, and 500 francs.

Avez-vous un billet de deux cents francs?
Do you have a two hundred-franc bill?

Des billets de cinq cents francs, ça vous va?
Five-hundred-franc bills, is that all right with you?

VOCABULAIRE

l'argent *(m.)*	money
l'argent liquide	cash
les devises étrangères *(f. pl.)*	foreign currency
les chèques de voyage *(f. pl.)*	traveler's checks
la monnaie	change (money)
faire de la monnaie	to make change
avoir de la monnaie	to have change
les petites coupures *(f. pl.)*	small bills
la banque	bank
le gardien	guard
le guichetier	teller
le guichet	window
la caisse	cashier
le compte	account
le chèque	check
signer	to sign
endosser	to endorse, to sign
toucher un chèque	to cash a check
le compte chèque	checking account
le compte épargne	savings account
un investissement	investment
ouvrir	to open
fermer	to close
le bureau de change	the exchange bureau
le taux de change	exchange rate
le taux d'intérêt	interest rate
changer	to change (money)
prêter	to lend
emprunter	to borrow
un franc	one franc

un centime	one centime (a hundredth of a franc)
le billet	bill (money)
un billet de cent francs	a one hundred-franc bill
la pièce	coin
une pièce de cinquante centimes	a fifty-centime coin
gagner de l'argent	to make/to earn money
compter	to count
gratuit	free (of charge)
le jour férié	holiday
24 heures sur 24	around the clock
cinq sur sept	five out of seven
au fait	by the way
Comment?	How?
Combien?	How much?
Pourquoi?	Why?
Que?	What?
Où?	Where?
Quand?	When?
en face de	across
à côté de	next to
loin de	far from
près de	near
en bas	at the bottom
en haut	at the top
sur	on
sous	under

EXERCICES

A. *Voici des réponses. Poser les questions d'après le modèle en utilisant l'inversion.* (Here are some answers. Ask the appropriate question following the example and using the inversion.)

MODÈLE: *Je pars à onze heures. (quand)*
        Quand partez-vous?

1. *Elle s'appelle Evelyne. (comment)*
2. *Je veux des chèques de voyage. (que)*
3. *Il veut changer cinq mille francs. (combien)*
4. *Vous êtes en retard. (pourquoi)*
5. *Ils vont à la banque. (où).*

B. *Répondre aux questions en utilisant les suggestions.*

MODÈLE: *Où est le bureau de change? (dans la gare)*
   Le bureau de change est dans la gare.

1. *Combien de dollars, Éric, veut-il changer? (deux cents dollars)*
2. *Combien de francs, le guichetier, donne-t-il à Éric? (douze mille francs)*
3. *Quels billets, l'employé, donne-t-il à Éric? (trois billets de deux cents francs et quatre billets de cent francs et de la petite monnaie)*
4. *Qu'est-ce qu'il montre au guichetier? (son passeport)*
5. *Est-ce qu'il y a des billets de trois cents francs? (non)*

C. *Répondre aux questions avec la forme correcte du verb "ouvrir" et "fermer."*

MODÈLE: *La banque _____ les jours fériés. (fermer)*
   La banque ferme les jours fériés.

1. *A quelle heure _____ la banque? (ouvrir)*
2. *Le bureau de change _____ à minuit. (fermer)*
3. *Les grands magasins _____ à dix heures. (ouvrir)*
4. *Nous _____ le 14 juillet. (fermer)*
5. *À quelle heure _____ vous? (ouvrir)*

D. *Choisir "changer" ou "changer de."* (Choose between *changer* and *changer de.*)

MODÈLE: *Il _____ toujours idée.*
   Il change toujours d'idée.

1. *Nous _____ train à Lyon.*
2. *Elle _____ six cents dollars.*
3. *Attends! Je _____ chapeau.*
4. *Elle _____ le décor de son bureau.*
5. *Ce pays _____ gouvernement.*

E. *Changer la preposition pour son opposé.* (Change the preposition to one of opposing meaning.)

MODÈLE: *J'habite loin de mon bureau.*
   J'habite près de mon bureau.

1. *L'argent est sur la table.*
2. *La banque est près du magasin.*
3. *Il faut signer en bas de la page.*
4. *Je suis devant le guichet.*
5. *Les chambres sont au-dessus.*

NOTE CULTURELLE

Banks in France are generally open from nine in the morning to five in the afternoon on weekdays, and some are even open on Saturdays.

Not every bank has an exchange bureau. The ones that do have a *Change* sign in the window. As the rate and fees vary from one bank to another, you may want to shop around before you exchange your money. *Bureau de change* offices, which are usually open until midnight (some around the clock, even), are close to most tourist attractions and in train stations. Foreign currency can also be exchanged at airports and hotels, though usually at a lower rate.

LA CLÉ DES EXERCICES

A. 1. *Comment s'appelle-t-elle?* 2. *Que voulez-vous?* 3. *Combien veut-il changer?* 4. *Pourquoi êtes-vous en retard?* 5. *Où vont-ils?*

B. 1. *Éric veut changer deux cents dollars.* 2. *Le guichetier donne douze mille francs à Éric.* 3. *L'employé donne à Éric trois billets de deux cents francs et quatre billets de cent francs et de la petite monnaie.* 4. *Il montre son passeport au guichetier.* 5. *Non, il n'y a pas de billets de trois cents francs.*

C. 1. *À quelle heure ouvre la banque?* 2. *Le bureau de change ferme à minuit.* 3. *Les grands magasins ouvrent à dix heures.* 4. *Nous fermons le 14 juillet.* 5. *À quelle heure ouvrez-vous?*

D. 1. *Nous changeons de train à Lyon.* 2. *Elle change six cents dollars.* 3. *Attends! Je change de chapeau.* 4. *Elle change le décor de son bureau.* 5. *Ce pays change de gouvernement.*

E. 1. *L'argent est sous la table.* 2. *La banque est loin du magasin.* 3. *Il faut signer en haut de la page.* 4. *Je suis derrière le guichet.* 5. *Les chambres sont au-dessous.*

LEÇON 18

LE MARCHÉ.   The Market.

A. DIALOGUE

Faire le marché.

MME LAULIAC: **Vous avez des haricots verts?**

LE MARCHAND: **Bien sûr, combien en voulez-vous?**

MME LAULIAC: **J'en voudrais une livre et demie.**

LE MARCHAND: **Voilà, Madame.**

MME LAULIAC: **Donnez-moi aussi un kilo de pommes de terre.**

LE MARCHAND: **Voilà. Il vous faut autre chose?**

MME LAULIAC: **Euh . . . Combien coûtent les asperges?**

LE MARCHAND: **Dix-huit francs la botte.**

MME LAULIAC: **Donnez-moi une botte d'asperges et un bouquet de persil.**

LE MARCHAND: **Et avec ça?**

MME LAULIAC: **C'est tout.**

LE MARCHAND: **J'ai de très beaux champignons aujourd'hui, Madame.**

MME LAULIAC: **Des champignons . . . Ah oui, j'en ai besoin pour ma blanquette de veau. Donnez-m'en 500 grammes.**

LE MARCHAND: **Voilà, une livre de champignons.**

MME LAULIAC: **Je vous dois combien?**

LE MARCHAND: **Soixante-sept francs cinquante.**

Shopping for Food.

MRS. LAULIAC: Do you have any green beans?

MERCHANT: Certainly. How much would you like?

MRS. LAULIAC: I would like a pound and a half.

MERCHANT: Here you are, Madam.

MRS. LAULIAC: Give me a kilo of potatoes also.

MERCHANT: Here you are. Do you need anything else?

MRS. LAULIAC: Uh . . . how much is the asparagus?

MERCHANT: Eighteen francs a bunch.

MRS. LAULIAC: Give me a bunch of asparagus and a bunch of parsley.

MERCHANT: Anything else?

MRS. LAULIAC: That's all.

MERCHANT: I have very fine mushrooms today, Madam.

MRS. LAULIAC: Mushrooms? Oh yes, I need some for my veal stew. Give me a pound.

MERCHANT: Here you are, a pound of mushrooms.

MRS. LAULIAC: How much do I owe you?

MERCHANT: Sixty-seven francs fifty.

B. GRAMMAIRE ET USAGE

1. THE PRONOUN *EN*

a. The pronoun *en* (some) is used to replace the partitive article *de* combined with a noun.

He takes some sugar. → *Il prend du sucre.*

He takes some. → *Il en prend.*

J'ai besoin d'asperges.
I need asparagus.

J'en ai besoin.
I need some.

Nous buvons du thé.
We drink tea.

Nous en buvons.
We drink some.

b. When *en* replaces a quantity, the quantity expression remains.

Je voudrais une livre et demie de champignons.
I would like a pound and a half of mushrooms.

J'en voudrais une livre et demie.
I would like a pound and a half.

Nous mangeons beaucoup de légumes.
We eat a lot of vegetables.

Nous en mangeons beaucoup.
　　We eat a lot of them.

Elle achète une botte d'asperges.
　　She buys a bunch of asparagus.

Elle en achète une botte.
　　She buys a bunch.

　　c. *En* precedes the verb in the negative form. The *ne* of the negation comes right after the subject and the *pas* after the verb.

Nous en achetons.
　　We buy some.

Nous n'en achetons pas.
　　We don't buy any.

Tu en veux.
　　You want some.

Tu n'en veux pas.
　　You don't want any.

　　d. In the inversion, *en* always precedes the verb.

En voulez-vous un kilo?
　　Do you want a kilo?

En avez-vous une douzaine?
　　Do you have a dozen?

2. THE POSITION OF CONSECUTIVE OBJECT PRONOUNS

　　a. When a verb has two objects, they can be replaced by two object pronouns.

Vous donnez les haricots à Mme Lauliac.
　　You are giving the beans to Mrs. Lauliac.

Vous les lui donnez.
　　You are giving them to her.

　　They appear in the following order.

me		
te	le	
se	la	lui
nous	l'	y before en
vous	les	leur

The pronouns *me, te, se, le* replace the vowel with an apostrophe before *en* and *y*.

Je vous le donne.
I'm giving it to you.

Le vendeur le lui donne.
The salesman gives it to him.

Il m'en donne une livre.
He gives me a pound.

Il y en a trois.
There are three of them.

Nous le leur montrons.
We show it to them.

b. The object pronouns follow the same position in the negative command form as above.

Ne le leur donnez pas.
Don't give it to them.

Ne lui en parlons pas.
Let's not speak to him about it.

Ne vous y promenez pas.
Don't take a walk there.

c. But in affirmative commands, the order is: direct object before indirect object, before *y*, before *en*.

Donnez-m'en un.
Give me one.

Parlez-lui-en.
Talk to him about it.

Rends-le-lui.
Give it back to him.

Donnez-les-leur.
Give them to them.

d. The pronouns *y* and *en* are not used consecutively except with the verb form *il y a*.

Est-ce qu'il y a des cerises?
Are there cherries?

Oui, il y en a.
Yes, there are some.

Non, il n'y en a pas.
No, there are not any.

3. WEIGHTS AND MEASURES

a. To indicate weights and measures, French uses the metric system.

un kilogramme, un kilo (kg) = 2.2 pounds
un gramme (g) = .035 ounces
une livre = ½ *kilo* = 500 grams (approximately 1 pound)
un litre (liquid) = 1.06 quarts
4 litres = 1.06 gallons
un mètre = 1.09 yards

Je voudrais une livre de raisins.
I would like a pound of grapes.

Donnez-moi deux kilos de pommes de terre.
Give me two kilos of potatoes.

b. Here are some other useful measures.

une douzaine de	a dozen
un morceau de	a piece of
une tranche de	a slice of
une bouteille de	a bottle of
une boîte de	a can of; a box of
un paquet de	a packet of
une botte de	a bunch of
un bouquet de	a bunch of
un panier de	a basket of
une poignée de	a handful of
une cuillerée	a spoonful of

Note that expressions of quantity, like *beaucoup, un peu,* etc., take *de* + the noun.

Je voudrais deux bouteilles de lait et un morceau de fromage.
I would like two bottles of milk and a piece of cheese.

4. PRICES AND PAYING

a. Some expressions.

Combien coûte ce melon?	How much does this melon cost?
Combien coûtent les fraises?	How much are the strawberries?

Ça coûte combien?	How much is it?
Ça fait combien?	How much does it come to?
Ça fait cinquante francs.	It comes to fifty francs.
Ça vous fait cent francs.	It comes to one hundred francs.
Ces pêches font combien le kilo?	How much are these peaches a kilo?
Elles font 20 francs.	They are twenty francs.

VOCABULAIRE

---

faire le marché	to go shopping, to go to the market
le marché	the market
le marchand, la marchande	seller
Ils font combien le kilo?	How much are they a kilo?
coûter	to cost
Combien ça coûte?	How much is it?
le fruit	fruit
la pêche	peach
la cerise	cherry
le raisin *(m.)*	grape
la pomme	apple
la banane	banana
la poire	pear
l'orange *(f.)*	orange
le légume *(m.)*	vegetable
la pomme de terre	potato
la carotte	carrot
les* haricots verts *(m.)*	stringbeans
les petits pois *(m.)*	peas
les épinards *(m.)*	spinach
le lait	milk
le fromage	cheese
la crème	cream
le beurre	butter
les œufs[1] *(m.)*	eggs
le litre	liter, quart
le kilogramme	kilogram
la livre	pound
le gramme	gram
la douzaine	dozen
le bouquet	bouquet, bunch
la botte	bunch, bundle

---

[1] In the singular, *œuf* is pronounced with an open *eu* sound and the *f* is sounded; in the plural it is pronounced with a closed *eu* sound and the *f* is silent (rhymes with *deux*).

la bouteille	bottle
la boîte	box, can
le paquet	packet
le morceau	piece
la tranche	slice

EXERCICES

A. *Répondre aux questions à la forme affirmative en utilisant "en."*

MODÈLE: *Est-ce que vous voulez des champignons?*
Oui, j'en veux.

1. *Est-ce qu'on prend du lait?*
2. *Combien de kilos de pommes de terre voulez-vous? (deux)*
3. *Avez-vous besoin d'asperges?*
4. *Combien avez-vous d'enfants? (trois)*
5. *Vous avez de la monnaie?*

B. *Remplacer les mots soulignés par "en."*

MODÈLE: *Il ne prend pas de sucre dans son café.*
Il n'en prend pas dans son café.

1. *Achetez-vous beaucoup de légumes frais?*
2. *Nous ne mangeons pas d'escargots.*
3. *Buvez-vous du thé le matin?*
4. *Y a-t-il du foie gras dans votre région?*
5. *Je n'ai pas besoin de persil.*

C. *Remplacer les mots soulignés en utilisant deux pronoms.*

MODÈLE: *Le client demande le prix au marchand.*
Le client le lui demande.

1. *Il donne le bouquet de fleurs à Catherine.*
2. *La vendeuse recommande des champignons sauvages à la cliente.*
3. *Le marchand vend du champagne à M. et Mme Lauliac.*
4. *La mère donne les clés de la voiture à mon frère et moi.*
5. *Il apporte la blanquette de veau à ses amis pour la soirée.*

D. *Mettre les phrases suivantes à la forme impérative en remplaçant les deux objets.*

MODÈLE: *Vous donnez des gâteaux aux enfants.*
Donnez-leur-en.

1. *Tu n'apportes pas de vin à l'hôtesse.*
2. *Vous rendez la monnaie aux clients.*
3. *Tu donnes les livres de cuisine à ta soeur.*
4. *Vous me donnez un kilo de cerises.*
5. *Nous n'achetons pas cette chemise à Julien.*

E. *Faire correspondre les colonnes A et B en récrivant des phrases complètes.*

MODÈLE: *J'achète des framboises. / Un panier.*
J'achète un panier de framboises.

A	B
1. *Donnez-moi du jambon.*	a. *une botte*
2. *Je voudrais des asperges.*	b. *un demi-litre*
3. *Elle voudrait du lait.*	c. *une douzaine*
4. *Il me faut du fromage.*	d. *cinq kilos*
5. *Je veux des œufs.*	e. *un beau morceau*
6. *Il me faut des pommes de terre.*	f. *trois belles tranches*

NOTE CULTURELLE

Despite the popularity of *supermarchés* and *hypermarchés,* neighborhood markets are frequented daily by the French who still demand fresh products. In Paris, almost every neighborhood has indoor or outdoor markets and small gourmet stores. If you travel throughout the country, you will see that even the most remote towns have a weekly market. Even if you are not planning to buy anything, they are worth a visit.

The concern for the environment, as well as the high price of paper goods, keeps the traditional shopping basket in every French pantry. Therefore, in case you decide to buy something, don't forget to bring your own fishnet bag, shopping bag or basket, as plastic or paper bags usually are not provided.

LA CLÉ DES EXERCICES

A. 1. *Oui, on en prend.* 2. *J'en veux deux.* 3. *Oui, j'en ai besoin.* 4. *J'en ai trois.* 5. *Oui, j'en ai.*
B. 1. *En achetez-vous beaucoup?* 2. *Nous n'en mangeons pas.* 3. *En buvez-vous le matin?* 4. *Y en a-t-il dans votre région?* 5. *Je n'en ai pas besoin.*
C. 1. *Il le lui donne.* 2. *La vendeuse lui en recommande.* 3. *Le marchand leur en vend.* 4. *La mère nous les donne.* 5. *Il la leur apporte.*
D. 1. *Ne lui en apporte pas.* 2. *Rendez-la-leur.* 3. *Donne-les-lui.* 4. *Donnez-m'en un kilo.* 5. *Ne la lui achetons pas.*
E. 1. *Donnez-moi trois belles tranches de jambon.* 2. *Je voudrais une botte d'asperges.* 3. *Elle voudrait un demi-litre de lait.* 4. *Il me faut un beau morceau de fromage.* 5. *Je veux une douzaine d'œufs.* 6. *Il me faut cinq kilos de pommes de terre.*

LEÇON 19
LE LOGEMENT. Housing.

A. DIALOGUE

À la recherche d'un appartement.

MARK: **Moi, je préfère l'appartement qui donne sur la Tour Eiffel. C'est le plus spacieux.**

JIM: **L'appartement du cinquième étage? Il n'est pas plus grand que celui du premier!**

MARK: **Mais si! Il a deux chambres, une salle à manger, un salon, et une cuisine qui est aussi grande que le salon.**

JIM: **Tu ne manges que des plats préparés. Tu n'as pas besoin d'une cuisine de quinze mètres carrés!**

MARK: **En tout cas, la salle de bain est en meilleur état que l'autre. Il y a plus de placards et l'appartement est moins sombre.**

JIM: **Tu exagères! Il y a autant de lumière dans l'un que dans l'autre. N'oublie pas qu'il n'y a pas d'ascenseur!**

MARK: **C'est le meilleur exercice possible! Aussi, le loyer est moins cher que celui du premier.**

JIM: **Bon, d'accord, on le prend! Mais c'est toi qui montes les provisions.**

Looking for an Apartment.

MARK: I prefer the apartment that looks out on the Eiffel Tower. It's more spacious.

JIM: The apartment on the sixth floor? It's no larger than the one on the second floor!

MARK: Yes, it is! It has two bedrooms, a dining room, a living room, and a kitchen which is as large as the living room.

JIM: You only eat ready-made meals. You don't need a fifteen-square-meter kitchen!

MARK: In any case, the bathroom is in better condition than the other one. There are many more closets and the apartment is much less dark.

JIM: You're exaggerating! There is as much light in the one as in the other. And don't forget that there is no elevator!

MARK: It's the best possible exercise! Also the rent is cheaper than the one on the second floor.

JIM: Okay. Let's take it! But you'll have to carry up the groceries.

B. GRAMMAIRE ET USAGE

1. COMPARATIVES

To compare things or people, French uses *plus* (more), *moins* (less) and *aussi* (as) followed by the adjective and *que* (than).

La cuisine est plus grande que le salon.
  The kitchen is larger than the living room.

Cet appartement est plus cher que l'autre.
  This apartment is more expensive than the other one.

La cuisine est moins grande que le salon.
  The kitchen is smaller than the living room.

Celle-ci est moins spacieuse que celle-là.
  This one is less spacious than that one.

La cuisine est aussi grande que le salon.
  The kitchen is as large as the living room.

Il est aussi intelligent que son frère.
  He is as bright as his brother.

As in English, the other item being compared can be omitted.

L'appartement est aussi cher.
  The apartment is just as expensive.

Il est plus grand.
  It's bigger.

Il est moins sombre.
  It's less dark.

Amounts of things can also be compared.

autant de + noun + *que*   as much . . . as/as many . . . as

Il y a autant de pièces dans cet appartement que dans l'autre.
  There are as many rooms in this apartment as in the other one.

plus de + noun + *que*   more . . . than

Il y a plus de lumière dans cette maison que dans l'autre.
    There is more light in this house than in the other one.

moins de + noun + *que*   less . . . than

Il y a moins de place dans cette pièce-ci que dans celle-là.
    There's less space in this room than in that one.

When adverbs are used instead of adjectives, the same rule applies.

Elle monte l'escalier plus vite que moi.
    She climbs the stairs faster than I.

Il travaille moins efficacement que son collègue.
    He works less efficiently than his colleague.

Je ne me lève pas aussi tôt que toi.
    I don't get up as early as you do.

The adverb *bien* has an irregular comparative of superiority.

Ils jouent mieux que nous.
    They play better than we do.

Marc travaille mieux que son frère.
    Marc works better than his brother.

But the comparatives of inferiority and equality remain the same.

Elle chante moins bien que moi.
    She sings less well than I do.

Vous dansez aussi bien que lui.
    You dance as well as he does.

2. SUPERLATIVES

Superlatives compare three or more things. They express the idea of the
most, the best, the least (e.g., He is the greatest.).

a. There are superlatives of superiority and inferiority.

Superiority: *le (la, les)* + *plus* + adjective

Inferiority: *le (la, les)* + *moins* + adjective

le plus beau   the most beautiful
le moins beau   the least beautiful

| *la plus grande* | the largest |
| *la moins grande* | the smallest |

| *les plus chers* | the most expensive |
| *les moins chers* | the least expensive |

Where English uses "in" after a superlative, French uses *de*.

C'est la plus grande ville du monde.
It's the largest city in the world.

C'est le plus bel appartement de l'immeuble.
It's the most beautiful apartment in the building.

C'est le quartier le plus cher de Paris.
It's the most expensive neighborhood in Paris.

   b. The superlatives of *bon* and *mauvais* are formed by adding the appropriate article before *meilleur* and *pire* or *plus mauvais*. Note that *pire* is used with abstract concepts, and *plus mauvais* is used with concrete items.

C'est le meilleur hôtel du monde.
It's the best hotel in the world.

Ce sont les meilleurs appartements du quartier.
These are the best apartments in the neighborhood.

C'est le pire remède. (abstract)
It's the worst remedy.

C'est le plus mauvais gâteau! (concrete)
It's the worst cake!

   c. The superlative of adverbs is given by *le* + *plus* / *moins* + adverb.

C'est lui qui court le plus vite.
It's he who runs the fastest.

C'est le pire!
It's the worst!

Note that the *le* is invariable.

3. ORDINAL NUMBERS

   a. Ordinal numbers (first, second, third, etc.) follow, for the most part, a regular pattern. Only *premier* (first) and *dernier* (last) agree with the noun they modify. Other ordinal numbers end in *-ième*. The *f* of *neuf* (nine) becomes *v*.

premier, première (1er, 1ère)	first
deuxième (2e or *2ème)*	second
troisième (3e or *3ème)*	third
quatrième	fourth
cinquième	fifth
sixième	sixth
septième	seventh
huitième	eighth
neuvième	ninth
dixième	tenth
onzième	eleventh
vingtième	twentieth
vingt et unième	twenty-first
vingt-deuxième	twenty-second
trentième	thirtieth
quarantième	fortieth
centième	hundredth
dernier, dernière	last

Nous allons célébrer son trentième anniversaire.
We are going to celebrate his thirtieth birthday.

Ils habitent dans le onzième arrondissement.
They live in the eleventh district.

C'est la première fois que vous visitez ce musée?
Is this the first time you are visiting this museum?

b. To express "on the fifth floor," French uses *au (à + le)*. (In France, the first floor is called *le rez-de-chaussée* (ground floor); *le premier étage* corresponds to our second floor, *le deuxième étage* to our third, etc.)

L'appartement se trouve au cinquième étage.
The apartment is on the sixth floor.

Le restaurant se trouve au troisième étage?
Is the restaurant on the fourth floor?

4. MEASURES: SQUARE METERS

Square footage is expressed in *mètres carrés* (square meters) in French. One meter is 39.37 inches, one foot is 0.3 meter.

L'appartement fait soixante mètres carrés.
The apartment measures sixty square meters.

La maison fait 150 mètres carrés.
The house measures 150 square meters.

5. THE WORD "ROOM"

French has several words for the word "room": *la pièce, la salle, la chambre, la place, le lieu,* etc. The usage varies according to its meaning in the sentence.

In a generic sense "room" is translated as *la pièce.*

C'est un appartement de quatre pièces.
It's a four-room apartment.

La salle designates a large room or hall.

Il y a quarante personnes dans la salle.
There are forty people in the room.

But the term *la salle à manger* means dining room, and *la salle de bain* stands for bathroom.

La chambre means bedroom.

Elle vient de faire repeindre sa chambre.
She just had her bedroom repainted.

Cet hôtel a plus de cent chambres.
This hotel has more than 100 rooms.

And *la place* stands for room in the sense of space.

Je n'ai pas assez de place pour mes livres.
I don't have enough room for my books.

Avez-vous assez de place?
Do you have enough room?

Finally, *le lieu* is often used figuratively.

Il y a encore lieu d'espérer.
There is still room for hope.

6. DONNER / DONNER SUR

We've seen the verb *donner* many times:

Donnez-moi des champignons.
Give me some mushrooms.

Il me donne des directions.
He gives me directions.

Pourriez-vous me donner un renseignement?
Could you give me some information?

Yet, if *donner* is used with the preposition *sur,* it takes on the meaning "to look on" or "to face":

L'appartement donne sur la Tour Eiffel.
The apartment looks out on the Eiffel Tower.

L'hôtel donne sur la mer.
The hotel faces the ocean.

Je voudrais une chambre qui donne sur le jardin.
I would like a room that looks out on the garden.

VOCABULAIRE

l'appartement *(m.)*	apartment
l'agence immobilière *(f.)*	real estate agency
à la recherche	in search of
chercher	to look for
le loyer	the rent
louer	to rent
donner sur	to look on, to face
oublier	to forget
cher	expensive
la pièce	room
un trois-pièces	a three-room apartment
le salon	living room
la salle à manger	dining room
la chambre à coucher	bedroom
la salle de bain	bathroom
la cuisine	kitchen, cooking
les plats préparés *(m. pl.)*	ready-made food
le placard	closet
la terrasse	terrace
l'étage *(m.)*	floor
l'ascenseur	elevator

au rez-de-chaussée	on the ground floor
au premier étage	on the second floor
pratique	practical, convenient
commode	convenient (also, chest of drawers, dresser)
bruyant	noisy
calme	quiet
sombre	dark
spacieux	spacious
carré	square
la vue	view
la lumière	light
le quartier	neighborhood
les provisions	groceries, supplies
monter	to go up (stairs)
meilleur*(e)*	better (adj.)
mieux	better (adv.)
dernier, dernière	last
l'un*(e)* . . . l'autre	the one . . . the other
d'accord	all right
en tout cas	in any case
autant . . . que	as much . . . as

EXERCICES

A. *Comparer.*

MODÈLE: *Un appartement à Paris / un appartement à Dijon. (cher)*
Un appartement à Paris est plus cher qu'un appartement à Dijon.

1. *La chambre sur le jardin/la chambre sur la rue. (bruyante)*
2. *Le salon / la cuisine. (spacieux)*
3. *L'appartement à 3 000 F / l'appartement à 5 000 F. (beau)*
4. *La ville de Paris / la ville de Bordeaux. (grande)*
5. *L'autobus / le TGV. (rapide)*

B. *Utiliser le comparatif d'égalité "aussi . . . que."*

1. *Les maisons aux États-Unis / les maisons en France. (chères)*
2. *La cuisine japonaise / la cuisine vietnamienne. (bonne)*
3. *La salle à manger / le salon. (grande)*
4. *Jim / Mark. (occupé)*
5. *Mon ami Pierre / mon ami Sébastien. (gentil)*

C. *Compléter en utilisant un comparatif de supériorité.*

MODÈLE: La cuisine est en _____ *état que la salle de bain. (bon)*
La cuisine est en meilleur état que la salle de bain.

1. *Il joue au tennis* _____ *que moi. (bien)*
2. *La situation économique est* _____ *dans ce pays-ci que dans celui-là. (mauvais)*
3. *La cuisine française est* _____ *que la cuisine anglaise. (bon)*
4. *Ma grand-mère chante* _____ *que ma tante. (bien)*
5. *Le sirop pharmaceutique est* _____ *que la limonade. (mauvais)*

D. *Composer des phrases superlatives avec les éléments proposés.* (Create superlative sentences with the elements suggested.)

MODÈLE: C'est un bon hôtel. (la ville)
C'est le meilleur hôtel de la ville.

1. *C'est un beau château. (la région)*
2. *C'est une ville chère. (le monde)*
3. *C'est une grande pièce. (l'appartement)*
4. *Ce sont de beaux appartements. (l'arrondissement)*
5. *C'est une pièce sombre. (la maison)*

E. *Utiliser le nombre ordinal qui convient.* (Use the appropriate ordinal number.)

MODÈLE: C'est sa (2) année d'étude au Conservatoire.
C'est sa deuxième année d'étude au Conservatoire.

1. *Le restaurant se trouve au (3) étage de la Tour Eiffel.*
2. *L'anniversaire de Véronique est le (1) juillet.*
3. *Leur nouvel appartement est au (25) étage.*
4. *Ils font leurs courses dans le (8) arrondissement.*
5. *On va célébrer le (60) anniversaire de mariage de mes grand-parents!*

F. *Traduire en français.*

1. His mother gives him ready-made meals.
2. Their apartment faces the most beautiful park in Paris.
3. Jim gives him the groceries.
4. The living room looks out on the garden.
5. Our hotel room looks out on the oldest bridge in town.

NOTE CULTURELLE

If you plan on renting or buying an apartment in Paris, use the classified ads *(petites annonces)* in the major newspapers or contact a real estate agent. While apartments found through the classified section in the papers are usually cheaper, getting one is quite an ordeal. You must get up quite early and wait in line to get a chance to see these apartments.

A rather popular and low-cost way for visitors to stay in a French home is to exchange homes. While you stay in a French family's home, they stay in yours. This way of visiting France will give you an insight into the French way of life.

For more information, contact the French Embassy or the Chamber of Commerce in your area or any specialized agency such as the International Home Exchange Service, (415) 435-3497.

LA CLÉ DES EXERCICES

A. 1. *La chambre sur le jardin est moins bruyante que la chambre sur la rue.* 2. *Le salon est plus spacieux que la cuisine.* 3. *L'appartement à 3000 F est moins beau que l'appartement à 5 000 F.* 4. *La ville de Paris est plus grande que la ville de Bordeaux.* 5. *L'autobus est moins rapide que le TGV.*

B. 1. *Les maisons aux États-Unis sont aussi chères que les maisons en France.* 2. *La cuisine japonaise est aussi bonne que la cuisine vietnamienne.* 3. *La salle à manger est aussi grande que le salon.* 4. *Jim est aussi occupé que Mark.* 5. *Mon ami Pierre est aussi gentil que mon ami Sébastien.*

C. 1. *Il joue au tennis mieux que moi.* 2. *La situation économique est pire dans ce pays-ci que dans celui-là.* 3. *La cuisine française est meilleure que la cuisine anglaise.* 4. *Ma grand-mère chante mieux que ma tante.* 5. *Le sirop pharmaceutique est plus mauvais que la limonade.*

D. 1. *C'est le plus beau château de la région.* 2. *C'est la ville la plus chère du monde.* 3. *C'est la plus grande pièce de l'appartement.* 4. *Ce sont les plus beaux appartements de l'arrondissement.* 5. *C'est la pièce la plus sombre de la maison.*

E. 1. *Le restaurant se trouve au troisième étage de la Tour Eiffel.* 2. *L'anniversaire de Véronique est le premier juillet.* 3. *Leur nouvel appartement est au vingt-cinquième étage.* 4. *Ils font leurs courses dans le huitième arrondissement.* 5. *On va célébrer le soixantième anniversaire de mariage de mes grands-parents.*

F. 1. *Sa mère lui donne des plats préparés.* 2. *Leur appartement donne sur le plus beau parc de Paris.* 3. *Jim lui donne les provisions.* 4. *Le salon donne sur le jardin.* 5. *Notre hôtel donne sur le plus vieux pont de la ville.*

LEÇON 20
À L'HOTEL.   At the Hotel.

A. DIALOGUE

Changer de chambre.

CONCIERGE: **La chambre ne vous convient pas?**

MLLE DUBOIS: **Il n'y a ni chauffage ni eau chaude.**

CONCIERGE: **Je suis désolé. Il doit y avoir un problème avec le radiateur.**

MLLE DUBOIS: **Avez-vous une autre chambre au même étage?**

CONCIERGE: **Oui, mais elle donne sur la rue. Il ne me reste plus rien de libre sur le jardin.**

MLLE DUBOIS: **Non, il y a trop de bruit. Je dois absolument me lever tôt demain.**

CONCIERGE: **J'ai une chambre grand luxe au sixième. Nous vous compterons[1] le même prix.**

MLLE DUBOIS: **Merci. Est-ce qu'il est possible d'aller au Palais des Congrès à pied ou est-ce que je dois prendre un taxi?**

CONCIERGE: **Ce n'est pas impossible à faire, mais vous devez compter une bonne demi-heure!**

MLLE DUBOIS: **Réveillez-moi à six heures et faites-moi monter un petit déjeuner complet.**

CONCIERGE: **Entendu. Bonne nuit, Mademoiselle.**

Changing Rooms.

CONCIERGE: You don't like your room?

MISS DUBOIS: There is neither heat nor hot water.

CONCIERGE: I am sorry. There must be a problem with the radiator.

MISS DUBOIS: Do you have another room on the same floor?

CONCIERGE: Yes, but it faces the street. I have nothing left that overlooks the garden.

[1] *Compterons* is the future tense of the first person plural of *compter,* to count: "we will count." The future tense will be discussed in *Leçon* 31.

MISS DUBOIS: No, there's too much noise. I absolutely must get up very
early tomorrow.

CONCIERGE: I have a luxury room on the seventh floor. We'll charge you
the same price.

MISS DUBOIS: Thank you. Is it possible to walk to the Palais des Congrès
from here, or should I take a taxi?

CONCIERGE: It is not an impossible thing to do, but you must give yourself
a good half hour.

MISS DUBOIS: Wake me at six o'clock and bring me a full breakfast.

CONCIERGE: Sure. Good night, Miss.

B. GRAMMAIRE ET USAGE

1. *C'EST* AND *IL EST* + ADJECTIVE + INFINITIVE

C'est and *il est* (it is) can both be used with an adjective and the infinitive,
but they are not interchangeable.

a. *C'est* + adjective + *à* + infinitive.
C'est refers to an idea already mentioned.

Aller à pied au Palais des Congrès? C'est impossible!
Walking to the Palais des Congrès? It's impossible!

Cet hôtel est complet? C'est difficile à croire!
This hotel is full? It's hard to believe.

Apprendre le japonais, c'est difficile!
Learning Japanese is difficult!

Je leur téléphone? Non, c'est inutile.
Shall I call them? No, it's useless.

b. *Il est* + adjective + *de* + infinitive.
Il est introduces an idea which has not been mentioned before.

Il est facile d'aller à La Défense.
It's easy to get to La Défense.

Il est difficile de trouver un hôtel à Paris pendant les Salons.
It's hard to find a hotel in Paris during the trade shows.

Il est impossible de comprendre leur attitude.
It is impossible to understand their attitude.

Il est difficile d'apprendre le japonais.
It is difficult to learn Japanese.

Il est inutile de me réveiller trop tôt.
There is no need to wake me up too early.

2. THE VERB *DEVOIR*

a. The verb *devoir* (must, to have to) presents quite a few difficulties due to its many nuances of meaning. It takes on different meanings according to its context. First, here are the forms.

DEVOIR   MUST, TO HAVE TO

I must (have to)	*je dois*	we must	*nous devons*
you must	*tu dois*	you must	*vous devez*
he/she/one must	*il/elle/on doit*	they must	*ils/elles doivent*

b. As indicated above, *devoir* usually implies obligation (must, to have to).

Il doit travailler cinq jours par semaine.
He has to work five days a week.

Vous devez être à l'heure pour votre rendez-vous
You have to be on time for your appointment.

c. But *devoir* can also be used to indicate probability (to be supposed to, scheduled to).

Le fauteuil doit être prêt jeudi.
The armchair is supposed to be ready on Thursday.

Le train doit arriver à 23 h 40.
The train is supposed to arrive at 11:40 P.M.

d. And *devoir* can be used to show debt (to owe).

Combien est-ce que je vous dois?
How much do I owe you?

Il me doit cinquante francs.
He owes me fifty francs.

Elle doit la vie à son médecin.
She owes her life to her doctor.

3. *QUELQUE CHOSE DE* AND *RIEN DE* + ADJECTIVE

To express phrases like "something funny" *(quelque chose d'amusant),* "nothing nice" *(rien de beau),* French uses *de* + masculine adjective after *quelque chose* or *rien.*

195

Il ne me reste plus rien de libre.
   I have nothing available.

Avez-vous quelque chose de passionnant à lire?
   Do you have anything fascinating to read?

Il mange quelque chose de bon.
   He is eating something good.

Je n'ai rien d'intéressant à vous proposer.
   I don't have anything interesting to suggest.

4. THE VERB *RESTER*

The regular -*er* verb *rester* means "to stay," "to remain."

Il reste deux jours.
   He's staying two days.

Je reste à la maison.
   I'm staying home.

To express the idea of staying, French will sometimes use other verbs. Let's look at the following example.

a. Do not use *rester* to mean to stay at a hotel. Use *descendre*.

Je descends à l'hôtel Crillon.
   I'm staying at the Hotel Crillon.

b. *Rester* is also used in the impersonal expression *il reste* (there remains).

Il reste une chambre de libre.
   There's one room left.

Il ne reste rien.
   There's nothing left.

c. Like *il faut,* the impersonal expression *il reste* can take an object pronoun to indicate a person.

Il me reste deux jours.
   I have two days left.

Il nous reste une chambre.
   We have one room left.

5. *NI ... NI*

The negative adverbs *ni . . . ni* (neither . . . nor) precede the nouns they negate: *Il n'y a ni chauffage ni eau chaude.* (There is neither heat nor hot water.) If the definite article, *le, la* or *les,* is used, it remains in the sentence. As in any negation, the *ne* precedes the verb. Note that *pas* is not used here.

Il aime l'hôtel et la chambre.
He likes the hotel and the room.

Il n'aime ni l'hôtel ni la chambre.
He likes neither the hotel nor the room.

The indefinite article *un, une* or *des* will disappear in the negative.

Il y a du chauffage et de l'eau chaude.
There is heat and hot water.

Il n'y a ni chauffage ni eau chaude.
There is neither heat nor hot water.

Elle lit les journaux français et les journaux américains.
She reads French and American papers.

Elle ne lit ni les journaux français ni les journaux américains.
She reads neither French nor American papers.

Elle commande du café et des croissants.
She orders coffee and croissants.

Elle ne commande ni café ni croissants.
She orders neither coffee nor croissants.

VOCABULAIRE

l'hôtel *(m.)*	hotel
l'hôtel (quatre) étoiles	a (four)-star hotel
l'auberge *(f.)*	inn
le séjour	a stay, sojourn
faire une réservation	to make a reservation
confirmer une réservation	to confirm a reservation
descendre dans un hôtel	to stay at a hotel
Il y a une chambre de libre.	There is a room available.
Il reste une chambre.	There's one room left.
une chambre avec salle de bain	a room with a private bath
une chambre avec douche	a room with a shower
le petit déjeuner compris	breakfast included
le petit déjeuner non compris	breakfast not included
le petit déjeuner complet	full breakfast
la réception	front desk

le standard	the switchboard, the operator
monter la valise	to take the bag to the room
Pouvez-vous descendre mes valises?	Can you take my suitcases down?
l'eau *(f.)*	water
le chauffage	heat, heating system
le radiateur	radiator
la climatisation	air conditioning
le bruit	noise
régler la note	to settle the bill
le prix	price
convenir	to be suitable
devoir	to have to, must; to owe
rester	to stay
se lever	to get up
donner sur	to look onto, to face
compter	to charge, to count
tôt	early
quelque chose	something
ne . . . aucun	none at all, not a single . . . , no
ne . . . ni . . . ni	neither . . . nor

EXERCICES

A. *Compléter les phrases avec le verbe "devoir."*

1. *Vous _____ prendre l'autobus numéro 8 pour aller au Jardin des Plantes.*
2. *Combien est-ce que je vous _____?*
3. *Nous vous _____ mille excuses.*
4. *Elle _____ passer une semaine avec nous cet été.*
5. *Je ne _____ pas me coucher trop tard ce soir.*

B. *Faire correspondre les colonnes A et B.*

A

1. *Il reste une semaine*
2. *Est-ce qu'il vous reste*
3. *Il ne vous reste*
4. *Il nous reste*
5. *Il reste deux kilos de pommes de terre*

B

a. *deux semaines de vacances.*
b. *avec nous.*
c. *dans le réfrigérateur.*
d. *une chambre de libre?*
e. *rien?*

C. *Utiliser "il est" ou "c'est."*

1. *_____ difficile de trouver un hôtel à cette saison.*
2. *Elle veut vendre sa maison? _____ incroyable!*
3. *Changer de chambre? _____ très facile à faire.*

4. *Tout ce bruit dans l'hôtel, _____ inacceptable!*
5. *_____ impossible de faire un réservation avant le mois de septembre.*

D. *Mettre à la forme négative en utilisant "ni . . . ni."*

1. *Il y a un réfrigérateur et une télévision.*
2. *Vous aimez l'hôtel et le quartier.*
3. *Elle mange du pain et des croissants.*
4. *Ils aiment l'appartement du troisième et l'appartement du quatrième.*
5. *Ils commandent du vin et du champagne.*

NOTE CULTURELLE

Hotels in France range from five-star luxury hotels to hotels offering only the bare essentials. In Paris, hotels are usually very expensive, but with some research it is possible to find hotels offering reasonable rates. A few castles and manors in the country have been turned into luxury hotels. Modern hotels offering all modern amenities, from air conditioned rooms to fax machines and fast-food restaurants, can be found all over France.

LA CLÉ DES EXERCICES

A. 1. *devez* 2. *dois* 3. *devons* 4. *doit* 5. *dois*
B. 1. *Il reste une semaine avec nous.* 2. *Est-ce qu'il vous reste une chambre de libre?* 3. *Il ne vous reste rien?* 4. *Il nous reste deux semaines de vacances.* 5. *Il reste deux kilos de pommes de terre dans le réfrigérateur.*
C. 1. *Il est* 2. *C'est* 3. *C'est* 4. *c'est* 5. *Il est*
D. 1. *Il n'y a ni réfrigérateur ni télévision.* 2. *Vous n'aimez ni l'hôtel ni le quartier.* 3. *Elle ne mange ni pain ni croissants.* 4. *Ils n'aiment ni l'appartement du troisième ni l'appartement du quatrième.* 5. *Ils ne commandent ni vin ni champagne.*

QUATRIÈME RÉVISION

A. *Répondre en utilisant le pronom indirect.*

MODÈLE: Téléphonez-vous à M Benoît tous les jours? (oui)
Oui, je lui téléphone tous les jours.

1. *Répondez-vous à tous vos clients? (oui)*
2. *Avez-vous laissé un message à Éric? (non)*
3. *Est-ce qu'il parle à M Benoît? (oui)*
4. *Vous a-t-il donné la clé de la chambre? (non)*
5. *Ont-ils répondu à Carole? (oui)*

B. *Répondre en utilisant un pronom objet direct ou indirect, ou les deux.*

MODÈLE: *Est-ce qu'il a donné le message à Mlle Chabrol? (oui)*
Oui, il le lui a donné.

1. *Est-ce que l'agent a recommandé l'appartement à Laurent et Marc? (oui)*
2. *Est-ce que Vincent peut parler à Jean? (non)*
3. *Est-ce que la secrétaire a donné les documents à Jacques? (oui)*
4. *Ont-ils apporté ce bouquet de fleurs à Mme Benoît? (oui)*
5. *Conseillez-vous ce remède à vos patients? (non)*

C. *Répondre en utilisant le pronom "en."*

MODÈLE: *A-t-elle mangé des escargots? (oui)*
Oui, elle en a mangé.

1. *Prenez-vous de la vitamine C? (oui)*
2. *Aimez-vous donner des conseils? (non)*
3. *Mangez-vous beaucoup de fruits? (oui)*
4. *Est-ce qu'il boit du vin blanc? (non)*
5. *Avez-vous changé des dollars? (oui)*

D. *Écrire les chiffres ordinaux en toutes lettres.*

MODÈLE: *la semaine (4) / la quatrième semaine*

1. *l'étage (16)*
2. *l'arrondissement (8)*
3. *la ville (1)*
4. *la rue (2) à gauche*
5. *la place (30)*

E. *Compléter les phrases avec la forme correcte du verbe.*

1. *Nous _____ par carte de crédit. (payer)*
2. *Christine _____ Monique au téléphone. (appeler)*
3. *Nous _____ d'hôtel. (changer)*
4. *Sandra _____ un compte chèque. (ouvrir)*

F. *Comparer les éléments proposés.*

MODÈLE: *Cet appartement / grand / l'autre. (+)*
Cet appartement est plus grand que l'autre.

1. *Un hôtel cinq étoiles / cher / une petite auberge. (+)*
2. *Le salon / grand / la salle à manger. (−)*
3. *Cette petite chambre / agréable / la grande chambre. (=)*
4. *Cette maison-ci / sombre / cette maison-là. (−)*

G. *Relier les deux colonnes.*

A

1. *Voilà une pièce d'un franc.*
2. *Je vous en donne un morceau.*

B

a. Do you have any French money?
b. You know how to count?

3. *Vous avez de la monnaie?*   c. Here's a one-franc coin.
4. *Vous savez compter?*   d. Do you have any change?
5. *Vous avez de l'argent français?*   e. I give you a piece.

H. *Récrire les phrases avec un superlatif.*

MODÈLE: *C'est un hôtel cher. (le quartier)*
       C'est l'hôtel le plus cher du quartier.

   1. *C'est un bel hôtel. (la ville)*
   2. *C'est une grande église. (le monde)*
   3. *C'est un bon joueur. (le pays)*
   4. *C'est un livre intéressant. (l'année)*
   5. *C'est un film ridicule. (le festival)*

I. *Mettre les phrases à la forme négative.*

MODÈLE: *Il mange des raisins et des pommes.*
       Il ne mange ni raisins ni pommes.

   1. *Elle achète des asperges et des haricots.*
   2. *Ils ont acheté une maison et un appartement.*
   3. *Nous aimons le veau et le boeuf.*
   4. *Elles boivent du thé et du café.*
   5. *Vous aimez l'appartement du troisième et du huitième.*

LA CLÉ DES EXERCICES

A. 1. *Oui, je leur réponds.* 2. *Non, je ne lui ai pas laissé de message.* 3. *Oui, il lui parle.* 4. *Non, il ne m'a pas donné la clé de la chambre.* 5. *Oui, ils lui ont répondu.*
B. 1. *Oui, l'agent le leur a recommandé.* 2. *Non, Vincent ne peut pas lui parler.* 3. *Oui, la secrétaire les lui a donnés.* 4. *Oui, ils le lui ont apporté.* 5. *Non, je ne le leur conseille pas.*
C. 1. *Oui, j'en prends.* 2. *Non, je n'aime pas en donner.* 3. *Oui, j'en mange beaucoup.* 4. *Non, il n'en boit pas.* 5. *Oui, j'en ai changé.*
D. 1. *le seizième étage* 2. *le huitième arrondissement* 3. *la première ville* 4. *la deuxième rue à gauche* 5. *la trentième place.*
E. 1. *payons* 2. *appelle* 3. *changeons* 4. *ouvre*
F. 1. *Un hôtel cinq étoiles est plus cher qu'une petite auberge.* 2. *Le salon est moins grand que la salle à manger.* 3. *Cette petite chambre est aussi agréable que la grande chambre.* 4. *Cette maison-ci est moins sombre que cette maison-là.*
G. 1.—c 2.—e 3.—d 4.—b 5.—a
H. 1. *C'est le plus bel hôtel de la ville.* 2. *C'est la plus grande église du monde.* 3. *C'est le meilleur joueur du pays.* 4. *C'est le livre le plus intéressant de l'année.* 5. *C'est le film le plus ridicule du festival.*

I. 1. *Elle n'achète ni asperges ni haricots.* 2. *Ils n'ont acheté ni maison ni appartement.* 3. *Nous n'aimons ni le veau ni le boeuf.* 4. *Elles ne boivent ni thé ni café.* 5. *Vous n'aimez ni l'appartement du troisième ni du huitième.*

LECTURE

UN VOYAGE[1] EN NORMANDIE

Paul est allé dans une agence de voyage.[2] Il désire faire un voyage en Normandie parce qu'il n'a jamais visité cette région. Il s'est renseigné[3] sur les curiosités[4] de la région et a acheté un billet pour une excursion en autocar.[5] D'abord, il va visiter Rouen: la cathédrale de Notre-Dame,[6] l'église Jeanne d'Arc,[7] et le Gros-Horloge.[8] Puis il va voir des peintures[9] de Sisley, Renoir, Monet, et Gericault au Musée des Beaux-Arts.[10] Il va aller au Havre, à Bayeux, où se trouve les tapisseries de Bayeux,[11] et à Arromanches, au Musée du Débarquement. Enfin, il va visiter le Mont-Saint-Michel, l'abbaye à la fois romanesque et gothique qui se trouve en haut d'un énorme rocher.[12] Paul s'intéresse particulièrement à cette partie du voyage parce qu'il adore l'architecture. L'église a été achevée en 1144, mais de nouvelles constructions ont été ajoutées[13] au 13ème, 15ème et 16ème siècles.[14] Le village aux rues très étroites[15] est très pittoresque. Aussi, on y mange de très bons fruits de mer![16] Bon Voyage[17] Paul!

VOCABULAIRE

1.	*le voyage*	trip
2.	*l'agence de voyage*	travel agency
3.	*se renseigner*	to inquire
4.	*les curiosités*	sights
5.	*l'autocar*	tour bus
6.	*la cathédrale de Notre-Dame*	Cathedral of Notre-Dame
7.	*l'église Jeanne d'Arc*	the church of Joan of Arc
8.	*le Gros-Horloge*	the Great Clock (giant Renaissance clock)
9.	*la peinture*	painting
10.	*le musée des Beaux-Arts*	Museum of Fine Arts
11.	*les tapisseries de Bayeux*	the tapestries of Bayeux
12.	*le rocher*	rock
13.	*ajouter*	to add
14.	*le siècle*	century
15.	*étroit*	narrow
16.	*les fruits de mer*	seafood
17.	*Bon voyage!*	Have a good trip!

LEÇON 21

LA SANTÉ. Health.

A. DIALOGUE

Chez le médecin.

DOCTEUR: **Qu'est-ce qui ne va pas? Vous avez du mal à marcher.**

MME LAURENT: **J'ai très mal à la jambe.**

DOCTEUR: **Qu'est-ce qui[1] vous est arrivé? Vous êtes tombée?**

MME LAURENT: **Non, je ne suis pas tombée. Hier, j'étais au club de forme où j'ai fait beaucoup d'exercice. J'ai suivi un cours de danse moderne, j'ai couru et j'ai nagé un peu.**

DOCTEUR: **Allongez-vous. Je vais vous examiner.**

MME LAURENT: **Aïe!!!**

DOCTEUR: **Vous n'avez rien de cassé mais vous avez une inflammation musculaire.**

MME LAURENT: **Qu'est-ce que je dois faire? C'est grave?**

DOCTEUR: **Non, mais il vaut mieux cesser toute forme d'exercice et prendre des comprimés anti-flammatoires trois fois par jour. Voilà votre ordonnance.**

MME LAURENT: **Merci, docteur.**

DOCTEUR: **Revenez me voir dans une semaine si vous avez toujours des douleurs.**

At the doctor's.

DOCTOR: What's wrong? You seem to have trouble walking.

MRS. LAURENT: My leg hurts.

DOCTOR: What happened to you? Did you fall?

MRS. LAURENT: No, I didn't fall. Yesterday, I was at the health club where I exercised a lot. I took a modern dance class, I ran, and I swam a bit.

DOCTOR: Lie down. I am going to examine you.

MRS. LAURENT: Ouch!!!

DOCTOR: Nothing is broken, but your muscles are a bit inflamed.

[1] Relative pronouns will be discussed in *Leçon* 21.

MRS. LAURENT: What should I do? Is it serious?

DOCTOR: No, but it would be better to stop all exercise and take anti-inflammatory pills three times a day. Here's your prescription.

MRS. LAURENT: Thank you, doctor.

DOCTOR: Come back to see me in a week if you still have pain.

B. GRAMMAIRE ET USAGE

1. THE VERB *SUIVRE*

Suivre (to follow) is a verb used in many common expressions. First, let's look at its conjugation.

SUIVRE TO FOLLOW

I follow	*je suis*	we follow	*nous suivons*
you follow	*tu suis*	you follow	*vous suivez*
he/she/one follows	*il/elle/on suit*	they follow	*ils/elles suivent*

Here are some of the ways *suivre* is used in French.

Suivez le guide!
Follow the guide!

Si vous voulez bien me suivre.
Please follow me.

Suivez les instructions avec soin.
Follow the instructions carefully.

Il suit un cours de français.
He is taking a French class.

Veuillez faire suivre mon courrier.
Please forward my mail.

Nous suivons le boulevard.
We walk along the boulevard.

2. THE *PASSÉ COMPOSÉ*

To talk about situations in the past, French has several different past tenses. To express a completed past action, French uses the *passé composé,* which is formed with a conjugated form of *avoir* or *être* plus the past participle.

a. The past participle of regular *-er* verbs is formed by dropping the *-er* of the infinitive and adding an *é* ending.

parler	*parl-er*	*parlé*
regarder	*regard-er*	*regardé*

Most verbs take *avoir* in the *passé composé*.

MARCHER   TO WALK

I walked	*j'ai marché*	we walked	*nous avons marché*
you walked	*tu as marché*	you walked	*vous avez marché*
he/she/ one walked	*il/elle/on a marché*	they walked	*ils/elles ont marché*

b. Each regular verb group forms the past participle in a regular way.

GROUP	INFINITIVE	PAST PARTICIPLE
1st group	*aimer*	*aimé*
2nd group	*finir*	*fini*
3rd group	*partir*	*parti*
4th group	*vendre*	*vendu*

J'ai travaillé.
　　I worked. / I have worked.

J'ai choisi.
　　I chose. / I have chosen.

J'ai attendu.
　　I waited. / I have waited.

Nous avons fini.
　　We finished. / We have finished.

Ils ont vendu la maison.
　　They sold. / They have sold the house.

c. There are two ways to translate the *passé composé* into English:

J'ai mangé dans ce restaurant.
　　I ate in this restaurant.
　　I have eaten in this restaurant.

Il est entré dans la classe.
　　He entered the classroom.
　　He has entered the classroom.

d. Many past participles are irregular and have to be memorized.

INFINITIVE	PAST PARTICIPLE	INFINITIVE	PAST PARTICIPLE
avoir	*eu*	*pouvoir*	*pu*
être	*été*	*vouloir*	*voulu*
connaître	*connu*	*devoir*	*dû*
lire	*lu*	*prendre*	*pris*
savoir	*su*	*apprendre*	*appris*
faire	*fait*	*comprendre*	*compris*
voir	*vu*	*pleuvoir*	*plu*
boire	*bu*	*suivre*	*suivi*
dire	*dit*	*ouvrir*	*ouvert*
falloir	*fallu*	*courir*	*couru*

Il a compris la leçon.
    He understood the lesson.

Nous avons lu le livre.
    We read the book.

J'ai couru.
    I ran.

Il a suivi un cours de danse.
    He took a dance class.

e. A certain number of verbs take the verb *être* in the *passé composé*. A rule of thumb for distinguishing auxiliaries might help: all reflexive, reciprocal,[2] and intransitive verbs expressing movement (except *quitter,* to leave) use *être* in the *passé composé*. Here is a list of the most important verbs expressing movement.

Aller (to go), *venir* (to come), *monter* (to go up), *descendre* (to do down), *arriver* (to arrive), *partir* (to leave), *sortir* (to go out), *naître* (to be born), *mourir* (to die), *entrer* (to enter), *rester* (to stay), *retourner* (to go back), *revenir* (to come back), *tomber* (to fall).

When using *être,* the past participle agrees in gender and number with the subject.

ARRIVER TO ARRIVE

I arrived	*je suis arrivé(e)*	we arrived	*nous sommes arrivé(e)s*
you arrived	*tu es arrivé(e)*	you arrived	*vous êtes arrivé(e)(s)*
he/she/one arrived	*il/elle/on est arrivé(e)*	they arrived	*ils/elles sont arrivé(e)s*

[2] See also *Leçon 22.*

Je suis tombé(e) hier.
  I fell yesterday.

Elle est allée chez le médecin.
  She went to the doctor's.

Ils sont arrivés à l'hôtel.
  They arrived at the hotel.

Nous sommes allé(e)s au cinéma.
  We went to a movie.

  f. In the *passé composé,* the negation *ne . . . pas* is placed around *avoir* or *être.*

Il n'a pas parlé au pharmacien.
  He did not talk to the pharmacist.

Je ne suis pas tombée.
  I didn't fall.

Nous ne sommes pas allés en Italie.
  We did not go to Italy.

Tu n'as pas vu le médecin?
  You did not see the doctor?

  g. To put a verb in the *passé composé* in the interrogative form, the subject is placed after the auxiliary *avoir* or *être.*

A-t-elle consulté un médecin?
  Did she see a doctor?

Avez-vous pris des comprimés?
  Did you take some pills?

À quelle heure êtes-vous revenu?
  At what time did you come back?

3. *AVOIR MAL À* VERSUS *AVOIR DU MAL À*

  a. To refer to the state of one's body, French uses the construction *avoir mal à.* The definite article, rather than a possessive adjective, is used with the part of the body.

J'ai mal à la jambe.
  My leg hurts.

Elle a mal à la tête.
  She has a headache.

Il a mal à l'estomac.
  He has a stomach ache.

b. *Avoir du mal à* is a construction followed by a verb which means to have trouble doing something.

Il a du mal à respirer.
He has trouble breathing.

Nous avons du mal à marcher.
We have trouble walking.

Il a du mal à cesser de fumer.
He has trouble quitting smoking.

4. ONOMATOPOEIA

aïe	ouch	**crac**	bang
vlan	wham bang	**bing**	smack
boum	bang, wallop	**cocorico**	cock-a-doodle-do
tic-tac	tick-tock	**dring**	ding-a-ling
miaou	meow	**paf**	ding-a-ling
meuh	moo		

VOCABULAIRE

le médecin	doctor
le médicament	medicine
le comprimé	pill
le sirop	syrup
prendre rendez-vous	to make an appointment
la salle d'attente	waiting room
examiner le malade	to examine the patient
consulter	to consult
une ordonnance	a prescription
suivre	to follow
suivre les instructions (f.)	to follow the instructions
le rhume	a cold
la grippe	flu
le stress	stress
la douleur	pain
se sentir	to feel
Ça ne va pas?	You're not feeling well?
grave	serious
tomber	to fall
marcher	to walk
suivre	to follow

208

courir	to run
nager	to swim
cesser	to stop
s'allonger	to lie down
obtenir	to obtain
il vaut mieux	it would be better
il faut	one must
avoir du mal à	to have trouble
aïe	ouch
la tête	head
la jambe	leg
le pied	foot
la santé	health
casser	to break
se casser la jambe	to break one's leg
couper	to cut

EXERCICES

A. *Mettre les phrases au passé composé.*

MODÈLE: *Il travaille samedi.*
        Il a travaillé samedi.

1. *Le médecin donne une ordonnance à Mme Laurent.*
2. *Ils cessent de prendre ces médicaments.*
3. *Le patient attend son tour.*
4. *Je parle au pharmacien.*
5. *Nous demandons de l'aspirine.*

B. *Compléter avec le participe passé approprié.*

MODÈLE: *Il a (boire) le sirop.*
        Il a bu le sirop.

1. *Il a (falloir) prendre un rendez-vous.*
2. *J'ai (devoir) suivre ses conseils.*
3. *Nous avons (prendre) trois comprimés.*
4. *Vous avez (voir) le nouveau club de forme.*
5. *Elle a (avoir) une inflammation musculaire.*

C. *Compléter les phrases au passé composé. Choisir l'auxiliaire "être" ou "avoir."*

MODÈLE: *Je _____ (aller) au cours de danse.*
        Je suis allé(e) au cours de danse.

1. *Elle _____ (tomber) dans la rue.*
2. *Nous _____ (partir) en vacances en France.*

3. *Ils* _____ *(suivre) les conseils du pharmacien.*
4. *Nous* _____ *(arriver) en retard.*
5. *Tu* _____ *(avoir) un accident.*
6. *Vous* _____ *(retourner) chez le médecin.*
7. *Je* _____ *(rester) à l'hôpital une semaine.*
8. *Elle* _____ *(naître) à la maternité.*
9. *Il* _____ *(pleuvoir) dimanche après-midi.*
10. *Nous* _____ *(descendre) dans un grand hôtel.*

D. *Mettre les phrases à la forme interrogative en utilisant l'inversion.*

MODÈLE: *Vous avez pris l'avion.*
Avez-vous pris l'avion?

1. *Tu es monté au sixième étage.*
2. *Vous avez eu du mal à obtenir un rendez-vous.*
3. *Il a ouvert une nouvelle clinique.*
4. *Nous sommes restés une demi-heure dans la salle d'attente.*
5. *Ils ont fait beaucoup d'exercice.*

E. *Mettre les phrases à la forme négative.*

1. *Nous avons pris de l'aspirine.*
2. *Ils ont trouvé un remède.*
3. *J'ai eu un gros rhume cet hiver.*
4. *Elle a pu prendre le médicament.*
5. *Il est venu en avion.*

F. *Compléter avec le verbe "suivre" au présent.*

1. *Nous* _____ *toujours les conseils de notre professeur.*
2. *Tu* _____ *un cours d'italien.*
3. *Elle* _____ *l'avenue de la Gare.*
4. *Je* _____ *les instructions.*
5. *Vous* _____ *le guide.*

NOTE CULTURELLE

The French health care system is socialized. Every French citizen is covered by the so-called *sécurité sociale*. All medical care, including dental care—visits to the doctor or dentist of your own choice, prescriptions, even post-maternity spas for new mothers—is covered by the state insurance system. A regular preventive visit to the doctor is quite affordable, even for foreigners who might not be insured.

A. 1. *Le médecin a donné une ordonnance à Mme Laurent.* 2. *Ils ont cessé de prendre ces médicaments.* 3. *Le patient a attendu son tour.* 4. *J'ai parlé au pharmacien.* 5. *Nous avons demandé de l'aspirine.*

B. 1. *fallu* 2. *dû* 3. *pris* 4. *vu* 5. *eu*

C. 1. *est tombée* 2. *sommes partis* 3. *ont suivi* 4. *sommes arrivé(e)s*
    5. *as eu* 6. *êtes retourné(e)(s)* 7. *suis resté(e)* 8. *est née* 9. *a plu*
    10. *sommes descendu(e)s*

D. 1. *Es-tu monté au sixième étage?* 2. *Avez-vous eu du mal à obtenir un rendez-vous?* 3. *A-t-il ouvert une nouvelle clinique?* 4. *Sommes-nous restés une demi-heure dans la salle d'attente?* 5. *Ont-ils fait beaucoup d'exercices?*

E. 1. *Nous n'avons pas pris d'aspirine.* 2. *Ils n'ont pas trouvé un remède.*
    3. *Je n'ai pas eu de gros rhume cet hiver.* 4. *Elle n'a pas pu prendre le médicament.* 5. *Il n'est pas venu en avion.*

F. 1. *suivons* 2. *suis* 3. *suit* 4. *suis* 5. *suivez*

LEÇON 22

LES VOITURES. Cars.

A. DIALOGUE

En panne.

SÉBASTIEN: **Tu es encore tombé en panne!**

JULIEN: **Ah, quelle histoire! Je me suis arrêté sur l'autoroute pour prendre un café et je n'ai pas pu redémarrer. J'ai essayé pendant plus d'une demi-heure.**

SÉBASTIEN: **Alors, qu'est-ce que tu as fait?**

JULIEN: **Je me suis fait remorquer.**

SÉBASTIEN: **Tu as pourtant fait réparer le moteur il y a un mois, avant de partir pour la Corse!**

JULIEN: **Je sais. J'ai fait vérifier les pneus, changer l'huile, régler les phares . . . Cette voiture d'occasion me coûte les yeux de la tête!**

SÉBASTIEN: **Tu conduis trop vite peut-être?**

JULIEN: **Pas du tout. J'ai passé mon permis il y a seulement deux ans et je suis très prudent. Au fait, tu rentres chez toi?**

SÉBASTIEN: **Je vais faire le plein d'essence et je rentre. Je te dépose?**

JULIEN: **Volontiers.**

Car Trouble.

SÉBASTIEN: Your car broke down again!

JULIEN: Oh, what a story! I stopped on the highway to have a cup of coffee, and I could not start up again. I tried for a half hour.

SÉBASTIEN: Well, what did you do?

JULIEN: I got it towed.

SÉBASTIEN: You had the motor fixed a month ago, before leaving for Corsica!

JULIEN: I know. I had the tires checked, the oil changed, the headlights fixed. This used car is costing me an arm and a leg!

SÉBASTIEN: Perhaps you drive too fast?

JULIEN: Not at all. I got my driver's license only two years ago, and I am very cautious. By the way, are you going home?

SÉBASTIEN: I am going to fill up my tank and then go home. Can I drop you off?

JULIEN: With pleasure.

B. GRAMMAIRE ET USAGE

1. REFLEXIVE VERBS IN THE *PASSÉ COMPOSÉ*

a. Reflexive and reciprocal verbs are conjugated with *être* in the *passé composé*. They agree in gender and number with the subject.

S'ARRÊTER   TO STOP

I stopped	*je me suis arrêté(e)*	we stopped	*nous nous sommes arrêté(e)s*
you stopped	*tu t'es arrêté(e)*	you stopped	*vous vous êtes arrêté(e)(s)*
he/she/ one stopped	*il/elle/on s'est arrêté(e)*	they stopped	*ils/elles se sont arrêté(e)s*

Je me suis arrêté sur l'autoroute.
   I stopped on the highway.

Elle s'est levée très tôt.
   She got up very early.

Nous nous sommes bien amusés.
   We had a great time.

Il s'est fait remorquer.
   He got his car towed.

b. In the negative, reflexive verbs, like other verbs, take the negation *ne . . . pas* around the conjugated verb.

Il ne s'est pas arrêté à Nice.
   He did not stop in Nice.

Tu ne t'es pas occupé des pneus.
   You did not take care of the tires.

Il ne s'est jamais promené dans ce parc.
   He never took a walk in this park.

c. In the interrogative form, the subject is placed right after the conjugated reciprocal or reflexive verb.

S'est-elle fait remorquer?
    Did she have her car towed?

Vous êtes-vous ennuyé à la soirée?
    Were you bored at the party?

Se sont-ils arrêtés devant le château?
    Did they stop in front of the castle?

2. THE CAUSATIVE CONSTRUCTION: *FAIRE* + THE INFINITIVE

This construction expresses the notion of either having something done by someone or causing something to be done by someone. Let's look at a few examples.

Je répare la voiture.
    I am fixing the car.

Je fais réparer la voiture.
    I am having the car fixed.

Il vérifie le niveau d'huile.
    He is checking the oil.

Il fait vérifier le niveau d'huile.
    He is having the oil checked.

Vous envoyez des fleurs.
    You send flowers.

Vous faites envoyer des fleurs.
    You are having flowers sent.

Il peint son appartement.
    He is painting his apartment.

Il fait peindre son appartement.
    He is having his apartment painted.

The causative construction also expresses the notion of causing someone to do something.

Le bébé mange.
    The baby is eating.

Elle fait manger le bébé.
    She feeds the baby.

Il travaille sur le projet.
He is working on the project.

Il les fait travailler sur le projet.
He is having them work on the project.

Les étudiants lisent le poème.
The students read the poem.

Le professeur fait lire le poème aux étudiants.
The professor has the students read the poem.

3. *IL Y A* AND *PENDANT* + *PASSÉ COMPOSÉ*

a. To express a completed action that took place some time ago in the past, French uses the *passé composé* + *il y a* + amount of time.

J'ai acheté cette voiture il y a trois ans.
I bought this car three years ago.

J'ai passé mon permis il y a six mois.
I got my license six months ago.

Nous sommes allés en France il y a trois ans.
We went to France three years ago.

b. To express a specific duration of time in the past, French uses the *passé composé* + *pendant* + amount of time.

J'ai essayé pendant une demi-heure.
I tried for a half hour.

Il s'est arrêté pendant deux heures.
He stopped for two hours.

c. Do not confuse *pendant* with *depuis* studied in lesson 14. To express an action or situation that began in the past and is still going on in the present, French uses the present tense + *depuis* + amount of time (see lesson 14).

Elle essaie de le joindre depuis une demi-heure.
She has been trying to reach him for a half hour.

4. THE VERB *CONDUIRE*

Conduire (to drive), like *construire* (to build) and *produire* (to produce), is conjugated according to the following pattern:

CONDUIRE   TO DRIVE

I drive	*je conduis*		we drive	*nous conduisons*
you drive	*tu conduis*		you drive	*vous conduisez*
he/she/one drives	*il/elle/on conduit*		they drive	*ils/elles conduisent*

Tu conduis trop vite.
    You drive too fast.

Vous conduisez bien.
    You're a good driver.

Il construit une maison.
    He is building a house.

Ils produisent du pétrole.
    They produce oil.

VOCABULAIRE

la voiture	car
conduire	to drive
le permis de conduire	driver's license
faire démarrer	to start the car
redémarrer	to start up again
rouler	to drive
rouler à 90 km à l'heure	to do 55 miles an hour
la vitesse	speed
ralentir	to slow down
klaxonner	to sound one's horn
marcher	to work; to run (machine)
La voiture marche bien.	The car runs well.
La voiture consomme peu.	The car is fuel-efficient.
l'essence	gas
la station-service	gas station
faire le plein	fill the tank
l'huile *(f.)*	oil
faire changer l'huile	to have the oil changed
tomber en panne	to break down
remorquer	to tow
réparer	to repair
le garage	garage
le garagiste	attendant (gas station)
le mécanicien	mechanic
vérifier	to check

le moteur	motor
les freins (m.)	brakes
le pneu	tire
la pression des pneus	tire pressure
gonfler	to inflate
J'ai un pneu crevé.	I have a flat tire.
le phare	headlight
régler	to fix
le feu arrière	tail light
les essuie-glaces	windshield wipers
le pare-choc	bumper
la bougie	sparkplug
le niveau d'eau	water level
la batterie	battery
avoir un accident	to have an accident
déposer	to drop off someone
les ennuis	problems
prudent	cautious
la voiture d'occasion	secondhand car
pourtant	yet
seulement	only
Ça coûte les yeux de la tête.	It costs an arm and a leg. (It costs the eyes of the head.)
volontiers	with pleasure, gladly

EXERCICES

A. *Répondre aux questions en utilisant "pendant" ou "il y a."*

MODÈLE: *Pierre a acheté sa maison _____ cinq ans.*
Pierre a acheté sa maison il y a cinq ans.

1. *Il a passé son examen _____ deux ans.*
2. *J'ai attendu le mécanicien _____ une demi-heure.*
3. *Nous avons voyagé en Corse _____ dix ans.*
4. *Il a changé l'huile _____ trois mois.*
5. *Vous avez regardé la télévision samedi après-midi _____ trois heures.*

B. *Transformer les phrases avec une construction causative.*

MODÈLE: *Je répare ma voiture.*
Je fais réparer ma voiture.

1. *Je change l'huile.*
2. *Il gonfle les pneus.*

3. *Nous vérifions le moteur.*
4. *Vous réglez les phares.*
5. *Elle lave la voiture.*

C. *Mettre les verbes au passé composé.*

MODÈLE: *Nous nous faisons remorquer.*
Nous nous sommes fait remorquer.

1. *Tu t'arrêtes devant la Tour Eiffel.*
2. *Nous nous levons très tôt.*
3. *Ils se promènent sur les boulevards.*
4. *Vous occupez-vous de ce projet?*
5. *Elle ne se couche pas avant minuit.*

D. *Conjuguer les verbes suivants au présent.*

MODÈLE: *Il _____ trop vite. (conduire)*
Il conduit trop vite.

1. *Nous _____ sur les petites routes. (conduire)*
2. *Tu _____ une étagère? (construire)*
3. *Je te _____ chez le médecin. (conduire)*
4. *Ce pays _____ beaucoup de grands artistes. (produire)*
5. *Vous _____ une grosse voiture. (conduire)*

NOTE CULTURELLE

In general, speed limits are higher in France than in the United States. On highways and expressways *(autoroutes)* you are allowed to go as fast as 130 km/h, or 80 miles per hour. On other main roads, the speed limit is 90 km/h, or about 55 miles an hour. Within city limits, do not go faster than 50 km/h, about 30 miles an hour.

The driving rules *(code de la route)* in France are not very different from the ones in the United States, except that the French are very fond of *ronds-points* —rotaries or traffic circles one must use in order to turn onto a road.

LA CLÉ DES EXERCICES

A. 1. *il y a* 2. *pendant* 3. *il y a* 4. *il y a* 5. *pendant*
B. 1. *Je fais changer l'huile.* 2. *Il fait gonfler les pneus.* 3. *Nous faisons vérifier le moteur.* 4. *Vous faites régler les phares.* 5. *Elle fait laver la voiture.*
C. 1. *Tu t'es arrêté(e) devant la Tour Eiffel.* 2. *Nous nous sommes levé(e)s très tôt.* 3. *Ils se sont promenés sur les boulevards.* 4. *Vous êtes-vous occupé(e)(s) de ce projet?* 4. *Elle ne s'est pas couchée avant minuit.*
D. 1. *conduisons* 2. *construis* 3. *conduis* 4. *produit* 5. *conduisez*

LEÇON 23
LES CAFÉS ET RESTAURANTS.   Cafés and Restaurants.

A. DIALOGUE

À la terrasse d'un café.

MARIE: **Tu te souviens, ils étaient toujours assis à cette table.**

RENÉ: **Qui donc?**

MARIE: **Sartre et Beauvoir!**

RENÉ: **C'est vrai! Ils buvaient du café toute la journée. Et ils parlaient de politique avec tous leurs amis.**

MARIE: **Il avait toujours une montagne de livres à ses côtés.**

RENÉ: **Et elle portait les siens dans un grand sac en cuir.**

MARIE: **Tu te souviens du jour où ils ont offert un verre à tous les clients?**

RENÉ: **Quelle mémoire! Moi, je me souviens que tu commandais toujours le même sandwich.**

MARIE: **Un jambon-beurre. Et le tien, c'était un sandwich au pâté de campagne avec des cornichons. Tu mourais toujours de faim et tu avalais tout en cinq minutes.**

RENÉ: **Si on s'offrait un sandwich en souvenir du bon vieux temps?**

MARIE: **Avec plaisir.**

At a sidewalk café.

MARIE: Do you remember? They always sat at this table.

RENÉ: Who?

MARIE: Sartre and Beauvoir!

RENÉ: You're right. They used to drink coffee all day long. And they talked about politics with their friends.

MARIE: He always had a mountain of books at his side.

RENÉ: And she carried hers in a large leather bag.

MARIE: Do you remember the day they bought a drink for all the customers?

RENÉ: What a memory! I remember that you always ordered the same sandwich.

MARIE: Ham with butter. And yours was a pâté de campagne sandwich with cornichons. You were always starving, and you swallowed everything in five minutes.

RENÉ: Should we treat ourselves to a sandwich in memory of the good old days?

MARIE: With pleasure.

B. GRAMMAIRE ET USAGE

1. THE IMPERFECT TENSE

To describe past actions, we learned to use the *passé composé* in lesson 21. Another past tense used in French is *l'imparfait* (the imperfect). This tense is used to describe an action that was continuous or habitual.

a. To form the imperfect, take the *nous* form of the verb in the present tense, drop the *nous* ending (e.g., *ons* for first group regular verbs) and keep the stem to add the corresponding imperfect endings.

The endings of the imperfect are:

-ais	*-ions*
-ais	*-iez*
-ait	*-aient*

Let's take the verb *passer* (to spend time) as an example.

nous passons → *pass* → *je passais*

PASSER   TO SPEND

I spent/I was spending	*je passais*
you spent/you were spending	*tu passais*
he/she/one spent/he/she/one was spending	*il/elle/on passait*
we spent/we were spending	*nous passions*
you spent/you were spending	*vous passiez*
they spent/they were spending	*ils passaient*

Note that there are two ways to translate the imperfect into English: the simple past and the past continuous tense.

b. Regular verbs in *-ger* add an *e* after the *g* in all forms of the singular and in the third-person plural to keep the *g* sound soft (like the s in pleasure). No *e* is needed in the *nous* and *vous* forms since *g* + *i* is always soft.

I ate	*je mangeais*	we ate	*nous mangions*
you ate	*tu mangeais*	you ate	*vous mangiez*
he/she/one ate	*il/elle/on mangeait*	they ate	*ils/elles mangeaient*

c. Regular verbs in *-cer* take a cedilla on the *c* in all singular forms and in the third-person plural to keep the *c* sound soft (like the s̲ in sin̲g). No cedilla is needed in the *nous* and *vous* forms since *c* + *i* are always soft.

COMMENCER TO BEGIN

I began	*je commençais*	we began	*nous commencions*
you began	*tu commençais*	you began	*vous commenciez*
he/she/ one began	*il/elle/on commençait*	they began	*ils/elles commençaient*

d. Most irregular verbs form the imperfect regularly, from the *nous* form of the present tense.

je prenais	I took	*j'allais*	I went
je voyais	I saw	*j'avais*	I had
je buvais	I drank	*je disais*	I said

e. Only *être* is an exception; its stem is *ét-*.

ÊTRE TO BE

I was	*j'étais*	we were	*nous étions*
you were	*tu étais*	you were	*vous étiez*
he/she/one was	*il/elle/on était*	they were	*ils/elles étaient*

f. The imperfect is used to describe an action that was performed in the past habitually.

Je passais des heures dans ce café.
   I used to spend hours in this café.

Tu commandais toujours le même plat.
   You would always order the same dish.

The imperfect is used when an action or a duration is interrupted by another action.

Elle lisait un livre quand soudain le téléphone a sonné.
   She was reading a book when suddenly the phone rang.

Il dînait au restaurant quand un de ses amis est entré.
He was having dinner in a restaurant when a friend of his walked in.

The imperfect describes two simultaneous actions in the past.

Nous lisions pendant qu'ils regardaient la télévision.
We were reading while they were watching TV.

Ils parlaient de politique pendant qu'ils dînaient.
They were talking about politics while they were having dinner.

The imperfect is used to describe the state of things or minds.

Elle portait une robe noire.
She was wearing a black dress.

Ils étaient fatigués.
They were tired.

Il faisait chaud.
It was warm.

The imperfect used with a *si* + *on* construction means "what about."

Si on s'offrait une bonne bouteille de vin?
What about treating ourselves to a good bottle of wine?

Si on allait au cinéma cet après-midi?
What about going to the movies this afternoon?

Si on commandait du champagne?
What about ordering champagne?

2. POSSESSIVE PRONOUNS

a. Possessive pronouns replace nouns used with possessive adjectives. They agree in gender and number with the noun they replace.

| | SINGULAR | | PLURAL | |
	MASC.	FEM.	MASC.	FEM.
mine	*le mien*	*la mienne*	*les miens*	*les miennes*
yours	*le tien*	*la tienne*	*les tiens*	*les tiennes*
his/hers/its	*le sien*	*la sienne*	*les siens*	*les siennes*
ours	*le nôtre*	*la nôtre*	*les nôtres*	*les nôtres*
yours	*le vôtre*	*la vôtre*	*les vôtres*	*les vôtres*
theirs	*le leur*	*la leur*	*les leurs*	*les leurs*

C'est mon sandwich. Voilà le tien.
This is my sandwich. Here's yours.

Il a son sac. Elle a le sien.
    He has his bag. She has hers.

Nous aimons notre maison. Elle aime la sienne.
    We like our house. She likes hers.

Ils prennent leur voiture. Nous prenons la nôtre.
    They take their car. We take ours.

    b. When the possessive pronoun is preceded by *à* or *de,* the article is contracted in the usual way.

Elle parle à ses amis, et moi, je parle aux miens.
    She talks to her friends, and I talk to mine.

Nous avons besoin de nos documents, et vous, vous avez besoin des vôtres.
    We need our documents, and you need yours.

    c. However, if no distinction is made as to the owner, the most common way of expressing possession is using *être* + *à* + the stressed pronoun.

Ce sac est à moi.
    This bag is mine.

Ces livres sont à moi.
    These books are mine.

    d. If there is a distinction, the possessive pronoun will be used.

C'est le mien, ce n'est pas le tien!
    It's mine, it's not yours!

Cet album de photos est le mien, celui-là est le vôtre.
    This photo album is mine, that one is yours.

3. *TOUT* AS ADJECTIVE AND PRONOUN

    a. The adjective *tout* + the definite article means "every" or "all." Both *tout* and its definite article agree in gender and number with the noun they qualify.

	SINGULAR	PLURAL
MASC.	*tout*	*tous*
FEM.	*toute*	*toutes*

Il passe tout son temps au bureau.
    He spends all his time in his office.

Il mange toute la journée.
He eats all day long.

Ils ont offert un verre à tous les clients.
They bought a drink for all the customers.

Toutes les tables sont prises.
All the tables are taken.

b. Although it refers to a large number of people, the pronoun *tout le monde,* "everyone," takes the verb in the singular.

Tout le monde est assis à la terrasse du café.
Everyone is sitting on the terrace of the café.

Tout le monde est allé à la campagne ce week-end.
Everyone went to the country this weekend.

c. The pronoun *tout* remains invariable when it means "everything" in a general, collective way.

Il veut tout voir.
He wants to see everything.

Tout va bien.
All is well.

Note: When the pronoun *tout* is used in the plural, referring to people or things, the final *s* is pronounced.

Ils sont tous ici.
They are all here.

Elle les achète tous.
She is buying them all.

Nous tous!
All of us!

Whereas if *tous* is an adjective, the *s* is not pronounced.

Il boit du café tous les matins.
He drinks coffee every morning.

Ils vont en France tous les ans.
They go to France every year.

Elle se lève à six heures tous les matins.
She gets up at 6 A.M. every morning.

d. In the *passé composé,* the pronoun *tout* is placed between the auxiliary and the past participle.

Ils ont tout mangé.
They ate everything.

Elle a tout lu.
She has read everything.

e. Here are some expressions with *tout.*

pas du tout	not at all	*tout à coup*	suddenly
en tout cas	in any case	*tout à fait*	quite, entirely
tout de suite	immediately	*tout le monde*	everybody
après tout	after all	*tout droit*	straight ahead
à tout jamais	for ever	*à tout à l'heure*	see you later

5. THE VERB *MOURIR*

Mourir (to die) is an irregular *-ir* verb and takes the following forms:

MOURIR   TO DIE

I die/am dying	*je meurs*	we die/are dying	*nous mourons*
you die/are dying	*tu meurs*	you die/are dying	*vous mourez*
he/she/one dies/is dying	*il/elle/on meurt*	they die/are dying	*ils/elles meurent*

The verb *mourir* has as many idioms as its English equivalent "to die."

mourir de faim	to starve (die of hunger)
mourir de soif	to die of thirst
mourir d'ennui	to die of boredom
mourir de rire	to laugh yourself to death
mourir de chaleur	to die of the heat
mourir d'amour	to die of a broken heart
mourir de fatigue	to be exhausted to death
mourir debout	to die with one's boots on (standing up)
mourir d'envie	to die to do something

Je meurs de faim.
I am starving.

On était morts de rire.
We laughed ourselves to death.

VOCABULAIRE

un express	an espresso
un chocolat	a cup of hot chocolate
un thé	a cup of tea
le croissant	croissant
le serveur, la serveuse	waiter, waitress
le/la client(e)	customer
à la terrasse	on the terrace, outside
à l'intérieur	inside
l'apéritif	before-dinner drink
le digestif	after-dinner drink
prendre un verre	to have a drink
À la vôtre. / À votre santé	Cheers / To your health
À la tienne.	To your health. (fam.)
le jus de fruit	fruit juice
la glace	ice
une glace	an ice cream
glacé	frozen, cold (also, iced as in a cake)
les cacahuètes *(m. pl.)*	peanuts
un sandwich	sandwich
un sandwich au jambon	a ham sandwich
un saucisson-beurre	a hard sausage and butter sandwich
le croque-monsieur	a hot ham and cheese open-faced sandwich
le cornichon	pickle
la mémoire	memory
le bon vieux temps	the good old days
se souvenir	to remember
mourir (de faim)	to die (of hunger)
passer du temps	to spend time
être assis	to be sitting
commander	to order
avaler	to swallow
s'offrir	to offer oneself, to treat oneself
avoir l'habitude	to be used to
porter	to carry, to wear
le sac	bag, handbag
le cuir	leather
Qui donc?	Who then?
toute la journée	all day long
autrefois	formerly
toujours	always

tout   everything
le côté   the side

EXERCICES

A. *Compléter avec le pronom possessif.*

MODÈLE: Son ami est américain, _____ est italien. (theirs)
Son ami est américain, le leur est italien.

1. *Je ne prends pas ma voiture parce que Georges prend _____.* (his)
2. *"Comment est ton café, Georges? _____ est froid."* (mine)
3. *Les enfants ont pris leurs bicyclettes mais nous avons oublié _____.*
   (ours)
4. *À ta santé!—À _____!* (yours)
5. *Ton sac est en cuir, _____ est en plastique.* (hers)

B. *Compléter avec l'imparfait du verbe.*

MODÈLE: Elle _____ un sandwich au pâté. (prendre)
Elle prenait un sandwich au pâté.

1. *Dans le temps, je _____ beaucoup de sport. (faire)*
2. *Quand nous _____ plus jeunes, nous _____ beaucoup de café. (être;*
   boire)
3. *Elles _____ souvent dans ce restaurant. (venir)*
4. *Ils _____ quand leur ami est arrivé. (manger)*
5. *Tu te souviens quand on _____ au café tous les matins? (aller)*

C. *Faire des phrases en utilisant la construction "si" + "on."*

MODÈLE: On achète une bouteille de champagne.
Si on achetait une bouteille de champagne?

1. *On va au théâtre.*
2. *On commande des escargots.*
3. *On téléphone à Jacques.*
4. *On s'offre du foie gras.*
5. *On fait un voyage au Népal.*

D. *Répondre aux questions avec l'adjectif "tout."*

MODÈLE: Est-ce qu'il a mangé les cornichons?
Oui, il a mangé tous les cornichons.

1. *Est-ce que les sacs sont en cuir?*
2. *Avez-vous lu les livres?*
3. *Ont-ils préparé les sandwichs?*
4. *Est-ce que les amis sont arrivés?*
5. *A-t-il offert un verre aux clientes?*

E. *Conjuguer le verbe "mourir" au présent.*

MODÈLE: Il _____ *d'ennui.*
       Il meurt d'ennui.

  1. *Nous* _____ *de faim.*
  2. *Tu* _____ *d'envie de voir ce film? C'est impossible!*
  3. *Il fait si chaud ici, on* _____ *de soif.*
  4. *Tous les grands romantiques* _____ *d'amour.*
  5. *Je* _____ *de faim. Allons au restaurant.*

NOTE CULTURELLE

Cafés are an essential feature in French social life. People of all ages sit at the tables sipping coffee or other beverages at any time of the day or night. Most cafés have a terrace that spills onto the sidewalk, and people love to sit and gaze at the passers-by. The café is a place to have breakfast, a quick lunch, afternoon tea, or an apéritif in the evening. Usually, cafés do not serve hot meals but the café-brasseries do. One of the real pleasures is that you can sit at a table for as long as you wish for the price of just a cup of coffee.

LA CLÉ DES EXERCICES

A. 1. *la sienne* 2. *Le mien* 3. *les nôtres* 4. *la tienne* 5. *le sien*
B. 1. *faisais* 2. *étions; buvions* 3. *venaient* 4. *mangeaient* 5. *allait*
C. 1. *Si on allait au théâtre?* 2. *Si on commandait des escargots?* 3. *Si on téléphonait à Jacques?* 4. *Si on s'offrait du foie gras?* 5. *Si on faisait un voyage au Népal?*
D. 1. *Oui, tous les sacs sont en cuir.* 2. *Oui, j'ai lu tous les livres.* 3. *Oui, ils ont préparé tous les sandwichs.* 4. *Oui, tous les amis sont arrivés.* 5. *Oui, il a offert un verre à toutes les clientes.*
E. 1. *mourons* 2. *meurs* 3. *meurt* 4. *meurent* 5. *meurs*

LEÇON 24
LE SPORT. Sports.

A. DIALOGUE

Un tournoi de tennis.

BRUNO: **Tu as regardé le tennis à la télé dimanche?**

LUC: **Oui, je l'ai regardé, bien sûr.**

BRUNO: **Qu'est-ce que tu penses du joueur argentin?**

LUC: **Il a un assez bon service, mais il ne court pas assez vite.**

BRUNO: **Il a quand même gagné plusieurs manches!**

LUC: **Oui, mais il manque de technique.**

BRUNO: **Tu as vu la finale?**

LUC: **Non, malheureusement, je l'ai manquée.**

BRUNO: **C'est dommage! L'Australien a joué à merveille. Il les a tous battus.**

LUC: **Au fait, tu as reçu ta nouvelle raquette?**

BRUNO: **Oui, je l'ai reçue la semaine dernière mais je ne l'ai pas encore essayée. Tu veux jouer avec moi dimanche matin?**

LUC: **D'accord.**

BRUNO: **Je vais réserver un court pour dix heures. Pense à apporter tes balles!**

A Tennis Tournament.

BRUNO: Did you watch the tennis match on television on Sunday?

LUC: Yes, I watched it, of course.

BRUNO: What do you think of the Argentinian player?

LUC: He has a good enough service, but he doesn't run fast enough.

BRUNO: Still, he won several sets.

LUC: Yes, but he lacks technique.

BRUNO: Did you see the final?

LUC: No, unfortunately, I missed it.

BRUNO: What a pity! The Australian played marvelously. He beat them all.

LUC: By the way, have you received your new racket?

BRUNO: Yes, I received it last week, but I have not tried it yet. Do you want to play with me on Sunday morning?

LUC: Okay.

BRUNO: I'll reserve a court for ten o'clock. Remember to bring your tennis balls!

B. GRAMMAIRE ET USAGE

1. DIRECT OBJECT PRONOUNS IN THE *PASSÉ COMPOSÉ*

a. In the *passé composé*, direct object pronouns are placed just before the auxiliary *être* or *avoir*.

J'ai regardé le match.
I watched the game.

Je l'ai regardé.
I watched it.

Elles ont réservé le court.
They reserved the court.

Elles l'ont réservé.
They reserved it.

Il a battu son adversaire.
He beat his opponent.

Il l'a battu.
He beat him.

b. When used with *avoir,* the past participle is invariable unless the direct object pronoun precedes the verb. In that case it agrees in gender and number with the noun it replaces.

Elle a manqué la finale.
She missed the final game.

Elle l'a manquée.
She missed it.

Il a gagné la première manche.
He won the first set.

Il l'a gagnée.
He won it.

230

Nous avons reçu la raquette.
We received the racket.

Nous l'avons reçue.
We received it.

Ils ont essayé les nouvelles balles.
They tried the new balls.

Ils les ont essayées.
They tried them.

2. INTERROGATIVE PRONOUNS

Interrogative pronouns are used in questions. To know which one to use, you must know whether the pronoun is a subject, a direct object, or the object of a preposition, and whether it refers to a person or a thing.

	PERSONS	THINGS
subject	*qui*	*qu'est-ce qui*
direct object	*qui*	*que/qu'est-ce que*
object of a preposition	*qui*	*quoi*

Qui est ce joueur?
Who is that player? (subject; person)

Qu'est-ce qui se passe?
What's happening? (subject; thing)

Qui préfères-tu?
Whom do you prefer? (direct object; person)

Qu'est-ce que tu fais?/Que fais-tu?
What are you doing? (direct object; thing)

Pour qui es-tu?
Who are you for? For whom are you? (object of a preposition; person)

De quoi parles-tu?
What are you talking about? (object of preposition; thing)

3. THE VERB *PENSER*

Penser (to think) is used in various constructions, using no preposition or the prepositions *à* or *de* (to think of, to think about). Let's take a look at a few examples.

a. With the preposition *à, penser* means to think about someone or something.

Il pense à son prochain tournoi.
  He is thinking about his next tournament.

Elle pense à ses amis français.
  She is thinking about her French friends.

Nous pensons à toi.
  We are thinking about you.

b. With the preposition *de, penser* means to have an opinion, a judgment about something or someone.

Que pensez-vous de ce nouveau joueur italien?
  What do you think about this new Italian player?

Qu'est-ce que tu penses du tournoi d'hier?
  What do you think about yesterday's tournament?

Que pensez-vous du nouveau directeur?
  What do you think of the new director?

c. If *penser* is followed by a verb, it is used without a preposition; in that case, it means "to plan."

Il pense acheter une nouvelle maison.
  He is planning to buy a house.

d. *Penser* can also be followed by *à* plus a verb, meaning "don't forget."

Pense à apporter tes balles.
  Don't forget to bring your balls.

4. THE VERB *MANQUER*

Manquer (to miss) is one of the most difficult verbs, as it takes on many different meanings. Let's look at the different possibilities.

a. *Manquer* can mean "to miss," "to be late for something."

Il a manqué l'avion.
  He missed the plane.

Ils ont manqué le début du concert.
  They missed the beginning of the concert.

b. *Manquer* can mean "to regret the absence."

232

Ma meilleure amie me manque.
I miss my best friend.

Nos voyages en Orient nous manquent.
We miss our trips to the Orient.

Note that the word order is changed. The object becomes the subject and vice versa. Literally, "I miss you" is transposed as "You are missing to me."

c. *Manquer* can mean "to lack," "to be deficient."

Il manque de courage.
He lacks courage.

Ils manquent d'imagination.
They lack imagination.

La soupe manque de sel.
The soup has not enough salt.

d. *Manquer à* can mean "to fail to do."

Il a manqué à ses responsabilités.
He failed to do his responsibilities.

Ils ont manqué à leur devoir.
They failed to do their duty.

VOCABULAIRE

le sport	sports
le tournoi	tournament
le match	match, game
la manche	set (sports)
la partie	match (sports)
l'équipe *(f.)*	team
le joueur	player
l'adversaire	the adversary; the opponent
le spectateur, *la spectatrice*	spectator
le stade	stadium
lá télé	television
le tennis	tennis
le football	soccer
jouer *(au tennis)*	to play (tennis)
la raquette	racket
le ballon	ball (inflated)
la balle	ball

le score	score
lancer le ballon	to pass/to throw the ball
courir	to run
vite	fast
se terminer	to end, to come to an end
remporter la victoire	to be victorious; to win
gagner	to win
battre	to beat
le vainqueur	winner
le vaincu	loser
être vaincu	to be beaten, to be defeated
perdre	to lose
manquer	to lack
au fait	by the way
C'est dommage!	What a pity!
penser de	to have an opinion about
Qu'est-ce que tu en penses?	What do you think about it?
Je pense que . . .	I think that . . .
penser à	to think about

EXERCICES

A. *Compléter les phrases avec les pronoms interrogatifs qui conviennent.*

MODÈLE: _____ *tu penses du match?*
        Qu'est-ce que tu penses du match?

   1. _____ *est ce joueur?*
   2. _____ *tu fais en ce moment?*
   3. _____ *se passe?*
   4. _____ *ils pensent du nouveau joueur italien?*
   5. *Avec* _____ *est-ce que vous vous êtes coupé le doigt?*

B. *Remplacer l'objet direct par un pronom et faire accorder.* (Replace the direct object with a pronoun and make the agreement.)

MODÈLE: Il a regardé les matches.
        Il les a regardés.

   1. *Elle a acheté cette raquette.*
   2. *Nous avons battu tous les autres joueurs.*
   3. *Vous avez manqué la première manche.*
   4. *J'ai gagné le match.*
   5. *Vous avez manqué les trois premiers matchs.*

C. *Compléter avec "penser à" ou "penser de."*

1. *Qu'est-ce que vous pensez _____ leur attitude?*
2. *Elle pense _____ ses prochaines vacances.*
3. *Nous pensons _____ prochain match.*
4. *Que penses-tu _____ sa nouvelle raquette?*
5. *Pense _____ réserver le court avant jeudi soir.*

D. *Traduire.*

1. They missed the first set.
2. He failed to do his duty.
3. I missed the train.
4. Do you miss Paris?
5. I miss you a lot.

NOTE CULTURELLE

Soccer and rugby are the favorite sports of the French. Every young boy has played soccer at school or on the weekends. The French love to watch these games on television or in the stadium. They are played in most European countries, and French spectators follow the international competition eagerly. The greatest time for soccer is *la Coupe du Monde,* the world cup.

LA CLÉ DES EXERCICES

A. 1. *Qui* 2. *Qu'est-ce que* 3. *Qu'est-ce qui* 4. *Qu'est-ce qu'* 5. *quoi*
B. 1. *Elle l'a achetée.* 2. *Nous les avons battus.* 3. *Vous l'avez manquée.* 4. *Je l'ai gagné.* 5. *Vous les avez manqués.*
C. 1. *de* 2. *à* 3. *au* 4. *de* 5. *à*
D. 1. *Ils ont manqué la première manche.* 2. *Il a manqué à son devoir.* 3. *J'ai manqué le train.* 4. *Paris te manque? / Est-ce que Paris te manque?* 5. *Tu me manques beaucoup. / Vous me manquez beaucoup.*

LEÇON 25

DANS LA RUE.   On the Street.

A. DIALOGUE

Un embouteillage.

KARINE: Nous t'attendons depuis deux heures! Qu'est-ce qui t'est arrivé?

PATRICK: Quelle histoire! Je traversais la place de la Victoire quand soudain j'ai vu une foule de gens en blouse blanche.

KARINE: Un accident?

PATRICK: Non, c'était une manifestation des étudiants de médecine.

KARINE: Pourquoi manifestaient-ils?

PATRICK: Je ne sais pas vraiment.

KARINE: Qu'est-ce que tu as fait?

PATRICK: Je me suis arrêté, naturellement.

KARINE: Cela a dû provoquer des embouteillages épouvantables!

PATRICK: Tu parles! Et j'attendais tranquillement quand tout à coup un étudiant qui portait un drôle de chapeau s'est approché de ma voiture.

KARINE: Qu'est-ce qu'il voulait?

PATRICK: Il voulait me donner un tract.

KARINE: Et tu ne l'as pas pris!

PATRICK: Évidemment non! J'étais furieux car je savais que j'allais être en retard pour ton dîner.

KARINE: Ne t'en fais pas, nous t'avons gardé quelques bons restes.

A Traffic Jam.

KARINE: We have been waiting for you for two hours! What happened to you?

PATRICK: What a story! I was driving through the Place de la Victoire, when suddenly I saw a crowd of people dressed in white coats.

KARIN: Was it an accident?

236

PATRICK: No, it was a demonstration of medical students.

KARINE: Why were they demonstrating?

PATRICK: I don't really know.

KARINE: What did you do?

PATRICK: I stopped, of course.

KARINE: It must have created an incredible traffic jam!

PATRICK: You're telling me! And while I was waiting, suddenly, a student who was wearing a strange hat walked up to my car.

KARINE: What did he want?

PATRICK: He wanted to give me a pamphlet.

KARINE: And you did not take it!

PATRICK: Of course not! I was furious as I knew I was going to be late for your dinner.

KARINE: Don't worry; we kept some leftovers for you.

B. GRAMMAIRE ET USAGE

1. USING THE *PASSÉ COMPOSÉ* AND THE IMPERFECT

We have seen that the *passé composé* indicates a single event in the past whereas the imperfect is used for describing a state of mind or being or a process in the past. Yet, when a duration or a continuing action is interrupted by another action, the *passé composé* and the imperfect are used together. The continuing action is in the imperfect, whereas the interrupting action is in the *passé composé*.

Je traversais la place de la Victoire quand soudain j'ai vu des étudiants.
I was crossing the Place de la Victoire when suddenly I saw some students.

J'attendais l'autobus quand tout à coup il s'est approché de moi.
I was waiting for the bus when suddenly he walked up to me.

Il regardait le match quand elle est entrée dans la pièce.
He was watching the game when she walked into the room.

Nous marchions dans le parc quand tout à coup nous avons vu un lapin.
We were walking in the park when suddenly we saw a rabbit.

2. ADVERBS

a. We have already encountered many adverbs like *bien, mal, beaucoup,* etc. Let's look at a few examples of other French adverbs. Almost always, French adverbs are formed by adding the suffix *-ment* to the feminine form of an adjective. If the adjective already ends with an *e,* just add the suffix *-ment* to the adjective.

rapide	→	*rapidement*	fast
difficile	→	*difficilement*	with difficulty
facile	→	*facilement*	easily
probable	→	*probablement*	probably

Otherwise, put the adjective in the feminine form and add *-ment.*

naturel	→	*naturelle*	→	*naturellement*	(naturally)
heureux	→	*heureuse*	→	*heureusement*	(happily, fortunately)
actif	→	*active*	→	*activement*	(actively)
sérieux	→	*sérieuse*	→	*sérieusement*	(seriously)
lent	→	*lente*	→	*lentement*	(slowly)
doux	→	*douce*	→	*doucement*	(softly, slowly)

b. Adjectives ending in *ent* and *ant* take *emment* or *amment* for the adverb form.

intelligent	→	*intelligemment*	(intelligently)
patient	→	*patiemment*	(patiently)
brillant	→	*brillamment*	(brilliantly)
constant	→	*constamment*	(constantly)
récent	→	*récemment*	(recently)

c. A certain number of adverbs present irregularities. Here are a few examples.

vrai	→	*vraiment*	(really)
gentil	→	*gentiment*	(nicely)
profond	→	*profondément*	(deeply)
bref	→	*brièvement*	(briefly)
précis	→	*précisément*	(precisely)

3. POSITION OF ADVERBS

Adverbs are usually placed after verbs in the present and other simple tenses (future, imperfect, etc.).

Il conduit rapidement.
  He drives fast.

Elle travaille sérieusement.
  She is working seriously.

Ils marchaient lentement.
  They walked slowly.

Elle va faire l'exercice facilement.
  She'll do this exercise easily.

Tu attends patiemment.
  You are waiting patiently.

However, in the *passé composé* and other compound tenses, adverbs of quality *(bien)*, quantity *(beaucoup)*, and frequency *(toujours)* are placed between the auxiliary verb *(avoir* or *être)* and the past participle.

Il parle beaucoup.
  He speaks a lot.

Il a beaucoup parlé.
  He spoke a lot.

Elle voyage souvent en Hollande.
  She often travels to Holland.

Elle a souvent voyagé en Hollande.
  She has often traveled to Holland.

On mange bien dans ce restaurant.
  We eat well in this restaurant.

On a bien mangé dans ce restaurant.
  We ate well in this restaurant.

Il prend toujours le métro.
  He always takes the subway.

Il a toujours pris le métro.
  He always took the subway.

In the negative, the adverb is placed after *pas.*

Elle n'est pas souvent allée à la campagne l'année dernière.
  She did not go to the country often last year.

Il n'a pas beaucoup travaillé en mai.
  He did not work much in May.

However the position of the adverbs ending in *ment* can be switched if one wishes to stress the action.

Il leur a lentement expliqué le fonctionnement de la machine.
He slowly explained to them how the machine works.

Ils ont méticuleusement examiné l'étiquette.
They meticulously examined the label.

Some adverbs are often used at the beginning or the end of a sentence.

Évidemment, nous avons dû attendre plus d'une heure.
Obviously, we had to wait more than an hour.

Malheureusement, ils ont manifesté Place de la Victoire hier matin.
Unfortunately, they demonstrated at the Place de la Victoire yesterday morning.

4. PEUT-ÊTRE

If the adverb *peut-être* (maybe) is placed at the beginning of a sentence, subject and verb must be reversed.

Il va peut-être venir à la soirée.
Maybe he'll come to the party.

Peut-être viendra-t-il à la soirée.
Maybe he'll come to the party.

In modern spoken French, one tends to keep *peut-être* after the verb in a simple tense (present, imperfect) or between the auxiliary and the past participle in the *passé composé*.

Ils sont peut-être allés chez Gérard.
Maybe they went to Gérard's.

Elle va peut-être arriver en retard.
Maybe she'll arrive late.

VOCABULAIRE

l'embouteillage *(m.)*	traffic jam
attendre	to wait
traverser	to drive through, to cross
une foule de gens	a crowd of people
l'accident *(m.)*	accident
la manifestation	demonstration
le tract	pamphlet
s'arrêter	to stop
s'approcher	to come up to, to approach

240

s'inquiéter	to worry
provoquer	to create, to incite, to provoke
épouvantable	incredible, awful
tranquillement	quietly, tranquilly
intelligemment	intelligently
patiemment	patiently
brillamment	brilliantly
constamment	constantly
récemment	recently
naturellement	naturally
heureusement	happily, fortunately
activement	actively
sérieusement	seriously
lentement	slowly
doucement	softly, slowly
tout à coup	suddenly
drôle	odd looking, funny looking
furieux	furious
être en retard	to be late
garder	to keep
les restes *(m. pl.)*	leftovers
soudain	suddenly
Quelle histoire!	What a story!
Évidemment non!	Of course not! Obviously not!

EXERCICES

A. *Compléter les phrases avec le passé composé ou l'imparfait.*

1. *Tout à coup, une voiture _____ à toute vitesse. (arriver)*
2. *Tout _____ très vite. (se passer)*
3. *Où étiez-vous? Je _____ dans un magasin. (être)*
4. *Pourquoi ne pouvait-il pas s'arrêter? Parce qu'il _____ trop vite. (rouler)*
5. *Pendant ce temps, nous _____ dans le magasin. (attendre)*

B. *Transformer les adjectifs en adverbes.*

1. *Il travaille (sérieux).*
2. *Nous attendons (patient).*
3. *Il parle (doux).*
4. *Vous roulez (lent).*
5. *Ils ont acheté cette voiture (récent).*

C. *Mettre les phrases au passé composé.*

MODÈLE: *Ils travaillent trop.*
Ils ont trop travaillé.

1. *Vous allez souvent dans ce bistro.* (plural)
2. *Nous mangeons très bien.*
3. *Tu voyages beaucoup.*
4. *Ils travaillent sérieusement.*
5. *Tu nous gardes toujours les bons restes.*

D. *Commencer la phrase par peut-être.*

MODÈLE: *Ils vont arriver en retard.*
Peut-être vont-ils arriver en retard.

1. *Ils manifestent parce qu'ils ne sont pas contents.*
2. *Vous savez pourquoi il y a des embouteillages.*
3. *Elle veut parler aux étudiants.*
4. *Il va nous garder des restes.*
5. *Vous pouvez nous dire pourquoi ils manifestent.*

E. *Traduire.*

1. We were waiting for the bus when the students arrived.
2. I was at the place de la Victoire when the demonstration started.
3. They saved me some leftovers.
4. What did you do? (familiar)
5. She was watching television when her friend Patrick called.

NOTE CULTURELLE

In an emergency in France, one should call the police. All phones, public and private, show the telephone number of the police. The police are connected to the hospital emergency service.

LA CLÉ DES EXERCICES

A. 1. *est arrivée* 2. *s'est passé très vite* 3. *j'étais* 4. *roulait* 5. *attendions*
B. 1. *sérieusement* 2. *patiemment* 3. *doucement* 4. *lentement*
5. *récemment*
C. 1. *Vous êtes souvent allés dans ce bistro.* 2. *Nous avons très bien mangé.*
3. *Tu as beaucoup voyagé.* 4. *Ils ont travaillé sérieusement.* 5. *Tu nous as toujours gardé les bons restes.*
D. 1. *Peut-être manifestent-ils parce qu'ils ne sont pas contents.* 2. *Peut-être savez-vous pourquoi il y a des embouteillages.* 3. *Peut-être veut-elle parler aux étudiants.* 4. *Peut-être va-t-il nous garder des restes.* 5. *Peut-être pouvez-vous nous dire pourquoi ils manifestent.*
E. 1. *Nous attendions l'autobus quand les étudiants sont arrivés.* 2. *J'étais place*

de la Victoire quand la manifestation a commencé. 3. Ils m'ont gardé des restes. 4. Qu'est-ce que tu as fait? 5. Elle regardait la télévision quand son ami Patrick a téléphoné.

CINQUIÈME RÉVISION

A. *Mettre au passé composé.*

MODÈLE: *Elle _____ à huit heures. (partir)*
    Elle est partie à huit heures.

  1. *Il _____ mal à la tête hier. (avoir)*
  2. *Nous _____ toute la journée. (conduire)*
  3. *Est-ce que tu _____ chez le médecin? (aller)*
  4. *Ils _____ les instructions. (suivre)*
  5. *Ils _____ ce matin. (arriver)*

B. *Mettre à la forme causative.*

MODÈLE: *Je ne lave pas ma voiture.*
    Je la fais laver.

  1. *Je ne répare pas ma voiture.*
  2. *Tu ne changes pas les freins.*
  3. *Elle n'a pas vérifié l'huile.*
  4. *Nous ne réservons pas notre court de tennis.*
  5. *Elle n'écrit pas ses lettres.* .

C. *Mettre les verbes à l'imparfait.*

MODÈLE: *Je _____ en France en mars. (être)*
    J'étais en France en mars.

  1. *Autrefois, il _____ beaucoup de viande rouge. (manger)*
  2. *Chaque jour, nous _____ ici. (déjeuner)*
  3. *Quand il était étudiant, il _____ beaucoup de sport. (faire)*
  4. *Ils _____ toujours le même repas. (commander)*
  5. *Nous _____ des heures à la terrasse des cafés. (passer)*

D. *Compléter les phrases avec le passé composé ou l'imparfait.*

MODÈLE: *Nous _____ la ville (traverser) quand il _____ à pleuvoir.*
    (commencer)
    Nous traversions la ville quand il a commencé à pleuvoir.

  1. *Autrefois, nous _____ souvent au restaurant. (aller)*
  2. *L'accident _____ très vite. (arriver)*
  3. *Nous nous promenions dans le parc quand soudain nous _____ (voir) Phillipe.*

4. *Quand il était jeune, il* _____ *beaucoup de tennis. (faire)*
5. *Est-ce que vous* _____ *de lire le livre de Sartre? (finir)*

E. *Faire des phrases en utilisant "avoir mal à" ou "avoir du mal à."*

MODÈLE: *Il* _____ *tête.*
         Il a mal à la tête.

1. *Ils* _____ *comprendre l'accent provençal.*
2. *Vous* _____ *jambe.*
3. *Elle* _____ *dents.*
4. *Tu* _____ *apprendre la leçon.*
5. *Elle* _____ *main gauche.*

F. *Compléter les phrases avec un pronom possessif.*

MODÈLE: *Elle porte ses livres et il porte* _____.
         Elle porte ses livres et il porte les siens.

1. *Je n'ai pas pris mon sac. Tu as pris* _____?
2. *Anne est contente de sa voiture, mais Julien n'est pas content de* _____.
3. *Nous n'avons pas notre voiture mais mes parents ont* _____.
4. *J'ai pris mes balles de tennis et vous, avez-vous pris* _____?
5. *Tu as payé ton voyage et moi, j'ai payé* _____.

G. *Faire l'accord du participe passé quand c'est nécessaire.*

MODÈLE: *Elle est (aller) aux Deux Magots.*
         Elle est allée aux Deux Magots.

1. *Elle a gagné toutes les manches? Oui, elle les a toutes (gagner)!*
2. *Elle s'est (laver) les mains.*
3. *Je connais ces équipes. Je les ai (voir) le mois dernier.*
4. *Vous avez regardé les matchs à la télé? Oui, je les ai (regarder).*
5. *Tu as apporté tes balles de tennis? Oui, je les ai (apporter).*

H. *Composer des phrases en utilisant la forme si + on.*

MODÈLE: *Nous mangeons au restaurant.*
         Si on mangeait au restaurant?

1. *Nous allons à l'opéra.*
2. *Nous visitons ce château.*
3. *Nous jouons au golf.*
4. *Nous commandons du foie gras.*
5. *Nous téléphonons à Karine.*

A. 1. *a eu*   2. *avons conduit*   3. *es allé*   4. *ont suivi*   5. *sont arrivés*
B. 1. *Je la fais réparer.* 2. *Tu les fais changer.* 3. *Elle l'a fait vérifier.* 4. *Nous le faisons réserver.* 5. *Elle les fait écrire.*
C. 1. *mangeait*   2. *déjeunions*   3. *faisait*   4. *commandaient*   5. *passions*
D. 1. *allions*   2. *est arrivé très vite*   3. *avons vu*   4. *faisait*   5. *avez fini*
E. 1. *ont du mal à*   2. *avez mal à la*   3. *a mal aux*   4. *as du mal à*
   5. *a mal à la*
F. 1. *le tien*   2. *la sienne*   3. *la leur*   4. *les vôtres*   5. *le mien*
G. 1. *gagnées*   2. *lavé*   3. *vues*   4. *regardés*   5. *apportées*
H. 1. *Si on allait à l'opéra?* 2. *Si on visitait ce château?* 3. *Si on jouait au golf?*
   4. *Si on commandait du foie gras?* 5. *Si on téléphonait à Karine?*

LEÇON 26

CHEZ LE COIFFEUR.   At the Hair Salon.

A. DIALOGUE

La grande nouvelle.

CÉCILE: Frédéric, je suis désolée d'être si en retard!

FRÉDÉRIC: Ne vous en faites pas, ce n'est pas grave. Tout le monde est en retard aujourd'hui!

CÉCILE: J'ai une grande nouvelle à vous annoncer . . . je vais me remarier en mai.

FRÉDÉRIC: Félicitations!

CÉCILE: Merci. Frédéric, je voudrais essayer des coiffures différentes.

FRÉDÉRIC: Avec vos cheveux, on a l'embarras du choix. Vous voulez une mise en plis, un chignon, des tresses, une coupe très courte?

CÉCILE: J'aimerais une coiffure élégante mais pratique pour ne pas être obligée de me repeigner toute la journée. Un chignon n'est pas une mauvaise idée.

FRÉDÉRIC: Commençons donc par un chignon.

CÉCILE: J'aimerais également une teinte un peu plus claire pour dissimuler quelques cheveux blancs.

FRÉDÉRIC: Je suis sûr que votre fiancé aura[1] le coup de foudre pour votre nouvelle coiffure.

Great News

CÉCILE: Frédéric, I'm sorry to be so late!

FRÉDÉRIC: Don't worry, it doesn't matter. Everyone is late today!

CÉCILE: I have a great piece of news to tell you . . . I am going to remarry in May.

FRÉDÉRIC: Congratulations!

CÉCILE: Thanks. Frédéric, I'd like to try a few different hairstyles.

FRÉDÉRIC: With your hair, we have a great many choices. Would you like a set, a bun, braids, a very short cut?

[1] The future tense will be discussed in *Leçon* 31.

CÉCILE: I would love an elegant but practical hairstyle so I won't have to keep combing my hair all day long. A bun isn't a bad idea.

FRÉDÉRIC: Well then, let's start with a bun.

CÉCILE: I'd also like a slightly lighter color to hide some of the grey hair.

FRÉDÉRIC: I am sure your fiancé will fall in love with your new hairstyle.

B. GRAMMAIRE ET USAGE

1. REFLEXIVE VERBS IN THE INFINITIVE

We've studied reflexive verbs in lessons 13 and 22, where you learned that the reflexive pronoun always precedes the verb.

Elle se lève tôt tous les matins.
She gets up early every morning.

Je me promène dans le jardin.
I take a walk in the garden.

If another verb precedes the reflexive verb, the latter will be in the infinitive, but the reflexive pronoun will still have to agree with the subject of the first verb.

J'aime me lever tôt.
I like to get up early.

Elle va se marier en mai.
She is going to get married in May.

Nous voulons nous recoiffer.
We want to redo our hair.

Il a envie de se coucher.
He feels like going to sleep.

Tu dois te préparer.
You must get ready.

On ne peut pas s'ennuyer avec lui.
One cannot get bored with him.

Vous aimez vous reposer le dimanche.
You like to rest on Sundays.

In the negative or interrogative form, the first verb will be either negative or interrogative, and the reflexive verb will remain in the infinitive, always preceded by the reflexive pronoun.

Tu n'as pas besoin de te presser.
   You don't need to hurry.

Vous ne pouvez pas vous lever si tard.
   You can't get up so late.

A-t-il oublié de se brosser les dents?
   Did he forget to brush his teeth?

Voulez-vous vous teindre les cheveux?
   Do you want to color your hair?

Peut-il se préparer en cinq minutes?
   Can he get ready in five minutes?

Espère-t-il s'amuser à leur soirée?
   Does he hope to have fun at their party?

2. THE VERB *COMMENCER*

We studied the forms of the verb *commencer* (to start) in lesson 8. Now let's focus on its different usages.

a. If the verb *commencer* is followed by a direct object, no preposition is used.

Il commence son travail à huit heures.
   He starts his job at 8 A.M.

Nous commençons le troisième chapitre.
   We are starting the third chapter.

b. If the preposition *à* is used, *commencer* means to begin an action.

Il commence à pleuvoir.
   It is starting to rain.

Vous avez déjà commencé à manger?
   Did you already start eating?

Nous avons commencé à travailler à dix heures.
   We started to work at 10 A.M.

c. The preposition *par* is used when *commencer* means the beginning of a series of actions.

Commençons par un chignon.
   Let's start with a bun.

Il faut commencer par le commencement.
   One must start with the beginning.

248

Par quoi voulez-vous commencer? Des escargots ou des artichauts?
What do you want to start with? Snails or artichokes?

3. APOLOGIZING

Here are a few common apologies.

Excusez-moi.
I'm sorry. Excuse me.

Excusez-moi d'arriver en retard.
I'm sorry to be late.

Pardon.
Excuse me. Pardon (me).

Toutes mes excuses.
My apologies.

The following expressions give your apology more emphasis.

Je suis navré.
I'm terribly sorry.

Je suis désolé.
I'm terribly sorry.

Je suis navré d'être en retard.
I'm terribly sorry to be late.

Je suis désolé de ne pas pouvoir venir.
I'm terribly sorry that I can't come.

The usual polite answer to apologies is:

Je vous en prie.
Please, it's nothing.

Ce n'est pas grave.
It's not serious.

4. LATE / EARLY / ON TIME

These expressions translate differently according to the way they are used.

a. When referring to people, use *être* plus *en retard* (late); *en avance* (early); or *à l'heure* (on time).

Je suis en retard de cinq minutes.
I am five minutes late.

Elle est toujours à l'heure.
She is always on time.

Il est arrivé en retard.
He arrived late.

Elle est en avance.
She is early.

b. When referring to transportation, "on time" is the same, but for "late" and "early" use *avoir du retard* or *de l'avance*.

Notre vol a du retard.
Our flight is late.

Le train avait une heure de retard.
The train was one hour late.

Le taxi était à l'heure.
The taxi was on time.

L'autobus a dix minutes d'avance.
The bus is ten minutes early.

c. When refering to machines or mechanisms, use the verbs *retarder* (late) and *avancer* (early).

Ma montre retarde de dix minutes.
My watch is ten minutes late.

Ma montre est à l'heure.
My watch is on time.

Leur réveil avance d'un quart d'heure.
Their alarm clock is fifteen minutes fast.

d. When early means arriving ahead of time.

Les restaurants sont pleins le samedi; il vaut mieux arriver en avance.
Restaurants are full on Saturdays; it's better to arrive early.

Elle avait une heure d'avance.
She arrived an hour early.

e. When something will occur, or has occurred, use *au début de* (early) or *à la fin de* (late).

Il va se marier au début de l'automne.
He is going to get married in the early fall.

Elle est allée en France à la fin des années 60.
She went to France in the late 60s.

Vers la fin de sa vie, il est allé en Chine.
In the later years of his life, he went to China.

f. Here are some idiomatic expressions with "early" and "late."

Mieux vaut tard que jamais.
Better late than never

Tôt ou tard.
Sooner or later.

Au plus tard.
At the latest.

Le plus tôt possible.
As soon as possible.

5. IDIOMATIC EXPRESSIONS WITH *COUP*

In learning the French language, you'll encounter a lot of idiomatic expressions with *coup*.

C'était le coup de foudre.
It was love at first sight.

Il m'a donné un coup de fil.
He gave me a ring.

Le joueur lui a donné un coup de pied.
The player kicked him.

Il a un bon coup de fourchette.
He is a big eater.

Nous jetons un coup d'oeil.
We're taking a look.

Je te donne un coup de main?
Shall I give you a hand?

Revenez demain pour un coup de peigne.
Come back tomorrow for a little combing.

VOCABULAIRE

le coiffeur pour dames	ladies' hairdresser
le coiffeur pour hommes	men's hairdresser
les cheveux *(m. pl.)*	hair
la coiffure	hairdo, hairstyle
l'embarras du choix	a great many choices
la mise en plis	set (with curlers)

le chignon	bun
les tresses *(f. pl.)*	braids
la permanente	permanent
les cheveux blancs	gray hair
un salon de coiffure	a beauty salon
le shampooing	shampoo
la coupe	haircut
se faire couper les cheveux	to get a haircut
repeigner	to recomb
dissimuler	to hide
la nuque	nape of the neck
la frange	bangs
la barbe	beard
la raie	part
le volume	volume
la laque	hairspray
le baume démêlant	hair conditioner (untangler)
le brushing	blow dry
rincer	to rinse
friser	to curl
le coup de foudre	love at first sight
le fiancé	fiancé
la fiancée	fiancée
se marier	to get married
se remarier	to remarry
Félicitations!	Congratulations!
se confier à	to confide in someone
une grande nouvelle	a great piece of news
Ce n'est pas grave.	It doesn't matter.
les excuses *(f.pl.)*	apologies
s'excuser	to apologize
Pardon.	Excuse me. Pardon.
Je suis désolé.	I'm terribly sorry.
Ne vous en faites pas.	Don't worry (about it).
Toutes mes excuses.	My apologies.
Je vous en prie, ce n'est rien.	Please. It's nothing.

EXERCICES

A. *Compléter avec "à" ou "par."*

MODÈLE: *Il a commencé* _____ *pleuvoir vers midi.*
        Il a commencé à pleuvoir vers midi.

252

1. _____ quoi est-ce que tu veux commencer?
2. Elle a commencé _____ étudier le français à 10 ans.
3. À quelle heure commences-tu _____ travailler aujourd'hui?
4. Tu veux commencer _____ le plus simple ou _____ le plus difficile?
5. Je venais de commencer _____ regarder le film quand le téléphone a sonné.

B. *Mettre les verbes au présent puis récrire les phrases en ajoutant le verbe "vouloir."* (Put the verbs in the present tense then write the sentences adding the verb *vouloir*.)

MODÈLE: *Je (se coucher) de bonne heure.*
        Je me couche de bonne heure.
        Je veux me coucher de bonne heure.

1. *Ils (se marier) en septembre.*
2. *Vous (se lever) très tôt.*
3. *Nous (se reposer) pendant nos vacances.*
4. *Est-ce que tu (se recoiffer)?*
5. *Elle (ne pas se faire couper) les cheveux.*

C. *Relier colonne A et B.*

A	B
1. *Ça vous va très bien.*	a. I'm terribly sorry.
2. *Toutes mes excuses.*	b. Please, it's nothing.
3. *Mieux vaut tard que jamais.*	c. Congratulations.
4. *Je suis navré.*	d. That suits you very well.
5. *Félicitations.*	e. My apologies.
6. *Je vous en prie.*	f. Better late than never.

D. *Compléter en utilisant une expression de temps.*

MODÈLE: *Elle _____ toujours à l'heure.*
        Elle est toujours à l'heure.

1. *Notre avion _____ une heure de retard.*
2. *Elle _____ toujours en retard.*
3. *Il faut arriver un peu _____ pour avoir une bonne place au concert dans le parc.*
4. *Je suis désolé d'être en retard; ma montre _____ 20 minutes.*
5. *Notre directeur est très ponctuel. Il faut toujours _____ à l'heure.*

E. *Remplacer par une expression idiomatique avec "coup."* (Replace with an idiomatic expression with *coup*.)

1. *Il adore manger.*
2. *Regardez par la fenêtre.*
3. *Vous allez lui téléphoner ce soir?*

4. *Ils sont tombés amoureux immédiatement.*

5. *Est-ce que tu peux m'aider cet après-midi?*

NOTE CULTURELLE

In France, beauty salons range from the friendly neighborhood parlor to high-fashion salons that have since also established themselves in the United States.

Hairdressers often consider themselves artists and like to be treated with a certain respect. Even in a small salon, the hairdresser will not wash your hair himself but ask an assistant to do so. The custom prescribes that you tip the assistant with a small amount. The hairdresser himself expects a 10% tip unless, of course, s/he owns the place.

LA CLÉ DES EXERCICES

A. 1. *Par* 2. *à* 3. *à* 4. *par; par* 5. *à*

B. 1. *Ils se marient en septembre.* / *Ils veulent se marier en septembre.* 2. *Vous vous levez très tôt.* / *Vous voulez vous lever très tôt.* 3. *Nous nous reposons pendant nos vacances.* / *Nous voulons nous reposer pendant nos vacances.*
4. *Est-ce que tu te recoiffes?/Est-ce que tu veux te recoiffer?* 5. *Elle ne se fait pas couper les cheveux.* / *Elle ne veut pas se faire couper les cheveux.*

C. 1.—d 2.—e 3.—f 4.—a 5.—c 6.—b

D. 1. *a* 2. *est* 3. *en avance* 4. *retarde de* 5. *être*

E. 1. *Il a un bon coup de fourchette.* 2. *Jetez un coup d'oeil par la fenêtre.*
3. *Vous allez lui passer un coup de fil ce soir?* 4. *C'était le coup de foudre.*
5. *Est-ce que tu peux me donner un coup de main cet après-midi?*

LEÇON 27
CHEZ LE DENTISTE.   At the Dentist's.

A. DIALOGUE

J'ai mal aux dents.

LE DENTISTE: Qu'est-ce qui ne va pas?

LE PATIENT: J'ai une dent qui me fait très mal depuis hier.

LE DENTISTE: Ouvrez la bouche, s'il vous plaît. Où avez-vous mal, exactement?

LE PATIENT: Je crois que c'est la première molaire inférieure à côté de la couronne.

LE DENTISTE: Ah! Vous avez encore toutes vos dents de sagesse! La dent que vous m'indiquez est en bien mauvais état. Le plombage est parti et je vois une bien vilaine carie.

LE PATIENT: Vous n'allez pas l'arracher!

LE DENTISTE: Non, ne vous inquiétez pas! Je vais simplement remplacer le plombage. D'abord, une petite piqûre de novocaïne. . . .

LE PATIENT: Allez-y, je vous en prie! Je ne peux pas supporter la douleur! Si vous me faites mal, j'aurai une dent contre vous.

LE DENTISTE: Vous n'allez rien sentir! Voilà. Et n'oubliez pas de fixer un rendez-vous pour un détartrage le plus tôt possible.

I have a toothache.

DENTIST: What's wrong?

PATIENT: I have a tooth that has been bothering me since yesterday.

DENTIST: Open your mouth, please. Where, exactly, does it hurt?

PATIENT: I think it is the first lower molar next to the crown.

DENTIST: Oh! You still have all your wisdom teeth! The tooth you are talking about is in very bad shape. The filling has fallen out, and I see a nasty cavity.

PATIENT: You're not going to pull it out!

DENTIST: No, don't worry! I am simply going to replace the filling. First a little injection of novocaine . . .

PATIENT: Please, go ahead. I can't stand pain! If you hurt me, I will hold a grudge against you.

DENTIST: You aren't going to feel a thing! Here we are. And don't forget to set an appointment for a cleaning as soon as possible.

B. GRAMMAIRE ET USAGE

1. THE RELATIVE PRONOUNS *QUI* AND *QUE*

Qui (who, whom), *que* (that, what), *où* (where) and *ce qui, ce que* (what) are the relative pronouns used in French.

a. A relative pronoun refers back to a noun in the main clause.

Je connais la personne qui parle.
I know the person who is talking.

A relative pronoun links a dependent clause to a main clause. For example:

The dentist whom you saw is very nice.

    dependent clause: whom you saw

    main clause: The dentist . . . is very nice.

In this sentence, the relative pronoun is "whom"; it refers back to its antecedent, "the dentist."

In English, a relative pronoun can often be omitted: The dentist you saw is very nice.

In French, however, the relative pronoun must always be expressed: *Le dentiste que vous avez vu est très gentil.*

b. A relative pronoun may have as its antecedent either a person or a thing and may be the subject or the direct object of the verb in the dependent clause.

ANTECEDENT	SUBJECT	DIRECT OBJECT
person	*qui* who	*que* whom
thing	*qui* that, which	*que* that, which

Let's take each case at a time. First, the antecedent = person; relative pronoun = subject:

256

C'est le dentiste qui a arraché cette dent.
He's the dentist who pulled out that tooth.

Le patient qui a mal aux dents consulte le dentiste.
The patient who has a toothache sees the dentist.

Now, the antecedent = person; relative pronoun = direct object:

C'est le joueur que j'ai vu au match.
He's the player whom I saw at the game.

Le dentiste que vous m'avez recommandé est formidable.
The dentist you recommended is wonderful.

Antecedent = thing; relative pronoun = subject:

Voilà la dent qui me fait mal.
Here's the tooth that hurts me.

Il faut arracher la molaire qui a une carie.
We must pull out the molar with the cavity.

Antecedent = thing; relative pronoun = direct object:

Voilà la dent que le dentiste va m'arracher.
Here's the tooth that the dentist is going to pull out.

Le rendez-vous que j'ai pris est pour vendredi.
The appointment I made is for Friday.

2. THE RELATIVE PRONOUNS *CE QUI* AND *CE QUE*

Ce qui and *ce que* are indefinite relative pronouns. In English, they both translate into "what." They do not have a specific antecedent; they refer to things, ideas or situations but never to people.

a. *Ce qui* is used as the subject of the dependent clause.

Ce qui me fait mal, c'est la deuxième molaire.
What hurts me is the second molar.

Ce qui est sur la table a l'air délicieux.
What is on the table looks delicious.

Je ne comprends pas ce qui est écrit sur ce papier.
I don't understand what is written on this paper.

Il ne sait pas ce qui s'est passé.
He does not know what happened.

b. *Ce que* is used as the direct object of the dependent clause:

Voilà ce que je vais faire.
Here's what I'll do.

Il dit toujours ce qu'il pense.
He always says what he thinks.

Ce que je ne comprends pas, c'est son attitude!
What I don't understand, is his attitude!

Ce que vous dites est intéressant.
What you are saying is interesting.

3. *OÙ*

a. *Où* (where) is a relative pronoun referring back to a place.

Savez-vous où il habite?
Do you know where he lives?

Dites-moi où vous avez mal.
Tell me where it hurts.

Il ne nous a pas dit où il allait prendre ses vacances.
He did not tell us where he was going to take his vacation.

b. *Où* is also used after an expression of time such as *le jour* (the day), *l'année* (the year), *le moment* (the moment). In this case it means "when." ("When" is often omitted in English.)

Le jour où je suis partie en vacances, j'avais mal aux dents.
The day (when) I left for vacation, I had a toothache.

Le moment où le dentiste m'a fait une piqûre de novocaïne, je me suis sentie mieux.
The moment (when) the dentist gave me a shot of novocaine, I felt better.

4. *AVOIR MAL À / FAIRE MAL*

When you want to express that a part of your body is hurting, you use *avoir* + *mal* + *à* (to ache).[1]

J'ai mal à la tête.
I have a headache.

J'ai mal aux dents.
I have a toothache.

---

[1] See also *Leçon 21.*

Il a mal au dos.
He has a backache.

Nous avons mal aux pieds.
Our feet hurt.

If someone is causing you pain, use *faire mal* (to hurt) plus the indirect pronoun *(me, te, lui, nous, vous, leur)*.

Docteur, vous me faites mal.
Doctor, you're hurting me.

Ne lui fais pas mal.
Don't hurt him / her.

5. IDIOMATIC EXPRESSIONS WITH *DENT*

As with many parts of the body in French, *dent* (tooth) is rich in idiomatic expressions. Here are a few of them.

Elle a une dent contre son frère.
She holds a grudge against her brother.

Ils ont les dents longues.
They are ambitious.

Il ment comme un arracheur de dents.
He lies through his teeth.

Ils n'ont pas desserré les dents de toute la soirée.
They did not utter a word the whole evening.

Quand les poules auront des dents . . .
When pigs fly . . .

Oeil pour oeil, dent pour dent.
An eye for an eye, a tooth for a tooth.

6. THE VERB *VOIR*

Voir (to see) is an irregular verb. It is conjugated as follows.

	VOIR TO SEE		
I see	*je vois*	we see	*nous voyons*
you see	*tu vois*	you see	*vous voyez*
he/she/one sees	*il/elle/on voit*	they see	*ils/elles voient*

Voir takes *avoir* in compound tenses such as the *passé composé* and *plus-que-parfait*[1] (pluperfect): *j'ai vu.*

Je vois une carie.
   I can see a cavity.

Ils ont vu le Musée d'Orsay.
   They saw the Orsay Museum.

Elle voit Pierre le samedi.
   She sees Pierre on Saturdays.

VOCABULAIRE

chez le dentiste	at the dentist's
la bouche	mouth
la mâchoire	jaw
la dent	tooth
les dents de sagesse	wisdom teeth
la dent du haut	upper tooth
la dent du bas	lower tooth
la molaire inférieure	lower molar
la canine	canine tooth
avoir une dent contre	to hold a grudge against
la carie	cavity
la rage de dents	toothache (raging)
la couronne	crown
le plombage	filling
Qu'est-ce qui ne va pas?	What's wrong?
avoir mal aux dents	to have a toothache
Un plombage est parti.	A filling has come out.
la gencive	gum
l'infection *(f.)*	infection
être infecté	to be infected
l'anesthésie *(f.)*	anesthesia
une anesthésie locale	a local anesthetic
la piqûre	injection
sentir	to feel
s'inquiéter de	to worry
nettoyer	to clean
le détartrage	cleaning (of teeth)
arracher	to pull out
remplacer	to replace
supporter	to tolerate

[1] The *plus-que-parfait* is introduced in *Leçon* 29.

enlever	to take out, to pull out, to remove
fixer un rendez-vous	to make an appointment
vilain	nasty
en haut	above
en bas	below
devant	in front
le côté	side
du côté droit	on the right
du côté gauche	on the left side
au-dessous	underneath, below
au-dessus	above

EXERCICES

A. *Compléter avec "qui" ou "que."*

MODÈLE: *Voilà la personne _____ va vous aider.*
Voilà la personne qui va vous aider.

1. *J'ai beaucoup aimé le livre _____ tu m'as donné.*
2. *C'est la dent _____ me fait très mal.*
3. *Les enfants _____ mangent peu de bonbons n'ont pas mal aux dents.*
4. *La dent _____ vous me montrez n'a pas de carie.*
5. *Le dentiste _____ est à côté de chez moi est excellent.*
6. *L'église _____ se trouve sur votre droite date du 12ème siècle.*
7. *Le coiffeur _____ me coupe les cheveux s'appelle Michel.*
8. *Le rendez-vous _____ vous avez oublié était important.*

B. *Compléter avec "ce qui" ou "ce que."*

MODÈLE: *Je ne sais pas _____ il veut.*
Je ne sais pas ce qu'il veut.

1. *_____ est insupportable, c'est la douleur!*
2. *Ils ne savent pas _____ ils vont faire pendant leurs vacances.*
3. *_____ je vous recommande, c'est de bien vous brosser les dents.*
4. *Dites-moi _____ vous désirez essayer.*
5. *_____ me fait mal, c'est cette molaire.*
6. *_____ elle va annoncer, c'est une grande nouvelle.*
7. *_____ vous allez sentir, c'est la piqûre de novocaïne.*
8. *Savez-vous _____ ils boivent?*

C. *Compléter avec un pronom relatif.*

MODÈLE: *Le village _____ ils habitent est magnifique.*
Le village où ils habitent est magnifique.

1. *J'ai beaucoup aimé le livre* _____ *tu m'as offert.*
2. *Les gens* _____ *sont invités sont très agréables.*
3. *Je vais voir* _____ *je vais faire.*
4. *Nous sommes partis le jour* _____ *ils sont arrivés.*
5. _____ *je voudrais, c'est une piqûre de novocaïne.*
6. *La couronne* _____ *je vais vous poser est en or.*
7. _____ *je vois c'est que vous avez grand besoin d'un détartrage!*
8. *Ils n'ont pas décidé* _____ *ils prépareront pour dîner.*

D. *Compléter avec le verbe "voir."*

MODÈLE: *Tu (voir) son nouveau chapeau? (passé composé)*
   Tu as vu son nouveau chapeau?

1. *Ils (voir) tous les films du festival. (passé composé)*
2. *Tu (voir) mes amis trois fois par semaine? (présent)*
3. *Nous ne le (voir) pas souvent. (présent)*
4. *Est-ce que vous (voir) M Laurent de temps en temps? (présent)*
5. *Je (ne pas voir) mon ami depuis des mois. (passé composé)*

NOTE CULTURELLE

In France, most dental work is covered by the health insurance provided by the state. If you have no insurance, you will find the fees quite reasonable.

LA CLÉ DES EXERCICES

A. 1. *que* 2. *qui* 3. *qui* 4. *que* 5. *qui* 6. *qui* 7. *qui* 8. *que*
B. 1. *Ce qui* 2. *ce qu'* 3. *Ce que* 4. *ce que* 5. *Ce qui* 6. *Ce qu'*
   7. *Ce que* 8. *ce qu'*
C. 1. *que* 2. *qui* 3. *ce que* 4. *où* 5. *Ce que* 6. *que* 7. *Ce que* 8. *ce qu'*
D. 1. *ont vu* 2. *vois* 3. *voyons* 4. *voyez* 5. *n'ai pas vu*

LEÇON 28

LE CINÉMA. The Movies.

A. DIALOGUE

Aller au cinéma.

BENOÎT: **Si on allait voir le dernier film de Francis Coppola?**

AMÉLIE: **Si c'est le film dont Marie m'a parlé, c'est hors de question!**

BENOÎT: **C'est un film excellent!**

AMÉLIE: **Tu peux me dire pourquoi tu n'aimes que les films dans lesquels il y a tant de violence?**

BENOÎT: **Marie ne comprend rien au cinéma.**

AMÉLIE: **De quoi s'agit-il, dans ce film?**

BENOÎT: **Il s'agit tout simplement d'une histoire d'amour!**

AMÉLIE: **De toute façon, dans notre quartier, tous ces films sont doublés, ce qui est insupportable!**

BENOÎT: **Bon, quel film aimerais-tu vraiment voir?**

AMÉLIE: **Le film auquel je pensais . . .**

BENOÎT: **Je sais, je sais . . . Tu veux voir le dernier film de Tavernier avec Philippe Noiret et Fanny Ardant.**

AMÉLIE: **Comment as-tu deviné?**

———————————

Going to the Movies.

BENOÎT: What about going to see the latest film by Francis Coppola?

AMÉLIE: If it's the film that Marie told me about, it's out of the question!

BENOÎT: It's an excellent film!

AMÉLIE: Can you tell me why you only like films in which there is so much violence?

BENOÎT: Marie doesn't understand anything about movies.

AMÉLIE: What is this film about?

BENOÎT: It's simply a love story!

AMÉLIE: Anyway, in our neighborhood, all these films are dubbed, which is unbearable!

BENOÎT: Well, which film would you really like to see?

AMÉLIE: The film I was thinking about . . .

BENOÎT: I know, I know . . . You want to see the last film by Tavernier with Phillipe Noiret and Fanny Ardant.

AMÉLIE: How did you guess?

B. GRAMMAIRE ET USAGE

1. THE RELATIVE PRONOUN *LEQUEL*

a. You've already studied the relative pronouns *qui* and *que*. But in French, if a preposition precedes the relative pronoun (for, to, which, etc.), you use *lequel* (which). It is used to refer to things; with rare exceptions, to refer to people you can use either *qui* or *lequel*.

La compagnie distribue des films.
The company distributes films.

Il travaille pour la compagnie.
He is working for the company.

Now, if we connect the two clauses:

La compagnie pour laquelle il travaille distribue des films.
The company for which he is working distributes films.

Lequel agrees in gender and number with the antecedent.

	SINGULAR	PLURAL
MASC.	*lequel*	*lesquels*
FEM.	*laquelle*	*lesquelles*

J'aime les films dans lesquels il n'y a pas de violence.
I like films in which there is no violence.

La chaise sur laquelle il est assis était à ma grand-tante.
The chair on which he is sitting belonged to my great-aunt.

b. The preposition *à* combines with certain forms of *lequel*.

	SINGULAR		PLURAL	
MASC.	*auquel*	to which	*auxquels*	to which
FEM.	*à laquelle*	to which	*auxquelles*	to which

Je pense à un film.
I am thinking about a film.

C'est le film auquel je pense.
It's the film I am thinking about.

C'est la littérature à laquelle elle s'intéresse.
It's the literature in which she is interested.

If it refers to a person, you have the choice between *qui* or *lequel*.

C'est la jeune femme avec laquelle (avec qui) il est allé au cinéma.
This is the young woman with whom he went to the theater.

C'est l'ami avec lequel (avec qui) je dîne ce soir.
It's the friend with whom I am having dinner tonight.

2. THE RELATIVE PRONOUN *DONT*

a. *Dont* can take on a possessive meaning (whose).

The following two sentences express two separate ideas.

Je connais les parents de ce jeune homme.
I know this young man's parents.

Le jeune homme étudie le cinéma.
The young man is a film student.

Now, let's try to connect the two ideas.

Le jeune homme dont je connais les parents étudie le cinéma.
The young man whose parents I know is a film student.

J'ai oublié le nom de cette actrice.
I forgot the name of this actress.

Elle joue très bien.
She acts very well.

L'actrice dont j'ai oublié le nom joue très bien.
The actress whose name I forgot acts very well.

b. With verbs using the preposition *de,* the relative pronoun *dont* is used. Some of these verbs are: *parler de, avoir besoin de, il s'agit de, se souvenir de, s'approcher de, jouer de, manquer de,* etc.

Le film est violent.
  The film is violent.

Je parle du film.
  I am talking about the film.

Le film dont je parle n'est pas violent.
  The film I'm talking about isn't violent. (of which)

Le film dont il s'agit a reçu un prix au festival de Cannes.
  The film in question won a prize at the Cannes festival.

Le château dont nous nous approchons date du 16ème siècle.
  The castle we are approaching dates back to the 16th century.

Ce dont vous parlez est passionnant.
  What you are talking about is fascinating.

3. NE . . . QUE

Ne . . . que (only) is an adverb which indicates a restriction. It is not a negation and must not be confused with *ne . . . pas, ne . . . rien* and other negations. Let's compare:

Il va au cinéma le dimanche.
  He goes to the movies on Sundays.

Il ne va pas au cinéma le dimanche.
  He does not go to the movies on Sundays.

Il ne va au cinéma que le dimanche.
  He goes to the movies only on Sundays.

The *ne* is placed after the subject and the *que* right before the restricted object, here *dimanche.*

Tu n'aimes regarder que les films violents.
  You only like to watch violent films.

Ils ne voient que des films doublés.
  They only see dubbed films.

Il ne prend des vacances avec ses parents qu'en été.
  He takes a vacation with his parents only in summer.

Elle n'a aimé, dans tous les films du festival, que celui de Godard.
  Of all the films at the festival, she only liked Godard's.

4. IL S'AGIT DE

Il s'agit de (it is a matter of, it is a question of, it is about) is a very useful idiomatic expression.

De quoi s'agit-il?
What is it about?

Dans ce film, il s'agit de la vie d'un grand pianiste.
This film is about the life of a great pianist.

Il faut prendre une décision; il s'agit de ton avenir.
You have to make a decision; your future is at stake.

Il ne s'agit pas d'argent!
It's not a matter of money!

Il ne s'agit pas de ça!
That's not the point!

Il ne s'agit pas de plaisanter!
This is no time for joking!

VOCABULAIRE

le cinéma	cinema, movies; movie theater
le film	film; movie
le film policier	detective film
la violence	violence
le meurtre	murder
le documentaire	documentary
l'histoire	story; plot
l'histoire d'amour	love story
le cinéaste	film maker
le producteur	producer
l'auteur	author, writer
le metteur en scène	the director
l'acteur	actor
l'actrice	actress
la vedette	star
jouer	to play, to act (theater, movies)
jouer un rôle	to play a role, to act a part
tourner un film	to shoot a film
le tournage	shooting
l'éclairage	lighting
les accessoires	props
les décors	sets

les coulisses	backstage
les feux de la rampe	limelight
célèbre	famous
le *héros	hero
l'héroïne	heroine
l'aventure *(f.)*	adventure
la violence	violence
le roman policier	detective story
le prix	prize
à la fin	in the end
de toute façon	anyway
recommander	to recommend
deviner	to guess
il s'agit de	to be about, it is a matter of, it is a question of
dont	whose, of whom, of which
ne . . . que	only
comprendre quelque chose à	to have some understanding of
ne rien comprendre à	to understand nothing of

EXERCICES

A. *Faire des phrases avec "dont."*

MODÈLE: *Voilà la jeune fille. / Ses parents sont aux États-Unis.*
Voilà la jeune fille dont les parents sont aux États-Unis.

1. *Voilà l'auteur. / Ses parents sont nos amis.*
2. *Ils habitent dans une ville. / J'ai oublié le nom de la ville.*
3. *C'est une histoire. / Je t'ai déjà parlé de l'histoire.*
4. *C'est un film policier. / Elle se souvient très bien du film.*
5. *Elle parle d'un nouveau film. Je ne connais pas le nom de ce film.*

B. *Compléter les phrases avec la forme de "lequel" qui convient.*

MODÈLE: *Le livre sur _____ ce film est basé est de Victor Hugo.*
Le livre sur lequel ce film est basé est de Victor Hugo.

1. *C'est un film dans _____ il y a beaucoup d'aventures.*
2. *C'est une histoire _____ je ne comprends rien.*
3. *C'est un genre de film _____ je m'intéresse.*
4. *L'acteur _____ je pense est anglais.*
5. *La compagnie pour _____ il travaille est à Toulon.*

C. *Compléter avec un pronom relatif.*

MODÈLE: *Les films _____ passent dans ce quartier sont en version originale.*
Les films qui passent dans ce quartier sont en version originale.

1. *Le festival _____ ils s'intéressent commence le 15 septembre.*
2. *Le film _____ j'ai vu hier est merveilleux.*
3. *Le documentaire _____ elle parle, vient de sortir.*
4. *_____ est insupportable dans ce film, c'est la violence.*
5. *L'actrice _____ joue dans ce film a beaucoup de talent.*

D. *Écrire les phrases en utilisant "ne . . . que."*

MODÈLE: *Il va au cinéma le dimanche.*
Il ne va au cinéma que le dimanche.

1. *Elle aime les films d'aventure.*
2. *Ils voient des films américains.*
3. *On parle de ce film.*
4. *Comme acteur, elle aime Gérard Depardieu.*
5. *Le cinéma de notre quartier passe des films doublés.*

E. *Traduire.*

1. This film is about Paris' monuments.
2. What is it about?
3. It's a matter of choosing a good school.
4. His new book is about Hollywood actors.
5. Is it a matter of money?

NOTE CULTURELLE

Despite the growing number of VCRs, the French still love to go to the movies. The French film festivals in Cannes and Deauville are very popular all over the world. Major figures of French film, such as Godard, Truffaut, Tavernier, and Berri, have given the French film tradition an international reputation. Although the French still make great movies, the industry is in a severe crisis because of the strong competition coming from the United States. Many neighborhood theaters have already closed, and others will probably follow. To be able to compete on the American market, French filmmakers have started shooting their films in English. While French filmmakers look to America for models, American filmmakers seem to look upon French models: the trend of remakes from French films has been established with movies such as *Cousins, Three Men and a Baby, Point of No Return,* and *Breathless.*

A. 1. *Voilà l'auteur dont les parents sont nos amis.* 2. *Ils habitent dans une ville dont j'ai oublié le nom.* 3. *C'est une histoire dont je t'ai déjà parlé.* 4. *C'est un film policier dont elle se souvient très bien.* 5. *Elle parle d'un nouveau film dont je ne connais pas le nom.*

B. 1. *lequel*   2. *à laquelle*   3. *auquel*   4. *auquel*   5. *laquelle*

C. 1. *auquel*   2. *que*   3. *dont*   4. *Ce qui*   5. *qui*

D. 1. *Elle n'aime que les films d'aventure.* 2. *Ils ne voient que des films américains.* 3. *On ne parle que de ce film.* 4. *Comme acteur, elle n'aime que Gérard Depardieu.* 5. *Le cinéma de notre quartier ne passe que des films doublés.*

E. 1. *Dans ce film, il s'agit des monuments de Paris.* 2. *De quoi s'agit-il?* 3. *Il s'agit de choisir une bonne école.* 4. *Dans son nouveau livre, il s'agit des acteurs de Hollywood.* 5. *S'agit-il d'argent?*

LEÇON 29

LE TOURISME. Tourism.

A. DIALOGUE

Un voyage féerique.

NATHALIE: **Alors, le Mont-Saint-Michel vous a plu?**

YVES: **C'était féerique. J'avais toujours rêvé de visiter ce site.**

NATHALIE: **Aviez-vous établi un itinéraire avant de partir?**

YVES: **Pas vraiment. Nous avons roulé un peu au hasard mais Deauville était une étape obligatoire car l'amie avec qui je voyageais adore les casinos.**

NATHALIE: **Ensuite, vous êtes retournés à Paris?**

YVES: **Oh non . . . Après avoir exploré la Normandie, nous avons décidé de mettre le cap sur la Bretagne.**

NATHALIE: **Il paraît que cette côte est magnifique.**

YVES: **Oui, des falaises spectaculaires et des kilomètres de rochers à escalader.**

NATHALIE: **J'en suis ravie, car nous avons l'intention d'y aller en septembre.**

YVES: **Je suis sûr que cette région va vous plaire. De plus, la cuisine est excellente. Vous pouvez faire une cure de crêpes et de cidre bouché.**

A Magical Trip.

NATHALIE: So, you enjoyed Mont-Saint-Michel?

YVES: It was magical. I had always dreamt of visiting that place.

NATHALIE: Had you mapped out an itinerary before going?

YVES: Not really. We drove around without a fixed destination, except that Deauville was a mandatory stop because the friend with whom I was traveling loves casinos.

NATHALIE: Then you went back to Paris?

YVES: Oh, no. After exploring Normandy, we decided to head for Brittany.

NATHALIE: I've heard the coast is splendid.

YVES: Yes, spectacular cliffs and miles of rocks for climbing.

NATHALIE: I am delighted because we intend to go there in September.

YVES: I am sure you'll enjoy that region. Moreover, the food is excellent. You can be on a diet of crepes and cider.

B. GRAMMAIRE ET USAGE

1. THE VERB *PLAIRE*

The verb *plaire* (to please, to enjoy) is an irregular verb.

PLAIRE   TO PLEASE, ENJOY

I please	*je plais*	we please	*nous plaisons*
you please	*tu plais*	you please	*vous plaisez*
he/she/one pleases	*il/elle/on plaît*	they please	*ils/elles plaisent*

Plaire uses the auxiliary *avoir* in the *passé composé: j'ai plu.*
To say that one merely likes something or someone, French often uses the verb *plaire.* The person who likes something or someone, becomes the indirect object. Literally, the verb *plaire* translates into "something or someone pleases."

Cette région plaît à Nathalie.
Nathalie likes this region. (Literally: This region pleases Nathalie.)

Le Mont-Saint-Michel t'a plu?
Did you like Mont-Saint-Michel?

Je suis sûr que ce château va te plaire.
I am sure you'll like this castle.

Elle fait ce qui lui plaît.
She does what she likes to do.

Le nouveau film de Claude Berri leur a beaucoup plu.
They really enjoyed Claude Berri's new film.

Ce nouvel acteur me plaît énormément.
I like this new actor very much.

Comment prononcez-vous ce mot, s'il vous plaît?
How do you pronounce this word, please?

b. As a reflexive verb, *se plaire* means "to enjoy being somewhere."

Il se plaît à Paris.
He enjoys living in Paris.

Je pense qu'il va se plaire ici.
I think he'll enjoy living here.

2. *APRÈS / AVANT* + INFINITIVE

a. French uses *avant* + *de* + present infinitive when English uses "before" + -ing form.

Aviez-vous fait des réservations avant de partir?
Did you make some reservations before leaving?

Avant de faire ce voyage, achetez un guide.
Before taking this trip, buy a guide book.

Avant d'aller en Normandie, achetez un parapluie.
Before going to Normandy, buy an umbrella.

Avant de vous coucher, lisez quelques pages de ce livre.
Before going to bed, read a few pages of this book.

b. French uses *après* followed by the past infinitive (*avoir* or *être*) + past participle of the verb to express "after" + the -ing form.

Après avoir exploré la Normandie, êtes-vous allé en Bretagne?
After exploring Normandy, did you go to Brittany?

The past participle used with *être* agrees in gender and number with the subject. If the verb is reflexive, don't forget the pronoun.

Elle s'est endormie après avoir lu le journal.
She fell asleep after reading the paper.

Après avoir mangé toutes ces crêpes, aviez-vous encore faim?
After eating all those crepes, were you still hungry?

Après être allés au Mont-Saint-Michel, nous avons suivi la côte.
After going to Mont-Saint-Michel, we followed the coast.

Après s'être arrêtés une heure, ils ont continué leur route.
After stopping an hour, they kept driving on.

3. THE PLUPERFECT

The *plus-que-parfait* (pluperfect) indicates a past action which happened before another past action started. For example, the English sentence, "I had finished my exercise when he arrived," would have to be translated into the pluperfect. To form the pluperfect, one uses the auxiliary *avoir* or *être* in the imperfect plus the past participle of the main verb.

273

I had called	*j'avais téléphoné*
you had called	*tu avais téléphoné*
he/she/one had called	*il/elle/on avait téléphoné*
we had called	*nous avions téléphoné*
you had called	*vous aviez téléphoné*
they had called	*ils/elles avaient téléphoné*

Nous avions établi un itinéraire avant de partir.
  We had mapped out our itinerary before leaving.

Elle n'avait pas fini son travail quand il est arrivé.
  She had not finished her work when he arrived.

Il s'est souvenu qu'il avait oublié l'anniversaire de sa soeur.
  He remembered he had forgotten his sister's birthday.

Il avait faim parce qu'il n'avait rien mangé pour le petit déjeuner.
  He was hungry because he had not eaten anything for breakfast.

Note: the pluperfect in English is not always used in the same way in French. In lesson 14, we saw expressions of continuity with *depuis* and the present tense. Let's look at a similar construction in the past. Compare the following two sentences and their translations.

Il roule depuis une heure sur cette route.
  He has been driving on this road for an hour.

Il roulait depuis une heure quand tout à coup il a vu la cathédrale.
  He had been driving for an hour when suddenly he saw the cathedral.

English uses the *plus-que-parfait* while French uses the *imparfait* when it refers to a continuing action in the past.

4. HASARD

Although the noun *hasard* bears a similar meaning to the word *hazard* in English, its more common usage is different.

Nous roulions au hasard.
  We were driving without a specific destination.

J'ai rencontré Yves dans la rue par hasard.
  I met Yves on the street by chance.

Quel hasard de vous rencontrer ici!
  What a coincidence meeting you here!

Elle ne laisse jamais rien au hasard.
    She never leaves anything to chance.

Savez-vous par hasard s'il est libre demain?
    Do you happen to know whether he is free tomorrow?

Si par hasard vous trouvez cet article, gardez-le-moi.
    If you happen to see that article, save it for me.

Ils détestent les jeux de hasard.
    They hate the games of chance.

VOCABULAIRE

le tourisme	tourism
le voyage	trip
l'agence de voyage *(f.)*	travel agency
établir un itinéraire	to map out an itinerary
un voyage organisé	a tour
le guide	guide, guidebook
le site	place
l'étape *(f.)*	stop-off
la région	region
la province	province
la côte	coast
le rocher	rock
la falaise	cliff
la grotte	grotto
la cave	cave
escalader	to climb
rêver	to dream
être ravi	to be delighted
visiter	to visit (a place)
explorer	to explore
la visite	visit
la visite guidée	guided tour
rendre visite à	to visit (a person)
raconter	to tell
pique-niquer	to have a picnic
avoir l'intention de	to intend to
se plaire	to enjoy being somewhere
féerique	magical
obligatoire	mandatory
faire une cure de	to take a cure of, to follow a regime of
le cidre	cider

retourner	to return to
rentrer	to come back/go back,
	to come home/go home
rouler	to drive
adorer	to love
paraître	to appear, to seem
mettre le cap	head for
au hasard	aimlessly
avant	before
après	after

EXERCICES

A. *Remplacer les phrases avec le verbe "plaire."*

MODÈLE: J'aime cette région.
      Cette région me plaît.

1. *J'aime les châteaux de la Loire.*
2. *Nous aimons le Mont-Saint-Michel.*
3. *Vous aimez la cuisine de cette région.*
4. *Elle aime Paris en mai.*
5. *J'ai beaucoup aimé la visite guidée.*

B. *Remplacer "avant de" par "après" dans les phrases suivantes.*

MODÈLE: Vous avez pris un chocolat chaud avant d'escalader les rochers.
      Vous avez pris un chocolat chaud après avoir escaladé les rochers.

1. *Elles sont allées au restaurant avant de visiter le château de Chambord.*
2. *Ils ont exploré l'Alsace avant d'aller dans les Alpes.*
3. *Elle a vu la maison de Balzac avant de retourner à Azay-le-Rideau.*
4. *Vous avez décidé de rester une semaine de plus avant de voir les Grottes de Lascaux.*
5. *Nous avons visité les caves avant de nous arrêter pour pique-niquer.*

C. *Mettre les verbes suivants au plus-que-parfait.*

MODÈLE: J'oublie mon passeport.
      J'avais oublié mon passeport.

1. *Nous voyageons en Normandie.*
2. *Vous racontez votre voyage à vos amis.*
3. *Nous partons en vacances.*
4. *Elle décide d'explorer les sites préhistoriques.*
5. *Je me lève très tôt.*

D. *Compléter les phrases avec le plus-que-parfait.*

MODÈLE: Ils _____ pendant des heures et ils étaient fatigués. (rouler)
   Ils avaient roulé pendant des heures et ils étaient fatigués.

1. *Nous _____ un itinéraire avant d'aller en Provence. (établir)*
2. *Je _____ mon projet quand mon patron m'en a donné un autre.
   (terminer)*
3. *Elle _____ déjà quand il a téléphoné. (partir)*
4. *Nous sommes retournés à l'hôtel parce qu'il _____ son appareil photo
   (oublier).*
5. *Nous _____ de dîner lorsqu'ils sont arrivés. (finir)*

NOTE CULTURELLE

Tourism is a major industry in France. Tourists from all over come to visit the
many beautiful regions of France. The regions of Normandy and Brittany are
very popular with foreign tourists. Quite a few British and American citizens
have acquired property such as renovated farms and barns in the area. The
Brittany coast, with its cliffs, is spectacular, and Mont-Saint-Michel is a must
any time of the year. Also, don't miss the fortress town of Saint-Malo.

With the tunnel between Great Britain and the Continent, the British have
no problem crossing the Channel to spend the weekend in their country home
in France.

LA CLÉ DES EXERCICES

A. 1. *Les châteaux de la Loire me plaisent.* 2. *Le Mont-Saint-Michel nous plaît.*
   3. *La cuisine de cette région vous plaît.* 4. *Paris en mai lui plaît.* 5. *La visite
   guidée m'a beaucoup plu.*
B. 1. *après avoir visité* 2. *après être allés* 3. *après être retournée* 4. *après
   avoir vu* 5. *après nous être arrêté(e)s*
C. 1. *Nous avions voyagé en Normandie.* 2. *Vous aviez raconté votre voyage à
   vos amis.* 3. *Nous étions partis en vacances.* 4. *Elle avait décidé d'explorer
   les sites préhistoriques.* 5. *Je m'étais levé(e) très tôt.*
D. 1. *avions établi* 2. *j'avais terminé* 3. *était déjà partie* 4. *avait oublié*
   5. *avions fini*

LEÇON 30
LES ARTICLES MÉNAGERS. Household Items.

A. DIALOGUE

Le bricolage.

JIM: Comme si ça ne suffisait pas de monter cinq étages à pied, en plus, je dois t'aider à faire du bricolage!

MARK: Je voudrais repeindre l'entrée et la cuisine, accrocher quelques affiches, et essayer de construire quelques étagères pour nos livres.

JIM: Jim, le roi du bricolage! Pourquoi investir tant d'énergie dans cet appartement? Tu as décidé de finir tes jours sous les toits de Paris?

MARK: Non, mais c'est plus agréable. Voyons . . . Il nous faut des clous, des crochets, un tournevis, de la colle . . . et un marteau, bien sûr!

JIM: Le propriétaire nous a dit de ne pas faire des trous dans les murs.

MARK: Ne t'inquiète pas. Je m'occupe de tout.

JIM: Tu plaisantes?

MARK: Non, non. Tu n'as qu'à passer un coup de balai, une fois les travaux finis.

Do-It-Yourself.

JIM: As if it were not enough to walk up five flights of stairs, I also have to help you tinker about!

MARK: I would like to repaint the foyer and the kitchen, hang a few posters, and try to build some shelves for our books.

JIM: Jim, the king of do-it-yourself! Why invest so much energy in this apartment? Have you decided to spend the rest of your life under the rooftops of Paris?

MARK: No, but it's more pleasant. Let's see. . . . We need nails, hooks, a screwdriver, some glue . . . and a hammer, of course.

JIM: The owner told us not to make holes in the walls.

MARK: Don't worry. I'll take care of everything.

JIM: You're kidding?

MARK: No, no. You'll only have to sweep when the job is done.

B. GRAMMAIRE ET USAGE

1. THE STRUCTURE VERB + PREPOSITIONS + INFINITIVE

As in English, some verbs may, and some verbs may not, be followed by a preposition. Very often, a verb which is followed by a preposition in English is not in French, and vice versa. Let's take a look at the following examples.

a. Let's look first at the case of a verb + no preposition + the infinitive. Many verbs do not require a preposition: *aimer* (to like, to love), *espérer* (to hope), *laisser* (to leave), *devoir* (to have to), *vouloir* (to want), *savoir* (to know), *pouvoir* (can), *faire* (to do, to make), *falloir* (to have to), *aller* (to go), *sembler* (to seem), and others.

J'espère trouver une étagère.
I hope to find a shelf.

Il faut acheter des clous.
We have to buy nails.

Je voudrais peindre le salon.
I'd like to paint the living room.

Nous allons passer un coup de balai.
We are going to sweep.

b. Now, let's look at a verb + the preposition *de* + the infinitive. Many verbs take the preposition *de*. Here are a few of them:

parler de: to talk about
décider de: to decide
dire de: to tell
s'inquiéter de: to worry
demander de: to ask
avoir envie de: to feel like

essayer de: to try
s'occuper de: to take care
avoir peur de: to fear
s'arrêter de: to stop
oublier de: to forget
finir de: to finish

Je m'occupe de tout.
I am taking care of everything.

Il essaie de rénover la maison.
He is trying to renovate the house.

Elle a décidé de faire un voyage.
She decided to take a trip.

Je lui ai demandé de m'aider.
I asked him to help me.

c. Finally, let's look at a verb + the preposition *à* + the infinitive.
A long list of verbs requires *à* before an infinitive.

commencer à: to start	*aider à:* to help
avoir à: to have to	*apprendre à:* to learn
s'habituer à: to get used to	*arriver à:* to manage
inviter à: to invite	*hésiter à:* to hesitate
s'attendre à: to expect	*encourager à:* to encourage
enseigner à: to teach	*réussir à:* to succeed

Tu dois m'aider à peindre.
You have to help me paint.

Elle apprend à conduire.
She is learning how to drive.

Il commence à s'inquiéter.
He is starting to get worried.

Vous hésitez à les appeler.
You hesitate to call them.

2. TELLING OR ASKING SOMEONE TO DO SOMETHING

a. To tell someone to do something, French uses the verb + the indirect object + *de* + the infinitive.

Madame Marti me dit d'acheter un tournevis.
Mrs. Marti tells me to buy a screwdriver.

Elle a dit à Robert de lui donner son numéro.
She told Robert to give her his number.

Il leur demande de trouver un marteau.
He asks them to find a hammer.

Nous avons demandé à nos parents de venir.
We asked our parents to come.

Elle a décidé de leur poser des questions.
She decided to ask them questions.

Dites-leur de ne pas mettre trop de colle.
Tell them not to put on too much glue.

b. To tell someone not to do something, French uses the negative infinitive. Both parts of the negation (*ne . . . pas, ne . . . rien, ne . . . jamais,* etc.) are placed before the infinitive.

Le propriétaire lui dit de peindre la cuisine en bleu.
The owner tells him to paint the kitchen blue.

Le propriétaire lui dit de ne pas peindre la cuisine en bleu.
The owner tells him not to paint the kitchen blue.

Let's look at other examples.

Il nous a dit de ne pas faire de bruit.
He told us not to make any noise.

Nous lui avons dit de ne pas s'inquiéter.
We told him not to worry.

Vous leur avez demandé de ne jamais téléphoner après minuit.
You told them never to call after midnight.

Il a peur de ne rien comprendre à la conférence.
He is afraid of understanding nothing at the conference.

Ils ont décidé de ne plus voyager en été.
They decided to no longer travel during the summer.

   c. Strict commands (as can be found on prohibitory signs, for example) are expressed with a straight infinitive.

Ne pas fumer dans les toilettes.
No smoking in the rest rooms.

Ne pas marcher sur la pelouse.
Keep off the grass.

3. INDEFINITE PRONOUNS

Indefinite pronouns refer to no one or nothing in particular, as in "someone" or "something" in English. The indefinite pronouns in French are *quelqu'un* (someone, somebody), *quelque chose de* + adjective (something), *quelques-uns, quelques-unes* (some), *un/une autre* (another), *plusieurs* (several), *certains . . . d'autres* (some . . . others), *chacun* (each), *quelque part* (somewhere), *aucun . . . ne* (not one, none), *ne . . . nulle part* (nowhere), *n'importe quoi* (anything), *n'importe qui* (anyone), and *n'importe où* (anywhere).

Here are a few example sentences.

Quelqu'un t'a téléphoné.
Somebody called you.

Il y a quelque chose de nouveau.
There is something new.

Quelques-unes de mes amies sont en France.
Some of my friends are in France.

Il faut une lampe pour l'entrée et une autre pour le salon.
We need a lamp for the foyer and another one for the living room.

Plusieurs étagères sont tombées.
Several shelves fell.

Certains aiment le bricolage, d'autres le détestent.
Some like to tinker about the house, others hate it.

Certaines femmes détestent le bricolage. (feminine)
Some women hate to tinker about the house.

Chacun à son goût.
To each his own.

On va trouver des articles ménagers quelque part.
We'll find household products somewhere.

Aucune quincaillerie n'est ouverte le dimanche dans ce village.
No hardware store is open in this town on Sundays.

Je ne les vois nulle part.
I don't see them anywhere.

Il fait n'importe quoi pour gagner de l'argent.
He does anything to make money.

N'importe qui peut le faire.
Anyone can do it.

Tu ne peux pas faire des trous n'importe où.
You can't make holes anywhere.

4. *-EINDRE* AND *-AINDRE* VERBS

The verbs ending in *-eindre* or *-aindre* like *peindre* (to paint), *teindre* (to dye), *craindre* (to fear), *feindre* (to feign) have an irregular conjugation.

PEINDRE   TO PAINT

I paint	*je peins*	we paint	*nous peignons*
you paint	*tu peins*	you paint	*vous peignez*
he/she/one paints	*il/elle/on peint*	they paint	*ils/elles peignent*

CRAINDRE   TO FEAR

I fear	*je crains*	we fear	*nous craignons*
you fear	*tu crains*	you fear	*vous craignez*
he/she/one fears	*il/elle/on craint*	they fear	*ils/elles craignent*

Ils peignent leur chambre à coucher.
They're painting their bedroom.

Gauguin a peint à Tahiti.
Gauguin painted in Tahiti.

Nous craignons le froid.
We fear the cold.

Vous ne craignez pas le danger.
You don't fear danger.

Elle s'est teint les cheveux.
She dyed her hair.

Ce bois se teint difficilement.
This wood is hard to stain.

Il feint de dormir.
He pretends he is sleeping.

Ils feignent de ne pas nous entendre.
They feign not to hear us.

VOCABULAIRE

la quincaillerie	hardware store
faire des achats	to shop, to make purchases
faire du bricolage	to tinker (around the house)
les articles ménagers	household items, things for the home
repeindre	to repaint
craindre	to fear
l'entrée	foyer
accrocher	to hang
l'affiche *(f.)*	poster
construire	to build
l'étagère *(f.)*	bookshelf
investir	to invest
l'énergie *(f.)*	energy
le toit	roof
le clou	nail
le crochet	hook
la vis	screw
le tournevis	screwdriver
la colle	glue
le marteau	hammer
le propriétaire	owner, landlord
un trou	hole

le mur	wall
passer un coup de balai	to sweep
s'occuper	to take care of
suffir	to be enough
aider à	to help
décider de	to decide
le roi	the king
quelques	some, a few
plusieurs	several
à pied	on foot
certain	some, certain
chaque	each
chacun, chacune	each one
quelqu'un	someone
quelque chose	something
quelque part	somewhere
ne . . . nulle part	nowhere

EXERCICES

A. 1. *Compléter les phrases avec la préposition qui convient.*

MODÈLE: Il faut _____ payer le loyer le premier du mois.
Il faut payer le loyer le premier du mois.

1. *Yves a réussi _____ construire l'étagère.*
2. *Nous avons décidé _____ repeindre la cuisine.*
3. *Il espère _____ trouver un nouvel appartement.*
4. *Ils s'habituent _____ monter cinq étages à pied.*
5. *Nous avons envie _____ accrocher de nouvelles affiches.*
6. *N'oublions pas _____ acheter du papier.*
7. *Il m'aide _____ faire les courses.*
8. *Vous devez _____ demander la permission au propriétaire.*
9. *Elle essaie _____ faire du bricolage.*
10. *Tu veux _____ aller à la quincaillerie samedi matin?*

B. *Mettre les verbes à l'infinitif à la forme négative.*

MODÈLE: Dis-lui de venir à huit heures.
Dis lui de ne pas venir à huit heures.

1. *Je lui dis d'acheter un autre marteau. (ne . . . jamais)*
2. *Dites-leur de venir voir l'appartement avant dix-huit heures. (ne . . . pas)*
3. *Demande-moi de le faire! (ne . . . pas)*

4. *Il a décidé de peindre l'entrée. (ne . . . pas)*
5. *Je lui demande de me téléphoner après onze heures. (ne . . . jamais)*
6. *Dis-leur d'accrocher des posters au mur. (ne . . . plus)*
7. *Je lui demande de passer un coup de balai dans la cuisine. (ne . . . pas)*
8. *Vous avez décidé de fumer. (ne . . . plus)*

C. *Répondre à l'affirmative.*

MODÈLE: *Vous n'avez vu personne?*
           Si, j'ai vu quelqu'un.

1. *Vous n'avez rien acheté?*
2. *Il n'a cherché nulle part?*
3. *Personne n'est venu?*
4. *Il n'y a rien de nouveau?*
5. *Tu ne prends rien?*

D. *Conjuguer les verbes suivants.*

1. *Vous (peindre) votre salle de bain.*
2. *Ne (craindre) rien!*
3. *Il (feindre) de ne rien comprendre.*
4. *Ils (repeindre) les murs.*
5. *Tu (se teindre) en blonde?*

NOTE CULTURELLE

The best places to find dinnerware, lamps, cooking utensils, and electronic kitchen tools are the so-called *grands magasins.* For items such as nails, glue, and paint, go to the hardware store *(la quincaillerie),* which can be found in every neighborhood. On the outskirts of most cities, there are big garden and tool supermarkets as well as do-it-yourself shopping malls.

LA CLÉ DES EXERCICES

A. 1. *à* 2. *de* 3. no preposition 4. *à* 5. *d'* 6. *d'* 7. *à* 8. no preposition 9. *de* 10. no preposition
B. 1. *de ne jamais acheter* 2. *de ne pas venir voir* 3. *de ne pas le faire* 4. *de ne pas peindre* 5. *de ne jamais me téléphoner* 6. *de ne plus accrocher* 7. *de ne pas passer* 8. *de ne plus fumer*
C. 1. *Si, j'ai acheté quelque chose.* 2. *Si, il a cherché quelque part.* 3. *Si, quelqu'un est venu.* 4. *Si, il y a quelque chose de nouveau.* 5. *Si, je prends quelque chose.*
D. 1. *peignez* 2. *crains/craignez* 3. *feint* 4. *repeignent* 5. *te teins*

A. *Compléter les phrases avec le pronom relatif qui convient.*

MODÈLE: *L'appartement _____ nous avons acheté est au cinquième étage.*
L'appartement que nous avons acheté est au cinquième étage.

1. *Il s'agit d'un jeune homme _____ est artiste.*
2. *Voici les livres _____ j'ai lus.*
3. *C'est la dent _____ me fait mal.*
4. *Voici l'ami avec _____ je suis allé à Paris.*
5. *Au moment _____ je suis entré, il s'est levé.*
6. *C'est le film _____ Amélie m'a parlé.*
7. *La compagnie pour _____ il travaille est suisse.*
8. *Je ne sais pas _____ il veut faire.*
9. *Les amis chez _____ nous avons passé le week-end, sont charmants.*
10. *Le voyage _____ nous avons fait en Normandie était merveilleux.*

B. *Refaire les phrases en utilisant "ne . . . que."*

MODÈLE: *Il voyage en été.*
Il ne voyage qu'en été.

1. *Elle aime les films étrangers.*
2. *Nous allons voyager en Bretagne.*
3. *Ils accrochent trois affiches.*
4. *Le dentiste arrache une dent.*
5. *Tu manges des crêpes pour le déjeuner?*

C. *Compléter les verbes avec une préposition quand c'est nécessaire.*

MODÈLE: *Il a dit à ses amis _____ venir en Normandie cet été.*
Il a dit à ses amis de venir en Normandie cet été.

1. *J'ai essayé _____ te téléphoner.*
2. *Nous avons peur _____ arriver en retard.*
3. *Ils s'habituent _____ vivre dans une petite ville.*
4. *Nous allons commencer _____ travailler demain.*
5. *J'ai déjà fini _____ accrocher les photos.*
6. *Ils refusent _____ y aller.*
7. *J'ai décidé _____ investir dans cette compagnie.*
8. *Elle veut _____ aller chez le coiffeur cet après-midi.*
9. *Nous avons envie _____ suivre cet itinéraire.*
10. *Pouvez-vous _____ recommander une bonne crêperie?*

D. *Conjuguez le verbe "voir" au temps indiqué.*

1. *Nous . . . beaucoup de films. (présent)*
2. *Il . . . ses amis pendant le week-end. (passé composé)*
3. *Tu . . . les falaises? (présent)*

286

4. *Je . . . mon dentiste cet après-midi. (futur immédiat)*
5. *Vous . . . le dernier film de Claude Berri? (passé composé)*

E. *Remplacer "avant" par "après."*

MODÈLE: *Elle finit la lettre avant de téléphoner.*
Elle finit la lettre après avoir téléphoné.

1. *Il répond avant de réfléchir.*
2. *Ils commencent à travailler avant de lire le journal.*
3. *Nous avons accroché des affiches avant de construire des étagères.*
4. *Vous êtes allés au casino avant de visiter le château.*
5. *J'ai établi mon itinéraire avant de réserver mon billet de train.*
6. *Tu es retourné à Deauville avant de descendre sur la Côte d'Azur.*
7. *Elle a mis le cap sur la Provence avant d'explorer le Massif Central.*
8. *Nous nous sommes repeignés avant de sortir.*
9. *Tu as fait des achats avant d'aller au cinéma.*
10. *Ils ont dîné au restaurant avant d'aller au cinéma.*

F. *Conjuguer les verbes suivants au présent.*

1. *Nous (peindre) notre nouvel appartement.*
2. *Cette région me (plaire) beaucoup.*
3. *Le dentiste me (faire) mal.*
4. *Il (craindre) la réaction du propriétaire.*
5. *Elle se (teindre) les cheveux?*

LA CLÉ DES EXERCICES

A. 1. *qui* 2. *que* 3. *qui* 4. *qui/lequel* 5. *où* 6. *dont* 7. *laquelle*
8. *ce qu'* 9. *qui* 10. *que*
B. 1. *Elle n'aime que les films étrangers.* 2. *Nous n'allons voyager qu'en Bretagne.* 3. *Ils n'accrochent que trois affiches.* 4. *Le dentiste n'arrache qu'une dent.* 5. *Tu ne manges que des crêpes pour le déjeuner?*
C. 1. *de* 2. *d'* 3. *à* 4. *à* 5. *d'* 6. *d'* 7. *d'* 8. no preposition
9. *de* 10. no preposition
D. 1. *voyons* 2. *a vu* 3. *vois* 4. *vais voir* 5. *avez vu*
E. 1. *après avoir réfléchi* 2. *après avoir lu* 3. *après avoir construit* 4. *après avoir visité* 5. *après avoir réservé* 6. *après être descendu* 7. *après avoir exploré* 8. *après être sortis* 9. *après être allé* 10. *après être allés*
F. 1. *peignons* 2. *plaît* 3. *fait* 4. *craint* 5. *teint*

LECTURE

LE CYCLISME [1] ET LE TOUR DE FRANCE

Le Tour de France est l'un des événements [2] les plus prestigieux du monde de cyclisme. L'enthousiasme des spectateurs [3] est sans pareil. [4] Bien avant l'arrivée [5] des cyclistes, la foule [6] s'assemble le long des rues avec anticipation. La plupart [7] s'installent [8] sur leurs chaises pliantes [9] en attendant leur passage. Mais les chaises sont vite oubliées [10] quand ils apprennent que l'équipe approche. [11] Tous se lèvent [12] pour voir les cyclistes en tête du peloton et applaudissent [13] lorsque [14] les cyclistes passent [15] à toute vitesse [16] à la poursuite de la victoire. [17] Évidemment, [18] la meilleure place est à l'arrivée, puisque [19] c'est là que les victoires sont célébrées et les pertes [20] sont lamentées.

VOCABULAIRE

1.	*le cyclisme*	cycling
2.	*l'événement*	event
3.	*le spectateur*	viewer
4.	*sans pareil*	without comparison
5.	*l'arrivée*	arrival
6.	*la foule*	crowd
7.	*la plupart*	most
8.	*s'installer*	to settle, to sit
9.	*la chaise pliante*	folding chair
10.	*oublier*	to forget
11.	*approcher*	to near
12.	*se lever*	to get up
13.	*applaudir*	to applaud
14.	*lorsque*	when
15.	*passer*	to pass by
16.	*à toute vitesse*	full speed
17.	*la victoire*	victory
18.	*évidemment*	obviously
19.	*puisque*	since
20.	*la perte*	loss

LEÇON 31
À L'AÉROPORT. At the Airport.

A. DIALOGUE

L'enregistrement des bagages.

EMPLOYÉE: **Vous enregistrez ces deux valises et ce sac, Monsieur?**

YANNICK: **Seulement les valises. Je voudrais garder ce sac comme bagage à main.**

EMPLOYÉE: **Voici vos deux cartes d'embarquement.**

YANNICK: **Deux cartes d'embarquement? Je croyais que c'était un vol sans escale.**

EMPLOYÉE: **Non, votre vol partira à 13h30 h à destination de Miami.**

YANNICK: **On passe par Miami?**

EMPLOYÉE: **Oui. Et quand vous arriverez en Floride à 17h20, vous aurez une correspondance pour Pointe-à-Pitre à 18h35.**

YANNICK: **Et si le vol a du retard?**

EMPLOYÉE: **Dès que vous serez arrivé à Miami, vous irez au comptoir d'Air France où nos hôtesses d'accueil seront à votre disposition.**

YANNICK: **A quelle heure est-ce que nous atterrirons à la Guadeloupe?**

EMPLOYÉE: **A 23 h. Votre vol part de la porte 36. L'embarquement des passagers commencera dans une heure. Bon voyage!**

Check-in.

EMPLOYEE: You're checking these two suitcases and this bag, sir?

YANNICK: Only the suitcases. I'd like to keep this bag as a carry-on.

EMPLOYEE: Here are your two boarding passes.

YANNICK: Two boarding passes? I thought it was a nonstop flight.

EMPLOYEE: No, your flight leaves for Miami at 1:30 P.M.

YANNICK: We're going through Miami?

EMPLOYEE: Yes. And when you arrive in Florida at 5:20 P.M., you have a connecting flight for Pointe-à-Pitre at 6:35 P.M.

YANNICK: What if the flight is late?

EMPLOYEE: As soon as you arrive in Miami, go to the Air France counter, where our hostesses will be available.

YANNICK: At what time do we land in Guadeloupe?

EMPLOYEE: At 11 P.M. Your flight leaves from gate 36. The passengers will start boarding in an hour. Have a good trip.

B. GRAMMAIRE ET USAGE

1. THE FUTURE TENSE

We have seen the immediate future with *aller* + the infinitive in lesson 6. Another way of expressing future events is with the proper future tense.

a. To form the future of regular verbs, add the future endings to the infinitive.

ARRIVER TO ARRIVE

I will arrive	*j'arriverai*	we will arrive	*nous arriverons*
you will arrive	*tu arriveras*	you will arrive	*vous arriverez*
he/she/one will arrive	*il/elle/on arrivera*	they will arrive	*ils/elles arriveront*

L'avion arrivera à 21 h.
The plane will arrive at 9 P.M.

Ils arriveront le 15 juillet.
They'll arrive on July 15.

b. When a verb ends in *re*, the *e* is dropped before the ending is added.

ATTENDRE TO WAIT

I will wait	*j'attendrai*	we will wait	*nous attendrons*
you will wait	*tu attendras*	you will wait	*vous attendrez*
he/she/one will wait	*il/elle/on attendra*	they will wait	*ils/elles attendront*

Nous attendrons ton arrivée.
We will wait for your arrival.

Jusqu'à quelle heure nous attendra-t-il?
Up to what time will he wait for us?

c. The *-er* verbs with spelling changes follow various patterns in the future tense.

-É + CONSONANT + *ER:*

je préférerai	I will prefer
ils répéteront (ré-pé-tron)	they will repeat

-E + CONSONANT + *ER:*
these verbs change *e* _____ *è*.

j'achèterai (ja-shè-tré)	I will buy
nous nous lèverons (lè-vron)	we will get up

APPELER and *JETER:*
these verbs double the consonant.

j'appellerai (ja-pèl-ré)	I will call
je jetterai (je-jet-ré)	I will throw

- VOWEL + *Y* + *ER:*
these verbs change *y* to *i* in front of a mute *e*.

je paierai	I will pay
nous essaierons	we will try
ils emploieront	they will use

d. Many irregular verbs in the present tense are regular in the future.

boire	*je boirai*	I will drink
conduire	*je conduirai*	I will drive
connaître	*je connaîtrai*	I will know
dire	*je dirai*	I will say
écrire	*j'écrirai*	I will write
lire	*je lirai*	I will read
mettre	*je mettrai*	I will put
ouvrir	*j'ouvrirai*	I will open
plaire	*je plairai*	I will please
prendre	*je prendrai*	I will take
suivre	*je suivrai*	I will follow

Vous garderez votre carte d'embarquement.
You'll keep your boarding pass.

Tu prendras le vol de 17 heures.
You'll take the 5 P.M. flight.

e. A large number of verbs have an irregular future stem which needs to be memorized.

INFINITIVE		FUTURE STEM	FUTURE	
aller	to go	*ir-*	*j'irai*	I will go
avoir	to have	*aur-*	*j'aurai*	I will have
courir	to run	*courr-*	*je courrai*	I will run
devoir	to have to	*devr-*	*je devrai*	I will have to
être	to be	*ser-*	*je serai*	I will be
envoyer	to send	*enverr-*	*j'enverrai*	I will send
faire	to do	*fer-*	*je ferai*	I will do
failoir	must	*faudr-*	*il faudra*	it will be necessary
mourir	to die	*mourr-*	*il mourra*	he will die
pleuvoir	to rain	*pleuvr-*	*il pleuvra*	it will rain
pouvoir	to be able	*pourr-*	*je pourrai*	I will be able
recevoir	to receive	*recevr-*	*je recevrai*	I will receive
savoir	to know	*saur-*	*je saurai*	I will know
tenir	to hold	*tiendr-*	*je tiendrai*	I will hold
venir	to come	*viendr-*	*je viendrai*	I will come
voir	to see	*verr-*	*je verrai*	I will see
vouloir	to want	*voudr-*	*je voudrai*	I will want

Ils viendront demain.
They'll come tomorrow.

Il faudra confirmer votre vol.
You'll have to confirm your flight.

Il y aura une correspondance.
There will be a connecting flight.

2. CONJUNCTIONS WITH THE FUTURE TENSE

In French, the future is used after *quand* (when), *lorsque* (when), *dès que*, *aussitôt que* (as soon as), *tant que* (as long as), where the present tense is used in English.

Quand vous arriverez en Floride, nous serons là pour vous accueillir.
When you arrive in Florida, we'll be there to welcome you.

Tant qu'il fera beau, nous resterons à la campagne.
As long as the weather is nice, we'll stay in the country.

Lorsque nous parlerons français, nous irons en France.
When we can speak French, we'll go to France.

Je vous téléphonerai dès que je saurai la date.
I will call you as soon as I know the date.

3. THE *FUTUR ANTÉRIEUR*

The *futur antérieur* (future perfect) describes an action which will have taken place before another future action. To form this compound tense, use the auxiliary *avoir* or *être* in the future plus the past participle.

TRAVAILLER TO WORK

I will have worked	*j'aurai travaillé*
you will have worked	*tu auras travaillé*
he/she/one will have worked	*il/elle/on aura travaillé*
we will have worked	*nous aurons travaillé*
you will have worked	*vous aurez travaillé*
they will have worked	*ils/elles auront travaillé*

As with the *passé composé,* the past participle agrees with the subject of the verb for reflexive verbs and verbs that use *être* as an auxiliary.

PARTIR TO LEAVE

I will have left	*je serai parti(e)*
you will have left	*tu seras parti(e)*
he/she/one will have left	*il/elle/on sera parti(e)*
we will have left	*nous serons parti(e)s*
you will have left	*vous serez parti(e)s*
they will have left	*ils/elles seront parti(e)s*

Dès que vous serez arrivé, allez au comptoir Air France.
As soon as you arrive, go to the Air France counter.

Quand vous aurez enregistré vos bagages, nous irons prendre un café.
When you have checked your luggage, we'll go for a cup of coffee.

Aussitôt qu'elle sera partie, appelez-moi.
As soon as she has left, call me.

4. THE VERB *PASSER*

a. *Passer* has many different uses in French. It can mean: to spend time, to take an exam, to hand something over, to make a call, etc. It is conjugated with *avoir* in the past tenses.

J'ai passé deux mois en Alsace.
I spent two months in Alsace.

Il a passé un examen lundi dernier.
He took an exam last Monday.

Passez-lui un coup de fil ce soir.
Give him a call tonight.

Qu'est-ce qu'on passe à la télé ce soir?
What's on TV tonight?

    b. *Passer* + a preposition takes on a different meaning and is conjugated with the auxiliary *être*.

Est-ce que nous passons par Lyon?
Are we going through Lyon?

Je suis passée devant le théâtre.
I walked past the theater.

Par où êtes-vous passé?
Which way did you go?

Nous sommes tous passés par là.
We've all been through it.

Il passe pour un séducteur.
He is regarded by his friends as a seducer.

Je passe sur les détails.
I'll skip the details.

VOCABULAIRE

l'aéroport *(m.)*	airport
la compagnie aérienne	airline
le comptoir	counter
le passager, la passagère	passenger
se présenter à l'enregistrement *(m.)*	to check in
être enregistré	to be checked in
faire enregistrer ses bagages *(m. pl.)*	to check one's luggage
le passeport	passport
le vol	flight
l'escale *(m.)*	stop-over
la porte	gate
l'avion *(m.)*	airplane

l'embarquement *(m.)*	boarding
la carte d'embarquement	boarding pass
monter à bord de l'avion	to board the plane
le siège	seat
le pilote	pilot
l'hôtesse *(de l'air) (f.)*	stewardess, flight attendant
le steward	steward
le personnel d'accueil	ground staff
attacher sa ceinture de sécurité	to fasten one's seat belt
les bagages *(m.pl.)*	luggage
le bagage à main	hand luggage
la valise	suitcase
le sac	bag
s'envoler	to fly off
atterrir	to land
la destination	destination
descendre d'avion	to deplane
passer la douane	to go through customs
la correspondance	connecting flight
confirmer	to confirm
passer par	to go through (a place)
prêt	ready
quand	when
lorsque	when
aussitôt que	as soon as
dès que	as soon as
sans	without

EXERCICES

A. *Remplacer le futur immédiat par le futur.*

MODÈLE: *Elle va attendre la correspondance.*
Elle attendra la correspondance.

1. *Je vais acheter un billet d'avion.*
2. *Nous allons arriver dans une semaine.*
3. *Ils vont repartir à la fin du mois.*
4. *Vous allez prendre l'avion le 12 novembre.*
5. *Tu ne vas pas regarder le programme.*

B. *Mettre les verbes au futur.*

MODÈLE: *Il est ravi de son voyage.*
Il sera ravi de son voyage.

1. *Cette province me plaît.*
2. *Nous suivons les directions*
3. *Ils boivent une tasse de café.*
4. *Elle va à la Guadeloupe le mois prochain.*
5. *Nous pouvons nous arrêter dans cette région.*
6. *Ils voient de très beaux châteaux.*
7. *Tu sais la nouvelle.*
8. *Vous faîtes un voyage en Floride.*
9. *Ils atterrissent dans un petit aéroport.*
10. *Vous recevez des brochures magnifiques.*

C. *Compléter avec le temps qui convient.*

MODÈLE: *Il se reposera quand il (aller) en vacances.*
Il se reposera quand il ira en vacances.

1. *Nous nagerons tous les jours quand nous (être) en Guadeloupe.*
2. *Ils resteront en Normandie tant qu'il y (avoir) du soleil.*
3. *J'irai en Italie lorsque je (parler) couramment l'italien.*
4. *Il prendra des vacances la semaine prochaine parce qu'il (être) fatigué.*
5. *Nous partirons dès que je (recevoir) mon passeport.*

D. *Mettre les verbes au futur antérieur.*

1. *Allez au comptoir quand vous (récupérer) vos bagages.*
2. *Présentez-vous à l'enregistrement dès que vous (arriver) à l'aéroport.*
3. *Je te donnerai mon livre aussitôt que je (finir) de le lire.*
4. *Ils passeront vous dire bonjour dès qu'ils (rentrer) de vacances.*
5. *Je vous appellerai aussitôt que je (enregistrer) mes bagages.*

E. *Mettre les phrases suivantes au passé composé.*

MODÈLE: *Nous passerons un examen en juin.*
Nous avons passé un examen en juin.

1. *Je passe un coup de fil à Yannick.*
2. *Nous passons deux semaines de vacances au Maroc.*
3. *Par où passez-vous pour aller à Perpignan?*
4. *Tu passeras un examen?*
5. *Vous passerez probablement devant une très vieille église.*

NOTE CULTURELLE

There are two French airlines, which are both state-owned: Air France, which services worldwide routes, and Air Inter, which services France only. Paris has two airports: Roissy Charles de Gaulle and Orly. Roissy Charles de Gaulle, located 30 miles north of Paris, is the hub for flights from northern Europe, America and the East. At Roissy you can catch a bus or a train to the center of Paris. Orly, located south of Paris, is a smaller airport, servicing most flights to and from southern Europe.

LA CLÉ DES EXERCICES

A. 1. *j'achèterai* 2. *nous arriverons* 3. *ils repartiront* 4. *vous prendrez*
   5. *tu ne regarderas pas*
B. 1. *plaira* 2. *suivrons* 3. *boiront* 4. *ira* 5. *pourrons* 6. *verront*
   7. *sauras* 8. *ferez* 9. *atterriront* 10. *recevrez*
C. 1. *serons* 2. *aura* 3. *parlerai* 4. *est* 5. *recevrai*
D. 1. *aurez récupéré* 2. *serez arrivé(e)(s)* 3. *j'aurai fini* 4. *seront rentrés*
   5. *j'aurai enregistré*
E. 1. *j'ai passé* 2. *nous avons passé* 3. *êtes-vous passé* 4. *tu as passé*
   5. *Vous êtes passé*

LEÇON 32
AU MUSÉE. At the Museum.

A. DIALOGUE

L'exposition.

PIERRE-HENRI: **Tu as de la chance d'être à Paris en ce moment. Le musée a réuni tous les chefs-d'œuvre de Degas pour cette exposition.**

BÉATRICE: **Vraiment?**

PIERRE-HENRI: **Oui, les tableaux d'Orsay et de nombreuses toiles provenant[1] de collections privées.**

GUIDE: **Une visite guidée commence à quatorze heures précises.**

PIERRE-HENRI: **Ça t'intéresse?**

BÉATRICE: **Non, c'est toi mon guide aujourd'hui.**

PIERRE-HENRI: **Si je devais changer de carrière, je ferais des études pour être conservateur.**

BÉATRICE: **Ce serait merveilleux d'être entouré d'objets d'art toute la journée. Moi, si je recommençais à zéro, je serais sculpteur.**

PIERRE-HENRI: **Peut-être deviendrais-tu la nouvelle Camille Claudel.**

BÉATRICE: **Alors, on commence par les sculptures?**

PIERRE-HENRI: **D'accord. Ça me ferait plaisir de te montrer les gravures au troisième et de t'inviter à déjeuner.**

BÉATRICE: **Qui pourrait refuser une telle offre?**

The Exhibit.

PIERRE-HENRI: You're lucky to be in Paris at this time of the year. The museum has gathered all the Degas masterpieces for this exhibition.

BÉATRICE: Really?

PIERRE-HENRI: Yes, paintings from the Orsay Museum and many works from private collections.

GUIDE: A guided tour will start at 2 P.M. sharp.

PIERRE-HENRI: Are you interested?

[1] The present participle will be dealt with in *Leçon* 34.

298

BÉATRICE: No, you're my guide today.

PIERRE-HENRI: If I had to change careers, I'd study to be a curator.

BÉATRICE: It would be wonderful to be surrounded with works of art all day long. If I were to start all over again, I would be a sculptor.

PIERRE-HENRI: Maybe you'd become the new Camille Claudel.

BÉATRICE: So, we'll start with the sculptures?

PIERRE-HENRI: Okay. I would enjoy showing you the etchings on the third floor and treating you to lunch.

BÉATRICE: Who could refuse such an offer?

B. GRAMMAIRE ET USAGE

1. THE PRESENT CONDITIONAL TENSE

a. The present conditional is formed by adding the endings of the imperfect to the future stem of a verb. Remember that for the verbs that are regular in the future, the stem is the infinitive.

PRESENT	FUTURE	PRESENT CONDITIONAL
je vais	*j'irai* (will go)	*j'irais* (would go)
je regarde	*je regarderai*	*je regarderais*
je deviens	*je deviendrai*	*je deviendrais*

AIMER   TO LOVE, TO LIKE

I would like	*j'aimerais*	we would like	*nous aimerions*
you would like	*tu aimerais*	you would like	*vous aimeriez*
he/she/one would like	*il/elle/on aimerait*	they would like	*ils/elles aimeraient*

b. The present conditional is often used to make a polite request.

J'aimerais voir la Joconde.
I would like to see the Mona Lisa.

Pourriez-vous nous aider?
Could you help us?

Il voudrait visiter le musée.
He would like to visit the museum.

Cela me ferait très plaisir.
I would be delighted.

The conditional is also used to express a suggestion, an obligation or duty.

Tu devrais voir cette exposition.
You should see this exhibit.

Vous devriez venir nous voir.
You should come and see us.

Nous devrions lui passer un coup de fil.
We should call him.

Elle ne devrait pas refuser une telle offre.
She should not turn down such an offer.

The present conditional is used in conditional sentences after clauses introduced by *si* (if) to express hypothetical situations.

Si j'avais le temps, j'irais au musée.
If I had the time, I would go to the museum.

If the main clause is the conditional tense, the *si* clause is in the imperfect.

Si je recommençais à zéro, je serais archéologue.
If I started from scratch, I would be an archeologist.

S'il était moins occupé, il irait au musée plus souvent.
If he were less busy, he would go to the museum more often.

Si tu changeais de carrière, qu'est-ce que tu ferais?
If you changed careers, what would you do?

c. In conditional sentences in French, certain tenses are combined with other tenses.

si + present + present

S'il pleut, je reste à la maison.
If it rains, I'm staying home.

si + present + future
Si on a de la chance, il y aura encore des billets.
If we're lucky, there'll still be some tickets.

si + present + present conditional
Si tu veux, on pourrait aller au Musée Pompidou.
If you want, we could go to the Pompidou Museum.

2. *SI* IN IDIOMATIC EXPRESSIONS

We learned in lesson 23 that if you want to suggest something, you can use *si* + *on* + imperfect.

Si on allait au musée?
What about going to the museum?

Si on l'invitait à déjeuner?
What about inviting him for lunch?

Similarly, if you want to express longing, use *si seulement* + imperfect:

Si seulement nous avions des billets!
If only we had tickets!

Si seulement je savais peindre!
If only I could paint!

Si seulement on pouvait voir cette exposition!
If only we could see this exhibit!

Si seulement il était venu!
If only he had come!

3. *FAIRE PLAISIR*

Faire plaisir[2] (to delight, to like) expresses the idea of liking, being delighted to do or get something.

Cela me fait plaisir de vous revoir.
I am happy to see you again.

Cela m'a fait plaisir de vous rencontrer.
I am pleased to have met you.

Cela me fera plaisir de faire leur connaissance.
I'll be delighted to meet them.

Cela lui ferait plaisir de vous montrer ses aquarelles.
He would be delighted to show you his watercolors.

Votre cadeau m'a fait très plaisir.
I liked your gift very much.

Qu'est-ce qui vous ferait plaisir pour votre anniversaire?
What would you like for your birthday?

4. PROFESSIONS

When describing someone's profession, no indefinite article is used.

Je serais sculpteur.
I would be a sculptor.

---

[2] Compare the usage of *plaire* in *Leçon* 29.

Il est pianiste.
He is a pianist.

Elle est conservateur.
She is a curator.

Yet, if you use an adjective with the profession, the article is needed.

Pierre-Henri est un guide excellent.
Pierre-Henri is an excellent guide.

Béatrice est une actrice célèbre.
Béatrice is a famous actress.

C'est un chanteur merveilleux.
He is a wonderful singer.

C'est une grande danseuse.
She is a great dancer.

VOCABULAIRE

le musée	museum
l'art *(m.)*	art
la peinture	painting (collective)
le tableau	a painting
la toile	canvas
la gravure	etching
l'aquarelle *(f.)*	watercolor
la sculpture	sculpture
le sculpteur	sculptor
le chef-d'œuvre	masterpiece
le conservateur	curator
la collection	collection
l'exposition *(f.)*	exposition
la visite guidée	guided tour
la galerie	gallery
le dessin	drawing
la statue	statue
la Joconde	Mona Lisa
les heures *(f.pl.)* **d'ouverture**	business hours
la fermeture	closing
l'offre *(f.)*	offer
montrer	to show
devenir	to become
provenir	to come from
entourer	to surround

changer	to change
changer de carrière	to change careers
commencer	to start, to begin
faire plaisir	to please
réunir	to gather, to assemble
avoir de la chance	to be lucky
tel, telle	such

EXERCICES

A. *Mettre les verbes au conditionnel présent.*

MODÈLE: *Vous (pouvoir) peut-être venir la semaine prochaine.*
Vous pourriez peut-être venir la semaine prochaine.

1. *Si je pouvais, je (aller) au Louvre cet après-midi.*
2. *Vous (devoir) venir avec nous.*
3. *Nous (aimer) voir les Impressionistes.*
4. *Cela nous (faire) très plaisir de faire sa connaissance.*
5. *Elle (vouloir) visiter le Musée d'Orsay.*

B. *Compléter les phrases avec l'imparfait et le conditionnel.*

MODÈLE: *Si nous (être) moins pressés, nous (rester) ici plus longtemps.*
Si nous étions moins pressés, nous resterions ici plus longtemps.

1. *Si tu (être) libre, nous (pouvoir) aller au Musée de la Villette.*
2. *S'il (changer) de profession, il (être) pianiste.*
3. *Elle (faire) le tour du monde si elle (avoir) le temps.*
4. *Si je (savoir) peindre, je (peindre) des tableaux abstraits.*
5. *Je (acheter) cet objet d'art s'il (coûter) moins cher.*

C. *Compléter avec le temps qui convient.*

MODÈLE: *Si nous avons le temps, nous (aller) au Musée de la Villette.*
Si nous avons le temps, nous irons au Musée de la Villette.

1. *Si tu as le temps, je te (montrer) quelques gravures.*
2. *S'il y avait encore des billets pour la conférence, nous (pouvoir) y aller.*
3. *Si on arrive en avance, il y (avoir) encore des places.*
4. *Je (acheter) une oeuvre d'art si je gagnais à la loterie.*
5. *Nous irons voir l'exposition au Grand Palais quand nous (être) à Paris.*

D. *Mettre les phrases suivants au temps indiqué.*

MODÈLE: *Cela leur (faire) énormément plaisir. (présent)*
Cela leur fait énormément plaisir.

1. *Cela lui (faire) plaisir de vous voir. (passé composé)*
2. *Cela nous (faire) très plaisir de vous revoir. (futur)*
3. *Qu'est ce qui te (faire) plaisir? (conditionnel)*
4. *Cela me (faire) plaisir de vous offrir ce livre. (présent)*
5. *Les fleurs que tu m'as envoyées me (faire) très plaisir. (passé composé)*

E. *Compléter avec l'article indéfini si nécessaire.*

MODÈLE: *Pierre est _____ bon danseur.*
        Pierre est un bon danseur.

1. *Jean est _____ acteur merveilleux.*
2. *Romain est _____ conservateur.*
3. *C'est _____ célèbre chanteur.*
4. *Corinne est _____ musicienne.*
5. *Ils sont _____ sculpteurs.*

NOTE CULTURELLE

Like museums in the United States, French museums have become a very important part of social life. The most well-known museum, undoubtedly, is *le Louvre,* which attracts more visitors than ever with its new *Pyramide.* Other rather well-known museums are the *Musée d'Art Moderne* and *le Centre Pompidou.* Fairly new museums are the *Musée de la Villette,* the *Musée d'Orsay,* and the *Institut du Monde Arabe.* Many museums offer lecture series and slide shows and are equipped with restaurants and cafés for your convenience.

LA CLÉ DES EXERCICES

A. 1. *j'irais* 2. *devriez* 3. *aimerions* 4. *ferait* 5. *voudrait*
B. 1. *étais / pourrions* 2. *changeait / serait* 3. *ferait / avait*
   4. *savais / peindrais* 5. *j'achèterais / coûtait*
C. 1. *montrerai* 2. *pourrions* 3. *aura* 4. *j'achèterais* 5. *serons*
D. 1. *a fait* 2. *fera* 3. *ferait* 4. *fait* 5. *m'ont fait*
E. 1. *Jean est un acteur merveilleux.* 2. *Romain est conservateur.* 3. *C'est un célèbre chanteur.* 4. *Corinne est musicienne.* 5. *Ils sont sculpteurs.*

LEÇON 33

FAIRE DE L'EXERCICE. Exercising.

A. DIALOGUE

Au club de forme.

FABIEN: **Tu aurais dû venir à mon club de forme ce matin.**

INÈS: **Quel est ta dernière performance?**

FABIEN: **Touche un peu ces muscles d'acier!**

INÈS: **Impressionnant!**

FABIEN: **Si tu m'avais vu à l'œuvre, tu aurais été fière de moi. J'ai soulevé des poids et haltères pendant plus d'une heure, j'ai fait toutes sortes d'exercices pour les jambes, les cuisses, le dos. . . .**

INÈS: **Oh! Je n'aurais jamais cru que tu étais tellement passionné de sport! Est-ce que tu fais de l'aérobic?**

FABIEN: **Rarement.**

INÈS: **As-tu entendu parler du prof américain, Jordan? C'est vraiment le meilleur prof d'aérobic.**

FABIEN: **Oui, j'ai entendu dire que ses classes étaient bondées.**

INÈS: **Tu sais, il a entraîné toutes les plus grandes vedettes de Hollywood!**

FABIEN: **Ah, je vois, c'est lui ton secret pour garder la taille mannequin!**

At the Health Club.

FABIEN: You should have come to my health club this morning.

INÈS: What is your latest performance?

FABIEN: Just feel these muscles of steel!

INÈS: Impressive!

FABIEN: If you had seen me at work, you would have been proud. I lifted weights and dumbbells for more than an hour. I did all kinds of exercises for the legs, the thighs, the back. . . .

INÈS: I would never have thought you were such an exercise buff! Do you do aerobics?

FABIEN: Rarely.

INÈS: Have you heard about the American instructor, Jordan? He is really the best aerobics instructor.

FABIEN: Yes, I heard his classes are packed!

INÈS: You know, he has trained all the greatest stars in Hollywood!

FABIEN: I see, he is the secret of your perfect figure!

B. GRAMMAIRE ET USAGE

1. THE PAST CONDITIONAL TENSE

a. The past conditional expresses the idea that an action would have been done if a certain condition had been fulfilled.

Je vous aurais téléphoné si j'avais eu votre numéro.
I would have called you if I had had your number.

It is formed with the present conditional of *avoir* or *être* + the past participle.

AIMER   TO LOVE, TO LIKE

I would have liked	*j'aurais aimé*
you would have liked	*tu aurais aimé*
he/she/one would have liked	*il/elle/on aurait aimé*
we would have liked	*nous aurions aimé*
you would have liked	*vous auriez aimé*
they would have liked	*ils/elles auraient aimé*

j'aurais fini
I would have finished

elle serait partie
she would have left

nous nous serions levés
we would have gotten up

b. The past conditional says what would have happened in the past if something else had occurred. The construction pattern is *si* + pluperfect . . . past conditional.

Si tu m'avais vu, tu aurais été fier de moi.
If you had seen me you would have been proud of me.

Si tu étais venue avec moi, je t'aurais montré notre club.
If you had come with me, I would have shown you our club.

Si tu t'étais couché plus tôt, tu ne serais pas si fatigué.
If you had gone to sleep earlier you would not be so tired.

2. THE VERB *DEVOIR* IN THE PAST CONDITIONAL

Devoir in the past conditional expresses moral obligation, regret, or remorse in the past.

Tu aurais dû y aller.
You should have gone there.

Ils auraient dû faire plus d'exercice.
They should have exercised more.

Vous n'auriez pas dû lui révéler votre secret.
You should not have revealed your secret to him.

N'aurais-tu pas dû lui donner des conseils?
Shouldn't you have given him some advice?

3. *ENTENDRE DIRE QUE / ENTENDRE PARLER DE*

a. Hearsay in French is expressed by using *entendre dire que* + the verb in the imperfect, pluperfect or conditional, according to the meaning of the sentence.

J'ai entendu dire que Marie habitait à Paris.
I heard Marie is living in Paris.

Although Marie is still living in Paris, French uses the imperfect after *entendre dire que* if the action is still going on.

Nous avons entendu dire qu'elle était en vacances.
We heard she is on vacation.

If the action is already completed, French uses the *plus-que-parfait*.

Nous avons entendu dire qu'il avait déménagé dans le 15ème.
We heard he had moved to the 15th district.

Elle a entendu dire qu'il avait quitté sa compagnie.
She heard he had left his company.

If the action has not yet taken place, the conditional will be used.

J'ai entendu dire qu'il serait à Moscou en juin.
I heard he would be in Moscow in June.

Il a entendu dire qu'elle participerait au championnat.
He heard she would participate in the championship.

b. When you hear about something or someone, you use *entendre parler de.*

Avez-vous entendu parler du nouveau professeur d'aérobic?
Have you heard about the new aerobics teacher?

Est-ce que tu as entendu parler de ce film?
Have you heard about that film?

Je n'en ai pas entendu parler.
I have not heard about it.

4. THE PARTS OF THE BODY

la tête	head	*le cœur*	heart
le visage	face	*le poumon*	lung
l'œil (m., les yeux)	eye	*le coude*	elbow
la bouche	mouth	*la jambe*	leg
les lèvres	lips	*le genou*	knee
la joue	cheek	*la cheville*	ankle
le nez	nose	*la hanche*	hip
la dent	tooth	*le pied*	foot
le menton	chin	*l'orteil (m.)*	toe
le cou	neck	*le poignet*	wrist
l'épaule (f.)	shoulder	*la main*	hand
la poitrine	chest	*le bras*	arm
la gorge	throat	*la peau*	skin
le muscle	muscle	*la cuisse*	thigh

Usually, when describing an action involving a part of the body the definite article, and not the possessive adjective, is used.

Il lève la jambe.
He raises his leg.

Elle baisse les bras.
She lowers her arms.

Il hausse les épaules.
He shrugs his shoulders.

308

VOCABULAIRE

le club de forme	health club
la performance	performance
faire de l'exercice	to exercise
s'entraîner	to train
soulever	to raise, to lift
entendre dire que	to hear that
entendre parler de	to hear about
garder	to keep
raconter	to tell
croire	to think, to believe
révéler	to reveal
toucher	to touch
déménager	to move
le secret	secret
la vedette	star
le mannequin	model (person)
l'acier	steel
les poids et haltères	weights and dumbbells
la taille	waist
le muscle	muscle
la jambe	leg
la cheville	ankle
le genou	knee
la cuisse	thigh
la hanche	hip
le ventre	belly
la poitrine	chest
les articulations	joints
la main	hand
le doigt	finger
le dos	back
le talon	heel
le cou	neck
bondé	crowded
fier	proud
passionné	passionate
rarement	rarely

EXERCICES

A. *Mettre les verbes suivants au conditionnel passé.*

MODÈLE: *Il fait des exercices.*
 Il aurait fait des exercices.

1. *Elle comprend l'explication.*
2. *Ils vont au club de forme.*
3. *Vous regardez le match.*
4. *Elle s'arrête de jouer au basket-ball.*
5. *Nous voyons les athlètes dans le club.*

B. *Compléter les phrases suivants avec la forme du verbe qui convient.*

MODÈLE: *Je (soulever) des poids si je (ne pas avoir) mal au dos.*
 J'aurais soulevé des poids si je n'avais pas eu mal au dos.

1. *Elle (s'entraîner) plus souvent si elle (avoir) le temps.*
2. *Tu lui (dire) ton secret s'il (jouer) dans ton équipe.*
3. *Vous (être) fier de moi si vous (voir) ma performance.*
4. *Ils (aller) au match s'il (ne pas pleuvoir).*
5. *Nous (suivre) son cours d'aérobic si nous (se lever) plus tôt.*

C. *Choisir entre le futur, le conditionnel présent, ou le conditionnel passé.*
(Choose between the future, the present, or past conditional.)

MODÈLE: *Si tu veux, nous (aller) au cinéma dimanche.*
 Si tu veux, nous irons au cinéma dimanche.

1. *Si tu suivais le cours, tu (être) en meilleure forme.*
2. *Si vous voulez, je (aller) au club de forme avec vous demain soir.*
3. *S'il avait su, il (s'inscrire) à ce club.*
4. *Elle (faire) de l'alpinisme si elle avait le temps.*
5. *S'il avait été plus prudent, il (ne pas se casser) le bras.*

D. *Compléter les phrases en les commençant par "j'ai entendu dire."*

MODÈLE: *Il travaille dans ce club.*
 J'ai entendu dire qu'il travaillait dans ce club.

1. *Ils font beaucoup d'exercices.*
2. *Elle s'entraîne avec les vedettes de Hollywood.*
3. *C'est son dernier spectacle.*
4. *Tu as mal au genou.*
5. *Il soulève des poids et haltères tous les jours.*

E. *Répondre avec "entendre parler de."*

MODÈLE: *Connaissez-vous ce professeur d'aérobic?*
 Oui, j'ai entendu parler de ce professeur d'aérobic.

1. *Connaissez-vous ce nouveau club de forme?*
2. *Connaissez-vous ce joueur de tennis?*
3. *Connaissez-vous les œuvres de cet artiste?*
4. *Connaissez-vous le directeur du club?*
5. *Connaissez-vous ce nouveau régime?*

F. *Traduire.*

1. You should have trained more. (Use *tu.*)
2. She should not have told him her secret.
3. Shouldn't you have talked to your doctor before doing this exercise? (Use *vous.*)
4. I should have called you.
5. We should have done more exercises.

NOTE CULTURELLE

Health clubs are becoming increasingly popular in France. As in the United States, people are more health conscious and make a serious attempt to exercise regularly. Therefore, exercise classes often replace the long lunch hour. Some companies offer special rates for their employees to join a health club. For those who can't, or don't want to, join a club, television offers exercise classes on a daily basis.

LA CLÉ DES EXERCICES

A. 1. *elle aurait compris*   2. *ils seraient allés*   3. *vous auriez regardé*   4. *elle se serait arrêtée*   5. *nous aurions vu*
B. 1. *se serait entraînée / avait eu*   2. *aurais dit / avait joué*   3. *auriez été / aviez vu*   4. *seraient allés / n'avait pas plu*   5. *aurions suivi / nous nous étions levé(e)s*
C. 1. *serais*   2. *irai*   3. *se serait inscrit*   4. *ferait*   5. *ne se serait pas cassé*
D. 1. *J'ai entendu dire qu'ils faisaient beaucoup d'exercices.*   2. *J'ai entendu dire qu'elle s'entraînait avec les vedettes de Hollywood.*   3. *J'ai entendu dire que c'était son dernier spectacle.*   4. *J'ai entendu dire que tu avais mal au genou.* 5. *J'ai entendu dire qu'il soulevait des poides et haltères tous les jours.*
E. 1. *Oui, j'ai entendu parler de ce nouveau club de forme.* 2. *Oui, j'ai entendu parler de ce joueur de tennis.* 3. *Oui, j'ai entendu parler des oeuvres de cet artiste.* 4. *Oui, j'ai entendu parler du directeur du club.* 5. *Oui, j'ai entendu parler de ce nouveau régime.*
F. 1. *Tu aurais dû t'entraîner plus.* 2. *Elle n'aurait pas dû lui dire son secret.* 3. *N'auriez-vous pas dû parler à votre médecin avant de faire cet exercice?* 4. *J'aurais dû vous téléphoner.* 5. *Nous aurions dû faire plus d'exercices.*

LEÇON 34
LES VACANCES. Vacation.

A. DIALOGUE

En Vacances.

SYLVAIN: **Max, quel est notre programme aujourd'hui?**

MAX: **Après avoir exploré les caves de Lascaux, nous visiterons le Musée National de la Préhistoire aux Eyzies.**

CHRISTEL: **Je croyais qu'on allait au Château de Hautefort?**

SYLVAIN: **On ne va tout de même pas passer nos vacances à visiter tous les châteaux de la région!**

MAX: **Vous verrez le château en passant mais il est en cours de restauration.**

SYLVAIN: **Chic alors! On aura plus de temps pour visiter les caves de Cahors!**

MAX: **Pas vraiment. En descendant sur Cahors, nous nous arrêterons à Rocamadour, un village médiéval perché sur une falaise.**

CHRISTEL: **N'est-ce pas un lieu de pèlerinage?**

MAX: **Oui, beaucoup de miracles ont eu lieu à Rocamadour.**

SYLVAIN: **Moi, je ne crois qu'aux miracles du légendaire vin noir de Cahors!**

On Vacation.

SYLVAIN: Max, what's our program for today?

MAX: After exploring the Caves of Lascaux, we'll visit the National Museum of Prehistory at Les Eyzies.

CHRISTEL: I thought we were going to the Hautefort Castle?

SYLVAIN: We're not going to spend our vacation visiting all the castles in the area!

MAX: You'll see the castle as we pass by, but it is being restored at the moment.

SYLVAIN: Terrific! We'll have more time to visit the wine cellars in Cahors!

312

MAX: Not really. As we drive down to Cahors, we'll make a stop at Rocamadour, a medieval village set high up on a cliff.

CHRISTEL: Isn't it a pilgrimage site?

MAX: Yes. Many miracles have taken place in Rocamadour.

SYLVAIN: The only miracles I believe in are those of the legendary black wine of Cahors!

B. GRAMMAIRE ET USAGE

1. THE PRESENT PARTICIPLE

The present participle indicates an action closely connected to the action of the main verb of the sentence.

a. The present participle is formed by adding *-ant* to the stem of the verb. The stem of the verb is found in the *nous* form of the present tense.

nous donnons	*donnant*	giving
nous finissons	*finissant*	finishing
nous rendons	*rendant*	returning
nous sortons	*sortant*	going out
nous buvons	*buvant*	drinking
nous voyons	*voyant*	seeing
nous choisissons	*choisissant*	choosing
nous allons	*allant*	going

Some verbs have irregular present participles.

être	*étant*	being
avoir	*ayant*	having
savoir	*sachant*	knowing

b. The present participle can be used as an adjective or a verb. When used as an adjective, the present participle agrees with the noun it modifies.

une maison plaisante
   a pleasing house

une histoire intéressante
   an interesting story

des films amusants
   amusing films

313

When used as a verb, the present participle is invariable; it refers to the subject of the sentence.

Sachant cela, je ne fume plus.
Knowing this, I don't smoke anymore.

Comprenant que tout était perdu, il est parti.
When he understood that everything was lost, he left.

Here the participle explains why something happened; e.g., "<u>because</u> I know this, I don't smoke anymore."

c. *En* + the present participle is the most commonly used form. It describes two actions taking place simultaneously and signifies "while" or "upon."

Il dîne en regardant la télévision.
He is having dinner while watching television.

Vous verrez le château en passant.
You'll see the castle while driving by.

En allant à Marseille, nous nous sommes arrêtés à Toulouse.
On our way to Marseille, we stopped in Toulouse.

It can also express how something is done.

C'est en apprenant ces verbes par coeur que vous les saurez.
It's by memorizing these verbs that you'll know them.

Ils ont dit au revoir en nous remerciant de notre hospitalité.
They said good-bye by thanking us for our hospitality.

d. *Tout en* + present participle implies a tension between two actions. Two actions which are not usually correlated are going on at the same time.

Il écrit un rapport sérieux tout en écoutant la radio.
He is writing a serious report while listening to the radio.

Elle chante tout en travaillant.
She sings while working.

Il est impossible de parler au téléphone tout en écoutant le discours.
It's impossible to talk on the phone while listening to the speech.

2. USAGE OF THE INFINITIVE

While the "-ing" form is widely used in English, its equivalent, *-ant,* is often replaced by the infinitive in French.

Voyager dans cette région en hiver est difficile.
Traveling to this area in winter is difficult.

a. The infinitive as subject of a verb.

Faire de l'exercice est bon pour la santé.
Exercising is good for your health.

Voyager en Europe est très agréable.
Traveling throughout Europe is very pleasant.

Regarder des vieux films est très amusant.
Watching old movies is a lot of fun.

b. The infinitive after certain verbs of perception.

Max voit son ami quitter le musée.
Max sees his friend leaving the museum.

Nous l'avons entendu parler des caves de Lascaux.
We heard him talking about the Lascaux caves.

L'as-tu vue pleurer?
Did you see her crying?

c. The infinitive after prepositions.

You have already studied the use of the present or past infinitive with *après* and *avant de* in lesson 29. Here is a little reminder.

Elle a visité la Normandie avant de faire le tour de la Dordogne.
She visited Normandy before touring the Dordogne.

Je me suis arrêté à Rocamadour après avoir visité Cahors.
I stopped in Rocamadour after visiting Cahors.

d. The *-ant* form is replaced by the infinitive after all expressions of time.

Il a passé ses vacances à visiter les châteaux de la Vallée de la Loire.
He spent his vacation visiting the castles of the Loire Valley.

Nous avons passé l'après-midi à déguster les vins de la région.
We spent the afternoon tasting the wines of the region.

Elle a passé sa vie à étudier l'histoire médiévale.
She spent her life studying Medieval History.

Nous passerons notre temps à ne rien faire.
We'll spend our time doing nothing.

VOCABULAIRE

les vacances	vacation
la vacance	vacancy
à la campagne	in the country
à la montagne	in the mountains
à la mer	by the sea
à la plage	at the beach
l'autobus	city bus
l'autocar	bus (intercity)
le château	castle
la visite guidée	guided tour
l'église (f.)	church
la cathédrale	cathedral
la mosquée	mosque
le temple	temple, Protestant church
le pèlerinage	pilgrimage
le pèlerin	pilgrim
le miracle	miracle
la restauration	restoration
le lieu	place
le parc	park
le zoo	zoo
la falaise	cliff
la grotte	grotto
la cave	cave; wine cellar
la corniche	cornice, cliff road
l'étape (f.)	stop over (car)
déguster	to taste
s'arrêter	to stop
faire le tour de	to tour around
passer du temps	to spend time
être perché	to be perched high up
croire	to believe
croire aux miracles	to believe in miracles
croire en Dieu	to believe in God
légendaire	legendary
mediéval	medieval
en cours	in process
instructif	instructive
chic alors!	terrific!

EXERCICES

A. *Mettre les verbes au participe présent.*

MODÈLE: *Il est allé au château de Chenonceau en (arriver) en Touraine.*
Il est allé au château de Chenonceau en arrivant en Touraine.

1. *Avez-vous vu des ruines médiévales en (descendre) sur Toulouse?*
2. *Ils ont mangé du fromage en (déguster) les vins de Cahors.*
3. *Elle a découvert des œuvres superbes en (visiter) les Caves de Lascaux.*
4. *Vous vous êtes arrêtés plusieurs fois en (faire) le tour de la Dordogne.*
5. *J'ai donné un pourboire au guide en le (remercier).*

B. *Compléter avec "en" ou "tout en" si c'est nécessaire.*

MODÈLE: *Ils ont regardé le paysage _____ conduisant dans la région.*
Ils ont regardé le paysage en conduisant dans la région.

1. *_____ sortant du château, j'ai vu Sylvain.*
2. *Il écrit sa dissertation _____ écoutant la radio.*
3. *_____ sachant que le guide était un expert de la préhistoire, nous avons décidé de suivre la visite guidée.*
4. *Pourrions-nous nous arrêter à Rocamadour _____ allant à Cahors?*
5. *_____ ayant fini l'exploration de cette province, il sont retournés à Paris.*

C. *Refaire les phrases en utilisant l'expression "passer son temps."*

MODÈLE: *Tu regardes la télévision.*
Tu passes ton temps à regarder la télévision.

1. *Nous étudions l'histoire ancienne.*
2. *Elle a visité l'exposition.*
3. *Vous dégusterez les vins de la région.*
4. *Ils font le tour de la France.*
5. *Il attend des miracles.*

D. *Traduire.*

1. Seeing the restoration of this castle is of great interest.
2. Did you see Max taking pictures of the pilgrimage?
3. Before starting the tour, the guide gave us a brochure.
4. Traveling with a friend is a lot of fun.
5. Learning the history of Les Eyzies was very instructive.

NOTE CULTURELLE

Most French people who work in a corporation or for the government have at least five weeks of paid vacation. Many people take three weeks in the summer and the rest sometime during the year. Although they used to, many companies no longer close their offices and plants during one of the summer months, as it is too expensive to do so. Thus, France is no longer "closed down" in August.

When the French go on vacation, the destination varies—the beaches of the Northern coast of Brittany, and the beautiful beaches on the Atlantic shore are both packed during the summer. The South of France seems to be quite popular with tourists, and is therefore very crowded in the months of July and August. During the winter holidays, the French look for the sun and therefore travel to Morocco and Tunisia, two destinations which are almost as popular in France as Florida is in the United States.

LA CLÉ DES EXERCICES

A. 1. *descendant* 2. *dégustant* 3. *visitant* 4. *faisant* 5. *remerciant*
B. 1. *En* 2. *tout en* 3. no preposition 4. *en* 5. no preposition
C. 1. *Nous passons notre temps à étudier l'histoire ancienne.* 2. *Elle a passé son temps à visiter l'exposition.* 3. *Vous passerez votre temps à déguster les vins de la région.* 4. *Ils passent leur temps à faire le tour de la France.* 5. *Il passe son temps à attendre des miracles.*
D. 1. *Voir la restauration de ce château est d'un grand intérêt.* 2. *Avez-vous vu Max prendre des photos du pèlerinage?* 3. *Avant de commencer la visite, le guide nous a donné une brochure.* 4. *Voyager avec un ami est très amusant.* 5. *Apprendre l'histoire des Eyzies était très instructif.*

LEÇON 35
LES MÉDIAS. The Media.

A. DIALOGUE

Les Informations.

CHRISTINE: **Que lis-tu de si passionnant?**

HUBERT: **Un article dans *Le Monde* sur l'agriculture. La situation est tragique, c'est à vous rendre malade! Le président du sommet européen a dit qu'une réforme était indispensable.**

CHRISTINE: **Moi aussi, je suis plongée dans l'agriculture.**

HUBERT: **L'agriculture dans *Elle, Madame Figaro?***

CHRISTINE: **Non, je lis *Nice-Matin*. En vacances, il faut bien lire le quotidien régional!**

HUBERT: **Que pense *Nice-Matin* des problèmes agricoles?**

CHRISTINE: **Il s'agit de la fête du citron de Menton. Le maire a déclaré que la fête était à l'heure européene. Les chars, décorés de milliers d'agrumes, arborent tous les drapeaux de la CE.**

HUBERT: **Une façon comme une autre d'utiliser les surplus!**

CHRISTINE: **Non, non, l'article a dit qu'une partie des 120 tonnes de citrons était distribuée aux œuvres de bienfaisance et qu'avec le reste on faisait du vin! Si on y allait?**

The News.

CHRISTINE: What are you reading that is so fascinating?

HUBERT: An article in *Le Monde* on agriculture. The situation is tragic. It's sickening. The president of the European Summit said a reform was essential.

CHRISTINE: I'm also reading about agriculture.

HUBERT: Agriculture in *Elle, Madame Figaro?*

CHRISTINE: No, I am reading *Nice-Matin*. One must read the local daily paper when on vacation.

HUBERT: What does *Nice-Matin* say about agricultural problems?

CHRISTINE: It's about the lemon festival in Menton. The mayor said the festival was going international. The floats, decorated with thousands of citrus fruit, display all the EC flags.

HUBERT: It's one way to use the agricultural surplus!

CHRISTINE: No, the article said that part of the 120 tons of lemons was given to charity, the rest was used to make wine. How about us going there?

B. GRAMMAIRE ET USAGE

1. THE SEQUENCE OF TENSES

When a verb introduces a second clause, the two verbs follow a certain sequence of tenses. Let's look at the following examples.

a. If the first verb of the sentence is in the present, the verb of the second sentence can be in the:

PRESENT

Je pense qu'il lit le journal.
I think he is reading the paper.

Je crois qu'elle est à Paris.
I think she is in Paris.

FUTURE

Il pense qu'il viendra.
He thinks he will come.

Vous pensez qu'il ira au festival?
Do you think he'll go to the festival?

PASSÉ COMPOSÉ

Nous croyons qu'il est parti.
We think he left.

Elle pense qu'il est allé à Menton.
She thinks he went to Menton.

b. If the first verb of the sentence is in the past (*passé composé*, imperfect, pluperfect), the second verb in the sentence can be in the:

IMPERFECT

J'ai pensé qu'il était à Nice.
I thought he was in Nice.

Il a cru que vous étiez en vacances.
He thought you were on vacation.

320

Nous avions pensé qu'il viendrait.
We had thought he would come.

Il avait cru qu'elle serait ici.
We had thought she would be here.

Nous croyions qu'il était parti.
We thought he had gone.

Elle pensait qu'elle avait déménagé.
She thought she had moved.

2. REPORTED SPEECH

In reported or indirect speech (as opposed to speech that is quoted directly), French follows a certain sequence of tenses. Reported speech usually follows verbs like these:

dire que	to say that, to tell
écrire que	to write that
annoncer que	to announce that
déclarer que	to declare that
demander si	to ask whether
répondre que	to answer that

a. When you report someone's speech, the tense used in the dependent clause changes from the tense used in the direct quote, regardless of whether the introductory phrase is in the past or the present. For example:

Direct: *Le président du sommet dit: "Une réforme est indispensable."*
The president of the Summit says: "A reform is essential."

Indirect: *Le président du sommet a dit qu'une réforme était indispensable.*
The president of the Summit said that a reform was essential.

Direct: *Il a dit: "On fait du vin avec le reste."*
He said: "One makes wine with the rest."

Indirect: *Il a dit qu'on faisait du vin avec le reste.*
He said that one made wine with the rest.

The following sequence of tenses is applied: If the direct speech is in the present tense, the indirect speech is in the imperfect.

Il a répondu: "C'est certain."
He answered, "It's certain."

Il a répondu que c'était certain.
He answered that it was certain.

If the direct speech is in the future, the indirect speech is in the conditional.

Il a dit: "Nous comprendrons bientôt."
He said, "We will soon understand."

Il a dit que nous comprendrions bientôt.
He said we would soon understand.

If the direct speech is in the *passé composé,* the indirect speech is in the pluperfect.

On a annoncé: "Le ministre a démissioné."
They announced: "The minister has resigned."

On a annoncé que le ministre avait demissioné.
They announced that the minister had resigned.

b. For questions in reported speech, the changes are as follows:

Est-ce que in direct speech becomes *si* in indirect speech.

Je demande: "Est-ce que vous partez?"
I ask, "Are you leaving?"

Je demande si vous partez.
I ask whether you're leaving.

Qu'est-ce que in direct speech becomes *ce que* in indirect speech.

Je demande: "Qu'est-ce qu'il va faire?"
I ask, "What will he do?"

Je demande ce qu'il va faire.
I ask what he will do.

Qu'est-ce qui becomes *ce qui.*

Je demande: "Qu'est-ce qui vous intéresse?"
I ask, "What interests you?"

Je demande ce qui vous intéresse.
I ask what interests you.

Other question words remain the same as in direct speech.

Je demande où nous allons.
I ask where we're going.

Il m'a demandé quand je partirais.
He asked me when I would leave.

On ne sait pas qui sera nommé.
We don't know who will be nominated.

Est-ce qu'il a dit comment on pouvait y remédier?
Did he say how we could remedy that?

Dites-nous à quelle heure vous arriverez.
Tell us at what time you'll arrive.

3. TO MAKE + ADJECTIVE

When using the verb to make + an adjective, such as to make sick, to make happy, French does not use *faire* but *rendre*.

La situation me rend malade.
The situation makes me sick.

Vous l'avez rendu très heureux.
You made him very happy.

Les nouvelles l'ont rendu triste.
The news made him sad.

4. VARIOUS TRANSLATIONS OF THE WORD "PAPER"

The word "paper" has a lot of meanings in English and cannot be translated into French easily.

Christine et Hubert lisent le journal.
Christine and Hubert are reading the (news)paper.

Les étudiants remettent leurs copies au professeur.
The students hand in their papers to the teacher.

Donne-moi un feuille de papier, s'il te plaît.
Please give me a piece of paper.

Tu dois le mettre par écrit.
You have to put this down on paper

VOCABULAIRE

les médias *(m. pl.)*	media
la presse	press
le journal, les journaux	newspaper, newspapers
l'hebdomadaire *(m.)*	weekly paper or news magazine

le quotidien	daily paper
le mensuel	monthly
le magazine	magazine
la nouvelle	a piece of news
les nouvelles	news
les actualités	news report
l'article *(m.)*	article
en première page	on the front page
la couverture	cover (paper)
les gros titres	headlines
le reportage	story
le reporter	reporter
l'interview	interview
interviewer	to interview
le sujet	subject
la radio	radio
à la radio	on the radio
à la télévision	on television
l'émission	program
la chaîne de télévision	TV channel
la CE	EC / European Community
le char	float
le citron	lemon
les agrumes	citrus fruit
le surplus	surplus, excess
l'oeuvre de bienfaisance	charity organization
le drapeau	flag
rendre	to make, to render
décorer	to decorate
arborer	to display
plonger	to dive
être plongé dans	to be absorbed in
déclarer	to declare, to state
passionnant	fascinating
indispensable	essential

EXERCICES

A. *Compléter avec le temps qui convient.*

MODÈLE: Il croit qu'elle (partir) pour Nice hier matin.
Il croit qu'elle est partie pour Nice hier matin.

1. *Je pense que Catherine (venir) demain.*
2. *Nous avons pensé qu'il (être) au musée.*
3. *Il avait espéré qu'elle (aller) avec lui à la fête du citron.*
4. *Le président du sommet a dit qu'il (falloir) réformer l'agriculture.*
5. *Nous pensons qu'ils (être) à Paris en ce moment.*

B. *Transformer les questions directes en questions indirectes.* (Rewrite the direct questions as reported questions.)

MODÈLE: *Hubert demande: "Qui est-ce qui va remplacer le ministre?"*
Hubert demande qui va remplacer le ministre.

1. *Mélanie demande: "Qu'est-ce qui se passe?"*
2. *Le reporter a demandé: "Qu'est-ce que vous allez faire?"*
3. *Alain veut savoir: "Comment peut-on remédier au problème?"*
4. *J'ai demandé: "Est-ce que nous irons à la fête?"*
5. *Je veux savoir: "Où est ce que je peux trouver un quotidien?"*
6. *Ils ont demandé au président: "Qu'est-ce que vous ferez pour les agriculteurs?"*

C. *Former des phrases selon le modèle suivant en utilisant le verbe "rendre" au temps indiqué.* (Make sentences according to the following example using the verb *rendre.*)

MODÈLE: *La situation / fou de rage. (passé composé)*
La situation m'a rendu fou de rage.

1. *Votre présence / heureux. (passé composé)*
2. *La mort de mon chien / triste. (passé composé)*
3. *Manger trop de chocolat / malade. (présent)*
4. *Leurs histoires / joyeux. (passé composé)*
5. *Cette nouvelle / furieux. (futur)*

D. *Compléter avec le mot qui convient.*

1. *Tous les matins, elle lit le _____ de la première à la dernière page.*
2. *Écris-moi les instructions sur ce morceau de _____.*
3. *L'examen est terminé, rendez-moi vos _____ tout de suite!*
4. *Il faut faire cette demande officielle _____, sinon vous n'aurez pas de réponse.*
5. *Est-ce que vous recyclez vos _____ après les avoir lus?*

NOTE CULTURELLE

The French are avid newspaper readers. The main newspapers are *Le Monde, Libération,* and *Le Figaro.* There are also many popular weekly news magazines, such as *L'Express, Le Point, Le Nouvel Observateur,* and *l'Evénement du Jeudi.* The women's magazines *Elle, Vogue, Marie-Claire,* and *Marie-France* enjoy popularity all over the world.

French television is continually increasing the availability of television channels. Until recently all channels were owned and operated by the state, but more and more television channels are now run privately. All over Europe, so-called European channels are being formed (Eurovision) that are both operated by and accessible to several European countries, making it possible to watch TV in several languages. Among the American shows that are exported, the CBS news broadcast and CNN enjoy popularity.

LA CLÉ DES EXERCICES

A. 1. *viendra* 2. *était* 3. *irait* 4. *fallait* 5. *sont*

B. 1. *Mélanie demande ce qui se passe.* 2. *Le reporter a demandé ce que vous alliez faire.* 3. *Alain veut savoir comment on peut remédier au problème.* 4. *J'ai demandé si nous irions à la fête.* 5. *Je veux savoir où je peux trouver un quotidien.* 6. *Ils ont demandé au président ce qu'il ferait pour les agriculteurs.*

C. 1. *Votre présence m'a rendu heureux.* 2. *La mort de mon chien m'a rendu triste.* 3. *Manger trop de chocolat me rend malade.* 4. *Leurs histoires m'ont rendu joyeux.* 5. *Cette nouvelle me rendra furieux.*

D. 1. *journal* 2. *papier* 3. *copies* 4. *par écrit* 5. *journaux*

SEPTIÈME RÉVISION

A. *Mettre les verbes au futur.*

MODÈLE: *Vous téléphonez à Sylvain.*
Vous téléphonerez à Sylvain.

1. *Nous sommes très contents de notre voyage.*
2. *Ils atterrissent à quinze heures.*
3. *Ils font un pèlerinage à Rocamadour.*
4. *Il a assez de temps pour visiter le château.*
5. *Elle va au comptoir d'Air France.*
6. *L'hôtesse vous donne une carte d'embarquement.*
7. *Elle est fière de ses enfants.*
8. *Nous voyons un film étranger une fois par semaine.*
9. *Les chars arborent des drapeaux.*
10. *Ça vous rend malade.*

B. *Mettre les verbes au temps qui convient.*

1. *Je passerai une semaine au bord de la mer quand je (aller) en vacances.*
2. *Revenez au comptoir aussitôt que vous (récupérer) vos valises.*
3. *Dès que tu (arriver), téléphone-moi.*
4. *Nous achèterons des timbres quand nous (trouver) une poste.*
5. *Je vous inviterai à déjeuner quand vous (être) à Paris.*

C. *Mettre les verbes au conditionnel présent.*

1. *Il (aller) en Italie s'il avait assez d'argent.*
2. *Vous (être) ravi s'il venait avec vous.*
3. *Si elle était libre en juin, elle (voyager) avec nous.*
4. *Si nous avions plus de temps, nous (aller) en Grèce.*
5. *Qu'est-ce que tu (faire), si tu décidais de changer de carrière?*

D. *Mettre les verbes aux temps qui convient.*

MODÈLE: *Nous achèterons le journal quand nous (être) en France.*
Nous achèterons le journal quand nous serons en France.

1. *Si je peux, je (prendre) le train demain matin.*
2. *Nous (partir) en vacances si nous avions le temps.*
3. *Si nous étions allés en France nous (voir) nos amis.*
4. *Si elle recommençait à zéro, elle (être) peintre.*
5. *Je (faire) du ski nautique si je pouvais.*
6. *Qu'est-ce que tu (prendre) comme vêtements si tu allais en Alsace en hiver?*
7. *Le président (faire) des réformes s'il avait un plus gros budget.*
8. *Nous (aller) à la fête du citron quand nous serons à Menton.*
9. *Ils (accepter) votre offre si vous aviez été plus raisonnable.*
10. *Je (garder) ton secret si tu promets de garder le mien.*

E. *Compléter avec le participe présent.*

MODÈLE: *Il s'rête à Lyon en (descendre) à Marseille.*
Il s'arrête à Lyon en descendant à Marseille.

1. *Il s'est fait mal en (tomber).*
2. *J'ai vu Christel en (sortir) du magasin.*
3. *Vous serez en meilleure forme en (faire) de l'exercice.*
4. *Téléphonez à Yannick en (arriver) à la Guadeloupe.*
5. *Fabien a rencontré Inès en (s'entraîner) dans un club de forme.*

F. *Traduire.*

1. She spent her vacation reading.
2. Have you heard about this new book?
3. She exercises while listening to modern music.
4. I heard he is in Paris. Do you know if it's true?
5. Would you spend a year studying French if you had the time?

G. *Mettre les verbes suivants au passé composé.*

1. *Je passe des vacances extraordinaires.*
2. *Nous passons par Tours pour aller à La Rochelle.*
3. *Vous passez un examen de français?*
4. *Je passe devant la Tour Eiffel.*
5. *À l'examen oral, tu passes avant moi.*

A. 1. *serons*   2. *atterriront*   3. *feront*   4. *aura*   5. *ira*   6. *donnera*
   7. *sera*   8. *verrons*   9. *arboreront*   10. *rendra*

B. 1. *j'irai*   2. *aurez récupéré*   3. *seras arrivé*   4. *aurons trouvé*   5. *serez*

C. 1. *irait*   2. *seriez*   3. *voyagerait*   4. *irions*   5. *ferais*

D. 1. *prendrai*   2. *partirions*   3. *aurions vu*   4. *serait*   5. *ferais*
   6. *prendrais*   7. *ferait*   8. *irons*   9. *auraient accepté*   10. *garderai*

E. 1. *tombant*   2. *sortant*   3. *faisant*   4. *arrivant*   5. *s'entraînant*

F. 1. *Elle a passé ses vacances à lire.* 2. *Avez-vous entendu parler de ce nouveau livre?* 3. *Elle fait de l'exercice en écoutant de la musique moderne.* 4. *J'ai entendu dire qu'il était à Paris. Savez-vous si c'est vrai?* 5. *Passeriez-vous une année à étudier le français si vous aviez le temps?*

G. 1. *J'ai passé*   2. *Nous sommes passé(e)s*   3. *Vous avez passé*   4. *Je suis passé(e)*   5. *tu es passé(e)*

LEÇON 36
AU MARCHÉ AUX PUCES.   At the Flea Market.

A. DIALOGUE

Marchander.

ALAIN: **Regarde ce miroir!**

MARCHANDE: **Vous avez bon goût, monsieur. C'est un miroir Empire.**

SERGE: **Je doute que ce soit un miroir d'époque.**

ALAIN: **Ah . . . peu importe, il est magnifique. Toi qui ne savais pas quoi m'offrir pour mon anniversaire . . . Je serais ravi que tu m'en fasses cadeau.**

SERGE: **Combien coûte ce miroir, s'il vous plaît?**

MARCHANDE: **Mille cinq cents francs.**

SERGE: **Mille cinq cents francs!**

ALAIN: **Il faut que tu marchandes un peu, voyons!**

SERGE: **Bien que ce soit ton quarantième anniversaire, je n'ai aucune intention de me lancer dans de telles extravagances! Tu tiens vraiment à ce que je te l'offre?**

ALAIN: **Essaie de faire baisser le prix!**

SERGE: **Tu ne veux pas qu'on aille jeter un coup d'œil aux autres stands?**

ALAIN: **D'accord. Pourvu que le miroir soit toujours là quand on reviendra!**

————————————

Bargaining.

ALAIN: Look at this mirror!

MERCHANT: You have great taste, sir. It's from the Empire period.

SERGE: I doubt it is a period piece.

ALAIN: It does not matter, it's beautiful. You who don't know what to get me for my birthday . . . I'd be delighted if you got it for me.

SERGE: How much is this mirror, please?

MERCHANT: Fifteen hundred francs.

SERGE: Fifteen hundred francs!

ALAIN: Come on, you've got to bargain a little.

SERGE: Although it's your fortieth birthday, I have no intention of such excessive spending! You really want me to buy it for you?

ALAIN: Try to bring the price down!

SERGE: Don't you want to take a look at the other booths?

ALAIN: Okay. Let's hope the mirror will still be here when we come back!

B. GRAMMAIRE ET USAGE

1. THE SUBJUNCTIVE

The mood of a verb expresses how a speaker views a fact or event. A verb can have several moods: The indicative states an objective fact; the imperative gives commands; the conditional says what will happen, if. . . . The present, *passé composé,* imperfect, and future tenses that you have studied are all tenses of the indicative. You will now study another mood, the subjunctive. It expresses how the speaker feels about the event described. It is much more commonly used in French than in English. Let's compare the indicative and subjunctive moods.

INDICATIVE

J'ai vu une commode.
I saw a dresser.

Cette commode est chère.
This dresser is expensive.

Je sais que c'est un meuble d'époque.
I know it's a period piece.

SUBJUNCTIVE

Je voudrais que tu voies cette commode.
I would like you to see this dresser.

J'ai peur que cette commode soit chère.
I'm afraid this dresser is expensive.

Je doute que ce soit un meuble d'époque.
I doubt it is a period piece.

For regular verbs, the present subjunctive is formed by adding the subjunctive endings to the stem. The stem is found by dropping the *-ent* from the third-person plural of the present indicative. The endings for the subjunctive are: *e, es, e, ions, iez, ent.* Let's take the verb *regarder* (to look at, to watch) as an example.

REGARDER   TO WATCH → *ILS REGARDENT* → *REGARD-*

I watch	*je regarde*	we watch	*nous regardions*
you watch	*tu regardes*	you watch	*vous regardiez*
he/she/one watches	*il/elle/on regarde*	they watch	*ils/elles regardent*

FINIR   TO FINISH → *ILS FINISSENT* → *FINISS-*

I finish	*je finisse*	we finish	*nous finissions*
you finish	*tu finisses*	you finish	*vous finissiez*
he/she/one finishes	*il/elle/on finisse*	they finish	*ils/elles finissent*

PARTIR   TO LEAVE

I leave	*je parte*
we leave	*nous partions*

VENDRE   TO SELL

I sell	*je vende*
we sell	*nous vendions*

Many irregular verbs form the present subjunctive like the regular verbs.

conduire	to drive	*je conduise*
connaître	to know	*je connaisse*
courir	to run	*je coure*
craindre	to fear	*je craigne*
dire	to say	*je dise*
écrire	to write	*j'écrive*
lire	to read	*je lise*
mettre	to put	*je mette*
ouvrir	to open	*j'ouvre*
plaire	to please	*je plaise*
rire	to laugh	*je rie*
suivre	to follow	*je suive*

But many irregular verbs have irregular stems in the present subjunctive. The irregular stem must be memorized but the conjugation follows the regular pattern. *Avoir* and *être* are completely irregular.

ÊTRE	*AVOIR*	*FAIRE*
je sois	*j'aie*	*je fasse*
tu sois	*tu aies*	*tu fasses*
il/elle/on soit	*il/elle/on ait*	*il/elle/on fasse*
nous soyons	*nous ayons*	*nous fassions*
vous soyez	*vous ayez*	*vous fassiez*
ils/elles soient	*ils/elles aient*	*ils/elles fassent*

ALLER	VENIR	PRENDRE
j'aille	*je vienne*	*je prenne*
tu ailles	*tu viennes*	*tu prennes*
il/elle/on aille	*il/elle/on vienne*	*il/elle/on prenne*
nous allions	*nous venions*	*nous prenions*
vous alliez	*vous veniez*	*vous preniez*
ils/elles aillent	*ils/elles viennent*	*ils/elles prennent*

POUVOIR	SAVOIR	DEVOIR
je puisse	*je sache*	*je doive*
tu puisses	*tu saches*	*tu doives*
il/elle/on puisse	*il/elle/on sache*	*il/elle/on doive*
nous puissions	*nous sachions*	*nous devions*
vous puissiez	*vous sachiez*	*vous deviez*
ils/elles puissent	*ils/elles sachent*	*ils/elles doivent*

VOULOIR	BOIRE	VOIR
je veuille	*je boive*	*je voie*
tu veuilles	*tu boives*	*tu voies*
il/elle/on veuille	*il/elle/on boive*	*il/elle/on voie*
nous voulions	*nous buvions*	*nous voyions*
vous vouliez	*vous buviez*	*vous voyiez*
ils/elles veuillent	*ils/elles boivent*	*ils/elles voient*

e. The three main concepts which require the subjunctive in the dependent clause are wish, emotion, and doubt. All verbs expressing the notion of wish and desire, such as *vouloir* (to want), *désirer* (to wish), *aimer* (to like), etc., are followed by the subjunctive.

Je veux que tu viennes avec moi au marché aux puces.
I want you to come with me to the flea market.

J'aimerais que tu m'offres ce livre.
I would like you to give me this book.

Nous souhaitons qu'elle puisse venir.
We hope she can come.

All verbs expressing emotion, such as *être* (to be) followed by *content* (happy), *triste* (sad), *désolé* (sorry), *ravi* (delighted), and *avoir peur* (to fear), are also followed by the subjunctive.

Je suis content que vous soyez là.
I'm happy you are there.

Je serais ravi que tu m'en fasses cadeau.
I would be delighted if you bought it for me.

Tu as peur qu'elle soit en retard?
Are you afraid she is going to be late?

Verbs expressing doubt, such as *je doute* (I doubt), *je ne suis pas sûr* (I am not sure), *je ne crois pas* (I don't think), etc., are also followed by the subjunctive.

Il doute qu'elle puisse l'accompagner.
He doubts she can come along with him.

Je ne crois pas qu'il soit libre samedi.
I doubt he will be free on Saturday.

Some impersonal expressions, verbs, verbal expressions, and conjunctions are always followed by the subjunctive. Here are a few impersonal expressions.

il faut	one must
il vaut mieux	it is better
il est important	it is important
il est temps	it is time
il est possible	it is possible
il est impossible	it is impossible
il est naturel	it is natural
il est rare	it is rare
il est étrange	it is strange

Il faut que vous marchandiez un peu!
You have to bargain a little.

Il est possible que ce soit une commode d'époque.
It is possible it is a period dresser.

Not all impersonal verbs require the subjunctive. Those that express certainty and probability, and the phrase *il me semble que,* are followed by the indicative.

il est certain	it is certain
il est évident	it is evident
il est sûr	it is sure
il est vrai	it is true
il est probable	it is probable
il me semble	it seems to me

Il est évident que Serge doit marchander.
It is evident that Serge must bargain.

Il est vrai que ce style me plaît.
It is true I like this style.

Some conjunctions are always followed by the subjunctive:

afin que	so that, in order to
pour que	so that, in order that
bien que	although
quoique	although
pourvu que	provided, let's hope
à moins que	unless
sans que	without
avant que . . . (ne)	before
jusqu'à ce que	until

Bien que ce soit ton quarantième anniversaire, je n'avais pas l'intention de t'offrir ce miroir.
Although it is your fortieth birthday, I didn't intend to give you this mirror.

Pourvu que le miroir soit toujours là.
Let's hope the mirror will still be there.

2. IDIOMATIC EXPRESSIONS WITH "EYE"

L'œil (eye; plural: *les yeux*) is used in many practical idiomatic expressions. Let's look at a few of them.

Je l'ai vu de mes propres yeux.
I saw it with my own eyes.

Il la cherchait des yeux.
He was looking around for her.

Cette armoire coûte les yeux de la tête.
This armoire costs an arm and a leg.

Il a les yeux plus grands que le ventre.
His eyes are bigger than his stomach.

Il m'a fait un clin d'œil.
He winked at me.

Ce miroir m'a tapé dans l'œil.
This mirror took my fancy.

Oeil pour œil, dent pour dent.
An eye for an eye, a tooth for a tooth.

C'est trop tape-à-l'œil.
　It's too flashy.

Nous avons pu voir l'exposition à l'œil.
　We were able to see the exhibit for free.

Elle n'a pas froid aux yeux.
　She is adventurous.

On ne voit pas ça du même œil que lui.
　We don't see that in the same light as he does.

Je jette simplement un coup d'œil.
　I am just taking a quick look.

VOCABULAIRE

les antiquités *(f.)*	antiques
le magasin d'antiquités	antique store
le marché aux puces	flea market
un antiquaire	an antique dealer
le stand	booth
le style Louis XV	Louis XV style
le meuble	piece of furniture
les meubles	furniture
la commode	dresser
le fauteuil	armchair
la chaise	chair
la table	table
le lit	bed
le coffre	chest
le secrétaire	secretary, writing desk
le buffet	buffet
l'armoire	wardrobe
la coiffeuse	dressing table
la lampe	lamp
le miroir	mirror
le lustre	chandelier
le vase	vase
cher, chère	expensive
bon marché	cheap
coûter	to cost
marchander	to bargain
baisser	to decrease, to lower
faire baisser le prix	to lower the price
offrir	to offer, to give a present

faire cadeau de	to offer
jeter un coup d'œil	to glance, to take a quick look
revenir	to come back
avoir du goût	to have some taste
d'accord	all right
pour que	so that, in order that
afin que	so that, in order that
sans que	without
à moins que	unless
bien que	although
quoique	although
pourvu que	provided that

EXERCICES

A. *Mettre les verbes au subjonctif.*

MODÈLE: *Il faut que tu (apprendre) le subjonctif.*
Il faut que tu apprennes le subjonctif.

1. *Il faut que nous (prendre) des vacances.*
2. *Il faut que vous (savoir) marchander.*
3. *Il faut qu'il (aller) en France.*
4. *Il faut que je (venir) vous voir.*
5. *Il ne faut pas que tu (avoir) peur de marchander.*
6. *Il ne faut pas que nous (être) en retard.*
7. *Il faut que vous (faire) baisser le prix.*
8. *Il faut qu'ils (avoir) beaucoup d'argent pour acheter cette armoire.*
9. *Il faut que vous (revenir) la semaine prochaine.*
10. *Il faut que nous leur (téléphoner) avant demain.*

B. *Faire des phrases avec les éléments suggérés.*

MODÉLE: *Nous vous accompagnerons/pourvu que/il/faire beau.*
Nous vous accompagnerons pourvu qu'il fasse beau.

1. *Je l'aiderai quoique/je/ne pas avoir/le temps.*
2. *Nous achèterons le lustre sans que/il/le savoir.*
3. *Ils attendront jusqu'à ce que/Serge/revenir.*
4. *Nous achèterons la commode à moins que/vous/être pas d'accord.*
5. *Il ira au marché aux puces/bien que/il/faire froid.*

C. *Choisir l'indicatif ou le subjonctif pour les expressions impersonnelles qui suivent.*

1. *Il est certain que Marc (arriver) demain.*
2. *Il est possible que nous (pouvoir) venir la semaine prochaine.*

3. *Il est évident qu'ils (savoir) parler français.*
4. *Il est étonnant que cette chaise (être) si bon marché.*
5. *Il vaut mieux que nous (aller) chez un autre antiquaire.*
6. *Il est important qu'elle (savoir) le prix.*
7. *Il est étrange qu'ils (ne pas être) encore là.*
8. *Il est impossible que vous (refuser) notre invitation.*
9. *Il est naturel qu'il (avoir) peur de commencer ce nouveau travail.*
10. *Il est probable qu'il (ne pas venir) ce soir.*

D. *Traduire.*

1. I doubt she can come with us to the flea market.
2. Although he is eighty, he is very active.
3. I want him to go with me to the antique dealer.
4. He is happy you are doing the bargaining for him. *(vous)*
5. They fear the mirror won't be there when they come back.

NOTE CULTURELLE

Buying antiques or browsing through antique shops is a great pleasure in Paris. There are many antique dealers in the neighborhood of Saint-Germain-des-Prés and along the banks of the Seine. The very large and well-established flea market *(marché aux puces)* of Saint-Ouen in the northeastern section of Paris, has everything from secondhand clothes and furniture to genuine antiques. The antique dealers expect prospective buyers to be knowledgeable and to bargain only within reason.

LA CLÉ DES EXERCICES

A. 1. *prenions* 2. *sachiez* 3. *aille* 4. *vienne* 5. *aies* 6. *soyons*
7. *fassiez* 8. *aient* 9. *reveniez* 10. *téléphonions*
B. 1. *Je l'aiderai quoique je n'aie pas le temps.* 2. *Nous achèterons le lustre sans qu'il le sache.* 3. *Ils attendront jusqu'à ce que Serge revienne.* 4. *Nous achèterons la commode à moins que vous ne soyez pas d'accord.* 5. *Il ira au marché aux puces bien qu'il fasse froid.*
C. 1. *arrivera* 2. *puissions* 3. *savent* 4. *soit* 5. *allions* 6. *sache*
7. *ne soient pas* 8. *refusiez* 9. *ait* 10. *ne viendra pas*
D. 1. *Je doute qu'elle puisse venir avec nous au marché aux puces.* 2. *Bien qu'il ait quatre-vingts ans, il est très actif.* 3. *Je veux qu'il aille avec moi chez l'antiquaire.* 4. *Il est heureux que vous marchandiez pour lui.* 5. *Ils ont peur que le miroir ne soit pas là quand ils reviendront.*

LEÇON 37

LA POLITIQUE. Politics.

A. DIALOGUE

Parler politique.

M. LANÇON: **Pour qui allez-vous voter, Mme Pradel?**

MME PRADEL: **J'ai bien peur de ne pas pouvoir vous répondre.**

M. LANÇON: **Vous boycottez les élections?**

MME PRADEL: **Non, mais il y a tant de candidats qu'on connaît à peine! Je regrette qu'aucun parti n'ait vraiment abordé les problèmes de fond.**

M. LANÇON: **Je crois que le programme de la gauche est assez séduisant: baisse de l'impôt sur le revenu, réforme de l'enseignement et de la sécurité sociale.**

MME PRADEL: **Et la création d'emplois, l'aide aux PME[1] et PMI,[2] l'augmentation du nombre de crèches? Comment peut-on voter pour un candidat sans connaître toutes ses intentions?**

M. LANÇON: **Vous savez bien que les politiciens ne peuvent pas tenir toutes leurs promesses.**

MME PRADEL: **La politique, c'est toujours la même histoire: plus ça change plus ça continue!**

Discussing Politics.

MR. LANÇON: For whom are you voting?

MRS. PRADEL: I am afraid I may not be able to give you an answer.

MR. LANÇON: Are you boycotting the elections?

MRS. PRADEL: No, but there are so many candidates we hardly know! I am sorry no party has really addressed the basic problems.

MR. LANÇON: I think the platform of the left is rather attractive: income tax reduction, reform of the educational and the social security system.

MRS. PRADEL: What about creating new jobs, helping small companies and small industries, increasing the number of day care centers? How can you vote for a candidate without knowing all of his or her intentions?

[1] PME = *petites et moyennes entreprises,* i.e. small to medium-sized companies.

[2] PMI = *petites et moyennes industries,* i.e. small to medium-sized industries.

MR. LANÇON: You know that politicians cannot keep all of their promises.

MRS. PRADEL: With politics it's always the same story: the more things change, the more they remain the same!

B. GRAMMAIRE ET USAGE

1. THE SUBJUNCTIVE AND THE INFINITIVE

French uses the infinitive instead of the subjunctive in dependent clauses describing the subjunctive mood, if the subject of the dependent clause is the same as in the main clause. Let's compare verbs of desire, emotion, and doubt followed by the subjunctive and the infinitive.

SUBJUNCTIVE

Je veux que tu sois là.
I want you to be there.

J'ai peur qu'il ne puisse pas vous répondre.
I fear he cannot answer you.

Je ne crois pas qu'il puisse venir.
I don't think he can come.

INFINITIVE

Je veux être là.
I want to be there.

J'ai peur de ne pas pouvoir vous répondre.
I fear I cannot answer you.

Je ne crois pas pouvoir venir.
I don't think I can come.

Thus, many common conjunctions that take the subjunctive have a prepositional counterpart used with the infinitive when the subject in the main and dependent clauses is the same.

pour que + subjunctive	*pour* + infinitive
afin que + subjunctive	*afin de* + infinitive
avant que + subjunctive	*avant de* + infinitive
sans que + subjunctive	*sans* + infinitive
à moins que + suibjunctive	*à moins de* + infinitive

For example:

SUBJUNCTIVE

Je téléphonerai avant qu'il parte.
I'll call before he leaves.

INDICATIVE:

Je téléphonerai avant de partir.
I'll call before I leave.

With the other conjunctions, *bien que, quoique, jusqu'à ce que,* and *à condition que,* which do not have a prepositional counterpart, the subjunctive is always used, even when the subject is the same.

Je voterai pour lui bien que je ne le connaisse pas très bien.
I'll vote for him although I don't know him very well.

Quoique les politiciens fassent beaucoup de promesses, ils les tiennent rarement.
Although politicians make a lot of promises, they rarely keep them.

2. THE PAST SUBJUNCTIVE

In conversational French, only two subjunctive tenses are used, the present and the past. The imperfect of the subjunctive is mainly used in literature.

The past subjunctive is formed with the subjunctive of the auxiliary verb *avoir/être* + the past participle.

PARLER   TO SPEAK

I spoke	*j'aie parlé*		we spoke	*nous ayons parlé*
you spoke	*tu aies parlé*		you spoke	*vous ayez parlé*
he/she/one spoke	*il/elle/on ait parlé*		they spoke	*ils/elles aient parlé*

PARTIR   TO LEAVE

I left	*je sois parti(e)*		we left	*nous soyons parti(e)s*
you left	*tu sois parti(e)*		you left	*vous soyez parti(e)s*
he/she/one left	*il/elle/on soit parti(e)*		they left	*ils/elles soient parti(e)s*

Il est dommage qu'il n'ait pas obtenu plus de voix.
It is a shame he did not get more votes.

Nous regrettons qu'il n'ait pas abordé les problèmes de fond.
We are sorry he did not address the basic problems.

340

The present subjective is used in all cases where the action in the subordinate clause takes place at the same time or after the action in the main clause.

J'aimerais qu'il obtienne plus de voix.
I would like him to get more votes.

The past subjunctive is used only when the action in the subordinate clause has taken place before the action in the main clause.

Je suis contente qu'ils aient gagné.
I'm happy that they won.

Nous regrettons que vous n'ayez pas pu venir.
We regret that you weren't able to come.

3. THE SUBJUNCTIVE VERSUS THE INDICATIVE

Affirmative verbs of thinking and believing *(penser, croire, trouver)* always take the indicative:

Je pense qu'ils n'ont pas de programme.
I think they don't have a program.

Nous trouvons qu'il y a trop d'erreurs.
We think there are too many mistakes.

When these verbs are in an interrogative or a negative form and the notion of doubt prevails, they are usually followed by the subjunctive.

Trouvez-vous que leur programme soit bon?
Do you think that their program is good?

Je ne pense pas qu'ils aient des solutions valables.
I don't think they have any worthwhile solutions.

Croyez-vous que ce soit possible?
Do you believe it's possible?

4. THE VERBS *CONNAÎTRE* AND *SAVOIR*

As you have learned in earlier chapters, both *connaître* and *savoir* mean "to know." However, they are used differently. Let's look first at *savoir*.

Savoir means to be aware of or informed about a situation.

Je sais pourquoi ils ont voté pour lui.
I know why they voted for him.

Savoir means to know how to do something through repetition.

Ils savent jouer au tennis.
They know how to play tennis.

Savoir is used with a conjunction.

Je sais pourquoi il a boycotté les élections.
I know why he boycotted the elections.

Je ne sais pas s'il gagnera.
I don't know if he'll win.

Savoir is used when the knowledge refers to needed study.

Il sait le poème.
He knows the poem.

Now let's look at *connaître*. *Connaître* means to be familiar with someone or something.

Je connais les chansons de Jacques Brel.
I know (am familiar with) Jacques Brel's songs.

Connaître means to be acquainted with.

Je connais le candidat du parti écologiste.
I know the candidate of the environmental party.

Je connais très bien Paris.
I know Paris very well.

VOCABULAIRE

la politique	politics
le pouvoir	power
le gouvernement	government
gouverner	to govern
le président	president
le politicien	politician
l'élection *(f.)*	election
la voix	vote (tallied)
le vote	vote
les élections présidentielles	presidential elections
les élections municipales	municipal elections
le premier tour	first round
le second tour	second round

le candidat, la candidate	candidate
conservateur *(m.)*, conservatrice *(f.)*	conservative
gagner les élections	to win the elections
perdre les élections	to lose the elections
la promesse	promise
tenir ses promesses	to keep one's promises
les affaires étrangères	foreign affairs
être élu	to be elected
aborder	to address (a problem)
le parti	party
la gauche	the left
la droite	the right
le centre	the center
la coalition	coalition
le programme	program, platform
la réforme	reform
l'intention *(f.)*	intention
l'augmentation *(f.)*	increase
la crèche	day care center
l'emploi *(m.)*	employment
l'impôt *(m.)*	tax
le revenu	income
l'enseignement *(m.)*	teaching, education
la sécurité sociale	social security
le boycott	boycott
boycotter	to boycott
voter	to vote
séduisant	attractive
tant de	so many
à peine	hardly
PME	small to medium-sized companies
PMI	small to medium-sized industries

EXERCICES

A. *Choisir entre le subjonctif ou l'infinitif.*

MODÈLE: *Je ne voterai pas _____ être sûr de son intégrité. (à moins de / que)*
              Je ne voterai pas à moins d'être sûr de son intégrité.

    1. *M. Lançon veut attendre _____ / se décider. (avant de / que)*
    2. *Vous votez _____ connaître son programme? (sans / sans que)*
    3. *Il apprend le français _____ pouvoir travailler en France.*
        (afin de / afin que)
    4. *Elle travaille _____ ses enfants / aller aux États-Unis.*
        (pour / pour que)
    5. *Il sera député _____ la droite / reprendre le pouvoir.*
        (à moins de/ à moins que)
    6. *Leur parti ne sera pas élu _____ avoir des solutions valables.*
        (sans / sans que)

B. *Mettre les phrases au subjonctif présent ou passé.*

MODÈLE: *Je crains qu'elle (manquer) le train ce matin. (passé)*
              Je crains qu'elle ait manqué le train ce matin.

    1. *Nous regrettons qu'il (partir) hier. (passé)*
    2. *J'ai peur que nous (arriver) en retard. (présent)*
    3. *Je suis content qu'ils (gagner) les dernières élections. (passé)*
    4. *Nous aimerions que vous (voter) pour lui. (présent)*
    5. *Il regrette que tu (perdre) ton poste de ministre. (passé)*
    6. *Nous sommes ravis que tu (changer) d'avis. (passé)*

C. *Choisir l'indicatif ou le subjonctif.*

MODÈLE: *Je crois qu'elle (changer d'avis).*
              Je crois qu'elle changera d'avis.

    1. *Je ne pense pas qu'ils (avoir) un bon programme.*
    2. *Je crois qu'ils (gagner) les élections demain.*
    3. *Trouvez-vous que la politique française (être) complexe?*
    4. *Pensez-vous qu'il (venir) ce soir?*
    5. *Je ne crois pas qu'il (avoir) assez de voix pour gagner l'élection*
        municipale.

D. *Compléter avec "savoir" ou "connaître."*

    1. *Nous _____ vaguement cette chanson.*
    2. *Nous ne _____ pas pourquoi il a perdu tant de voix.*
    3. *Il _____ très bien danser.*
    4. *_____-vous si les impôts vont augmenter cette année?*
    5. *Nous voudrions mieux _____ cette région.*

E. *Traduire.*

1. He is afraid he doesn't know who he'll vote for.
2. I won't vote for him unless he promises to open more day care centers.
3. She wants to address these questions.
4. Do you know these candidates?
5. We are happy she won the election.

NOTE CULTURELLE

France has a presidential system of government. The president is elected by direct suffrage for a term of seven years. He appoints a prime minister who is responsible to him and to the parliament. However the parliament, *l'Assemblée nationale,* has the power to make the prime minister resign if his party is in the minority.

The *RPR, Rassemblement pour la République,* and the *UDF, Union pour la Démocratie Française,* are conservative parties and form the political right wing, *la droite,* in France. The *PS, Parti Socialiste,* and the *PC, Parti Communiste,* are the main parties of the political left, *la gauche.* There are many smaller parties on both the right and left wing of politics.

Such plurality of parties makes it necessary to hold elections in two rounds. Whichever party and whichever candidate is elected in the first round has a chance to go on to the second round, where the final selections take place.

LA CLÉ DES EXERCICES

A. 1. *avant de se décider*   2. *sans connaître*   3. *afin de pouvoir travailler*
   4. *pour que ses enfants aillent*   5. *à moins que la droite reprenne*   6. *sans*
B. 1. *soit parti*   2. *arrivions*   3. *aient gagné*   4. *votiez*   5. *aies perdu*
   6. *aies changé*
C. 1. *aient*   2. *gagneront*   3. *soit*   4. *vienne*   5. *ait*
D. 1. *connaissons*   2. *savons*   3. *sait*   4. *Savez*   5. *connaître*
E. 1. *Il a peur de ne pas savoir pour qui voter.* 2. *Je ne voterai pas pour lui à moins qu'il ne promette d'ouvrir plus de crèches.* 3. *Elle veut aborder ces questions.* 4. *Connaissez-vous ces candidats?* 5. *Nous sommes heureux qu'elle ait gagné l'élection.*

LEÇON 38

LES PROFESSIONS. Professions.

A. DIALOGUE

Une entretien.

LA DIRECTRICE: **Nous cherchons quelqu'un qui connaisse bien nos logiciels et qui puisse effectuer des déplacements dans toute l'Europe.**

GUILLAUME: **J'ai une licence en informatique, une maîtrise en gestion et j'adore voyager.**

LA DIRECTRICE: **Quels que soient vos diplômes, il faut que vous parliez l'anglais couramment. Que vous soyez à Berlin, à Madrid ou à Rome, les réunions seront en anglais.**

GUILLAUME: **Cela ne devrait présenter aucun problème car j'ai vécu aux États-Unis pendant un an.**

LA DIRECTRICE: **Quoi qu'il en soit, pourriez-vous me dire pourquoi vous désirez travailler pour notre société?**

GUILLAUME: **À mon avis, votre approche globale correspond aux besoins de l'Europe actuelle et vos produits sont les meilleurs qui soient sur le marché international.**

LA DIRECTRICE: **Très bien. Je vous tiendrai au courant de notre décision, d'ici une semaine.**

A Job Interview.

DIRECTOR: We're looking for someone who knows our software and can travel throughout Europe.

GUILLAUME: I have a bachelor's in Computer Science, a master's in management, and I love to travel.

DIRECTOR: Whatever your degrees may be, you have to be fluent in English. Whether you are in Berlin, Madrid, or Rome, the meetings will be conducted in English.

GUILLAUME: That should not be a problem, as I lived in the United States for a year.

DIRECTOR: However that may be, could you tell me why you would like to work for our company?

GUILLAUME: In my opinion, your global approach meets the needs of today's Europe, and your products are the best one can find on the international market.

DIRECTOR: Very good. I'll let you know about our decision within a week.

B. GRAMMAIRE ET USAGE

1. THE SUBJUNCTIVE AFTER RELATIVE PRONOUNS

As you know, the indicative is normally used in relative clauses. However, the subjunctive is used in relative clauses when there is doubt or denial of the existence or attainability of the antecedent.

INDICATIVE:

Nous avons un employé qui sait parler anglais.
We have an employee who knows how to speak English.

Note the certainty here: the person clearly exists.

SUBJUNCTIVE:

Nous cherchons une personne qui sache parler l'anglais couramment.
We're looking for someone who knows how to speak English fluently.

In this case there is doubt: such a person may not be found.

Let's look at other examples.

Nous cherchons quelqu'un qui puisse voyager.
We're looking for someone who can travel.

Je cherche un ordinateur qui puisse résoudre ces équations.
I am looking for a computer that can solve these equations.

Nous aimerions engager un employé qui soit honnête.
We would like to hire an employee who is honest.

Nous cherchons quelqu'un qui connaisse bien nos logiciels.
We are looking for someone who knows our software well.

2. THE SUBJUNCTIVE AFTER THE SUPERLATIVE

In relative clauses where the antecedent is modified by a superlative or by the adjectives *seul* (only), *premier* (first), or *dernier* (last), the verb is usually in the subjunctive, unless it states an objective fact.

347

Votre société produit les meilleurs logiciels que je connaisse.
Your company makes the best software I know.

Ce sont les meilleurs produits qui soient sur le marché international.
These are the best products to be found on the international market.

C'est une des choses les plus fascinantes que l'on puisse faire.
It's one of the most thrilling things one can do.

Paris est la plus belle ville que j'aie jamais vue.
Paris is the most beautiful city I've ever seen.

3. THE SUBJUNCTIVE WITH EXPRESSIONS OF CONCESSION

The subjunctive is used to express the English indefinites "whatever," "whenever," and "wherever."

When "whatever" is used with a verb, French uses *quoi que* + the verb in the subjunctive (no agreement in gender or number).

Quoi que tu fasses, tu réussiras.
Whatever you do, you'll succeed.

Quoi qu'il dise, je ne le crois pas.
Whatever he says, I don't believe him.

When "whatever" is used with a noun, French uses *quel que* + the verb in the subjunctive; *quel* has to agree with the subject in gender and number.

Quels que soient vos diplômes, il faut que vous parliez anglais.
Whatever your degrees, you have to speak English.

Quelles que soient ses qualifications, nous l'engagerons.
Whatever her qualifications, we'll hire her.

Here are some other expressions of concessions with similar constructions.

Où qu'elle aille, elle trouvera du travail.
Wherever she goes, she'll find work.

Qui que vous soyez, vous pouvez faire une demande d'un emploi.
Whoever you are, you can apply for a job.

Quoi qu'il en soit, parlons de vous.
However that may be, let's talk about you.

Que vous soyez à Berlin ou à Madrid, les réunions seront en anglais.
Whether you are in Berlin or Madrid, the meetings will be in English.

4. THE SUBJUNCTIVE AS COMMAND

To express a command in the third person, French sometimes uses the subjunctive.

Qu'ils viennent.
Let them come.

Qu'elle entre.
Let her come in.

5. THE USE OF THE DEFINITE ARTICLE

a. The general rule in French is that the definite article indicates all particular nouns. It is repeated before every noun, even when English omits it.

Les ordinateurs sont très utiles.
Computers are very useful.

Les diplômes ne vous garantissent pas un emploi.
Degrees don't guarantee a job.

b. The article is used with the day of the week or the date:

Le mardi 5 mai.
Tuesday May 5.

Paris, le 12 juin.
Paris, June 12.

However, when the day of the week is given alone, as you know, the article is not used.

On se voit jeudi.
See you Thursday.

BUT:

On se voit le jeudi.
We see each other on Thursdays.

c. The article is used before names of languages, except when the language is introduced by *en* or when it follows the verb *parler.*

Nous apprenons le français.
We are learning French.

Traduisez en français.
Translate into French.

Ils parlent français et espagnol.
They speak French and Spanish.

But if *parler* is followed by an adverb, the definite article is used.

Nous parlons le français couramment.
We speak French fluently.

Ils parlent très bien le japonais.
They speak Japanese very well.

d. After the verb *être*, French does not use the definite article before names of professions.

Est-ce que vous voulez être informaticien?
Do you want to be a computer programmer?

Jacques est journaliste et Guillaume comptable.
Jacques is a journalist and Guillaume an accountant.

e. When speaking of a person, the definite article is used before titles indicating a profession.

Voici le docteur Dumas.
Here is Doctor Dumas.

Le président Mitterrand va parler à la télévision.
President Mitterrand will speak on television.

Monsieur le président, que comptez-vous faire contre la pollution?
Mister President, what do you intend to do to fight pollution?

Le général Moreau est allé à Londres.
General Moreau went to London.

Le capitaine Lenormand rencontrera le président.
Captain Lenormand will meet the president.

6. THE VERB *VIVRE*

Vivre (to live) is an irregular verb conjugated in the present tense as follows:

VIVRE   TO LIVE

I live	*je vis*	we live	*nous vivons*
you live	*tu vis*	you live	*vous vivez*
he/she/one lives	*il/elle/on vit*	they live	*ils/elles vivent*

In the *passé composé, vivre* is conjugated with *avoir: j'ai vécu.* The future tense is conjugated simply, *je vivrai, tu vivras . . .*

J'ai vécu aux États-Unis.
I lived in the United States.

Ils vivent ensemble depuis trois ans.
They have been living together for three years.

7. THE VERB *TENIR*

Tenir (to hold) is an irregular verb conjugated like *venir*. It is a very useful verb as it is used in many idiomatic expressions.

Je vous tiendrai au courant.
I'll keep you informed.

Il tient son document à la main.
He holds his document in his hand.

Les politiciens ne tiennent pas toujours leurs promesses.
Politicians don't always keep their promises.

Le directeur a tenu compte de leurs opinions.
The director took their opinions into account.

Il tient à ses amis / sa voiture.
He is attached to his friends / his car.

Je tiens à vous parler immédiatement.
I insist on talking to you immediately.

Elle tient de sa mère.
She takes after her mother.

VOCABULAIRE

la profession	profession
l'emploi *(m.)*	job, occupation, employment
l'avocat, l'avocate	lawyer
le/la comptable	accountant
la comptabilité	accounting
l'informatique *(f.)*	computer science
l'ordinateur *(m.)*	computer
le logiciel	software
l'ingénieur *(m.)*	engineer
l'employé(e) de banque	bank clerk
le/la fonctionnaire	civil servant
le vice-président	vice-president

le directeur du personnel	personnel manager
la société	company
la gestion	management
gérer	to manage (business)
la réunion	meeting
produire	to produce
le produit	product
le marché	market
le candidat, la candidate	applicant
les qualifications *(f.)*	qualifications
le diplôme	diploma
le C.V.	curriculum vitae, résumé
la licence	bachelor's degree
la maîtrise	master's degree
l'expérience *(f.)*	experience
les petites annonces *(f. pl.)*	classifieds, want ads
faire une demande d'emploi	to apply for a job
avoir une entrevue avec	to have an interview with
être muni de	to be equipped with
les déplacements *(m.)*	traveling, moving about
fabriquer	to make, to manufacture
vivre	to live
être au courant	to be informed
tenir au courant	to keep (someone) informed
parler couramment	to be fluent
l'avis *(m.)*	opinion
à mon avis	in my opinion

EXERCICES

A. *Compléter avec le subjonctif ou l'indicatif.*

MODÈLE: *Il a un secrétaire qui (savoir) bien classer ses documents.*
Il a un secrétaire qui sait bien classer ses documents.

1. *Nous cherchons quelqu'un qui (connaître) la comptabilité à la perfection.*
2. *Je connais une avocate qui (pouvoir) vous aider.*
3. *Y a-t-il beaucoup de fonctionnaires qui (savoir) le russe?*
4. *Pourriez-vous trouver des candidats qui (être) enthousiastes?*
5. *Nous voudrions une machine qui (pouvoir) résoudre ces problèmes.*

B. *Compléter avec la forme du verbe qui convient.*

MODÈLE: *C'est le plus beau musée que je (visiter) jamais.*
C'est le plus beau musée que j'aie jamais visité.

1. *C'est la meilleure société d'informatique que je (connaître).*
2. *Guillaume est le seul journaliste qui (vouloir) aller en Alaska.*
3. *Rome est la plus belle ville que je (voir) jamais.*
4. *C'est le temple le plus vieux qui (être).*
5. *C'est le dernier livre que vous (devoir) lire avant la fin de la semaine.*

C. *Utiliser l'article défini quand c'est nécessaire.*

MODÈLE: *Voilà _____ lieutenant Baron.*
   Voilà le lieutenant Baron.

1. *Monsieur _____ président, comment allez-vous?*
2. *Je vous présente _____ docteur Letessier.*
3. *Christian veut être _____ directeur d'entreprise.*
4. *Suzanne parle _____ italien couramment.*
5. *Ils sont _____ ingénieurs.*

D. *Compléter avec le verbe "vivre."*

1. *Ils _____ à la campagne.*
2. *Elle _____ tranquillement avec ses chats.*
3. *Vous _____ une vie compliquée.*
4. *On ne peut pas _____ d'amour et d'eau fraîche.*
5. *Est-ce que tu _____ toujours à Paris?*

E. *Compléter avec le verbe "tenir."*

1. *Elle _____ son fils par la main. (présent)*
2. *Ils _____ des propos scandaleux. (passé composé)*
3. *_____ vous de votre père ou de votre mère? (présent)*
4. *Nous _____ à vous remercier de votre gentillesse. (présent)*
5. *Je vous assure qu'ils _____ leurs promesses. (futur)*

NOTE CULTURELLE

There is more formality in professional and social relationships in France than there is in the United States. For job applications, this increased level of formality means that a letter of application must follow the rules of formal written address. It should begin with a formula such as: *"J'ai l'honneur de soumettre ma candidature au poste de . . . "* ("I have the honor of submitting my application to the position of . . . "), and it should end with the appropriate formula for expressing one's regards: *"Je vous prie, Monsieur le directeur, de trouver ici l'expression de mes salutations distinguées"* ("Sir, I hope you will find here the expression of my highest regards").

LA CLÉ DES EXERCICES

A. 1. *connaisse* 2. *pourra* 3. *sachent* 4. *soient* 5. *puisse*
B. 1. *connaisse* 2. *veuille* 3. *j'aie jamais vue* 4. *soit* 5. *deviez*
C. 1. *le* 2. *le* 3. no article 4. *l'* 5. no article
D. 1. *vivent* 2. *vit* 3. *vivez* 4. *vivre* 5. *vis*
E. 1. *tient* 2. *ont tenu* 3. *Tenez-* 4. *tenons* 5. *tiendront*

LEÇON 39
LES ÉCOLES ET LES UNIVERSITÉS. Schools and Universities.

A. DIALOGUE

L'étude du français.

PAUL: Vous êtes prêts pour l'examen?

LISA: Plus ou moins.

PAUL: Je suis sûre qu'elle va nous faire faire une dictée!

JIM: Une dictée!

PAUL: Ah oui! Mon ancien prof nous en faisait toujours faire une pour l'examen final.

LISA: J'ai beau lire des centaines de pages de littérature et d'histoire ancienne par semaine, je fais toujours des tas de fautes d'orthographe.

JIM: Et toi, Paul, tu sais les conjugaisons de tous les verbes?

PAUL: Sur le bout des doigts. Mme Hébert nous les a fait apprendre par coeur.

JIM: On a beau étudier cette langue, je doute qu'on ne la parle jamais couramment.

LISA: Mon pauvre Jim, tu es toujours cynique! On ne se débrouille pas mal quand même!

JIM: Bon, mes chers amis, si on réussit tous à l'examen, je vous offre un verre au Café Flore!

Studying French.

PAUL: Are you ready for the exam?

LISA: More or less.

PAUL: I am sure she'll have us do a dictation!

JIM: A dictation!

PAUL: Yes! My former teacher always had us do one for the final exam.

LISA: Although I read hundreds of pages of literature and ancient history every week, I always make lots of spelling mistakes.

JIM: Paul, do you know the conjugations of all the verbs?

PAUL: I know them perfectly. Mrs. Hébert had us learn them by heart.

JIM: However much we study this language, I doubt we'll ever be able to speak it fluently.

LISA: My poor Jim, you are always cynical! We are not doing badly at all.

JIM: Okay, my dear friends, if we all pass the exam, I'll buy you a drink at the Café Flore!

B. GRAMMAIRE ET USAGE

1. OBJECTS WITH THE CAUSATIVE *FAIRE*

We studied the causative form *faire* + the infinitive in lesson 22.

Je fais réparer la voiture.
I have the car fixed.

a. When replacing the object with an object pronoun, the pronoun precedes the verb faire.

Je fais réparer la voiture.
I have the car fixed.

Je la fais réparer.
I have it fixed.

Elle fait apprendre par coeur les conjugaisons des verbes.
She has the verb conjugations memorized.

Elle les fait apprendre par coeur.
She has them memorized.

b. When the direct and indirect pronouns are replaced, pronouns are placed in the usual order. (See lessons 16 and 18)

Elle nous faisait faire une dictée.
She had us do a dictation.

Elle nous en faisait faire une.
She had us do one.

Elle vous fait apprendre les verbes?
She makes you learn the verbs?

Elle vous les fait apprendre?
She makes you learn them?

Il leur fait passer l'examen.
He has them take the exam.

Il le leur fait passer.
He has them take it.

Faites-leur apprendre le poème.
Have them learn the poem.

Faites-le leur apprendre.
Have them learn it.

    c. As we've already studied, if the direct object is replaced by the direct object pronoun, the past participle agrees in gender and number with the object.

J'ai appris la leçon.
I learned the lesson.

Je l'ai apprise.
I learned it.

Elle a vu les fautes.
She saw the mistakes.

Elle les a vues.
She saw them.

    Yet, when the causative construction is used in the past tenses, the past participle remains invariable.

Il leur a fait apprendre les verbes.
He had them learn the verbs.

Il les leur a fait apprendre.
He had them learn them.

Elle nous a fait faire la dictée la plus difficile.
She had us do the most difficult dictation.

Elle nous l'a fait faire.
She had us do it.

2. ADJECTIVES PRECEDING OR FOLLOWING THE NOUN

The meaning of some adjectives changes, depending on whether they precede or follow the noun. Here are a few examples:

mon ancien professeur	my former teacher
l'histoire ancienne	ancient history
mes chers amis	my dear friends
un livre cher	an expensive book
mon pauvre Jim	my poor (unfortunate) Jim

357

les pays pauvres	poor countries
sa propre compagnie	his own company
une salle de classe propre	a clean classroom
la même dictée	the same dictation
le jour même de l'examen	the very day of the exam
un brave homme	a good man
un homme brave	a courageous man
différentes opinions	various opinions
des idées très différentes	very different ideas

3. AVOIR BEAU

a. *Avoir beau* (although, despite the fact, however much), an idiomatic expression which conveys an idea of concession, is widely used in modern spoken and written French. Let's look at a few examples:

Quoiqu'il fasse froid, nous irons faire une promenade.
      or
Il a beau faire froid, nous irons faire une promenade.
   Although it is cold, we'll go for a walk.

Quoique j'étudie cette langue, je ne la parle pas couramment.
      or
J'ai beau étudier cette langue, je ne la parle pas couramment.
   Although I study this language, I am not fluent.

Quoique nous lisions énormément, nous faisons des fautes.
      or
Nous avons beau lire énormément, nous faisons des fautes.
   No matter how much we study, we make mistakes.

Once you've grasped the construction, you'll soon realize that *avoir beau* is very handy if an irregular subjunctive has slipped your mind!

b. *Avoir beau* can be used with all tenses. Here are a few examples:

Il aura beau insister, ils ne lui donneront pas un coup de main.
   However much he insists, they won't give him a hand.

Elle avait beau manger toute la journée, elle ne grossissait pas.
   Although she ate all day long, she never put on weight.

J'ai eu beau lui dire de refuser l'offre, il l'a acceptée.
   Although I told him to turn down the offer, he accepted it.

4. IDIOMATIC EXPRESSIONS WITH *COEUR*

J'ai appris le poème par coeur.
    I learned the poem by heart.

Ma lettre lui a brisé le coeur.
    My letter broke his heart.

Elle a eu une opération à coeur ouvert.
    She had open-heart surgery.

Arrêtez-vous! J'ai toujours mal au coeur dans votre voiture!
    Stop! I always feel nauseous in your car!

Il a un coeur d'or / de pierre.
    He has a heart of gold / of stone.

Le château est au coeur de la ville.
    The castle is in the heart of the town.

Il a un coeur d'artichaut.
    He falls in love with every woman he meets.

Je vais lui dire ce que j'ai sur le coeur.
    I'm going to tell him what's on my mind.

VOCABULAIRE

un stage linguistique	language training
le cours	class
un professeur	teacher, professor
un élève	student (grade school)
un étudiant	student (college)
un ancien étudiant	alumni
les devoirs *(m.pl.)*	homework
la dictée	dictation
le verbe	verb
la conjugaison	conjugation
l'orthographe *(f.)*	spelling
la faute d'orthographe	spelling mistake
l'examen *(m.)*	exam
la salle de classe	classroom
le tableau	blackboard
la craie	chalk
le cahier	notebook
le bloc de papier	note pad
le stylo	pen
le crayon	pencil

l'ordinateur	computer
apprendre	to learn
enseigner	to teach
parler couramment	to be fluent
se débrouiller	to manage
offrir	to offer, to treat
douter	to doubt
passer un examen	to take an exam
réussir à un examen	to pass an exam
échouer à un examen	to fail an exam
ancien	former; ancient
cher	dear; expensive
pauvre	unfortunate; poor
propre	(one's) own; clean
brave	nice; brave
différent	different; various
même	same; very; even
cynique	cynical
prêt	ready
des tas de	piles of, lots of

EXERCICES

A. *Remplacer le nom souligné par un pronom.*

MODÈLE: Elle lui a fait chanter la chanson.
   Elle la lui a fait chanter.

1. *Nous avons fait couper l'arbre mort.*
2. *Il nous a fait faire quatre exercices.*
3. *Ce professeur fait passer les examens chaque semestre.*
4. *Mme Hébert leur fera apprendre tous les verbes irréguliers.*
5. *Ils ont fait construire la plus grande maison du village.*
6. *Nous lui ferons envoyer des fleurs pour son anniversaire.*
7. *Je lui fais copier dix fois le texte.*
8. *Le propriétaire leur a fait repeindre l'appartement.*
9. *Le professeur nous fait refaire le même exercice plusieurs fois.*
10. *Je dois faire réparer la télévision.*

B. *Relier le français et l'anglais.*

A

1. *sa maison propre*
2. *sa voiture chère*

B

a. her own house
b. an old city

3. *sa propre maison*   c. his dear car
4. *une ville ancienne*   d. her clean house
5. *sa chère voiture*   e. those poor (not rich) people
6. *ces pauvres gens*   f. your former teacher
7. *votre ancien professeur*   g. his expensive car
8. *ces gens pauvres*   h. those poor (unfortunate) people

C. *Substituer "quoique" par l'expression idiomatique "avoir beau."*

MODÈLE: *Quoiqu'il ne sache pas très bien jouer, il participera au tournoi.*
   Il a beau ne pas savoir très bien jouer, il participera au tournoi.

1. *Quoiqu'elle soit malade, elle assistera à la réunion.*
2. *Quoique nous fassions de notre mieux, je doute que nous réussissions à l'examen.*
3. *Quoiqu'il se couche tard, il se lève tôt.*
4. *Quoique je passe des heures à étudier, je fais encore des fautes.*
5. *Quoique vous appreniez par coeur les verbes, vous les oubliez parfois.*
6. *Quoique j'aie encore deux semaines de vacances, je n'irai pas en Australie.*
7. *Quoiqu'il ne fasse pas très chaud, nous irons à la plage.*
8. *Quoique vous soyez fatigué, vous devrez étudier toute la soirée.*
9. *Quoiqu'ils fassent des dictées chaque semaine, ils font des tas de fautes.*
10. *Quoiqu'il dorme dix heures par nuit, il est toujours fatigué.*

D. *Refaites les phrases en utilisant une expression idiomatique avec "coeur."*

1. *Elle est extrêmement généreuse.*
2. *Elle a beaucoup souffert en apprenant la nouvelle.*
3. *Je sais toutes les paroles de la chanson.*
4. *Elle ne cesse pas d'avoir des coups de foudre.*
5. *Il a la nausée.*

NOTE CULTURELLE

Language schools all over France cater to Americans and EC Europeans who want to learn French. However, French is no longer the language of diplomacy it used to be when it was spoken at the courts in Russia, the Middle East, and the Near East. The French language is under attack from the strong influence of English. The *académiciens* of the French Academy are waging a fruitless war against so-called Franglais. French is still spoken in the DOM *(Département d'Outre-Mer):* Guadeloupe, Martinique, French Guyana and Réunion (East Africa).

DOMs are full-fledged departments, where the French citizens vote and also receive the same benefits as the French on the mainland. TOMs *(Territoire d'Outre-Mer)* are ex-colonies, such as New Caledonia and French Polynesia, which have kept economic ties with France.

LA CLÉ DES EXERCICES

A. 1. *Nous l'avons fait couper.* 2. *Il nous en a fait faire quatre.* 3. *Ce professeur les fait passer chaque semestre.* 4. *Mme Hébert les leur fera apprendre.* 5. *Ils l'ont fait construire.* 6. *Nous lui en ferons envoyer pour son anniversaire.* 7. *Je le lui fais copier dix fois.* 8. *Le propriétaire le leur a fait repeindre.* 9. *Le professeur nous le fait refaire plusieurs fois.* 10. *Je dois la faire réparer.*

B. 1.—d 2.—g 3.—a 4.—b 5.—c 6.—h 7.—f 8.—e

C. 1. *Elle a beau être malade, elle assistera à la réunion.* 2. *Nous avons beau faire de notre mieux, je doute que nous réussissions à l'examen.* 3. *Il a beau se coucher tard, il se lève tôt.* 4. *J'ai beau passer des heures à étudier, je fais encore des fautes.* 5. *Vous avez beau apprendre par coeur les verbes, vous les oubliez parfois.* 6. *J'ai beau avoir encore deux semaines de vacances, je n'irai pas en Australie.* 7. *Il a beau ne pas faire très chaud, nous irons à la plage.* 8. *Vous avez beau être fatigué, vous devrez étudier toute la soirée.* 9. *Ils ont beau faire des dictées chaque semaine, ils font des tas de fautes.* 10. *Il a beau dormir dix heures par nuit, il est toujours fatigué.*

D. 1. *Elle a un coeur d'or.* 2. *La nouvelle lui a brisé le coeur.* 3. *J'ai appris la chanson par coeur.* 4. *Elle a un coeur d'artichaut.* 5. *Il a mal au coeur.*

LEÇON 40
LA LITTÉRATURE.   Literature.

A. SELECTED POETRY

La poésie

J'ai cueilli ce brin de bruyère
L'automne est morte souviens-t'en
Nous ne nous reverrons plus sur terre
Odeur du temps, brin de bruyère
Et souviens-toi que je t'attends

—Guillaume Apollinaire

je voudrais que mon amour meure
qu'il pleuve sur le cimetière
et les ruelles où je vais
pleurant celle qui crut m'aimer

—Samuel Beckett

L'autre jour au creux d'un vallon
Un serpent piqua Jean Frerron
Que croyez-vous qui arriva?
Ce fut le serpent qui creva

—Voltaire

Poetry

I picked this fragile sprig of heather
Autumn had died long since remember
Never again shall we see one another
Odor of time, sprig of heather
Remember I await our life.

—Guillaume Apollinaire

I would like my love to die
and the rain to be raining on the graveyard
and on me walking the streets
mourning her who thought she loved me.

—Samuel Beckett

The other day at the bottom of a hollow
A serpent bit Jean Frerron
What do you think came to follow?
The serpent died of the bite.

—Voltaire

B. GRAMMAIRE ET USAGE

1. WRITTEN FRENCH VERSUS SPOKEN FRENCH

Literary tenses are mostly used in written French, particularly in narratives. They are used in the writing of history and in literature, as for example, sometimes in formal lectures at the *Académie française.*

a. The *passé simple.* The *passé simple* is a literary tense and is never used in daily speech. In the sequence of tenses it plays the same role as the *passé composé:* It expresses a past act or a series of actions. Since the *passé simple* is used mostly in third-person narration, only the third-person singular and plural will be given here. For the complete forms, see the Appendix.

Il a parlé avec son ami. (passé composé)
  He spoke with his friend.

Il parla avec son ami. (passé simple)
  He spoke with his friend.

Qu'est-ce qui est arrivé? (passé composé)
  What happened?

Qu'est-ce qui arriva? (passé simple)
  What happened?

PARLER	TO SPEAK
il/elle/on parla	he/she/one spoke
ils/elles parlèrent	they spoke

FINIR	TO FINISH
il/elle finit	he/she finished
ils/elles finirent	they finished

PARTIR	TO LEAVE
il/elle partit	he/she left
ils/elles partirent	they left

VENDRE	TO SELL
il/elle vendit	he/she sold
ils/elles vendirent	they sold

CROIRE	TO BELIEVE
il/elle crut	he/she believed
ils/elles crurent	they believed

b. Some verbs have an irregular form in the *passé simple.*

avoir	to have	*il eut*	*ils eurent*
être	to be	*il fut*	*ils furent*
venir	to come	*il vint*	*ils vinrent*
faire	to do	*il fit*	*ils firent*
naître	to be born	*il naquit*	*ils naquirent*
mourir	to die	*il mourut*	*ils moururent*
prendre	to take	*il prit*	*ils prirent*
vouloir	to want	*il voulut*	*ils voulurent*
savoir	to know	*il sut*	*ils surent*
vivre	to live	*il vécut*	*ils vécurent*

Here are a few example sentences:

Il mourut de sa belle mort.
He died a natural death.

Elle naquit un soir d'automne.
She was born on an autumn night.

2. THE VERB *CUEILLIR*

Cueillir (to pick) is an irregular verb with useful derivatives: *accueillir* (to welcome), *recueillir* (to gather). Here is its conjugation in the present tense.

CUELLIR TO PICK

I pick	*je cueille*	we pick	*nous cueillons*
you pick	*tu cueilles*	you pick	*vous cueillez*
he/she/one picks	*il/elle/on cueille*	they pick	*ils/elles cueillent*

The *passé composé* is formed with *avoir: j'ai cueilli*
The future form is: *je cueillerai, tu cueilleras, . . .*

J'ai cueilli ce brin de bruyère.
I picked this fragile sprig of heather.

Elle a cueilli des fleurs dans le jardin.
She picked flowers in the garden.

Ils cueillent les pommes en septembre.
They pick apples in September.

Ils sont allés accueillir leurs amis à l'aéroport.
They welcomed their friends at the airport.

Je dois recueillir beaucoup de renseignements.
I need to gather a lot of information.

Le candidat a recueilli 300 000 voix.
The candidate won 300,000 votes.

In slang, *cueillir* means to arrest someone.

La police a cueilli le voleur.
The police picked up the thief.

3. THE PREFIX *RE-*

Adding the prefix *re-* to certain verbs indicates repetition.

voir	to see
revoir	to see again
faire	to do
refaire	to do over
dire	to say
redire	to say again
commencer	to start
recommencer	to start over
acheter	to buy
racheter	to buy back
appeler	to call
rappeler	to call back
venir	to come
revenir	to come back

| *lire* | to read |
| *relire* | to reread |

Elle a relu toutes les oeuvres de Flaubert.
    She has reread all of Flaubert's works.

Rappelez-moi demain.
    Call me back tomorrow.

Il est revenu hier soir.
    He came back last night.

Ils ont décidé de recommencer à zéro.
    They decided to start again from scratch.

VOCABULAIRE

la bruyère	heather
l'amour *(m.)*	love
la ruelle	alley, small street
le vallon	vale; hollow
la terre	earth; soil
l'odeur *(f.)*	odor, smell
le brin	sprig
le cimetière	cemetery
le serpent	serpent; snake
attendre	to wait
cueillir	to pick (flowers)
se souvenir	to remember
pleuvoir	to rain
pleurer	to cry
l'histoire *(f.)*	history; story
la monarchie	monarchy
le roi	king
la reine	queen
la règne	reign
l'empereur *(m.)*	emperor
la république	republic
le citoyen	citizen
le noble	noble
la bourgeoisie	middle class, bourgeoisie
le paysan	farmer, peasant
la paix	peace
la guerre	war
la bataille	battle
la victoire	victory
la défaite	defeat

le prisonnier	prisoner
la puissance	power
la misère	misery, poverty
la révolution	revolution
triompher	to triumph
établir	to establish
restaurer	to restore
durer	to last, to endure
le siècle	century
naître	to be born
être guillotiné	to be guillotined

EXERCICES

A. *Mettre les verbes au passé composé.*

MODÈLE: Il ne dit rien.
  Il n'a rien dit.

1. *Napoléon prit le pouvoir en 1799.*
2. *Il voulut conquérir l'Europe.*
3. *Louis-Philippe fut le dernier roi de France.*
4. *Les rois firent la guerre.*
5. *Les français connurent la prospérité au XXième siècle.*
6. *Louis XVI ne sut pas gouverner la France.*
7. *Au XVIIième siècle, la France devint une grande puissance.*
8. *Ils vécurent heureux.*
9. *Elles naquirent avant la Révolution.*
10. *Ils crurent que tout finirait mal.*

B. *Mettre les verbes au passé simple.*

MODÈLE: Il (revenir) de bonne heure.
  Il revint de bonne heure.

1. *Elle (naître) en 1968.*
2. *Napoléon (mourir) à Sainte-Hélène.*
3. *Ils (vivre) en France pendant des années.*
4. *Elle ne (savoir) quoi répondre.*
5. *Ils (être) très triste en apprenant la nouvelle.*

C. *Compléter avec le verbe qui convient.*

MODÈLE: Il _____ des fleurs pour sa mère.
  Il cueille des fleurs pour sa mère.

1. *Ils _____ des kilos de poires hier après-midi.*
2. *Il _____ l'information nécessaire d'ici la semaine prochaine.*

3. *Ce serait gentil d'aller l'_____ à la gare d'Austerlitz.*
4. *Chaque année, nous _____ de magnifiques bouquets de fleurs dans notre jardin.*
5. *Combien de voix est-ce que le candidat de gauche _____ aux dernières élections?*

NOTE CULTURELLE

France has an abundance of great poets. Some of the more famous ones from the 19th century are Mallarmé, Baudelaire, Verlaine, and Rimbaud. In the 20th century, Apollinaire, Prévert, Breton, Valéry, and Laforgues have enjoyed both popularity and critical acclaim.

France's national holiday is July 14, Bastille Day. This day is remembered as the beginning of modern republican France. It commemorates the popular uprising of 1789 that destroyed the Bastille, a prison and at the same time a powerful symbol of the monarchy (the *ancien régime*). To celebrate this day, a parade marches down the Champs-Elysées, and the *bal du 14 juillet* encourages everyone to dance in the squares and streets of Paris.

LA CLÉ DES EXERCICES

A. 1. *a pris*　2. *a voulu*　3. *a été*　4. *ont fait*　5. *ont connu*　6. *n'a pas su*
　　7. *est devenue*　8. *ont vécu*　9. *sont nées*　10. *ont cru*
B. 1. *naquit*　2. *mourut*　3. *vécurent*　4. *sut*　5. *furent*
C. 1. *ont cueilli*　2. *recueillera*　3. *accueillir*　4. *cueillons*　5. *a recueilli*

HUITIÈME RÉVISION

A. *Mettre les verbes au subjonctif présent.*

MODÈLE: *À quelle heure voulez-vous que nous (arriver).*
　　　　À quelle heure voulez-vous que nous arrivions.

1. *Il faut que vous (marchander) au marché aux puces.*
2. *Il vaut mieux que tu (aller) jeter un coup d'oeil toi-même.*
3. *Pourvu qu'ils (être) à l'heure.*
4. *Il a tout prévu pour que vous (pouvoir) passer un excellent moment.*
5. *Nous ne croyons pas qu'elle (réussir) à son examen.*
6. *Bien que nous (avoir) le temps, je doute que nous (aller) au marché.*
7. *Nous sommes ravis que vous (venir) nous voir cet été.*
8. *Quel dommage qu'il (faire) si froid!*
9. *Il est possible qu'elle (partir) avant midi.*
10. *Il est étrange que le TGV (avoir) tant de retard.*

B. *Indicatif ou subjonctif?*

1. *Il est impossible que nous (arriver) avant midi.*
2. *Il est certain qu'il vous (craindre).*
3. *Il est étonnant qu'il (faire) si chaud.*
4. *Elle sera contente où qu'elle (aller).*
5. *Nous espérons qu'ils le (faire) réparer demain.*
6. *Je pense qu'elle (acheter) ce miroir.*
7. *Il tient à ce que vous lui (téléphoner) ce soir.*
8. *Nous croyons que les politiciens (faire) les réformes qu'ils ont promises.*
9. *Elle veut que tu (repeindre) la cuisine.*
10. *Pensez-vous qu'il (être) vraiment honnête?*

C. *Mettre les phrases au temps qui convient.*

1. *Je connais une personne qui (savoir) le français et l'espagnol.*
2. *Y a-t-il quelqu'un qui (pouvoir) venir tout de suite?*
3. *Paris et Rome sont les plus belles villes que je (connaître).*
4. *Nous cherchons un ordinateur qui (pouvoir) résoudre ces problèmes.*
5. *Y a-t-il un train qui (être) plus rapide?*

D. *Mettre les verbes au subjonctif présent ou passé.*

MODÈLE: *Je regrette qu'il (perdre) l'élection.*
Je regrette qu'il ait perdu l'élection.

1. *Ne croyez-vous pas que le président (tenir) ses promesses l'an passé.*
2. *Je suis désolé que vous (ne pas pouvoir) venir hier.*
3. *Elle doute qu'il (finir) le travail avant demain.*
4. *Il est content que nous (pouvoir) voir l'exposition la semaine dernière.*
5. *Voulez-vous que nous (faire) une partie de tennis?*

E. *Compléter les phrases avec un article défini quand c'est nécessaire.*

1. *Elle veut être _____ médecin.*
2. *Bonjour, Monsieur _____ président.*
3. *Il parle _____ italien.*
4. *Elle n'a jamais suivi un cours mais elle parle _____ français couramment.*
5. *_____ général Mauriceau prononcera un discours aux Nations-Unies.*

F. *Compléter en utilisant "savoir" ou "connaître."*

1. *Ils _____ cette chanson par coeur.*
2. *Vous _____ l'édifice de l'Institut du Monde Arabe?*
3. *Tu _____ jouer au bridge?*
4. *Nous _____ qu'il a beaucoup de chances de gagner l'élection.*
5. *Je _____ très bien Guillaume et sa femme Aurélie.*

G. *Mettre au passé simple.*

MODÈLE: *Il demande la permission de sortir.*
Il demanda la permission de sortir.

1. *Il est très triste.*
2. *Qu'est-ce qui est arrivé?*
3. *Il croit l'aimer.*
4. *Elle a peur du serpent.*
5. *Ils parlent pendant des heures.*

H. *Conjuguer les verbes suivants.*

1. *Ils _____ avec leurs deux enfants dans une grande maison. (vivre; imparfait)*
2. *Nous _____ à ce que vous assistiez à notre réunion. (tenir; présent)*
3. *Il _____ avec ses chats dans sa maison de campagne. (vivre; présent)*
4. *Est-ce qu'il _____ ses promesses? (tenir; passé composé)*
5. *Elle _____ les fleurs de son jardin. (cueillir; futur)*

LA CLÉ DES EXERCICES

A. 1. *marchandiez* 2. *ailles* 3. *soient* 4. *puissiez* 5. *réussisse* 6. *ayons; allions* 7. *veniez* 8. *fasse* 9. *parte* 10. *ait*
B. 1. *arrivions* 2. *craint* 3. *fasse* 4. *aille* 5. *feront* 6. *achètera* 7. *téléphoniez* 8. *feront* 9. *repeignes* 10. *soit*
C. 1. *sait* 2. *puisse* 3. *connaisse* 4. *puisse* 5. *soit*
D. 1. *ait tenu* 2. *n'ayez pas pu* 3. *finisse* 4. *ayons pu* 5. *fassions*
E. 1. (no article) 2. *le* 3. (no article) 4. *le* 5. *Le*
F. 1. *savent* 2. *connaissez* 3. *sais* 4. *savons* 5. *connais*
G. 1. *fut* 2. *arriva* 3. *crut* 4. *eut* 5. *parlèrent*
H. 1. *vivaient* 2. *tenons* 3. *vit* 4. *a tenu* 5. *cueillera*

LECTURE

LES VINS FRANÇAIS

Guillaume est au rayon des vins[1] dans un grand supermarché de la région parisienne. Ce soir, c'est le deuxième anniversaire de mariage[2] de Guillaume et sa femme, Sophie. Ils vont célébrer l'occasion en dégustant du foie gras avec une bonne bouteille de Sauternes. Ensuite, pour le plat de résistance,[3] Guillaume va préparer un coq[4] au vin qu'il servira avec un Châteauneuf-du-Pape.

La France est renommée pour ses vins et ses fromages,[5] tous deux vieillis[6] avec une précision méticuleuse.[7] En dehors de Paris, vous découvrirez[8] un pays parsemé[9] de petites fermes[10] et de champs[11] à perte de vue. C'est ici que les vins français commencent leur long voyage.

VOCABULAIRE

1.	*le rayon des vins*	wine section
2.	*l'anniversaire de mariage*	wedding anniversary
3.	*le plat de résistance*	main dish
4.	*le coq*	rooster
5.	*le fromage*	cheese
6.	*vieilli*	aged
7.	*méticuleux*	meticulous
8.	*découvrir*	to discover
9.	*parsemé*	dotted
10.	*la ferme*	farm
11.	*le champ*	field

Félicitations!

Now that you have completed the course, you'll be able to use this manual as a reference book for expressions, grammar and usage. The appendixes that follow provide even more information for additional study. We also recommend that you review the material, looking carefully at sections that seemed difficult the first time around. Both sets of recordings will be of further use as you study and review at home, in your car, or while jogging. . . .

Keep up the good work!

APPENDIXES

A. GLOSSARY OF COUNTRIES, NATIONALITIES, AND CONTINENTS

FRANÇAIS–ANGLAIS

Names of languages are usually the same as the masculine form of the nationality: *Paul est anglais; il parle anglais.*

PAYS	COUNTRY	*NATIONALITÉ*
Algérie (f)	Algeria	*algérien*
Allemagne (f)	Germany	*allemand*
Angleterre (f)	England	*anglais*
Argentine (f)	Argentina	*argentin*
Autriche (f)	Austria	*autrichien*
Brésil (m)	Brazil	*brésilien*
Bulgarie (f)	Bulgaria	*bulgare*
Canada (m)	Canada	*canadien*
Chili (m)	Chile	*chilien*
Chine (f)	China	*chinois*
Colombie (f)	Colombia	*colombien*
Danemark (m)	Denmark	*danois*
Écosse (f)	Scotland	*écossais*
Égypte (f)	Egypt	*égyptien*
Espagne (f)	Spain	*espagnol*
États-Unis (m. pl.)	United States	*américain*
France (f)	France	*français*
Grèce (f)	Greece	*grec*
Hollande (f)	Holland	*hollandais*
Hongrie (f)	Hungary	*hongrois*
Inde (f)	India	*indien*
Irlande (f)	Ireland	*irlandais*
Italie (f)	Italy	*italien*
Japon (m)	Japan	*japonais*
Luxembourg (m)	Luxembourg	*luxembourgeois*
Maroc (m)	Morocco	*marocain*
Mexique (m)	Mexico	*mexicain*
Norvège (f)	Norway	*norvégien*
Pérou (m)	Peru	*péruvien*
Pologne (f)	Poland	*polonais*

Portugal (m)	Portugal	*portuguais*
Roumanie (f)	Rumania	*roumain*
Russie (f)	Russia	*russe*
Sénégal (m)	Senegal	*sénégalais*
Suède (f)	Sweden	*suédois*
Suisse (f)	Switzerland	*suisse*
Tunisie (f)	Tunisia	*tunisien*
Turquie (f)	Turkey	*turc*

CONTINENTS	CONTINENTS	*NATIONALITÉ*
Afrique (f)	Africa	*africain*
Amérique du nord (f)	North America	*nord-américain*
Amérique du sud (f)	South America	*sud-américain*
Asie (f)	Asia	*asiatique*
Australie (f)	Australia	*australien*
Europe (f)	Europe	*européen*

ENGLISH–FRENCH

COUNTRY	*PAYS*	*NATIONALITÉ*
Algeria	*Algérie (f)*	*algérien*
Germany	*Allemagne (f)*	*allemand*
England	*Angleterre (f)*	*anglais*
Argentina	*Argentine (f)*	*argentin*
Austria	*Autriche (f)*	*autrichien*
Brazil	*Brésil (m)*	*brésilien*
Bulgaria	*Bulgarie (f)*	*bulgare*
Canada	*Canada (m)*	*canadien*
Chile	*Chili (m)*	*chilien*
China	*Chine (f)*	*chinois*
Colombia	*Colombie (f)*	*colombien*
Denmark	*Danemark (m)*	*danois*
Scotland	*Écosse (f)*	*écossais*
Egypt	*Égypte (f)*	*égyptien*
Spain	*Espagne (f)*	*espagnol*
United States	*États-Unis (m. pl.)*	*américain*
France	*France (f)*	*français*
Greece	*Grèce (f)*	*grec*
Holland	*Hollande (f)*	*hollandais*
Hungary	*Hongrie (f)*	*hongrois*
India	*Inde (f)*	*indien*
Ireland	*Irlande (f)*	*irlandais*
Italy	*Italie (f)*	*italien*
Japan	*Japon (m)*	*japonais*
Luxembourg	*Luxembourg (m)*	*luxembourgeois*
Morocco	*Maroc (m)*	*marocain*
Mexico	*Mexique (m)*	*mexicain*
Norway	*Norvège (f)*	*norvégien*

Peru	*Pérou (m)*	*péruvien*
Poland	*Pologne (f)*	*polonais*
Portugal	*Portugal (m)*	*portuguais*
Rumania	*Roumanie (f)*	*roumain*
Russia	*Russie (f)*	*russe*
Senegal	*Sénégal (m)*	*sénégalais*
Sweden	*Suède (f)*	*suédois*
Switzerland	*Suisse (f)*	*suisse*
Tunisia	*Tunisie (f)*	*tunisien*
Turkey	*Turquie (f)*	*turc*

CONTINENTS	*CONTINENTS*	*NATIONALITÉ*
Africa	*Afrique (f)*	*africain*
North America	*Amérique du nord (f)*	*nord-américain*
South America	*Amérique du sud (f)*	*sud-américain*
Asia	*Asie (f)*	*asiatique*
Australia	*Australie (f)*	*australien*
Europe	*Europe (f)*	*européen*

B. GRAMMAR SUMMARY

1. SUBJECT PRONOUNS

I	*je*		we	*nous*
you [singular familiar]	*tu*		you [singular polite and plural of *tu*]	*vous*
he, it (masculine)	*il*		they (masculine)	*ils*
she, it (feminine)	*elle*		they (feminine)	*elles*
it, one (1)	*on*			

2. ARTICLES

a. Definite articles.

MASCULINE	*le (l')*
FEMININE	*la (l')*
PLURAL	*les*

b. Indefinite articles.

MASCULINE	*un*
FEMININE	*une*
PLURAL	*des*

c. Partitive articles.

$à + le = au$

Je vais à + le cinéma. = Je vais au cinéma.
I am going to the movies.

$à + la = à la$

Elle va à + la maison. = Elle va à la maison.
She is going home.

$à + l' = à l'$

Ils sont à + l'opéra. = Ils sont à l'opéra.
They are at the opera.

$à + les = aux$

Ils vont à + les Antilles. = Ils vont aux Antilles.
They are going to the Antilles.

$de + le = du$

Elle est de + le Canada. = Elle est du Canada.
She is from Canada.

$de + la = de la$

Je parle de + la maison. = Je parle de la maison.
I talk about the house.

$de + l' + de l'$

Je parle de + l'hôtel. = Je parle de l'hôtel.
I am talking about the hotel.

$de + les = des$

Ils viennent des + les USA. = Ils viennent des USA.
They come from the United States.

3. THE INTERROGATIVE ADJECTIVE *QUEL* (WHAT, WHICH)

	SINGULAR	PLURAL
MASCULINE	*quel*	*quels*
FEMININE	*quelle*	*quelles*

4. POSSESSIVE ADJECTIVES

	MASCULINE SINGULAR	FEMININE SINGULAR	MASCULINE AND FEMININE PLURAL
my	*mon salon*	*ma maison*	*mes livres*
your	*ton salon*	*ta maison*	*tes livres*
his/her/its	*son salon*	*sa maison*	*ses livres*
our	*notre salon*	*notre maison*	*nos livres*
your	*votre salon*	*votre maison*	*vos livres*
theirs	*leur salon*	*leur maison*	*leurs livres*

5. NUMBERS

0	*zéro*	11	*onze*	30	*trente*
1	*un*	12	*douze*	40	*quarante*
2	*deux*	13	*treize*	50	*cinquante*
3	*trois*	14	*quatorze*	60	*soixante*
4	*quatre*	15	*quinze*	70	*soixante-dix*
5	*cinq*	16	*seize*	80	*quatre-vingt*
6	*six*	17	*dix-sept*	81	*quatre-vingt-un*
7	*sept*	18	*dix-huit*	90	*quatre-vingt-dix*
8	*huit*	19	*dix-neuf*	100	*cent*
9	*neuf*	20	*vingt*	101	*cent un*
10	*dix*	21	*vingt et un*	1,000	*mille*

6. DEMONSTRATIVE PRONOUNS

this one/that one (masculine singular)	*celui*
this one/that one (feminine singular)	*celle*
these ones/those ones (masculine plural)	*ceux*
these ones/those ones (feminine plural)	*celles*

7. STRESSED PRONOUNS

me	*moi*	us	*nous*
you	*toi*	you	*vous*
him	*lui*	them (masculine)	*eux*
her	*elle*	them (feminine)	*elles*

8. DIRECT OBJECT PRONOUNS

me	*me*		we	*nous*	
you	*te*		you	*vous*	
him/it	*le*		them	*les*	
her/it	*la*				
him/her/it	*l'*				

9. INDIRECT OBJECT PRONOUNS

to me	*me*		to us	*nous*	
to you (familiar)	*te*		to you	*vous*	
			to them		
to him/her/it	*lui*		(masculine/feminine)	*leur*	

C. VERB CHARTS

1. FORMS OF THE REGULAR VERBS

A. CLASSES I, II, III

INFINITIVE	PRES. & PAST PARTICIPLES	PRESENT INDICATIVE	PRESENT SUBJUNCTIVE†	CONVERSATIONAL PAST	PAST SUBJUNCTIVE	IMPERFECT INDICATIVE
-er ending parler	parlant parlé	parl + e es e ons ez ent	parl + e es e ions iez ent	j'ai + parlé tu as il a nous avons vous avez ils ont	que j'aie + parlé que tu aies qu'il ait que nous ayons que vous ayez qu'ils aient	parl + ais ais ait ions iez aient
-ir ending finir	finissant fini	fin + is is it issons issez issent	finiss + e es e ions iez ent	j'ai + fini tu as il a nous avons vous avez ils ont	que j'aie + fini que tu aies qu'il ait que nous ayons que vous ayez qu'ils aient	finiss + ais ais ait ions iez aient
-re ending vendre	vendant vendu	vend + s s — ons ez ent	vend + e es e ions iez ent	j'ai + vendu tu as il a nous avons vous avez ils ont	que j'aie + vendu que tu aies qu'il ait que nous ayons que vous ayez qu'ils aient	vend + ais ais ait ions iez aient

† Like the past subjunctive, the present subjunctive verb is always preceded by *que* or *qu'* + the appropriate pronoun, as in "*Il faut que je parle*" and "*Je veux qu'il quitte la maison.*"

PAST PERFECT	FUTURE	FUTURE PERFECT	CONDITIONAL	CONDITIONAL PERFECT	IMPERATIVE
j'avais + parlé tu avais il avait nous avions vous aviez ils avaient	parler + ai as a ons ez ont	j'aurai + parlé tu auras il aura nous aurons vous aurez ils auront	parler + ais ais ait ions iez aient	j'aurais + parlé tu aurais il aurait nous aurions vous auriez ils auraient	parle parlons parlez
j'avais + fini tu avais il avait nous avions vous aviez ils avaient	finir + ai as a ons ez ont	j'aurai + fini tu auras il aura nous aurons vous aurez ils auront	finir + ais ais ait ions iez aient	j'aurais + fini tu aurais il aurait nous aurions vous auriez ils auraient	finis finissons finissez
j'avais + vendu tu avais il avait nous avions vous aviez ils avaient	vendr + ai as a ons ez ont	j'aurai + vendu tu auras il aura nous aurons vous aurez ils auront	vendr + ais ais ait ions iez aient	j'aurais + vendu tu aurais il aurait nous aurions vous auriez ils auraient	vends vendons vendez

B. VERBS ENDING IN -CER AND -GER

INFINITIVE	PRES. & PAST PARTICIPLES	PRESENT INDICATIVE	PRESENT SUBJUNCTIVE†	CONVERSATIONAL PAST	PAST SUBJUNCTIVE	IMPERFECT INDICATIVE
placer[1]	*plaçant* *placé*	*place* *places* *place* *plaçons* *placez* *placent*	*place* *places* *place* *placions* *placiez* *placent*	*j'ai* *tu as* *il a* *nous avons* + *placé* *vous avez* *ils ont*	*que j'aie* *que tu aies* *qu'il ait* *que nous ayons* + *placé* *que vous ayez* *qu'ils aient*	*plaçais* *plaçais* *plaçait* *placions* *placiez* *plaçaient*
manger[2]	*mangeant* *mangé*	*mange* *manges* *mange* *mangeons* *mangez* *mangent*	*mange* *manges* *mange* *mangions* *mangiez* *mangent*	*j'ai* *tu as* *il a* *nous avons* + *mangé* *vous avez* *ils ont*	*que j'aie* *que tu aies* *qu'il ait* *que nous ayons* + *mangé* *que vous ayez* *qu'ils aient*	*mangeais* *mangeais* *mangeait* *mangions* *mangiez* *mangeaient*

[1] Similarly conjugated: *commencer, lancer,* etc.
[2] Similarly conjugated: *plonger, ranger, arranger,* etc.

PAST PERFECT	FUTURE	FUTURE PERFECT	CONDITIONAL	CONDITIONAL PERFECT	IMPERATIVE
j'avais + *placé* *tu avais* *il avait* *nous avions* *vous aviez* *ils avaient*	*placer* + *ai* *as* *a* *ons* *ez* *ont*	*j'aurai* + *placé* *tu auras* *il aura* *nous aurons* *vous aurez* *ils auront*	*placer* + *ais* *ais* *ait* *ions* *iez* *aient*	*j'aurais* + *placé* *tu aurais* *il aurait* *nous aurions* *vous auriez* *ils auraient*	*place* *plaçons* *placez*
j'avais + *mangé* *tu avais* *il avait* *nous avions* *vous aviez* *ils avaient*	*manger* + *ai* *as* *a* *ons* *ez* *ont*	*j'aurai* + *mangé* *tu auras* *il aura* *nous aurons* *vous aurez* *ils auront*	*manger* + *ais* *ais* *ait* *ions* *iez* *aient*	*j'aurais* + *mangé* *tu aurais* *il aurait* *nous aurions* *vous auriez* *ils auraient*	*mange* *mangeons* *mangez*

C. VERBS ENDING IN -ER WITH CHANGES IN THE STEM

INFINITIVE	PRES. & PAST PARTICIPLES	PRESENT INDICATIVE	PRESENT SUBJUNCTIVE†	CONVERSATIONAL PAST	PAST SUBJUNCTIVE	IMPERFECT INDICATIVE
acheter[1]	*achetant* *acheté*	*achète* *achètes* *achète* *achetons* *achetez* *achètent*	*achète* *achètes* *achète* *achetions* *achetiez* *achètent*	*j'ai* *tu as* *il a* *nous avons* *vous avez* *ils ont* + *acheté*	*que j'aie* *que tu aies* *qu'il ait* *que nous ayons* *que vous ayez* *qu'ils aient* + *acheté*	*achet* + *ais* *ais* *ait* *ions* *iez* *aient*
appeler[2]	*appelant* *appelé*	*appelle* *appelles* *appelle* *appelons* *appelez* *appellent*	*appelle* *appelles* *appelle* *appelions* *appeliez* *appellent*	*j'ai* *tu as* *il a* *nous avons* *vous avez* *ils ont* + *appelé*	*que j'aie* *que tu aies* *qu'il ait* *que nous ayons* *que vous ayez* *qu'ils aient* + *appelé*	*appel* + *ais* *ais* *ait* *ions* *iez* *aient*
payer[3]*	*payant* *payé*	*paie/paye* *paies/payes* *paie/paye* *payons* *payez* *paient/payent*	*paie/paye* *paies/payes* *paie/paye* *payons* *payez* *paient/payent*	*j'ai* *tu as* *il a* *nous avons* *vous avez* *ils ont* + *payé*	*que j'aie* *que tu aies* *qu'il ait* *que nous ayons* *que vous ayez* *qu'ils aient* + *payé*	*pay* + *ais* *ais* *ait* *ions* *iez* *aient*
préférer[4]	*préférant* *préféré*	*préfère* *préfères* *préfère* *préférons* *préférez* *préfèrent*	*préfère* *préfères* *préfère* *préférions* *préfériez* *préfèrent*	*j'ai* *tu as* *il a* *nous avons* *vous avez* *ils ont* + *préféré*	*que j'aie* *que tu aies* *qu'il ait* *que nous ayons* *que vous ayez* *qu'ils aient* + *préféré*	*préfér* + *ais* *ais* *ait* *ions* *iez* *aient*

[1] Verbs like *acheter: mener, amener, emmener, se promener, lever, se lever, élever*
[2] Verbs like *appeler: se rappeler, jeter*
[3] Verbs like *payer: essayer, employer, ennuyer, essuyer, nettoyer* (See note below.)
[4] Verbs like *préférer: expérer, répéter, célébrer, considérer, suggérer, protéger*
* Verbs ending in *-oyer* may use *i* or *y* in the present (except for *nous* and *vous* forms), the future, and the conditional, as in *payer, essayer*. Verbs ending in *-oyer, -uyer* change *y* to *i* (as in *essayer, ennuyer, employer, nettoyer*). These changes are indicated by the use of italic.

	PAST PERFECT	FUTURE	FUTURE PERFECT	CONDITIONAL	CONDITIONAL PERFECT	IMPERATIVE
acheter	j'avais + acheté tu avais il avait nous avions vous aviez ils avaient	achèter + ai as a ons ez ont	j'aurai + acheté tu auras il aura nous aurons vous aurez ils auront	achèter + ais ais ait ions iez aient	j'aurais + acheté tu aurais il aurait nous aurions vous auriez ils auraient	achète achetons achetez
appeler	j'avais + appelé tu avais il avait nous avions vous aviez ils avaient	appeller + ai as a ons ez ont	j'aurai + appelé tu auras il aura nous aurons vous aurez ils auront	appeller + ais ais ait ions iez aient	j'aurais + appelé tu aurais il aurait nous aurions vous auriez ils auraient	appelle appelons appelez
payer	j'avais + payé tu avais il avait nous avions vous aviez ils avaient	paier or payer + ai as a ons ez ont	j'aurai + payé tu auras il aura nous aurons vous aurez ils auront	paier + ais or payer + ait ais ions iez aient	j'aurais + payé tu aurais il aurait nous aurions vous auriez ils auraient	paie/paye payons payez
préférer	j'avais + préféré tu avais il avait nous avions vous aviez ils avaient	préférer + ai as a ons ez ont	j'aurai + préféré tu auras il aura nous aurons vous aurez ils auront	préférer + ais ais ait ions iez aient	j'aurais + préféré tu aurais il aurait nous aurions vous auriez ils auraient	préfère préférons préférez

D. VERBS ENDING IN -OIR

INFINITIVE	PRES. & PAST PARTICIPLES	PRESENT INDICATIVE	PRESENT SUBJUNCTIVE†	CONVERSATIONAL PAST		PAST SUBJUNCTIVE		IMPERFECT INDICATIVE
recevoir[1]	recevant	reçois	reçoive	j'ai	+ reçu	que j'aie	+ reçu	recev + ais
	reçu	reçois	reçoives	tu as		que tu aies		ais
		reçoit	reçoive	il a		qu'il ait		ait
		recevons	recevions	nous avons		que nous ayons		ions
		recevez	receviez	vous avez		que vous ayez		iez
		reçoivent	reçoivent	ils ont		qu'ils aient		aient

FUTURE		FUTURE PERFECT		CONDITIONAL		CONDITIONAL PERFECT		IMPERATIVE
recevr + ai		j'aurai	+ reçu	recevr + ais		j'aurais	+ reçu	
as		tu auras		ais		tu aurais		reçois
a		il aura		ait		il aurait		
ons		nous aurons		ions		nous aurions		recevons
ez		vous aurez		iez		vous auriez		recevez
ont		ils auront		aient		ils auraient		

PAST PERFECT	
j'avais	+ reçu
tu avais	
il avait	
nous avions	
vous aviez	
ils avaient	

[1] Verbs like recevoir: devoir (dois, doive, dû).

E. VERBS ENDING IN -NDRE

INFINITIVE	PRES. & PAST PARTICIPLES	PRESENT INDICATIVE	PRESENT SUBJUNCTIVE†	CONVERSATIONAL PAST	PAST SUBJUNCTIVE	IMPERFECT INDICATIVE
craindre[1]	*craignant* *craint*	*crains* *crains* *craint* *craignons* *craignez* *craignent*	*craigne* *craignes* *craigne* *craignions* *craigniez* *craignent*	*j'ai* *tu as* *il a* *nous avons* *vous avez* *ils ont* + *craint*	*que j'aie* *que tu aies* *qu'il ait* *que nous ayons* *que vous ayez* *qu'ils aient* + *craint*	*craign* + *ais* *ais* *ait* *ions* *iez* *aient*
éteindre[2]	*éteignant* *éteint*	*éteins* *éteins* *éteint* *éteignons* *éteignez* *éteignent*	*éteigne* *éteignes* *éteigne* *éteignions* *éteigniez* *éteignent*	*j'ai* *tu as* *il a* *nous avons* *vous avez* *ils ont* + *éteint*	*que j'aie* *que tu aies* *qu'il ait* *que nous ayons* *que vous ayez* *qu'ils aient* + *éteint*	*éteign* + *ais* *ais* *ait* *ions* *iez* *aient*

[1] Verbs like *craindre*: *plaindre*, to pity. The reflexive form, *se plaindre*, means "to complain," and in the compound tenses is conjugated with *être*.
[2] Verbs like *éteindre*: *peindre*, to paint: *teindre*, to dye.

386

PAST PERFECT	FUTURE	FUTURE PERFECT	CONDITIONAL	CONDITIONAL PERFECT	IMPERATIVE
j'avais + *craint* *tu avais* *il avait* *nous avions* *vous aviez* *ils avaient*	*craindr* + *ai* *as* *a* *ons* *ez* *ont*	*j'aurai* + *craint* *tu auras* *il aura* *nous aurons* *vous aurez* *ils auront*	*craindr* + *ais* *ais* *ait* *ions* *iez* *aient*	*j'aurais* + *craint* *tu aurais* *il aurait* *nous aurions* *vous auriez* *ils auraient*	*crains* *craignons* *craignez*
j'avais + *éteint* *tu avais* *il avait* *nous avions* *vous aviez* *ils avaient*	*éteindr* + *ai* *as* *a* *ons* *ez* *ont*	*j'aurai* + *éteint* *tu auras* *il aura* *nous aurons* *vous aurez* *ils auront*	*éteindr* + *ais* *ais* *ait* *ions* *iez* *aient*	*j'aurais* + *éteint* *tu aurais* *il aurait* *nous aurions* *vous auriez* *ils auraient*	*éteins* *éteignons* *éteignez*

387

F. COMPOUND TENSES OF VERBS CONJUGATED WITH *ÊTRE*

CONVERSATIONAL PAST	PAST SUBJUNCTIVE	PAST PERFECT	FUTURE PERFECT	CONDITIONAL PERFECT
je suis allé(e)	que je sois allé(e)	j'étais allé(e)	je serai allé(e)	je serais allé(e)
tu es allé(e)	que tu sois allé(e)	tu étais allé(e)	tu seras allé(e)	tu serais allé(e)
il est allé	qu'il soit allé	il était allé	il sera allé	il serait allé
elle est allée	qu'elle soit allée	elle était allée	elle sera allée	elle serait allée
nous sommes allé(e)s	que nous soyons allé(e)s	nous étions allé(e)s	nous serons allé(e)s	nous serions allé(e)s
vous êtes allé(e)(s)	que vous soyez allé(e)(s)	vous étiez allé(e)(s)	vous serez allé(e)(s)	vous seriez allé(e)(s)
ils sont allés	qu'ils soient allés	ils étaient allés	ils seront allés	ils seraient allés
elles sont allées	qu'elles soient allées	elles étaient allées	elles seront allées	elles seraient allées

G. COMPOUND TENSES OF REFLEXIVE VERBS (ALL REFLEXIVE VERBS ARE CONJUGATED WITH *ÊTRE*)

CONVERSATIONAL PAST	PAST SUBJUNCTIVE	PAST PERFECT	FUTURE PERFECT	CONDITIONAL PERFECT
je me suis levé(e)	*que je me sois levé(e)*	*je m'étais levé(e)*	*je me serai levé(e)*	*je me serais levé(e)*
tu t'es levé(e)	*que tu te sois levé(e)*	*tu t'étais levé(e)*	*tu te seras levé(e)*	*tu te serais levé(e)*
il s'est levé	*qu'il se soit levé*	*il s'était levé*	*il se sera levé*	*il se serait levé*
elle s'est levée	*qu'elle se soit levée*	*elle s'était levée*	*elle se sera levée*	*elle se serait levée*
nous nous sommes levé(e)s	*que nous nous soyons levé(e)s*	*nous nous étions levé(e)s*	*nous nous serons levé(e)s*	*nous nous serions levé(e)s*
vous vous êtes levé(e)(s)	*que vous vous soyez levé(e)(s)*	*vous vous étiez levé(e)(s)*	*vous vous serez levé(e)(s)*	*vous vous seriez levé(e)(s)*
ils se sont levés	*qu'ils se soient levés*	*ils s'étaient levés*	*ils se seront levés*	*ils se seraient levés*
elles se sont levées	*qu'elles se soient levées*	*elles s'étaient levées*	*elles se seront levées*	*elles se seraient levées*

2. FREQUENTLY USED IRREGULAR VERBS

The correct auxiliary verb is indicated in parentheses below each verb. For compound tenses, use the appropriate form of the auxiliary verb + past participle.

INFINITIVE	PRES. & PAST PARTICIPLES	PRESENT INDICATIVE	PRESENT SUBJUNCTIVE	IMPERFECT INDICATIVE	FUTURE	CONDITIONAL	IMPERATIVE
acquérir to acquire (*avoir*)	*acquériant* *acquis*	*acquiers* *acquiers* *acquiert* *acquérons* *acquérez* *acquièrent*	*acquière* *acquières* *acquière* *acquérions* *acquériez* *acquièrent*	*acquér + ais* *ais* *ait* *ions* *iez* *aient*	*acquerr + ai* *as* *a* *ons* *ez* *ont*	*acquerr + ais* *ais* *ait* *ions* *iez* *aient*	*acquiers* *acquérons* *acquérez*
aller to go (*être*)	*allant* *allé(e)(s)*	*vais* *vas* *va* *allons* *allez* *vont*	*aille* *ailles* *aille* *allions* *alliez* *aillent*	*all + ais* *ais* *ait* *ions* *iez* *aient*	*ir + ai* *as* *a* *ons* *ez* *ont*	*ir + ais* *ais* *ait* *ions* *iez* *aient*	*va* *allons* *allez*
(s')asseoir† to sit (down) (*être*)	*asseyant* *assis(e)(s)*	*assieds* *assieds* *assied* *asseyons* *asseyez* *asseyent*	*asseye* *asseyes* *asseye* *asseyions* *asseyiez* *asseyent*	*assey + ais* *ais* *ait* *ions* *iez* *aient*	*asseyer + ai* *as* or *a* *assiér + a* *ons* or *assoir + ez* *ont*	*asseyer + ais* *ais* or *ait* *assiér + ait* *ions* or *assoir + ions* *iez* *aient*	*assieds-toi* *asseyons-nous* *asseyez-vous*

† There is a variant form of the conjugation of *s'asseoir* based on the present participle *assoyant* and first person singular *assois*, but this is rather archaic and is rarely used. *Assiér-* is frequently used. There are also two variant forms for the future stem: *assiér-* and *assoir-*. *Assiér-* is frequently used.

INFINITIVE	PRES. & PAST PARTICIPLES	PRESENT INDICATIVE	PRESENT SUBJUNCTIVE	IMPERFECT INDICATIVE	FUTURE	CONDITIONAL	IMPERATIVE
avoir to have (*avoir*)	*ayant* *eu*	*ai* *as* *a* *avons* *avez* *ont*	*aie* *aies* *ait* *ayons* *ayez* *aient*	*av* + *ais* *ais* *ait* *ions* *iez* *aient*	*aur* + *ai* *as* *a* *ons* *ez* *ont*	*aur* + *ais* *ais* *ait* *ions* *iez* *aient*	*aie* *ayons* *ayez*
battre to beat (*avoir*)	*battant* *battu*	*bats* *bats* *bat* *battons* *battez* *battent*	*batte* *battes* *batte* *battions* *battiez* *battent*	*batt* + *ais* *ais* *ait* *ions* *iez* *aient*	*battr* + *ai* *as* *a* *ons* *ez* *ont*	*battr* + *ais* *ais* *ait* *ions* *iez* *aient*	*bats* *battons* *battez*
boire to drink (*avoir*)	*buvant* *bu*	*bois* *bois* *boit* *buvons* *buvez* *boivent*	*boive* *boives* *boive* *buvions* *buviez* *boivent*	*buv* + *ais* *ais* *ait* *ions* *iez* *aient*	*boir* + *ai* *as* *a* *ons* *ez* *ont*	*boir* + *ais* *ais* *ait* *ions* *iez* *aient*	*bois* *buvons* *buvez*
conclure to conclude (*avoir*)	*concluant* *conclu*	*conclus* *conclus* *conclut* *concluons* *concluez* *concluent*	*conclue* *conclues* *conclue* *concluions* *concluiez* *concluent*	*conclu* + *ais* *ais* *ait* *ions* *iez* *aient*	*conclur* + *ai* *as* *a* *ons* *ez* *ont*	*conclur* + *ais* *ais* *ait* *ions* *iez* *aient*	*conclus* *concluons* *concluez*

INFINITIVE	PRES. & PAST PARTICIPLES	PRESENT INDICATIVE	PRESENT SUBJUNCTIVE	IMPERFECT INDICATIVE	FUTURE	CONDITIONAL	IMPERATIVE
conduire to drive to lead (*avoir*)	*conduisant* *conduit*	*conduis* *conduis* *conduit* *conduisons* *conduisez* *conduisent*	*conduise* *conduises* *conduise* *conduisions* *conduisiez* *conduisent*	*conduis* + *ais* *ais* *ait* *ions* *iez* *aient*	*conduir* + *ai* *as* *a* *ons* *ez* *ont*	*conduir* + *ais* *ais* *ait* *ions* *iez* *aient*	*conduis* *conduisons* *conduisez*
connaître to know (*avoir*)	*connaissant* *connu*	*connais* *connais* *connaît* *connaissons* *connaissez* *connaissent*	*connaisse* *connaisses* *connaisse* *connaissions* *connaissiez* *connaissent*	*connaiss* + *ais* *ais* *ait* *ions* *iez* *aient*	*connaîtr* + *ai* *as* *a* *ons* *ez* *ont*	*connaîtr* + *ais* *ais* *ait* *ions* *iez* *aient*	*connais* *connaissons* *connaissez*
courir to run (*avoir*)	*courant* *couru*	*cours* *cours* *court* *courons* *courez* *courent*	*coure* *coures* *coure* *courions* *couriez* *courent*	*cour* + *ais* *ais* *ait* *ions* *iez* *aient*	*courr* + *ai* *as* *a* *ons* *ez* *ont*	*courr* + *ais* *ais* *ait* *ions* *iez* *aient*	*cours* *courons* *courez*

INFINITIVE	PRES. & PAST PARTICIPLES	PRESENT INDICATIVE	PRESENT SUBJUNCTIVE	IMPERFECT INDICATIVE	FUTURE	CONDITIONAL	IMPERATIVE
croire to believe (*avoir*)	*croyant* *cru*	*crois* *crois* *croit* *croyons* *croyez* *croient*	*croie* *croies* *croie* *croyions* *croyiez* *croient*	*croy* + *ais* *ais* *ait* *ions* *iez* *aient*	*croir* + *ai* *as* *a* *ons* *ez* *ont*	*croir* + *ais* *ais* *ait* *ions* *iez* *aient*	*crois* *croyons* *croyez*
cueillir to gather to pick (*avoir*)	*cueillant* *cueilli*	*cueille* *cueilles* *cueille* *cueillons* *cueillez* *cueillent*	*cueille* *cueilles* *cueille* *cueillions* *cueilliez* *cueillent*	*cueill* + *ais* *ais* *ait* *ions* *iez* *aient*	*cueiller* + *ai* *as* *a* *ons* *ez* *ont*	*cueiller* + *ais* *ais* *ait* *ions* *iez* *aient*	*cueille* *cueillons* *cueillez*
devoir to owe to ought (*avoir*)	*devant* *dû*	*dois* *dois* *doit* *devons* *devez* *doivent*	*doive* *doives* *doive* *devions* *deviez* *doivent*	*dev* + *ais* *ais* *ait* *ions* *iez* *aient*	*devr* + *ai* *as* *a* *ons* *ez* *ont*	*devr* + *ais* *ais* *ait* *ions* *iez* *aient*	not used
dire to say to tell (*avoir*)	*disant* *dit*	*dis* *dis* *dit* *disons* *dites* *disent*	*dise* *dises* *dise* *disions* *disiez* *disent*	*dis* + *ais* *ais* *ait* *ions* *iez* *aient*	*dir* + *ai* *as* *a* *ons* *ez* *ont*	*dir* + *ais* *ais* *ait* *ions* *iez* *aient*	*dis* *disons* *dites*

393

INFINITIVE	PRES. & PAST PARTICIPLES	PRESENT INDICATIVE	PRESENT SUBJUNCTIVE	IMPERFECT INDICATIVE	FUTURE	CONDITIONAL	IMPERATIVE
dormir to sleep (*avoir*)	*dormant* *dormi*	*dors* *dors* *dort* *dormons* *dormez* *dorment*	*dorme* *dormes* *dorme* *dormions* *dormiez* *dorment*	*dorm* + *ais* *ais* *ait* *ions* *iez* *aient*	*dormir* + *ai* *as* *a* *ons* *ez* *ont*	*dormir* + *ais* *ais* *ait* *ions* *iez* *aient*	*dors* *dormons* *dormez*
écrire to write (*avoir*)	*écrivant* *écrit*	*écris* *écris* *écrit* *écrivons* *écrivez* *écrivent*	*écrive* *écrives* *écrive* *écrivions* *écriviez* *écrivent*	*écriv* + *ais* *ais* *ait* *ions* *iez* *aient*	*écrir* + *ai* *as* *a* *ons* *ez* *ont*	*écrir* + *ais* *ais* *ait* *ions* *iez* *aient*	*écris* *écrivons* *écrivez*
envoyer to send (*avoir*)	*envoyant* *envoyé*	*envoie* *envoies* *envoie* *envoyons* *envoyez* *envoient*	*envoie* *envoies* *envoie* *envoyions* *envoyiez* *envoient*	*envoy* + *ais* *ais* *ait* *ions* *iez* *aient*	*enverr* + *ai* *as* *a* *ons* *ez* *ont*	*enverr* + *ais* *ais* *ait* *ions* *iez* *aient*	*envoie* *envoyons* *envoyez*
être to be (*avoir*)	*étant* *été*	*suis* *es* *est* *sommes* *êtes* *sont*	*sois* *sois* *soit* *soyons* *soyez* *soient*	*ét* + *ais* *ais* *ait* *ions* *iez* *aient*	*ser* + *ai* *as* *a* *ons* *ez* *ont*	*ser* + *ais* *ais* *ait* *ions* *iez* *aient*	*sois* *soyons* *soyez*

INFINITIVE	PRES. & PAST PARTICIPLES	PRESENT INDICATIVE	PRESENT SUBJUNCTIVE	IMPERFECT INDICATIVE	FUTURE	CONDITIONAL	IMPERATIVE
faillir† to fail (*avoir*)	*faillant* *failli*	not used	not used	not used	*faillir* + *ai* *as* *a* *ons* *ez* *ont*	*faillir* + *ais* *ais* *ait* *ions* *iez* *aient*	not used
faire to do to make (*avoir*)	*faisant* *fait*	*fais* *fais* *fait* *faisons* *faites* *font*	*fasse* *fasses* *fasse* *fassions* *fassiez* *fassent*	*fais* + *ais* *ais* *ait* *ions* *iez* *aient*	*fer* + *ai* *as* *a* *ons* *ez* *ont*	*fer* + *ais* *ais* *ait* *ions* *iez* *aient*	*fais* *faisons* *faites*
falloir to be necessary, must (used only with *il*) (*avoir*)	no pres. part. *fallu*	*il faut*	*il faille*	*il fallait*	*il faudra*	*il faudrait*	not used
fuir to flee (*avoir*)	*fuyant* *fui*	*fuis* *fuis* *fuit* *fuyons* *fuyez* *fuient*	*fuie* *fuies* *fuie* *fuyions* *fuyiez* *fuient*	*fuy* + *ais* *ais* *ait* *ions* *iez* *aient*	*fuir* + *ai* *as* *a* *ons* *ez* *ont*	*fuir* + *ais* *ais* *ait* *ions* *iez* *aient*	*fuis* *fuyons* *fuyez*

† Used in expressions such as *Il a failli tomber.* He nearly fell (lit., he failed to fall).

(cont.)

INFINITIVE	PRES. & PAST PARTICIPLES	PRESENT INDICATIVE	PRESENT SUBJUNCTIVE	IMPERFECT INDICATIVE	FUTURE	CONDITIONAL	IMPERATIVE
haïr to hate (avoir)	haïssant haï	hais hais hait haïssons haïssez haïssent	haïsse haïsses haïsse haïssions haïssiez haïssent	haïss + ais ais ait ions iez aient	haïr + ai as a ons ez ont	haïr + ais ais ait ions iez aient	haïs haïssons haïssez
lire to read (avoir)	lisant lu	lis lis lit lisons lisez lisent	lise lises lise lisions lisiez lisent	lis + ais ais ait ions iez aient	lir + ai as a ons ez ont	lir + ais ais ait ions iez aient	lis lisons lisez
mettre to put to place (avoir)	mettant mis	mets mets met mettons mettez mettent	mette mettes mette mettions mettiez mettent	mett + ais ais ait ions iez aient	mettr + ai as a ons ez ont	mettr + ais ais ait ions iez aient	mets mettons mettez

INFINITIVE	PRES. & PAST PARTICIPLES	PRESENT INDICATIVE	PRESENT SUBJUNCTIVE	IMPERFECT INDICATIVE	FUTURE	CONDITIONAL	IMPERATIVE
mourir to die (*être*)	*mourant* *mort(e)(s)*	*meurs* *meurs* *meurt* *mourons* *mourez* *meurent*	*meure* *meures* *meure* *mourions* *mouriez* *meurent*	*mour* + *ais* *ais* *ait* *ions* *iez* *aient*	*mourr* + *ai* *as* *a* *ons* *ez* *ont*	*mourr* + *ais* *ais* *ait* *ions* *iez* *aient*	*meurs* *mourons* *mourez*
mouvoir† to move (*avoir*)	*mouvant* *mû*	*meus* *meus* *meut* *mouvons* *mouvez* *meuvent*	*meuve* *meuves* *meuve* *mouvions* *mouviez* *meuvent*	*mouv* + *ais* *ais* *ait* *ions* *iez* *aient*	*mouvr* + *ai* *as* *a* *ons* *ez* *ont*	*mouvr* + *ais* *ais* *ait* *ions* *iez* *aient*	*meus* *mouvons* *mouvez*
naître to be born (*être*)	*naissant* *né(e)(s)*	*nais* *nais* *naît* *naissons* *naissez* *naissent*	*naisse* *naisses* *naisse* *naissions* *naissiez* *naissent*	*naiss* + *ais* *ais* *ait* *ions* *iez* *aient*	*naîtr* + *ai* *as* *a* *ons* *ez* *ont*	*naîtr* + *ais* *ais* *ait* *ions* *iez* *aient*	*nais* *naissons* *naissez*
ouvrir to open (*avoir*)	*ouvrant* *ouvert*	*ouvre* *ouvres* *ouvre* *ouvrons* *ouvrez* *ouvrent*	*ouvre* *ouvres* *ouvre* *ouvrions* *ouvriez* *ouvrent*	*ouvr* + *ais* *ais* *ait* *ions* *iez* *aient*	*ouvrir* + *ai* *as* *a* *ons* *ez* *ont*	*ouvrir* + *ais* *ais* *ait* *ions* *iez* *aient*	*ouvre* *ouvrons* *ouvrez*

† *Mouvoir* is seldom used except in compounds like *émouvoir*, to move (emotionally).

INFINITIVE	PRES. & PAST PARTICIPLES	PRESENT INDICATIVE	PRESENT SUBJUNCTIVE	IMPERFECT INDICATIVE	FUTURE	CONDITIONAL	IMPERATIVE
partir to leave to depart (*être*)	*partant* *parti(e)(s)*	*pars* *pars* *part* *partons* *partez* *partent*	*parte* *partes* *parte* *partions* *partiez* *partent*	*part* + *ais* *ais* *ait* *ions* *iez* *aient*	*partir* + *ai* *as* *a* *ons* *ez* *ont*	*partir* + *ais* *ais* *ait* *ions* *iez* *aient*	*pars* *partons* *partez*
plaire to please (to be pleasing to) (*avoir*)	*plaisant* *plu*	*plais* *plais* *plaît* *plaisons* *plaisez* *plaisent*	*plaise* *plaises* *plaise* *plaisions* *plaisiez* *plaisent*	*plais* + *ais* *ais* *ait* *ions* *iez* *aient*	*plair* + *ai* *as* *a* *ons* *ez* *ont*	*plair* + *ais* *ais* *ait* *ions* *iez* *aient*	*plais* *plaisons* *plaisez*
pleuvoir to rain (used only with *il*) (*avoir*)	*pleuvant* *plu*	*il pleut*	*il pleuve*	*il pleuvait*	*il pleuvra*	*il pleuvrait*	not used
pouvoir† to be able, can (*avoir*)	*pouvant* *pu*	*peux (puis)*† *peux* *peut* *pouvons* *pouvez* *peuvent*	*puisse* *puisses* *puisse* *puissions* *puissiez* *puissent*	*pouv* + *ais* *ais* *ait* *ions* *iez* *aient*	*pourr* + *ai* *as* *a* *ons* *ez* *ont*	*pourr* + *ais* *ais* *ait* *ions* *iez* *aient*	not used
prendre to take (*avoir*)	*prenant* *pris*	*prends* *prends* *prend* *prenons* *prenez* *prennent*	*prenne* *prennes* *prenne* *prenions* *preniez* *prennent*	*pren* + *ais* *ais* *ait* *ions* *iez* *aient*	*prendr* + *ai* *as* *a* *ons* *ez* *ont*	*prendr* + *ais* *ais* *ait* *ions* *iez* *aient*	*prends* *prenons* *prenez*

† The interrogative of *pouvoir* in the first person singular is always *Puis-je?*

INFINITIVE	PRES. & PAST PARTICIPLES	PRESENT INDICATIVE	PRESENT SUBJUNCTIVE	IMPERFECT INDICATIVE	FUTURE	CONDITIONAL	IMPERATIVE
résoudre to resolve (*avoir*)	*résolvant* *résolu*	*résous* *résous* *résout* *résolvons* *résolvez* *résolvent*	*résolve* *résolves* *résolve* *résolvions* *résolviez* *résolvent*	*résolv* + *ais* *ais* *ait* *ions* *iez* *aient*	*résoudr* + *ai* *as* *a* *ons* *ez* *ont*	*résoudr* + *ais* *ais* *ait* *ions* *iez* *aient*	*résous* *résolvons* *résolvez*
rire to laugh (*avoir*)	*riant* *ri*	*ris* *ris* *rit* *rions* *riez* *rient*	*rie* *ries* *rie* *riions* *riiez* *rient*	*ri* + *ais* *ais* *ait* *ions* *iez* *aient*	*rir* + *ai* *as* *a* *ons* *ez* *ont*	*rir* + *ais* *ais* *ait* *ions* *iez* *aient*	*ris* *rions* *riez*
savoir to know (*avoir*)	*sachant* *su*	*sais* *sais* *sait* *savons* *savez* *savent*	*sache* *saches* *sache* *sachions* *sachiez* *sachent*	*sav* + *ais* *ais* *ait* *ions* *iez* *aient*	*saur* + *ai* *as* *a* *ons* *ez* *ont*	*saur* + *ais* *ais* *ait* *ions* *iez* *aient*	*sache* *sachons* *sachez*
suffire to be enough, to suffice (*avoir*)	*suffisant* *suffi*	*suffis* *suffis* *suffit* *suffisons* *suffisez* *suffisent*	*suffise* *suffises* *suffise* *suffisions* *suffisiez* *suffisent*	*suffis* + *ais* *ais* *ait* *ions* *iez* *aient*	*suffir* + *ai* *as* *a* *ons* *ez* *ont*	*suffir* + *ais* *ais* *ait* *ions* *iez* *aient*	*suffis* *suffisons* *suffisez*

INFINITIVE	PRES. & PAST PARTICIPLES	PRESENT INDICATIVE	PRESENT SUBJUNCTIVE	IMPERFECT INDICATIVE	FUTURE	CONDITIONAL	IMPERATIVE
suivre to follow (*avoir*)	*suivant* *suivi*	*suis* *suis* *suit* *suivons* *suivez* *suivent*	*suive* *suives* *suive* *suivions* *suiviez* *suivent*	*suiv* + *ais* *ais* *ait* *ions* *iez* *aient*	*suiv* + *ai* *as* *a* *ons* *ez* *ont*	*suivr* + *ais* *ais* *ait* *ions* *iez* *aient*	*suis* *suivons* *suivez*
(se)taire to be quiet, to say nothing (*être*)	*taisant* *tu(e)(s)*	*tais* *tais* *tait* *taisons* *taisez* *taisent*	*taise* *taises* *taise* *taisions* *taisiez* *taisent*	*tais* + *ais* *ais* *ait* *ions* *iez* *aient*	*tair* + *ai* *as* *a* *ons* *ez* *ont*	*tair* + *ais* *ais* *ait* *ions* *iez* *aient*	*tais-toi* *taisons-nous* *taisez-vous*
tenir to hold, to keep (*avoir*)	*tenant* *tenu*	*tiens* *tiens* *tient* *tenons* *tenez* *tiennent*	*tienne* *tiennes* *tienne* *tenions* *teniez* *tiennent*	*ten* + *ais* *ais* *ait* *ions* *iez* *aient*	*tiendr* + *ai* *as* *a* *ons* *ez* *ont*	*tiendr* + *ais* *ais* *ait* *ions* *iez* *aient*	*tiens* *tenons* *tenez*
vaincre to conquer (*avoir*)	*vainquant* *vaincu*	*vaincs* *vaincs* *vainc* *vainquons* *vainquez* *vainquent*	*vainque* *vainques* *vainque* *vainquions* *vainquiez* *vainquent*	*vainqu* + *ais* *ais* *ait* *ions* *iez* *aient*	*vaincr* + *ai* *as* *a* *ons* *ez* *ont*	*vaincr* + *ais* *ais* *ait* *ions* *iez* *aient*	*vaincs* *vainquons* *vainquez*

INFINITIVE	PRES. & PAST PARTICIPLES	PRESENT INDICATIVE	PRESENT SUBJUNCTIVE	IMPERFECT INDICATIVE	FUTURE	CONDITIONAL	IMPERATIVE
valoir to be worth (*avoir*)	*valant* *valu*	*vaux* *vaux* *vaut* *valons* *valez* *valent*	*vaille* *vailles* *vaille* *valions* *valiez* *vaillent*	*val* + *ais* *ais* *ait* *ions* *iez* *aient*	*vaudr* + *ai* *as* *a* *ons* *ez* *ont*	*vaudr* + *ais* *ais* *ait* *ions* *iez* *aient*	*vaux* † *valons* *valez*
venir to come (*être*)	*venant* *venu(e)(s)*	*viens* *viens* *vient* *venons* *venez* *viennent*	*vienne* *viennes* *vienne* *venions* *veniez* *viennent*	*ven* + *ais* *ais* *ait* *ions* *iez* *aient*	*viendr* + *ai* *as* *a* *ons* *ez* *ont*	*viendr* + *ais* *ais* *ait* *ions* *iez* *aient*	*viens* *venons* *venez*
vivre to live (*avoir*)	*vivant* *vécu*	*vis* *vis* *vit* *vivons* *vivez* *vivent*	*vive* *vives* *vive* *vivions* *viviez* *vivent*	*viv* + *ais* *ais* *ait* *ions* *iez* *aient*	*vivr* + *ai* *as* *a* *ons* *ez* *ont*	*vivr* + *ais* *ais* *ait* *ions* *iez* *aient*	*vis* *vivons* *vivez*
voir to see (*avoir*)	*voyant* *vu*	*vois* *vois* *voit* *voyons* *voyez* *voient*	*voie* *voies* *voie* *voyions* *voyiez* *voient*	*voy* + *ais* *ais* *ait* *ions* *iez* *aient*	*verr* + *ai* *as* *a* *ons* *ez* *ont*	*verr* + *ais* *ais* *ait* *ions* *iez* *aient*	*vois* *voyons* *voyez*

† The imperative of *valoir* is not often used.

401

D. LETTER WRITING

1. FORMAL INVITATIONS AND ACCEPTANCES

Monsieur et madame de Montour vous prient de leur faire l'honneur d'assister à un bal, donné en l'honneur de leur fille Marie-José, le dimanche huit avril à neuf heures du soir.

> *M. et Mme de Montour*
> *35 avenue Hoche*
> *75016 Paris*

R.S.V.P.

Mr. and Mrs. de Montour request the pleasure of your presence at a ball given in honor of their daughter, Marie-José, on Sunday evening, April eighth, at nine o'clock.

> Mr. and Mrs. de Montour
> 35 avenue Hoche
> Paris 75016

R.S.V.P.

R.S.V.P. stands for *Répondez s'il vous plaît.* Please answer.

NOTE OF ACCEPTANCE

Monsieur et madame du Panier vous remercient de votre aimable invitation à laquelle ils se feront un plaisir de se rendre.

Mr. and Mrs. du Panier thank you for your kind invitation and will be delighted to come.

2. THANK-YOU NOTES

le 14 mars 1993

Chère Madame,

Je tiens à vous remercier de l'aimable attention que vous avez eue en m'envoyant le charmant présent que j'ai reçu. Ce tableau me fait d'autant plus plaisir qu'il est ravissant dans le cadre de mon studio.
Je vous prie de croire à l'expression de mes sentiments de sincère amitié.

> *Renée Beaujoly*

March 14, 1993

Dear Mrs. Duparc,

I should like to thank you for the delightful present you sent me. The picture was all the more welcome because it fits in so beautifully with the other things in my studio.

Thank you ever so much.

Sincerely yours,
Renée Beaujoly

3. BUSINESS LETTERS

M Roger Beaumont
2 rue Chalgrin
Paris

> *le 6 novembre 1994*
> *M le rédacteur en chef*
> *"Vu"*
> *3 Blvd. des Capucines*
> *75009 Paris*

Monsieur,

Je vous envoie ci-inclus mon chèque de 250 frs., montant de ma souscription d'un abonnement d'un an à votre publication.

Veuillez agréer, Monsieur, mes salutations distinguées.

> *Roger Beaumont*

ci-inclus un chèque

> 2 Chalgrin Street
> Paris
> November 6, 1994

Circulation Department
"Vu"
3 Blvd. des Capucines
Paris 75009

Gentlemen:

Enclosed please find a check for 250 francs to cover a year's subscription to your magazine.

Sincerely yours,
Roger Beaumont

Enc.

Dupuis Aîné
3 rue du Quatre-Septembre
Paris 75002

le 30 septembre 1993
Vermont et Cie.
2 rue Marat
Bordeaux
Gironde

Monsieur,

En réponse à votre lettre du dix courant, je tiens à vous confirmer que la marchandise en question vous a été expédiée le treize août par colis postal.
Veuillez agréer, Monsieur, mes salutations distinguées.

Henri Tournaire

db/ht

---

3 Quatre-September St.
Paris 75002
September 30, 1993

Vermont and Co.
2 Marat Street
Bordeaux
Gironde

Gentlemen:

In reply to your letter of the tenth of this month, I wish to confirm that the merchandise was mailed to you by parcel post on August 13.

Sincerely yours,
Henri Tournaire

db/ht

4. INFORMAL LETTERS

le 5 mars 1994

Mon cher Jacques,

Ta dernière lettre m'a fait grand plaisir.
Tout d'abord laisse-moi t'annoncer une bonne nouvelle: je compte venir passer une quinzaine de jours à Paris au commencement d'avril et je me réjouis à l'avance à l'idée de te revoir ainsi que les tiens qui je l'espère, se portent bien.
Colette vient avec moi et se fait une grande joie à l'idée de connaître enfin ta femme, de cette manière nous pourrons laisser nos deux femmes potiner un après-midi et nous pourrons rester

ensemble comme nous faisions au lycée. Les affaires marchent bien en ce moment, espérons que ça continuera. Tâche de ne pas avoir trop de malades au mois d'avril, enfin il est vrai que ces choses-là ne se commandent pas.

Toute ma famille se porte bien, heureusement.

J'ai pris l'apéritif avec Dumont l'autre jour, qui m'a demandé de tes nouvelles. Son affaire marche très bien.

J'allais presque oublier le plus important, peux-tu me réserver une chambre au Grand Hôtel pour le cinq avril, je t'en saurais fort gré.

J'espère avoir le plaisir de te lire très bientôt.

Mes meilleurs respects à ta femme.

> *En toute amitié,*
> *André*

March 5, 1994

Dear Jack,

I was very happy to receive your last letter.

First of all, I've some good news for you. I expect to spend two weeks in Paris at the beginning of April and I'm looking forward to the prospect of seeing you and your family, all of whom I hope are well.

Colette's coming with me; she's delighted to be able at last to meet your wife. That way we shall be able to let our two wives gossip and we can spend the afternoon talking together as we used to at school. Business is pretty good right now. Let's hope it will keep up. Try not to get too many patients during the month of April, though I suppose that's a little difficult to arrange.

Fortunately, my family is doing well.

I had cocktails with Dumont the other day and he asked about you. His business is going well.

I almost forgot the most important thing. Can you reserve a room for me at the Grand Hotel for April the fifth? You'll be doing me a great favor.

I hope to hear from you soon. My best regards to your wife.

> Your friend,
> Andrew

Paris, le 3 avril 1993

Ma Chérie,

J'ai bien reçu ta lettre du trente et je suis heureuse de savoir que ta fille est tout à fait remise.
Rien de bien nouveau ici, sauf que Pierre me donne beaucoup de mal, enfin toi aussi tu as un fils de cet âge-là, et tu sais ce que je veux dire!
L'autre jour, j'ai rencontré Mme Michaud dans la rue, Dieu qu'elle a vieilli! Elle est méconnaissable!
Nous avons vu ton mari l'autre soir, il est venu dîner à la maison; il se porte bien et voudrait bien te voir de retour.
Tu as bien de la veine d'être à la montagne pour encore un mois. Que fais-tu de beau toute la journée à Chamonix? Y a-t-il encore beaucoup de monde là-bas? Il paraît que les de Villneque sont là. A Paris tout le monde parle des prochaines fiançailles de leur fille.
Nous sommes allés à une soirée l'autre soir chez les Clergeaud, cette femme ne sait pas recevoir, je m'y suis ennuyée à mourir.
Voilà à peu près tous les derniers potins de Paris, tu vois que je te tiens bien au courant, tâche d'en faire autant.
Embrasse bien Françoise pour moi.

Meilleurs baisers de ton amie,
Monique

Paris, April 3, 1993

Darling,

I received your letter of the thirtieth and I'm happy to learn that your daughter has completely recovered.

Nothing new here, except that Pierre is giving me a lot of trouble. You have a son of the same age, so you know what I mean.

The other day I ran into Mrs. Michaud in the street. My, how she's aged! She's unrecognizable!

We saw your husband the other night—he had dinner at our house. He's well and is looking forward to your coming home.

You're lucky to be staying in the mountains for another month! What do you do all day long in Chamonix? Is it still very crowded? It seems that the de Villneques are there. In Paris, the future engagement of their daughter is the talk of the town.

The other evening we went to a party given by the Clergeauds. She doesn't know how to entertain and I was bored to death.

That's about all of the latest Paris gossip. You see how well I keep you posted—try to do the same.

Give my love to Françoise.

Love,
Monique

5. FORMS OF SALUTATIONS AND COMPLIMENTARY CLOSINGS

SALUTATIONS

FORMAL

Monsieur l'Abbé,	Dear Reverend:
Monsieur le Député,	Dear Congressman:
Monsieur le Maire,	Dear Mayor (Smith):
Cher Professeur,	Dear Professor (Smith):
Cher Maître (Mon cher Maître),	Dear Mr. (Smith): (Lawyers are addressed as "Maître" in France.)
Monsieur,	Dear Sir:
Messieurs,	Gentlemen:
Cher Monsieur Varnoux,	My dear Mr. Varnoux:
Chère Madame Gignoux,	My dear Mrs. Gignoux:

INFORMAL

Mon Cher Roger	Dear Roger
Ma Chère Denise,	Dear Denise,
Chéri,	Darling *(m),*
Chérie,	Darling *(f.),*
Mon Chéri,	My darling (m.),
Ma Chérie,	My darling *(f.),*

COMPLIMENTARY CLOSINGS

FORMAL

1. *Agréez, je vous prie, l'expression de mes salutations les plus distinguées.*
   ("Please accept the expression of my most distinguished greetings.") Very truly yours.
2. *Veuillez agréer l'expression de mes salutations distinguées.*
   ("Will you please accept the expression of my distinguished greetings.") Very truly yours.
3. *Veuillez agréer, Monsieur, mes salutations empressées.*
   ("Sir, please accept my eager greetings.") Yours truly.
4. *Veuillez agréer, Monsieur, mes sincères salutations.*
   ("Sir, please accept my sincere greetings.") Yours truly.
5. *Agréez, Monsieur, mes salutations distinguées.*
   ("Sir, accept my distinguished greetings.") Yours truly.
6. *Votre tout dévoué.*
   ("Your very devoted.") Yours truly.

1. *Je vous prie de croire à l'expression de mes sentiments de sincère amitié.*
   ("Please believe in my feelings of sincere friendship.") Very sincerely.
2. *Meilleures amitiés.*
   ("Best regards.") Sincerely yours.
3. *Amicalement.*
   ("Kindly.") Sincerely yours.
4. *Mes pensées affectueuses* (or *amicales*).
   ("My affectionate *or* friendly thoughts.") Sincerely.
5. *En toute amitié.*
   ("In all friendship.") Your friend.
6. *Amitiés.*
   Regards.
7. *Affectueusement.*
   Affectionately.
8. *Très affectueusement.*
   ("Very affectionately.") Affectionately yours.
9. *Je vous prie de bien vouloir transmettre mes respects à Madame votre mère.*
   Please give my regards to your mother.
10. *Transmets mes respects à ta famille.*
    Give my regards to your family.
11. *Rappelle-moi au bon souvenir de ta famille.*
    Remember me to your family.
12. *Embrasse tout le monde pour moi.*
    ("Kiss everybody for me.") Give my love to everybody.
13. *Je t'embrasse bien fort.*   }   Love.
    Mille baisers.
14. *A bientôt.*
    See you soon.
15. *Grosses bises.*
    Kisses.
16. *Mille baisers.*
    A thousand kisses.
17. *Tu me manques.*
    I miss you.

6. FORM OF THE ENVELOPE

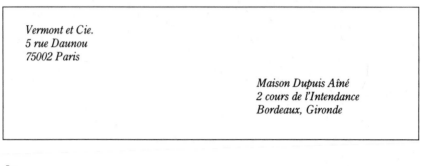

Vermont et Cie.
5 rue Daunou
75002 Paris

                                      Maison Dupuis Aîné
                                      2 cours de l'Intendance
                                      Bordeaux, Gironde

Or:

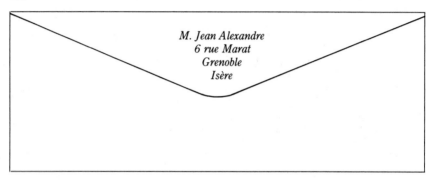

M. Jean Alexandre
6 rue Marat
Grenoble
Isère

M. Robert Marcatour
aux bons soins[1] *de M.P. Lambert*
2 rue du Ranelagh
75016 Paris

[1] *"In care of." Sometimes written as in English: c/o.*

410

GLOSSARY

FRENCH–ENGLISH

A

à *at, in*
  à bientôt *see you soon*
  à côté *next to*
  à droite *on the right*
  à gauche *on the left*
  à merveille *wonderfully*
  à peine *hardly*
  à pied *on foot*
  à vos souhaits *God bless you*
  à votre disposition *at your disposal*
aborder *to approach (a problem)*
accrocher *to hang*
l'accueil *(m) reception; welcome*
acheter *to buy*
l'acier *(m) steel*
actuel *present*
adorer *to love; to adore*
les affaires *(f.p.) business*
  la bonne affaire *a good deal*
l'affiche *(f) poster*
l'âge *(m) age*
l'agneau *(m) lamb*
agréable *pleasant*
les agrumes *(m.p.) citrus fruits*
aider *to help*
aimer *to love*
aller *to go*
  aller et retour *round trip*
  aller simple *one-way ticket*
l'allergie *(f) allergy*
allergique *allergic*
allonger (se) *to lie down*
alors *then*
l'amateur *(m) amateur; lover of*
américain *American*
l'ami (e) *friend*
l'amour *(m) love*
amuser (se) *to have fun*
l'an *(m) year*
anglais *English*
l'année *(f) year*
l'anniversaire *(m) birthday*
annoncer *to announce*
l'antiquaire *(m) antique dealer*
l'appartement *apartment*
appeler *to call*
apporter *to bring*
apprendre *to learn*
approcher (se) *to approach*

août *August*
après *after*
l'après-midi *(f) afternoon*
arborer *to display*
l'architecte *(m) architect*
l'architecture *(f) architecture*
l'argent *(m) money*
  l'argent liquide (m) *cash*
l'armoire *(f) armoire*
arracher *to pull*
arrêter (se) *to stop*
l'arrivée *(f) arrival*
arriver *to arrive*
l'artichaut *(m) artichoke*
l'article *(m) article*
l'ascenseur *(m) elevator*
l'asperge *(f) asparagus*
asseoir (se) *to sit*
assez *enough*
attendre *to wait*
atterrir *to land*
au fait *by the way*
au fond *in the back*
au hasard *at random*
au milieu *in the middle*
au revoir *good-bye*
l'aubergine *(f) eggplant*
l'augmentation *(f) raise*
augmenter *to raise*
aujourd'hui *today*
aussi *also*
autant *as much as*
l'autobus *(m) bus (intra-city)*
l'autocar *(m) bus (inter-city)*
l'automne *(m) fall*
l'autoroute *(f) highway*
autre *other*
autrefois *formerly*
avant *before*
avec *with*
l'avis *(m) opinion*
avoir *to have*
  avoir besoin *to need*
  avoir envie *to feel like*
  avoir l'air *to seem*
  avoir lieu *to take place*
  avoir l'intention *to intend*
  avoir l'occasion *to have the opportunity*
  avoir mal *to hurt*
  avoir peur *to fear*
avril *April*

B

le bagage *luggage*
baisser *to lower*
le balai *broom*
la balle de tennis *tennis ball*
la banque *bank*
battre *to beat*
beau *beautiful*
beaucoup *much; a lot*
le beau-frère *brother-in-law*
le beau-père *father-in-law*
la belle-mère *mother-in-law*
la belle-soeur *sister-in-law*
le besoin *need*
le beurre *butter*
bien *good; well*
  bien sûr *of course*
bientôt *soon*
le billet *ticket*
la blanquette de veau *veal stew*
bleu *blue*
le bœuf *beef*
boire *to drink*
la boisson *beverage*
bon *good*
bondé *crowded*
bonjour *good morning*
la bouche *mouth*
le boulot *job*
le bouquet *bunch; bouquet*
la bouteille *bottle*
la boutique *shop*
le bricolage *odd jobs*
le bruit *noise*
la bruyère *heather*
le bureau *office*
le bureau de change *exchange bureau*

C

Ça va? *How are you?*
la cabine d'essayage *dressing room*
le cadeau *gift*
le café *coffee*
la caisse *cash register*
la campagne *country*
le car *bus (inter-city)*
la carie *cavity*
carré *square*
la carrière *career*
la carte *card; map*
la carte de visite *business card*
le casino *casino*
casser *to break*
la cave *cave; wine cellar*
la CE *European Community*
celui *this one*
cesser *to stop*
la chaise *chair*
la chaleur *heat*

la chambre *room*
le champignon *mushroom*
la chance *chance*
changer *to change, to exchange*
le chanteur *singer*
le chapeau *hat*
le char *float*
charger *to load; to charge*
le chat *cat*
le château *castle*
chaud *hot*
le chauffage *heat*
le chef *chef*
le chef-d'œuvre *masterpiece*
la chemise *shirt (man's)*
le chemisier *shirt (woman's)*
cher *dear; expensive*
chercher *to look for*
chéri *darling*
les cheveux *(m.p.) hair*
chez *at someone's place*
le chien *dog*
le chignon *bun (hair)*
le chocolat *chocolate*
le choix *choice*
la chose *thing*
le cidre *cider*
le cimetière *cemetery*
le cinéma *cinema*
la circulation *traffic*
le citron *lemon*
clair *light; clear*
le clou *nail*
le club de forme *health club*
le cœur *heart*
le coiffeur *hairdresser*
la coiffure *hairstyle*
le collègue *colleague*
combien *how much*
commander *to order*
comme *as*
commencer *to begin; start*
comment *how*
la commode *dresser*
la compagnie *company*
comprendre *to understand*
le comprimé *pill*
compter *to count*
conduire *to drive*
confier (se) *to confide*
confortable *comfortable*
la connaissance *knowledge*
connaître *to know*
le conseil *advice*
conseiller *to advise*
le conservateur *curator*
continuer *to continue; to go on*
construire *to build*
contre *against*
le cornichon *pickle*
la correspondance *correspondence*
la côte *coast*

la côte d'Azur *Riviera*
coucher (se) *to sleep*
la couleur *color*
le coup *blow*
    le coup de fil *phone call*
    le coup de foudre *love at first sight*
    le coup d'œil *glance*
la coupe *cut*
le couple *couple*
  couramment *fluently*
le coureur *runner*
  courir *to run*
la couronne *crown*
le cours *class*
  court *short*
le court de tennis *tennis court*
le cousin *cousin*
la cousine *cousin*
  coûter *to cost*
la crèche *day care center*
le crochet *hook*
  croire *to believe*
les crustacés *shellfish*
  cueillir *to pick*
le cuir *leather*
la cuisine *kitchen; cooking*
la cuisse *thigh*

D

d'accord *all right*
d'ailleurs *besides*
la dame *lady*
  dans *in*
la danse *dance*
le danseur *dancer*
la date *date*
  débrouiller (se) *to manage*
  décembre *December*
  décider *to decide*
la décision *decision*
  déclarer *to declare*
le décor *decor*
  décorer *to decorate*
  déguster *to savor; to taste*
  délicieux *delicious*
  demain *tomorrow*
  demander *to ask*
  démarrer *to start (up)*
  demi *half*
la dent *tooth*
    la dent de sagesse *wisdom tooth*
le dentifrice *toothpaste*
le dentiste *dentist*
le déplacement *travel*
  déposer *to drop off*
  depuis *since*
  dernier *last*
  descendre *to go down; to get off*
  désirer *to desire; to wish*
  désolé *sorry*

le dessert *dessert*
le détartrage *cleaning (teeth)*
  détester *to hate*
  devant *in front of*
  devenir *to become*
  deviner *to guess*
les devises étrangères *(f.p.) currency*
  devoir *must; to have to*
la dictée *dictation*
  différent *different*
  dîner *to dine*
le dîner *dinner*
le diplôme *degree*
  dire *to say*
le directeur *director*
la direction *direction; management*
  distraire (se) *to entertain (oneself)*
  distribuer *to distribute*
la dizaine *ten (or so)*
le document *document*
le doigt *finger*
  donc *therefore; so*
  donner *to give*
  dont *whose; of which*
le dos *back*
  doubler *to pass (car); to dub*
la douleur *pain*
la douzaine *twelve (or so)*
le drapeau *flag*
  drôle *funny; strange*

E

l'eau *(f) water*
l'eau chaude *(f) hot water*
  effectuer *to carry out*
  également *also*
  élégant *elegant*
l'élection *(f) election*
  éloigné *far*
l'embarquement *(m) boarding*
  embarquer *to board*
l'embouteillage *(m) traffic jam*
  en *in, to*
    en bas *at the bottom; downstairs*
    en face *across (the street)*
    en solde *on sale*
    en tout cas *in any case*
  enchanté *delighted*
l'enfant *(m., f.) child*
l'ennui *(m) boredom*
  ennuyer (se) *to get bored*
  enregistrer *to check; to record*
l'enseignement *(m) teaching*
  enseigner *to teach*
  ensuite *then*
  entendre *to hear*
  entraîner (se) *to train*
  entre *between*
l'entrée *(f) entrance*
l'entreprise *(f) company*

l'entrevue (f) interview
environ about
envoler (se) to take off
épouvantable scary; awful
l'équitation (f) horseback riding
escalader to climb
l'escargot (m) snail
espérer to hope
l'essence (f) gas
établir to establish; to make
l'étage (m) floor
l'étagère (f) shelf
l'étape (f) stop
l'état (m) state
les Etats-Unis (m.p.) United States
l'été (m) summer
étranger strange
être to be
   être en retard to be late
   être obligé to have to
l'étude (f) study
l'étudiant, -e student
étudier to study
l'Europe (f) Europe
évidemment obviously
exactement exactly
exagérer to exagerate
l'examen (m) exam
excellent excellent
l'exercice (m) exercise
explorer to explore
l'exposition (f) exhibit
exquis exquisite

F

fabriquer to make; to manufacture
faire to do; to make
   faire (se) to get used to
   faire (s'en) to worry
   faire des achats to shop
   faire la cuisine to cook
   faire des courses to shop
   faire le plein to fill up (gas)
la falaise cliff
la famille family
fantastique fantastic
la faute error; mistake
le fauteuil armchair
féerique magical
les félicitations (f.p.) congratulations
féliciter to congratulate
la femme woman, wife
la fenêtre window
fermer to close
le festival festival
la fête party; celebration
fêter to celebrate
le feu fire
   le feu de circulation traffic light
février February

le fiancé fiancé
la fiancée fiancée
fier proud
le film film
finir to finish; to end
fixer un rendez-vous to make an appointment
la fleur flower
fleuri flowery
le foie liver
   le foie gras goose liver
la fois time
foncé dark
la forme shape
la foule crowd
le franc franc
français French
le frère brother
les frites french fries
froid cold
fumer to smoke
fumeur smoker
furieux furious

G

gagner to earn; to win
la gare train station
le gâteau cake
gauche left
   la gauche left (politics)
les gens people
la gestion management
global global
le goût taste
le gouvernement government
la graisse fat
grand large
le grand magasin department store
la grand-mère grandmother
le grand-père grandfather
grave serious
la gravure etching
la grippe flu
grossir to put on weight
le guichet window

H

habiter to live
l'habitude (f) habit
le *haricot (m) bean
le *haricot vert (m) green bean
hésiter to hesitate
l'heure (f) time
l'histoire (f) story; history
l'hiver (m) winter
le *homard lobster
l'homme (m) man
les *hors-d'oeuvre (m. p.) appetizers
l'hôtel hotel

l'hôtesse (de l'air) *(f)* *flight attendant*
l'huile *(f)* *oil*

I

ici *here*
l'idée *(f)* *idea*
il *he; it*
  il faut *one must*
  il s'agit *it is about*
  il vaut mieux *it is better*
  il y a *there is; there are*
impossible *impossible*
l'impôt *(m)* *tax*
impressionnant *impressive*
indiquer *to indicate*
l'informatique *(m)* *computer science*
inquiéter (se) *to worry*
inscrire (se) *to register*
insupportable *unbearable*
intéressant *interesting*
intéressé *interested*
intéresser (se) *to be interested*
investir *to invest*
l'invité *(m)* *guest*
inviter *to invite*
italien *Italian*
l'itinéraire *(m)* *itinerary*

J

jamais *never*
la jambe *leg*
le jambon *ham*
janvier *January*
le jardin *garden*
jaune *yellow*
jeter *to throw*
le jeu *game*
jeudi *Thursday*
joindre *to meet; to join*
jouer *to play*
le joueur *player*
le jour *day*
  le jour férié *holiday*
juillet *July*
juin *June*
jusqu'à *until*

K

le kilo *kilo*

L

laisser *to leave*
le lac *lake*
lancer *to throw*

le langage *language; speech*
la langue *language (of a people)*
légendaire *legendary*
lever (se) *to get up*
libre *free*
la licence *bachelor of Arts*
lire *to read*
le lit *bed*
la littérature *literature*
le livre *book*
la livre *pound*
le logiciel *software*
loin *far*
le loisir *leisure*
le loyer *rent*
la lumière *light*
lundi *Monday*

M

Madame *Madam*
Mademoiselle *Miss*
magnifique *magnificent*
mai *May*
la main *hand*
maintenant *now*
mais *but*
la maison *house*
la maîtrise *masters*
malade *sick*
malheureusement *unfortunately*
la manche *sleeve; set (of tennis)*
manger *to eat*
le manifestant *demonstrator*
la manifestation *demonstration (political)*
manifester *to demonstrate*
le mannequin *model*
manquer *to miss*
marchander *to bargain*
le marché *market*
  le marché aux puces *flea market*
marcher *to walk*
mardi *Tuesday*
marier (se) *to get married*
mars *March*
le marteau *hammer*
le match *game*
le matin *morning*
mauvais *bad*
le médecin *doctor*
la médecine *medicine*
le médicament *medicine*
meilleur *better*
même *same, even*
la mémoire *memory*
merci *thank you*
mercredi *Wednesday*
la mère *mother*
le message *message*
mettre le cap sur *to head to*
le meuble *furniture*

le midi *noon*
le miracle *miracle*
le miroir *mirror*
la mise en plis *set (hair)*
moins *less*
le mois *month*
la molaire *molar*
le moment *moment*
le monde *world*
la monnaie *change*
monsieur *sir*
la montagne *mountain*
monter *to climb*
montrer *to show*
le moteur *engine*
mourir *to die*
mourir de faim *to starve*
la mousse à raser *shaving cream*
le mur *wall*
le muscle *muscle*
le musée *museum*
la musique *music*

N

nager *to swim*
la naissance *birth*
la neige *snow*
le nom *name*
le nombre *number*
non *no*
le nord *north*
nouveau *new*
la nouvelle *(a piece of) news*
novembre *November*

O

l'objet *(m) object*
obligatoire *compulsory*
l'occasion *(f) opportunity*
occupé *busy*
occuper (se) *to take care*
octobre *October*
l'odeur *(f) smell*
l'œil *(m) eye*
l'œuvre *(f) work*
l'œuvre de bienfaisance *(f) charity organization*
l'offre *(f) offer*
offrir *to offer*
l'oncle *(m) uncle*
l'opéra *(m) opera*
l'ordonnance *(f) prescription*
organiser *to organize*
l'orthographe *(f) spelling*
où *where*
oublier *to forget*
oui *yes*
ouvrir *to open*

P

la page *page*
le pantalon *pants*
par *by*
par cœur *by heart*
paraître *to seem*
le parc *park*
le parent *relative*
les parents *parents*
parfait *perfect*
parler *to speak*
partager *to share*
le parti *political party*
participer *to participate*
partir *to leave*
le passager *passenger*
le passeport *passport*
passer *to spend; to pass by*
passionnant *fascinating*
pauvre *poor*
peigner *to comb*
peindre *to paint*
le pèlerinage *pilgrimage*
pendant *during; for*
penser *to think*
perché *perched*
le permis de conduire *driver's license*
le père *father*
le persil *parsley*
la personne *person*
petit *small*
le petit déjeuner *breakfast*
peu *little*
la peur *fear*
peut-être *maybe*
le phare *headlight*
la pharmacie *pharmacy*
le pharmacien *pharmacist*
la photo *picture*
la piqûre *injection*
le placard *closet*
plaire *to please*
plaisanter *to joke*
le plaisir *pleasure*
le plan *map*
la planche à voile *wind-surfing*
le plat *dish*
plein *full*
pleurer *to cry*
pleuvoir *to rain*
le plombage *filling*
plonger *to dive*
plus *more*
plusieurs *several*
le pneu *tire*
le poids *weight*
le poisson *fish*
le poivre *pepper*
le politicien *politician*
la politique *politics*
la pomme *apple*

la pomme de terre *potato*
le pont *bridge*
porter *to carry; to wear*
pour *for*
pourquoi *why*
pourtant *however*
pourvu *provided*
pousser *to push*
pouvoir *can; may*
préférer *to prefer*
premier *first*
prendre *to take*
préparer *to prepare*
près *close; near*
présenter *to introduce*
prêt *ready*
le printemps *spring*
le prix *price*
le problème *problem*
le produit *product*
le professeur *teacher; professor*
profiter *to take advantage*
le programme *program*
le projet *project*
la promesse *promise*
proposer *to suggest*
la protéine *protein*
la province *province*
les provisions *(f.p.) supplies*
provoquer *to trigger; to cause*
prudent *cautious*

Q

quand *when*
le quart *quarter*
le quartier *neighborhood*
quel *what*
quelque chose *something*
quelqu'un *someone*
la quincaillerie *hardware store*
quoi *what*
le quotidien *daily; daily paper*

R

raccrocher *to hang up*
raconter *to tell*
le radiateur *radiator*
rapide *fast*
rappeler *to call back*
la raquette *racket*
rarement *rarely*
ravi *delighted*
ravissant *delightful*
recevoir *to receive; entertain*
la recherche *search*
recommander *to recommend*
la réforme *reform*
refuser *to refuse*

regarder *to watch*
le régime *diet*
la région *region*
régler *to settle*
regretter *to regret*
le remède *remedy*
remorquer *to tow*
rencontrer *to meet*
le rendez-vous *appointment*
répondre *to answer*
la réponse *answer*
la réservation *reservation*
réserver *to reserve*
respirer *to breathe*
le restaurant *restaurant*
la restauration *restoration*
le reste *rest, remainder*
rester *to stay*
les restes *(m.p.) leftovers*
le retour *return*
retourner *to go back*
retrouver *to meet, to join*
la réunion *meeting*
réussir *to succeed*
réveiller (se) *to wake up*
revenir *to come back*
le revenu *income*
rêver *to dream*
revoir *to see again*
le rhume *cold*
rien *nothing*
la robe *dress*
le rocher *rock*
le roi *king*
rose *pink*
rouge *red*
rouler *to drive; to rule*
la route *road*
la rue *street*
la ruelle *small street*
rustique *rustic*

S

le sac *bag*
la saison *season*
la salle à manger *dining room*
le salon *living room*
samedi *Saturday*
la santé *health*
s'appeler *to be called*
savoir *to know*
le sculpteur *sculptor*
la sculpture *sculpture*
second *second*
le secret *secret*
le secrétaire *secretary; bureau*
la sécurité sociale *social security*
séduisant *attractive*
le séjour *stay*
le sel *salt*

la semaine *week*
sentir *to feel*
septembre *September*
le serpent *snake*
seulement *only*
signer *to sign*
s'il vous plaît *please*
le sirop *syrup*
la société *company*
la sœur *sister*
le soir *evening*
la soirée *evening; party*
le soleil *sun*
sombre *dark*
le son *sound*
sortir *to go out*
soulever *to lift*
sous *under*
le souvenir *memory; souvenir*
souvenir (se) *to remember*
souvent *often*
spacieux *spacious*
la spécialité *specialty*
le spectacle *performance*
spectaculaire *spectacular*
le sport *sport*
le stage *training*
le stand *booth*
le sucre *sugar*
le sud *south*
suffire *to suffice*
suisse *Swiss*
suivant *following*
suivre *to follow*
superbe *superb*
supporter *to bear; to stand*
sur *on*
la surprise *surprise*

T

la table *table*
le tableau *painting*
la taille *size*
tant *so much; so many*
la tante *aunt*
tard *late*
le tas *pile*
la tasse *cup*
le taux *rate*
le taux de change *rate of exchange*
la technique *technique*
teindre *to dye*
le teint *complexion*
la teinte *shade; color*
téléphoner *to call*
la télévision *television*
le temps *time, weather*
tenir *to hold*
tenir à *to insist; to want*
la terrasse *terrace*
la terre *earth*

la tête *head*
le thé *tea*
la toile *canvas; painting*
le toit *roof*
tomber *to fall*
tomber en panne *to break down (car)*
tôt *early*
toucher *to touch*
toujours *always*
tourner *to turn*
la tour *tower*
le tour *walk; stroll; trip*
le tournevis *screwdriver*
le tournoi *tournament*
tout *all*
tout de suite *right away*
tout le monde *everyone*
tout droit *straight ahead*
le trac *stage fright*
le travail *work*
travailler *to work*
les travaux *(m.p.) construction*
traverser *to cross*
très *very*
la tresse *braid*
triste *sad*
trop *too much*
le trou *hole*
trouver *to find*

U

utiliser *to use*

V

les vacances *vacation*
la valise *suitcase*
le vallon *valley*
la vedette *star*
le vendeur *salesperson*
vendre *to sell*
vendredi *Friday*
venir *to come*
le verbe *verb*
vérifier *to check*
le verre *glass*
vers *toward*
le vert *green*
la viande *meat*
la victoire *victory*
vieux *old*
la ville *town*
le vin *wine*
la violence *violence*
visiter *to visit*
vite *fast*
vivre *to live*
voici *here is*
voilà *there is*

la voile *sail*
voir *to see*
la voiture *car*
la voiture d'occasion *secondhand car*
le vol *flight*
volontiers *willingly*
voter *to vote*
vouloir *to want*
le voyage *travel*
voyager *to travel; journey, trip*
vrai *true*
vraiment *truly*

W

w.c. *rest rooms*

X

le xylophone *xylophone*

Y

le yaourt *yoghurt*

Z

zéro *zero*
le zoo *zoo*

ENGLISH–FRENCH

A

about *environ*
across *en face*
adore (to) *adorer*
advice *le conseil*
advise (to) *conseiller*
after *après*
afternoon *l'après-midi (m)*
against *contre*
age *l'age (m)*
all *tout*
allergic *allergique*
allergy *l'allergie (f)*
all right *d'accord*
also *aussi, également*
always *toujours*
amateur *l'amateur (m)*
American *américain*
announce (to) *annoncer*
answer *la réponse*
answer (to) *répondre*
antique dealer *l'antiquaire (m)*
apartment *l'appartement (m)*
appetizers *les *hors d'œuvre (m.p.)*
apple *la pomme*
appointment *le rendez-vous*
make an appointment (to) *fixer un rendez-vous*
approach (to) *aborder, (se) approcher*
April *avril*
architect *l'architecte (m)*
architecture *l'architecture (f)*
armchair *le fauteuil*
armoire *l'armoire (f)*
arrival *l'arrivée (f)*
arrive (to) *arriver*
artichoke *l'artichaut (m)*
article *l'article (m)*
as *comme*
as much as *autant que*

ask (to) *demander*
asparagus *asperge (f)*
at *à, de, chez*
at random *au hasard*
at the bottom *au fond, en bas*
at your disposal *à votre disposition*
attractive *séduisant*
August *l'août (m)*
aunt *la tante*
awful *épouvantable*

B

bachelor's degree *la licence*
back *le dos*
bad *mauvais*
bag *le sac*
bank *la banque*
bargain (to) *marchander*
be (to) *être*
be late (to) *être en retard*
bean *le *haricot (m)*
green bean *le *haricot vert*
bear (to) *supporter*
beat (to) *battre*
beautiful *beau (m.), belle (f.)*
become (to) *devenir*
bed *le lit*
beef *le bœuf*
before *avant*
begin (to) *commencer*
believe (to) *croire*
besides *d'ailleurs*
better *meilleur; mieux*
between *entre*
beverage *la boisson*
birth *la naissance*
birthday *l'anniversaire (m)*
blow *le coup*

blue *bleu*
board (to) *embarquer*
boarding *l'embarquement (m)*
book *le livre*
book (to) *réserver*
booth *le stand*
boredom *l'ennui (m)*
bottle *la bouteille*
bouquet *le bouquet*
braid *la tresse*
break (to) *casser*
  break down (to) *tomber en panne*
breakfast *le petit déjeuner*
breathe (to) *respirer*
bridge *le pont*
bring (to) *apporter*
broom *le balai*
brother *le frère*
brother-in-law *le beau-frère*
build (to) *construire*
bun *le chignon*
bunch *le bouquet*
bureau *le secrétaire*
bus *l'autobus (m), l'autocar (m), le car*
business *les affaires*
  business card *la carte de visite*
busy *occupé*
but *mais*
butter *le beurre*
buy (to) *acheter*
by *par*
  by heart *par coeur*
  by the way *au fait*

C

cake *le gâteau*
call *l'appel (m)*
call (to) *appeler, téléphoner*
  be called (to) *s'appeler*
  call back (to) *rappeler*
can *pouvoir*
canvas *la toile*
car *la voiture*
  secondhand car *la voiture d'occasion*
card *la carte*
  business card *la carte de visite*
career *la carrière*
carry (to) *porter*
  carry out (to) *effectuer*
cash *l'argent liquide (m)*
  cash register *la caisse*
casino *le casino*
castle *le château*
cat *le chat*
cause (to) *provoquer*
cautious *prudent*
cave *la caverne*
cavity *la carie*
celebrate (to) *célébrer; fêter*
celebration *la fête*

cemetery *la cimetière*
chair *la chaise*
chance *la chance*
change *la monnaie*
change (to) *changer*
charge (to) *charger*
charity association *l'organisation de bienfaisance (f)*
chef *le chef*
check *le chèque*
check (to) *vérifier*
child *l'enfant*
chocolate *le chocolat*
choice *le choix*
cider *le cidre*
cinema *le cinéma*
citrus fruits *les agrumes (m.p.)*
class *la classe; le cours*
clean (to) *nettoyer*
cleaning (tooth) *le détartrage*
clear *clair*
cliff *la falaise*
climb (to) *escalader, monter*
close (to) *fermer*
closet *le placard*
coast *la côte*
coffee *le café*
coin *la pièce*
cold *froid; le rhume*
colleague *le collègue*
color *la couleur, la teinte*
come (to) *venir*
  come back (to) *revenir*
comb *le peigne*
comb (to) *peigner*
comfortable *confortable*
company *l'entreprise, la société, la compagnie*
complexion *le teint*
compulsory *obligatoire*
computer *l'ordinateur (m)*
  computer science *l'informatique (f)*
confide (to) *se confier*
congratulate (to) *féliciter*
congratulations *les félicitations (f.p.)*
construction (work) *les travaux*
continue (to) *continuer*
cook (to) *faire la cuisine*
cooking *la cuisine*
correspondence *la correspondance*
cost (to) *coûter*
count (to) *compter*
country *la campagne*
couple *le couple*
cousin *le cousin; la cousine*
cross (to) *traverser*
crowd *la foule*
crowded *bondé*
crown *la couronne*
cry (to) *pleurer*
cup *la tasse*
curator *le conservateur*

currency *les devises étrangères (f.p.)*
cut *la coupe*
cut (to) *couper*

D

dance *la danse*
dance (to) *danser*
dancer *le danseur*
dark *sombre, foncé*
darling *chéri*
date *la date*
day *le jour*
day care center *la crèche*
daily *quotidien*
   daily paper *le quotidien*
dear *cher*
December *décembre*
decide (to) *décider*
decision *la décision*
declare (to) *déclarer*
décor *le décor*
decorate (to) *décorer*
degree *le diplôme*
delicious *délicieux*
delighted *enchanté, ravi*
delight *le délice*
delightful *ravissant*
demonstrate (to) *manifester*
demonstration (political) *la manifestation*
demonstrator *le manifestant*
dentist *le dentiste*
department store *le grand magasin*
desire (to) *désirer*
dessert *le dessert*
dictation *la dictée*
die (to) *mourir*
diet *le régime*
different *différent*
dine (to) *dîner*
dining room *la salle à manger*
dinner *le dîner*
direction *la direction*
director *le directeur*
dish *le plat*
display (to) *arborer*
distribute (to) *distribuer*
dive (to) *plonger*
do (to) *faire*
doctor *le médecin*
document *le document*
dog *le chien*
downstairs *en bas*
dream *le rêve*
dream (to) *rêver*
dress *la robe*
dress (to) *s'habiller*
dresser *la commode*
dressing room *la cabine d'essayage*
drink (to) *boire*
drive (to) *conduire, rouler*

driver's license *le permis de conduire*
drop off (to) *déposer*
dub (to) *doubler*
during *pendant*
dye (to) *teindre*

E

early *tôt*
earn (to) *gagner*
earth *la terre*
eat (to) *manger*
eggplant *l'aubergine (f)*
election *l'élection (f)*
elegant *élégant*
elevator *l'ascenseur (m)*
end (to) *finir*
engaged *fiancé*
engine *le moteur*
English *anglais*
enough *assez*
entertain (to) *recevoir*
   entertain oneself (to) *se distraire*
entrance *l'entrée (f)*
error *l'erreur (f), la faute*
establish *établir*
etching *la gravure*
Europe *l'Europe (f)*
European Community (EC) *la Communauté Européenne (CE)*
even *même*
evening *le soir; la soirée*
everyone *tout le monde*
exactly *exactement*
exagerate (to) *exagérer*
exam *l'examen (m)*
excellent *excellent*
exchange (to) *changer*
exchange bureau *bureau de change*
exercise *l'exercice (m)*
exercise (to) *faire de l'exercice*
exhibition *l'exposition (f)*
expensive *cher*
explore (to) *explorer*
exquisite *exquis*
eye *l'œil, les yeux (pl.)*

F

fall *l'automne (m)*
fall (to) *tomber*
family *la famille*
fantastic *fantastique*
far *loin, éloigné*
fascinating *fascinant*
fast *rapide, vite*
fat *la graisse*
father *le père*
father-in-law *le beau-père*

fear *la peur*
fear (to) *avoir peur*
February *février*
feel (to) *sentir*
  feel like (to) *avoir envie*
festival *le festival*
fiancé *le fiancé*
fiancée *la fiancée*
fill up (to) *faire le plein*
filling *le plombage*
film *le film*
find (to) *trouver*
finger *le doigt*
finish (to) *finir*
fire *le feu*
first *premier*
fish *le poisson*
flag *le drapeau*
flea market *le marché aux puces*
flight *le vol*
  flight attendant *le steward, l'hôtesse*
    (de l'air) (f.)
float *le char*
floor *l'étage (m)*
flower *la fleur*
flowery *fleuri*
flu *la grippe*
fluently *couramment*
follow (to) *suivre*
following *suivant*
for *pour*
foreign *étranger*
  foreign currency *les devises étrangères*
forget (to) *oublier*
formerly *autrefois*
franc *le franc*
France *la France*
free *libre*
French *français*
  French fries *les frites (f. pl.)*
Friday *vendredi*
friend *l'ami (e)*
full *plein*
funny *drôle*
furious *furieux*
furniture *les meubles (m.p.)*

G

game *le jeu, le match*
garden *le jardin*
gas *l'essence (f)*
get (to) *obtenir*
  get bored (to) *s'ennuyer*
  get married (to) *se marier*
  get off (to) *descendre*
  get up (to) *se lever*
  get used to (to) *s'habituer, se faire*
gift *le cadeau*
give (to) *donner*
glance *le coup d'œil*

glass *le verre*
global *global*
God *Dieu*
God bless you *à vos souhaits*
good *bon*
good-bye *au revoir*
go (to) *aller*
  go back (to) *retourner*
  go down (to) *descendre*
  go on (to) *continuer*
  go out (to) *sortir*
good *bon(ne), bien*
  good-bye *au revoir*
  good deal *la bonne affaire*
  good morning *bonjour*
goose *l'oie (f)*
  goose liver *le foie gras*
government *le gouvernement*
grandfather *le grand-père*
grandmother *la grand-mère*
green *vert*
guess (to) *deviner*
guest *l'invité*

H

habit *l'habitude (f)*
hair *les cheveux (m.p.)*
hairdresser *le coiffeur*
hairstyle *la coiffure*
half *demi*
ham *le jambon*
hammer *le marteau*
hand *la main*
hang (to) *accrocher*
  hang up (to) *raccrocher*
hardly *à peine*
hardware store *la quincaillerie*
hat *le chapeau*
hate (to) *détester*
have (to) *avoir*
  have fun (to) *s'amuser*
  have the opportunity (to) *avoir l'occasion*
  have to (to) *devoir, être obligé*
head *la tête*
head to (to) *mettre le cap sur*
headlight *le phare*
health *la santé*
  health club *le club de forme*
hear (to) *entendre*
heart *le coeur*
heat *la chaleur*
heather *la bruyère*
help (to) *aider*
here *ici*
  here is *voici, voilà*
hesitate (to) *hésiter*
highway *l'autoroute (f)*
history *l'histoire*
hold (to) *tenir*
hole *le trou*

holiday *le jour férié*
hook *le crochet*
hope (to) *espérer*
horse *le cheval*
horseback riding *l'équitation (f)*
hot *chaud*
hotel *l'hôtel (m)*
house *la maison*
how *comment*
  How are you? *Comment allez-vous?*
  How much? *Combien?*
however *pourtant*
hurt (to) *avoir mal*

I

idea *l'idée (f)*
impossible *impossible*
impressive *impressionnant*
in *dans*
  in any case *en tout cas*
  in front of *devant*
  in the back *au fond*
  in the middle *au milieu*
income *le revenu*
indicate (to) *indiquer*
injection *la piqûre*
insist (to) *tenir à*
intend (to) *avoir l'intention*
interested *intéressé(e)*
  be interested (to) *s'intéresser à*
interesting *intéressant*
interview *l'entrevue (f)*
introduce (to) *présenter*
introduction *les présentations (f.p.)*
invest (to) *investir*
invite (to) *inviter*
invitation *l'invitation (f)*
it is about *il s'agit de*
it is better *il vaut mieux*
Italian *italien*
itinerary *l'itinéraire (m)*

J

January *janvier*
job *le boulot*
join (to) *joindre, retrouver*
joke *la plaisanterie*
joke (to) *plaisanter*
July *juillet*
June *juin*

K

kilo *le kilo*
king *le roi*
kitchen *la cuisine*
know (to) *savoir; connaître*
knowledge *la connaissance*

L

lady *la dame*
lake *le lac*
lamb *l'agneau (m)*
land *la terre*
land (to) *atterrir*
language *la langue; le langage*
large *grand .*
last *dernier*
late *tard*
learn (to) *apprendre*
leather *le cuir*
leave (to) *partir; quitter, laisser*
left *gauche, la gauche (politics)*
leftovers *les restes (m.p.)*
leg *la jambe*
legendary *légendaire*
leisure *les loisirs (m.p.)*
lemon *le citron*
less *moins*
lie down (to) *s'allonger*
life *la vie*
lift (to) *soulever*
light *clair; la lumière*
literature *la littérature*
little *un peu*
live (to) *vivre; habiter*
liver *le foie*
  goose liver paté *le foie gras*
living room *le salon*
load (to) *charger*
lobster *le *homard*
look (to) *regarder*
  look for (to) *chercher*
love *l'amour (m)*
  love at first sight *le coup de foudre*
love (to) *aimer, adorer*
low *bas*
lower (to) *baisser*
luggage *les bagages (m.p.)*

M

Madam *Madame*
magical *féerique*
magnificent *magnifique*
make (to) *faire, établir, fabriquer*
manage (to) *se débrouiller*
management *la gestion, la direction*
manufacture (to) *fabriquer*
map *la carte, le plan*
March *mars*
market *le marché*
  flea market *le marché aux puces*
masterpiece *le chef-d'œuvre*
master's degree *la maîtrise*
may *pouvoir*
May *mai*
maybe *peut-être*
meat *la viande*

medicine *la médicine; les médicaments*
meet (to) *rencontrer; (re)joindre*
meeting *le réunion*
memory *la mémoire, le souvenir*
message *le message*
miracle *le miracle*
mirror *le miroir*
Miss *Mademoiselle*
miss (to) *manquer*
mistake *la faute*
model *le mannequin*
molar *la molaire*
moment *le moment*
Monday *lundi*
money *l'argent (m)*
month *le mois*
more *plus*
morning *le matin*
mother *la mère*
mother-in-law *la belle-mère*
mountain *la montagne*
mouth *la bouche*
much *beaucoup*
muscle *le muscle*
museum *le musée*
mushroom *le champignon*
music *la musique*
must *devoir*

N

nail *le clou*
name *le nom*
near *près*
need (to) *avoir besoin*
neighborhood *le quartier*
never *jamais*
new *nouveau*
news *la nouvelle*
next *prochain*
  next to *à côté de*
no *non*
noise *le bruit*
noon *le midi*
north *le nord*
nothing *rien*
November *novembre*
now *maintenant*
number *le nombre*

O

object *l'objet (m)*
obviously *évidemment*
odd job *le bricolage*
of course *bien sûr*
offer *l'offre (f)*
offer (to) *offrir*
office *le bureau*
often *souvent*

oil *l'huile (f)*
old *vieux (m), vieille (f)*
on *sur*
  on foot *à pied*
  on sale *en solde*
  on the left *à gauche*
  on the right *à droite*
one *un, une; on*
  one must *il faut*
only *seulement*
open (to) *ouvrir*
opinion *l'opinion (f)*
order (to) *commander*
other *autre*

P

page *la page*
pants *le pantalon*
pain *la douleur*
paint (to) *peindre*
painter *le peintre*
painting *la peinture; le tableau, la toile*
parent(s) *le(s) parent(s)*
park *le parc*
park (to) *garer*
participate (to) *participer*
parsley *le persil*
party *la soirée; la fête, le parti (political)*
pass (to) *dépasser; doubler*
  pass by (to) *passer*
passenger *le passager*
passport *le passeport*
people *les gens (m. p.)*
pepper *le poivre*
perched *perché*
perfect *parfait*
performance *le spectacle*
person *la personne*
pharmacist *le pharmacien*
pharmacy *la pharmacie*
phone *le téléphone*
phone call *le coup de téléphone*
photo *la photographie*
pick (to) *cueillir*
pickle *le cornichon*
picture *le tableau; l'image*
pile *le tas; la pile*
pilgrimage *le pèlerinage*
pill *le comprimé*
pink *rose*
play *le jeu*
play (to) *jouer*
player *le joueur*
pleasant *agréable*
please *s'il vous plaît*
please (to) *faire plaisir; plaire*
pleasure *le plaisir*
political party *le parti politique*
politician *le politicien*
politics *la politique*

poor *pauvre*
poster *l'affiche*
potato *la pomme de terre*
pound *la livre*
prefer (to) *préférer*
prepare (to) *préparer*
prescription *l'ordonnance (f)*
present *le cadeau (n); actuel (adj.)*
price *le prix*
problem *problème*
product *le produit*
professor *le professeur*
program *le programme*
project *le projet*
promise *la promesse*
promise (to) *promettre*
protein *la protéine*
proud *fier*
provided *pourvu que*
province *la province*
pull (to) *tirer, arracher*
push (to) *pousser*
put (to) *mettre*
put on weight (to) *grossir*

Q

quarter *le quart*

R

racket *la raquette*
radiator *le radiateur*
rain *la pluie*
rain (to) *pleuvoir*
raise *l'augmentation (f)*
raise (to) *augmenter*
rarely *rarement*
rate *le taux*
  rate of exchange *le taux de change*
receive (to) *recevoir*
reception *la réception, l'accueil (m)*
read (to) *lire*
ready *prêt*
recommend *recommander*
red *rouge*
reform *la réforme*
refuse (to) *refuser*
region *la région*
register (to) *s'inscrire*
relative *le parent*
regret (to) *regretter*
remedy *le remède*
remember (to) *se souvenir*
rent *le loyer*
rent (to) *louer*
reservation *la réservation*
reserve (to) *réserver*
restaurant *le restaurant*

rest rooms *les toilettes*
restoration *la restauration*
return *le retour*
return (to) *retourner; revenir*
right away *tout de suite*
Riviera *la côte d'Azur*
road *la route*
rock *le rocher*
roof *le toit*
room *la pièce, la chambre*
round trip *aller et retour*
run (to) *courir*
runner *le coureur*
rustic *rustique*

S

sad *triste*
sail *la voile*
same *même*
sale *les soldes (m.p.)*
  on sale *en solde*
salesperson *le vendeur*
salt *le sel*
Saturday *le samedi*
savor (to) *déguster*
say (to) *dire*
scary *effrayant, épouvantable*
screwdriver *le tournevis*
sculptor *le sculpteur*
sculpture *la sculpture*
search *la recherche*
season *la saison*
second *second*
  secondhand car *la voiture d'occasion*
secret *le secret*
secretary *le secrétaire*
see (to) *voir*
  see again (to) *revoir*
  see you soon *à bientôt*
seem (to) *sembler, avoir l'air, paraître*
sell (to) *vendre*
September *septembre*
serious *sérieux, grave*
set (of tennis) *la manche*
settle (to) *régler*
several *plusieurs*
shade *la teinte; l'ombre (f)*
shape *la forme*
share (to) *partager*
shaving cream *la mousse à raser*
shelf *l'étagère (f)*
shellfish *les fruits de mer (m.p.)*
shirt *la chemise; le chemisier*
shop *le magasin, la boutique*
shop (to) *faire des courses, faire des achats*
short *court*
show (to) *montrer*
sick *malade*
sign (to) *signer*
since *depuis*

sing (to) *chanter*
singer *le chanteur*
sir *monsieur*
sister *la sœur*
sister-in-law *la belle-sœur*
sit (to) *s'asseoir*
size *la taille*
sleep (to) *(se) coucher, dormir*
sleeve *la manche*
small *petit*
smell *l'odeur (f)*
smell (to) *sentir*
smoke (to) *fumer*
smoker *le fumeur*
snail *l'escargot (m)*
snake *le serpent*
snow *la neige*
so *donc*
social security *la sécurité sociale*
software *le logiciel*
some *quelques*
someone *quelqu'un*
something *quelque chose*
soon *bientôt*
sorry *désolé*
sound *le son*
south *sud*
speak (to) *parler*
spacious *spacieux*
specialty *la spécialité*
spectacular *spectaculaire*
spelling *l'orthographe (f)*
spend (to) *dépenser; passer*
sport *le sport*
spring *le printemps*
square *carré*
stage *la scène*
stage fright *le trac*
stand (to) *supporter*
star *la vedette*
start (to) *commencer, démarrer*
starve (to) *mourir de faim*
state *l'état (m)*
stay *le séjour*
stay (to) *rester*
steel *l'acier (m)*
stop *l'arrêt (m), l'étape (f)*
stop (to) *arrêter, cesser*
story *l'histoire (f)*
straight ahead *tout droit*
strange *étrange, drôle*
street *la rue*
   small street *la ruelle*
stroll *le tour*
student *l'étudiant (m)*
study *l'étude (f)*
study (to) *étudier*
succeed (to) *réussir*
suffice (to) *suffire*
sugar *le sucre*
suggest (to) *suggérer*
suitcase *la valise*

summer *l'été (m)*
sun *le soleil*
superb *superbe*
supplies *les provisions (f.p.)*
surprise *la surprise*
swim (to) *nager*
Swiss *suisse*
Switzerland *la Suisse*
syrup *le sirop*

T

table *la table*
take (to) *prendre*
   take care (to) *s'occuper*
   take place (to) *avoir lieu*
   take off (to) *s'envoler*
   take advantage (to) *profiter*
taste *le goût*
taste (to) *goûter, déguster*
tax *l'impôt (m)*
tea *le thé*
teach (to) *enseigner*
teacher *professeur*
teaching *l'enseignement (m)*
technique *la technique*
television *la télévision*
tell (to) *raconter*
ten (or so) *dix, la dizaine*
tennis *le tennis*
   tennis ball *la balle de tennis*
   tennis court *le court de tennis*
terrace *la terrasse*
thank you *merci*
then *puis; ensuite; alors*
there is/are *il y a*
therefore *donc*
thigh *la cuisse*
thing *la chose*
think (to) *penser*
this *ce*
   this one *celui*
throw (to) *jeter, lancer*
Thursday *jeudi*
ticket *le billet; le ticket*
   one-way ticket *aller simple*
time *l'heure; le temps; la fois*
tire *le pneu*
today *aujourd'hui*
tomorrow *demain*
too much *trop*
tooth *la dent*
   wisdom tooth *la dent de sagesse*
toothpaste *le dentifrice*
touch (to) *toucher*
tournament *le tournoi*
tow (to) *remorquer*
toward *vers*
tower *la tour*
town *la ville*
traffic *la circulation*

traffic jam *l'embouteillage (m)*
traffic light *le feu de circulation*
train *le train*
   train station *la gare*
train (to) *s'entraîner*
training *le stage; l'entraînement*
travel *le voyage, le déplacement*
travel (to) *voyager*
trigger (to) *déclencher, provoquer*
trip *le tour, le voyage*
true *vrai*
truly *vraiment*
Tuesday *mardi*
turn (to) *tourner*
twelve (or so) *douze, la douzaine*

U

unbearable *insupportable*
uncle *l'oncle (m)*
under *sous*
understand (to) *comprendre*
unfortunately *malheureusement*
United States *les Etats-Unis*
until *jusqu'à*
use (to) *utiliser*

V

vacation *les vacances*
valley *la vallée*
veal *le veau*
   veal stew *la blanquette de veau*
verb *le verbe*
very *très*
victory *la victoire*
violence *la violence*
visit *la visite*
visit (to) *visiter*
vote (to) *voter*

W

wait (to) *attendre*
wake up (to) *se réveiller*
walk *le tour, la promenade*
walk (to) *marcher*
wall *le mur*
want (to) *vouloir, tenir à*

watch (to) *regarder*
water *l'eau (f)*
   hot water *l'eau chaude (f.)*
wear (to) *porter*
week *la semaine*
weather *le temps*
Wednesday *mercredi*
weight *le poids*
welcome *l'accueil (m)*
well *bien*
what *quoi; que; quel*
when *quand*
where *où*
which one *lequel*
whose *dont*
why *pourquoi*
wife *la femme*
willingly *volontiers*
win (to) *gagner*
window *la fenêtre*
wind-surfing *la planche à voile*
wine *le vin*
wine cellar *la cave*
winter *l'hiver (m)*
wisdom *la sagesse*
   wisdom tooth *la dent de sagesse*
wish (to) *désirer*
with *avec*
without *sans*
woman *la femme*
work *le travail*
work (to) *travailler*
world *le monde*
worry *s'inquiéter, s'en faire*

X

xylophone *le xylophone*

Y

year *l'an (m); l'année (f)*
yellow *jaune*
yoghurt *le yaourt*

Z

zero *zéro*
zoo *le zoo*

INDEX